THE COMPLETE BOOK OF THE
WORLD CUP

THE COMPLETE BOOK OF THE

WORLD CUP

CRIS FREDDI

ALL THE FACTS, FIGURES AND MATCH REPORTS FROM EVERY TOURNAMENT

CollinsWillow

An Imprint of HarperCollins*Publishers*

First published in 1998 by
Collins Willow
an imprint of HarperCollins*Publishers*
London

Text copyright © Cris Freddi 1998
1 3 5 7 9 8 6 4 2

A CIP catalogue record for this book is available from
the British Library.

ISBN 0 00 218831 7

Created and produced by Flame Tree Publishing,
a part of The Foundry Creative Media Company Ltd,
The Long House, Antrobus Road,
Chiswick, London W4 5HY.
Grateful thanks to Dave Jones and Sonya Newland.

Printed and bound in Great Britain by
The Bath Press, Bath

Contents

Introduction

The *complete* book of the World Cup? No false modesty there, then. The kind of claim that can come back to haunt a writer. Even so, let's stick with it; this is the first book published in this country to contain all the main details for every match played in the World Cup finals – line-ups, referees, captains, coaches, attendances, goal times, substitute times. It's as complete as makes no difference.

Unfortunately, that doesn't involve claims of absolute accuracy. It's a strange animal, the World Cup. Although it began life in 1930, i.e. relatively recently by world football standards, it's always been rather patchily documented. Some excellent recent research, especially in Germany and Poland, has corrected some of the received wisdom, but even these latest efforts are sprinkled with errors, as are some of FIFA's own Official Reports. A minefield for researchers.

As a result, every piece of information here has been double-checked, using national sources where possible, e.g. Bulgarian publications and statisticians for Bulgarian line-ups. Where these findings differ from what's already been published, I've added footnotes to that effect. Any errors that emerge (all contributions welcome) will be given a full spotlight in the next edition.

The match reports themselves are based on video evidence where it's been available. As for the printed word, it sometimes bears little resemblance to what's happening on the screen – but I've made extensive use of it in the absence of film evidence and for off-the-field matters and players' recollections.

I've gone for a match-by-match format in preference to hundreds of pages of text followed by a great block of statistics. This way the prose and stats should feed off each other, adding context and

immediacy. The top line of each report comprises the date of the match, the name of the stadium and the city, the number of spectators, and the name and nationality of the referee. At the end of each team line-up, the team manager or coach is included. This is usually the man in sole charge of team selection and tactics, although sometimes these roles were divided between two or more individuals. Team captains are indicated by the letter (c) after their names. Results at half-time, full-time and – where applicable – extra-time are indicated in the scoreline. Goal times are in minutes unless specified as seconds.

Players' names

This is the first English publication to include the first name of every player, coach and referee. For the most part, players are shown by their first names and surnames in the usual European manner, including those commonly known by more than one forename: e.g. Jan Åge Fjørtoft, Jose Luis Lamadrid. Where possible, I've used a player's familiar name or diminutive rather than the formal version; e.g. Bobby not Robert, Jupp or Sepp not Josef, Enzo or Renzo instead of Lorenzo, Bora instead of Velibor or Borivoje. In most cases the formal name should be obvious (Jack Charlton was christened John, etc.) but where this isn't so, lack of space prevents an explanation. For example, Danny

INTRODUCTION

Blanchflower was christened Dennis, Ray Wilson was Ramon, and the Dutch thankfully shorten their long Latin names, e.g. from Josephus Franciscus Johannes Antonius van Run to 'Sjef'!

Even using diminutives isn't something you can do every time. In all countries, some players are known by their formal names (Alessandro Altobelli, Giovanni Lodetti, Giuseppe Bergomi) and some aren't (Sandro Mazzola, Gianni Rivera, Beppe Signori). As a result, I've had to make a decision – sometimes a compromise – with most players, often using a formal name where it's more recognizable in this country, e.g. Kurt Hamrin instead of Kurre, Karl-Erik Palmér instead of Kalle, Francisco Gento instead of Paco, etc. Bear with it, it's been a difficult juggling act.

A good many players, mainly Brazilians, Spanish, Portuguese, Turkish and some from North Africa, were known by their first names. These are shown with their surnames in brackets – Eusébio (Ferreira), Gérson (de Oliveira), etc. – and are referred to by just their first names in subsequent matches. Again, this includes players known by two forenames, e.g. Paulo César (Lima), José Augusto (de Almeida). To save space, there's been no attempt to list all the surnames of, say, the Brazilians (Sócrates had six!) except in a few famous cases: Pelé,

Garrincha, Zico and so on. Any player known by a nickname has inverted commas round it, followed by his forename and surname in brackets, e.g. 'Tostão' (Eduardo Gonçalves), 'Jairzinho' (Jair Ventura). The inverted commas disappear in a player's subsequent appearances.

For Spanish names, I've used the Basque spelling where appropriate (e.g. Goikoetxea and Alexanko rather than Goicoechea and Alesanco). As for translations from other scripts (Cyrillic for Bulgaria and the USSR, etc., Arabic, Hebrew and Greek), I've tried to be consistent but haven't been unduly concerned with matching the versions seen in other publications, especially those from abroad. A Polish book, for instance, writes the name Tsarev as Carew!

Two final points: unless otherwise mentioned, players with the same surname are unrelated; and the text includes a number of references to 'finals' (as in 'finals matches' and 'finals records'). This refers of course to World Cup finals tournaments, as opposed to qualifying rounds. The word 'Final' – with a

INTRODUCTION

capital 'F' – refers to the World Cup Final itself, the deciding game in each tournament and the most important football match in the world.

That's been the bottom line in producing this book – the enjoyment of covering the greatest sporting show on earth. For all the politics off the field and the regular violence on it, every tournament has produced enough world-class football to raise the spirits. It's been hard, while writing this, to avoid the repetition of words like 'brilliant', 'astounding' and 'breathtaking' – and frankly I haven't tried. The World Cup has been at the height of world sport for nearly 70 years and deserves a Complete Book at long last. This is the nearest thing yet.

CMG Freddi
Shepherd's Bush, May 1998

Abbreviations

ALG	ALGERIA	**ITA**	ITALY
ARG	ARGENTINA	**JPN**	JAPAN
AUS	AUSTRALIA	**LBY**	LIBYA
AUT	AUSTRIA	**MAU**	MAURITIUS
BEL	BELGIUM	**MEX**	MEXICO
BHR	BAHRAIN	**MLI**	MALI
BOL	BOLIVIA	**NIR**	NORTHERN IRELAND
BRZ	BRAZIL	**NKO**	NORTH KOREA
BUL	BULGARIA	**PAR**	PARAGUAY
CAM	CAMEROON	**PER**	PERU
CAN	CANADA	**POL**	POLAND
CHI	CHILE	**POR**	PORTUGAL
COL	COLOMBIA	**ROM**	ROMANIA
COS	COSTA RICA	**RUS**	RUSSIA
CZE	CZECHOSLOVAKIA	**SAU**	SAUDI ARABIA
DEN	DENMARK	**SCO**	SCOTLAND
ECU	ECUADOR	**SEN**	SENEGAL
EG	EAST GERMANY	**SNG**	SINGAPORE
EGY	EGYPT	**SPA**	SPAIN
EIR	REPUBLIC OF IRELAND	**SWE**	SWEDEN
ENG	ENGLAND	**SWI**	SWITZERLAND
ETH	ETHIOPIA	**SYR**	SYRIA
FIN	FINLAND	**TUN**	TUNISIA
FRA	FRANCE	**TUR**	TURKEY
GER	GERMANY	**UAE**	UNITED ARAB EMIRATES
GHA	GHANA	**URU**	URUGUAY
GUA	GUATEMALA	**USA**	UNITED STATES
HKG	HONG KONG	**USR**	USSR (SOVIET UNION)
HOL	HOLLAND	**VEN**	VENEZUELA
HUN	HUNGARY	**WAL**	WALES
IRN	IRAN	**WG**	WEST GERMANY
ISR	ISRAEL	**YUG**	YUGOSLAVIA

French for Beginners
Prologue

It was a glint in FIFA's eye from the start. When the governing body was formed in 1904, they reserved the exclusive right to organize a world championship – just when there was no real need for one. The Olympics were beginning to produce a universally accepted pecking order, the UK (a.k.a. England amateurs) beating Denmark in the 1908 and 1912 Finals. However, by the time of the 1929 FIFA Congress, football had outgrown the Games, partly because of the spread of professionalism. Time for a trophy of one's own.

Five countries didn't think so – the amateur Scandinavians and Estonia – but the other 25 members voted for a tournament to be held within a year. A host country was soon chosen and a stadium built within eight months, including three in the rainy season. Simple when you know it's necessary.

This probably had something to do with the French flair for getting things done. A Frenchman had inaugurated the modern Olympics, Robert Guérin was the first FIFA president, Jules Rimet one of his successors (1920-54). Henri Delaunay proposed an early World Cup resolution, Abel Lafleur sculpted the first trophy, France played in the first match. Thirty years later, they had a similar influence on the European Cup.

But if the French were the midwives, there was a country that called itself the father of football (acknowledging England as the mother), the natural choice for bringing up FIFA's baby.

The French team who played in the pioneering first match with Mexico. (l-r): standing: *Chantrel, Pinel, Thépot, Capelle, Mattler, Villaplane;* kneeling: *Liberati, Delfour, Maschinot, Laurent, Langiller.*

New World Order

Uruguay 1930

Almost as soon as they'd voted against the idea of a World Cup, Sweden applied to stage it; quick learners indeed. Italy applied too, along with Spain and Holland, only for all four to step aside once all the credentials were on the table. Uruguay were clearly the big players.

In some reports it comes across as a surprising decision, as if the game's showpiece had been offered to a Third World shanty town. In fact Montevideo was a thrusting city and port, still surviving the effects of the Wall Street Crash. 1930 was the centenary of Uruguayan independence and the country's exchequer was buoyant enough to build a grand new stadium and to guarantee the expenses of every country that took part.

The last was surely the clincher as far as FIFA were concerned, but it seems to have cut little ice with most of Europe. Regular jet travel was still in the future, so the financial guarantees persuaded only four countries to make the ocean voyage. With just 13 now taking part, the knockout system had to be replaced by four groups. The real contenders stayed at home: Hungary, Austria, Italy, Germany, Spain – while England and Scotland, as strong as anyone, weren't even eligible, having resigned from FIFA over the question of 'broken time' payments in 1928.

All of which didn't really matter very much. Even against Europe's finest, Uruguay would have been expected to win. In 1924 they'd played outside South America for the first time, winning the Olympic title in Paris. After thrashing Yugoslavia 7-0 and the hosts 5-1, they outplayed the Swiss 3-0 in the final, their stern defence buttressing some dazzling inter-passing up front. Four years later they won it again.

It wasn't just that they happened to have a strong pool of players. What really separated the leading South American countries from European opposition was a familiarity with tournaments arranged along World Cup lines; several matches played in the space of a month or so. Both continents took part in the Olympics every four years – but Uruguay and the rest were also involved in the Copa América, already staged 12 times since 1910 (50 years before the European Championship). Ideas on physical preparation and training camps were in advance of anything in most of Europe at the time.

So the hosts were firm favourites, with the only real opposition likely to come from Argentina, who'd taken them to a replay in the Olympic final two years earlier and beaten them 2-0 to win the Copa América in between. The other South American teams were makeweights, Mexico barely that, and the United States an unknown quantity (polite euphemism). The four European entries weren't particularly good, but at least they were there, and one or two were about to play more than just a bit-part in history.

Uruguay's captain José Nasazzi.

Group 1

Argentina, Chile, France, Mexico

■ 13 July 1930 • Pocitos, Montevideo • 4,444 •
Domingo Lombardi (URU)

▲ **FRANCE (3) 4**
Laurent 19, Langiller 40, Maschinot 42, 87
MEXICO (0) 1
Carreño 70

● FRANCE *Alexis Thépot, Étienne Mattler, Marcel Capelle,
Augustin Chantrel, Alexandre Villaplane (c), Edmond
Delfour, Marcel Pinel, Lucien Laurent, André Maschinot,
Ernest Liberati, Marcel Langiller.* Raoul Caudron.
MEXICO *Oscar Bonfiglio, Rafael Garza Gutiérrez (c),
Manuel Rosas, Efraín Amezcua, Alfredo Sánchez, Felipe
Rosas, Hilario López, José Ruiz, Dionisio Mejía, Juan
Carreño, Luis Pérez.* Juan Luque de Serrallonga (SPA).

France's win against Belgium the previous month
had been their first in 11 matches, and they were
accustomed to losing heavily against the stronger
European sides – but Mexico were even worse. The
only country they'd ever beaten was Guatemala, and
the one other time they'd dipped their toe in a
tournament, they'd lost 7-1 to Spain at the 1928
Olympics.

Still, the match had some history attached. With
no qualifying games necessary, this and the USA-
Belgium fixture were the first ever World Cup
matches (they kicked off at the same time). Laurent
scored the first ever goal, converting Liberati's cross
from the right. An injury to Alex Thépot led to
Chantrel playing in goal for the last hour, but even
with ten men France were too good. Mattler, a big
capable full-back, made a goal for Langiller, and

Maschinot shot home a pass by Delfour, who
doubled as the team's physical trainer. Carreño, a
stumpy Aztec, scored from Mejía's pass, but the
Mexicans weren't enjoying the conditions (it had
snowed the night before) and the speedy Langiller
crossed for Maschinot to finish off what amounted
to a training match for tougher things to come.
Manuel and Felipe Rosas were the first brothers to
play in the World Cup.

■ 15 July 1930 • Parque Central, Montevideo •
23,409 • Gilberto de Almeida Rego (BRZ)

▲ **ARGENTINA (0) 1**
Monti 81
FRANCE (0) 0

● ARGENTINA *Angel Bossio, José Della Torre, Ramón
Muttis, Juan Evaristo, Luis Monti, Pedro 'Arico' Suárez,
Natalio Perinetti, Francisco Varallo, Manuel (Nolo) Ferreira
(c), Roberto Cherro, Marino (Mario) Evaristo.* Francisco
Olazar, with Juan José Tramutola.
FRANCE *Thépot, Mattler, Capelle, Chantrel, Villaplane
(c), Delfour, Pinel, Laurent, Liberati, Maschinot, Langiller.*

In any normal tournament, the next match would
have been between the other two teams in the group.
Instead, the French were made to take on their
strongest opposition after only a day's rest. Whimsical
days indeed. In the event, they made a brave show of
it, resisting for over 80 minutes despite having little
luck – or much protection from the referee.

Argentina relied almost totally on pure skill up
front, leaving virtually all semblance of defence to
their famous centre-half Luisito Monti, a good long
passer out to the wings but essentially a destroyer – to
say the least. This was the dirtiest great player of his
generation, with a Desperate Dan jaw, no neck, and
legs that went right through a man – something they

---

did after only two minutes here. When Laurent had the temerity to try and dribble past Monti, his ankle was so badly injured that he limped throughout the match and couldn't play in the next. Then Thépot's injury flared up again and France were left with nine fit men for the remaining 70 minutes.

They nearly survived, partly because Argentina lacked a cutting edge. Ferreira was playing out of position and Cherro, normally so good in the air, was apparently taking medication for his nerves! The late goal came from a free-kick which Thépot didn't see. Sources disagree as to whether Pinel deflected it past him or just moved across his line of vision. Either way, Argentina were fortunate, especially when the referee had to restart the match after blowing for full-time six minutes early with France on the attack. Nevertheless, they were the better side, likely to improve as the tournament went on. Especially if they found a genuine striker.

Tramutola was the youngest coach in any finals tournament: 27 years 267 days.

■ 16 July 1930 • Parque Central, Montevideo • 9,249 • Henri Christophe (BEL)

▲ **CHILE (1) 3**
Vidal 4, 86, M. Rosas o.g. 51
MEXICO (0) 0

● CHILE *Roberto Cortés, Ulises Poirier, Victor Morales, Humberto Elgueta, Guillermo Saavedra, Arturo Torres, Carlos Schneeberger (c), Carlos Vidal, Eberardo Villalobos, Guillermo Subiabre, Tomás Ojeda.* György Orth (HUN).
MEXICO *Isidoro Sota, R. Garza Gutiérrez (c), M. Rosas, Amezcua, Sánchez, F. Rosas, López, Ruiz, Roberto Gayón, Carreño, Pérez.*

Easy as expected for Chile, beneficiaries of the first World Cup own goal, a Manuel Rosas header. Some old sources list the goalscorers as Vidal, Subiabre 2.

■ 19 July 1930 • Centenário, Montevideo • 42,100 • Anibal Tejada (URU)

▲ **CHILE (0) 1**
Subiabre 64
FRANCE (0) 0

● CHILE *Cortés, Ernesto Chaparro, Guillermo Riveros, A. Torres, Saavedra, Casimiro Torres, Schneeberger (c), Vidal, Villalobos, Subiabre, Ojeda.*
FRANCE *Thépot, Mattler, Capelle, Chantrel, Villaplane (c), Delfour, Célestin Delmer, Pinel, Liberati, Émile Veinante, Langiller.*

Again France held out determinedly. Ten minutes before half-time, Thépot, a genuine star of the tournament, saved Vidal's penalty, the first awarded in any World Cup match. The French were as dapper as ever, but injuries, tiredness and a reshuffled attack took their toll, and a single headed goal was enough. For Chile, a showdown with Argentina. For France, what else but *la gloire*.

Alex Villaplane, the French captain winning his last cap in this match, was later executed for collaborating with the Nazis.

■ 19 July 1930 • Centenário, Montevideo •
42,100 • Ulrico Saucedo (BOL)

▲ **ARGENTINA (3) 6**
Stábile 8, 17, 80, Zumelzú 10, 55, Varallo 53
MEXICO (1) 3
M. Rosas pen 37 pen 72, Gayón 78

● ARGENTINA *Bossio (c), Della Torre, Fernando Paternóster, Alberto Chividini, Adolfo Zumelzú, Rodolfo Orlandini, Carlos Peucelle, Guillermo Stábile, Varallo, Atilio Demaría, Carlos Spadaro.*
MEXICO *Bonfiglio, Francisco Garza Gutiérrez, R. Garza Gutiérrez (c), Raymundo Rodríguez, Sánchez, M. Rosas, Felipe Olivares, Carreño, Gayón, López, F. Rosas.*

■ 22 July 1930 • Centenário, Montevideo •
41,459 • John Langenus (BEL)

▲ **ARGENTINA (2) 3**
Stábile 12, 14, M. Evaristo 51
CHILE (1) 1
Arellano 15

● ARGENTINA *Bossio, Della Torre, Paternóster, J. Evaristo, Monti, Orlandini, Peucelle, Varallo, Stábile, Ferreira (c), M. Evaristo.*
CHILE *Cortés, Chaparro, Morales, A. Torres, Saavedra, C. Torres, Juan Aguilera, Vidal, Villalobos, Subiabre (c), Guillermo Arellano.*

Part of a double-header, played after the Chile-France match – so four penalties were awarded on the same ground on the same day, all three in this game for handball. Bonfiglio saved Paternóster's kick and Bossio saved Rosas' second but couldn't keep out the rebound. Mind you, Rosas did well to score at all; the penalty spot was apparently 16 yards out!

Argentina had found their goal poacher, albeit by accident. With Ferreira back in Buenos Aires taking a law exam (the past is another country, no question), they replaced him with the lean and craggy Stábile, who became the only player to score a hat-trick in the World Cup finals on his international debut, after which he couldn't be left out.

Some modern publications list Zumelzú as captain, but the leading Argentinian statistician disagrees, and Bossio is carrying the pennant in the team photo. The referee was also the manager ('person responsible') of the Bolivian squad; one of the linesmen was Costel Radulescu, the manager of Romania.

Again, much as expected – Chile no pushovers, Argentina always likely to qualify, Monti sure to cause mayhem. This time his activities provoked a mass punch-up (photographs show more than 30 officials and police on the pitch). Chile squared the ledger with a foul on Varallo while he was celebrating a goal! Old sources listed Subiabre as the Chilean goalscorer.

GROUP 1	P	W	D	L	F	A	PTS
Argentina	3	3	0	0	10	4	6
Chile	3	2	0	1	5	3	4
France	3	1	0	2	4	3	2
Mexico	3	0	0	3	4	13	0

Argentina qualified for the semi-finals.

MOST NEW CAPS

10	Brazil	1930	v Yugoslavia
10	Argentina	1934	v Sweden
9	Dutch East Indies	1938	v Hungary
8	Brazil	1934	v Spain

Group 2

Bolivia, Brazil, Yugoslavia

■ 14 July 1930 • Parque Central, Montevideo • 24,059 • Anibal Tejada (URU)

▲ **YUGOSLAVIA (2) 2**
Tirnanic 21, Bek 30
BRAZIL (0) 1
Preguinho 62

● YUGOSLAVIA *Milovan Jaksic, Milutin Ivkovic (c), Dragan Mihajlovic, Milorad Arsenijevic, Ljubisa Stevanovic, Momcilo Dokic, Aleksandar Tirnanic, Blagoje Marjanovic, Ivan Bek, Dorde Vujadinovic, Brane Sekulic.* Bosko Simonovic.
BRAZIL *Joel (de Oliveira), Alfredo Brilhante, 'Itália' (Luis Gervasoni), Hermógenes (Fonseca), Fausto (dos Santos), Fernando (Giudicelli), 'Poly' (Polycarpo Ribeiro), Nilo (Murtinho Braga), Araken (Patuska), 'Preguinho' (João Coelho Netto) (c), Téophilo (Bettencourt).* Píndaro (de Carvalho).

On the surface, a surprise result: a so-so European team beating the mighty Brazil – but there was more to it than that. Brazil hadn't played in a full international since 1925 and now fielded ten new caps.

When Joel couldn't stop Sekulic's shot, Tirnanic put in the rebound. He later had a goal disallowed. Quick and fit (average age only 21), Yugoslavia had three players good enough to play for French clubs, including one later capped by France under the name Yvan Beck.

Brazil scored through the multi-talented Preguinho (basketball, volleyball, water polo) but were frustrated by Jaksic, prominent throughout the tournament, and the huge, swarthy Ivkovic.

■ 17 July 1930 • Parque Central, Montevideo • 18,306 • Francisco Matteucci (URU)

▲ **YUGOSLAVIA (0) 4**
Bek 60, 67, Marjanovic 65, Vujadinovic 85
BOLIVIA (0) 0

● YUGOSLAVIA *Jaksic, Ivkovic (c), Mihajlovic, Arsenijevic, Stevanovic, Dokic, Tirnanic, Marjanovic, Bek, Vujadinovic, Dragutin Najdanovic.*
BOLIVIA *Jesús Bermúdez, Segundo Durandal, Casiano Chavarría, Juan Jorge Argote, Diógenes Lara, Jorge Luis Valderrama, Gumercindo Gómez, José Bustamante I, Rafael Méndez (c), Mario Alborta, René Fernández.* Ulrico Saucedo.

Bolivia, playing their only match against European opposition before 1977, made a colourful entrance, each player sporting a letter of the alphabet on the front of his white shirt, forming the words Viva Uruguay. One wore a thick white headband, another a black beret.

None of this camouflaged the fact that they were the weakest team in the competition, already established as the whipping boys of the Copa América. Eight were making their debuts, and the country had played a grand total of seven internationals, losing the lot.

They might have changed that if they'd had any luck here. Instead, they had four goals disallowed (!) and Gómez broke his leg in a challenge with Ivkovic. Yugoslavia needed only a draw and were happy to wait an hour for the goals to come. Brazil were out.

GROUP 2	P	W	D	L	F	A	PTS
Yugoslavia	2	2	0	0	6	1	4
Brazil	2	1	0	1	5	2	2
Bolivia	2	0	0	2	0	8	0

Yugoslavia qualified for the semi-finals.

Group 3

Peru, Romania, Uruguay

■ 20 July 1930 • Centenário, Montevideo •
25,466 • John Balway (FRA)

▲ **BRAZIL (1) 4**
Moderato 27, 73, Preguinho 57, 83
BOLIVIA (0) 0

● BRAZIL *Oswaldo Velloso, 'Zé Luiz' (José Luiz de Oliveira), Itália, Hermógenes, Fausto, Fernando, Benedicto (Dantas), 'Russinho' (Moacyr de Siqueira), Carlos de Carvalho Leite, Preguinho (c), Moderato (Visintainer).*
BOLIVIA *Bermúdez, Durandal, Chavarría, Renato Sáenz, Lara, Valderrama, Eduardo Reyes, Bustamante, Méndez (c), Alborta, Fernández.*

■ 14 July 1930 • Pocitos, Montevideo • 300 •
Alberto Warnken (CHI)

▲ **ROMANIA (1) 3**
Desu 50 sec, Stanciu 74, Kovács 85
PERU (0) 1
Souza Ferreira 60

● ROMANIA *Ion Lapusneanu, Adalbert Steiner, Rudolf Bürger, Ladislau Raffinsky, Alfred Eisenbeisser, Emerich Vogl, Nicolae Kovács, Adalbert Desu, Rudolf Wetzer (c), Constantin Stanciu, Stefan Barbu. Costel Radulescu.*
PERU *Juan Valdivieso, Mario de las Casas, Alberto Soria, Alberto Denegri, Plácido Galindo (c), Domingo García, José María Lavalle, Julio Lores, Alejandro Villanueva, Demetrio Neyra, Luis Souza Ferreira. Francisco Brú (SPA).*
▼ SENT OFF: *Galindo 70.*

With nothing at stake, Brazil sent out another five debutants, one of whom saved Sáenz's penalty with the score still 0-0, leaving Bolivia to wait 64 years for their first goal in the finals. Three from each side wore berets. Black players were only just beginning to filter into Brazilian national teams; the only one in 1930 was the strong centre-half Fausto, who was their best player.

Balway is believed to have been an Englishman living in Paris. Some sources call him Georges Balvay, but this seems to be an error. Sáenz is sometimes seen spelt Sáinz.

Essentially a curtain-raiser for the entrance of the hosts, the match produced the first World Cup sending-off and the smallest crowd. Although the official figure was 2,549, photographs of a completely empty stand, with very few spectators behind the goals, make 300 look about right.

Peru fielded six new caps, including Valdivieso who conceded a goal in the first minute of his international career – from Desu's 30-yard drive. After that came a series of brawls resulting in Steiner breaking a leg and skipper Galindo being sent off by a referee who lost control. Romania then scored twice against ten men.

A respected modern publication mentions Lizandro Nué Rodríguez coming on as substitute for Souza Ferreira after 80 minutes – but the leading Peruvian statistician says this is a definite error and Nué Rodríguez was never capped by Peru. Two sources, one old and one recent, list the Romanian goalscorers as Stanciu 2, Barbu – and the captains as Vogl and de las Casas. Eisenbeisser was commonly known as Fieraru, Kovács as Covaci, Raffinsky also spelt Rafinski. Lores, who later played for Mexico, is misprinted Flóres in some reports.

SMALLEST CROWDS

300	1930	Romania v Peru	Montevideo
2,000	1954	Turkey v S. Korea	Geneva
2,823	1958	Wales v Hungary	Stockholm
3,580	1950	Switzerland v Mexico	Pôrto Alegre
3,993	1938	Cuba v Romania	Toulouse
4,444	1930	France v Mexico	Montevideo

SMALLEST FOR A FINAL

45,124	1938	Italy v Hungary	Paris

■ 18 July 1930 • Centenário, Montevideo • 57,735 • John Langenus (BEL)

▲ **URUGUAY (0) 1**
Castro 60
PERU (0) 0

● URUGUAY *Enrique Ballestrero, José Nasazzi (c), Domingo Tejera, José Leandro Andrade, Lorenzo Fernández, Alvaro Gestido, Santos Urdinarán, Héctor Castro, Pedro Petrone, Pedro Cea, Santos Iriarte.* Alberto Suppici. PERU *Jorge Pardón, de las Casas, Antonio Maquilón (c), Denegri, Galindo, Eduardo Astengo, Lavalle, Lores, Villanueva, Neyra, Souza Ferreira.*

When Uruguay finally made their bow, five days after the first match, in front of the biggest crowd yet, they had an unfinished ground (three tiers in some places, two in others) and a team to match.

This was the first international played at the new stadium, on the same day as the name of the road leading to it: Avenida 18 Julio, the anniversary of independence. The team was more established than that: eight players had Olympic gold medals and the spine had been there for some time; the 'iron curtain' half-back line; the fearsome Nasazzi at the back; and several of the forwards. But there had been a change in goal, where Andrés Mazali, a star of both Olympic teams and one of the first keepers to patrol his penalty area, had been dropped from the team for breaking curfew. Caught sneaking home for a conjugal visit, he didn't play for Uruguay again. His replacement (misspelt Ballesteros in old sources) wasn't in the same class.

Up front too, things didn't click against Peru. Two of the inside-forward trio were finishers rather than starters: the famous Petrone, so clever at finding space that he was called the first player to play without the ball; and the combative Castro, who had lost his right hand to an electric saw while working as a carpenter. Petrone was off form, missing chances on a dusty pitch. Pardón made save after save ('Supermann' said one German publication), the best from Petrone at point-blank range. When Castro eventually scored, relief was all around. Apart from anything else, Uruguay had won at home for the first time since 1925!

Despite his sending-off against Romania, Galindo was allowed to play – but deprived of the captaincy (some sources say it was given to de las Casas). Seven of the Peruvians weren't capped again, including Pardón who was still only 20. Gestido's brother Oscar was the president of Uruguay!

■ 21 July 1930 • Centenário, Montevideo • 70,022 • Gilberto de Almeida Rego (BRZ)

▲ **URUGUAY (4) 4**
Dorado 7, Scarone 16, Anselmo 30, Cea 35
ROMANIA (0) 0

● URUGUAY *Ballestrero, Nasazzi (c), Ernesto Mascheroni, Andrade, Fernández, Gestido, Pablo Dorado, Héctor Scarone, Juan Pelegrino Anselmo, Cea, Iriarte.*
ROMANIA *Lapusneanu, Iosif Czako, Bürger, Corneliu Robe, Eisenbeisser, Vogl, Kovács, Desu, Wetzer (c), Raffinsky, Barbu.*

The formalities before the first Final. (l-r): linesman Henri Christophe (BEL), Uruguay's captain Nasazzi, referee Langenus in his famous plus-fours, Argentina's captain Ferreira, linesman Ulrico Saucedo (BOL).

Suppici added the last piece to his defence by giving a first cap to the leggy Mascheroni – and above all increased the skill quotient up front, bringing back Anselmo and the crinkly-haired Scarone, who was only six days younger than the manager but looked far older than 31. Less of a finisher by now (this was the last of his 29 goals, still the Uruguayan record), he compensated with cleverness and passing skills.

The forward line moved better from the start, playing the one-twos which had so impressed spectators in Europe, Cea scoring after completing such a move with Anselmo. Dorado, playing on the wrong wing, scored the first with his left foot. In the first half, Romania hadn't been able to cope with the inter-passing and Andrade's all-round strength; in the second, it's said they didn't have a shot on goal. One way or another, they were the first to know the hosts had re-established themselves as favourites.

GROUP 3	P	W	D	L	F	A	PTS
Uruguay	2	2	0	0	5	0	4
Romania	2	1	0	1	3	5	2
Peru	2	0	0	2	1	4	0
Uruguay qualified for the semi-finals.							

Group 4

Belgium, Paraguay, USA

■ 13 July 1930 • Parque Central, Montevideo •
18,436 • José Macías (ARG)

▲ **USA (2) 3**
McGhee 41, Florie 44, Patenaude 88
BELGIUM (0) 0

● USA *Jim Douglas, Alec Wood, George Moorhouse, Jim Gallagher, Raphael (Ralph) Tracy, Billy Gonsalves, Andy Auld, Jim Brown, Bert Patenaude, Tom Florie (c), Bart McGhee.* Robert Millar.
BELGIUM *Arnold Badjou, Théodore Nouwens, Nic Hoydonckx, Pierre Braine (c), Auguste Hellemans, Jean De Clercq, Louis Versijp, Bernard Voorhoof, Ferdinand Adams, Jacques Moeschal, Jean Diddens.* Hector Goetinck.

No great anticipation here. Belgium were without their best player, the great Raymond Braine, brother of the captain – and the USA had no form to speak of: seven new caps, no matches for two years, and before that an 11-2 thumping by Argentina in the Olympics.

But the Americans were the one real revelation of the tournament. Over the years, legends have grown up about their physiques (the French calling them 'shot putters', etc.). They don't look so gargantuan in photographs. Some hefty thighs here and there (Gonsalves, McGhee, Auld) but all quite human really.

They won because they were better, not just brawnier. Six of the team had played in Britain and their style was surprisingly modern, breaking out of massed defence with long passes to the wings. Belgium protested about both the first two goals but were well beaten.

Among the American players' clubs were Wieboldt Wonderbolts, Detroit Holley Carburettor, Curry Silver Tops and the Providence Gold Bugs (previously Providence Clamdiggers). Some old sources credit McGhee with both the first two goals.

■ 17 July 1930 • Parque Central, Montevideo •
18,306 • José Macías (ARG)

▲ **USA (2) 3**
Patenaude 10, 15, 50
PARAGUAY (0) 0

● USA *Douglas, Wood, Moorhouse, Gallagher, Tracy, Gonsalves, Auld, Brown, Patenaude, Florie (c), McGhee.*
PARAGUAY *Modesto Denis, Quiterio Olmedo, José Luis Miracca, Romilio Etcheverry, Eusebio Díaz, Francisco Aguirre, Lino Nessi, Diógenes Domínguez, Aurelio González, Delfín Benítez Cáceres, Luis Vargas Peña (c).* José Durand Laguna (ARG).

Even after their performance against Belgium, the Americans' second win was another surprise. Paraguay had finished runners-up in the Copa América, beating a full-strength Uruguay 3-0. Their ball skills were admired by the press, Vargas Peña was a tricky winger and the 19-year-old Benítez Cáceres was good enough to play for Argentina in 1934.

Here, though, they were hampered by a stiff wind and an injury to Denis – and González headed against the bar. Patenaude, the 20-year-old centre-forward, scored the first ever World Cup hat-trick. Some sources still credit him with only two goals, but his own team-mates maintained that he scored all three, and two contemporary South American newspapers confirmed it, one even printing diagrams of the three goals, all scored from left-wing crosses, the last with a 'violent' shot.

■ 20 July 1930 • Centenário, Montevideo •
9,000 • Ricardo Vallerino (URU)

▲ **PARAGUAY (1) 1**
Vargas Peña 40
BELGIUM (0) 0

● PARAGUAY *Pedro Benítez, Olmedo, Salvador Flóres,*
Santiago Benítez, Díaz, Tranquilino Garcete, Nessi, Gerardo
Romero, González, Benítez Cáceres, Vargas Peña (c).
BELGIUM *Badjou, Hoydonckx, Henri De Deken,*
P. Braine (c), Hellemans, Moeschal, Versijp, Gérard
Delbeke, Nouwens, Adams, Diddens.

Little to write home about, even in contemporary
reports. The official attendance figure was 25,466,
but the figure above is more realistic.

GROUP 4	P	W	D	L	F	A	PTS
USA	2	2	0	0	6	0	4
Paraguay	2	1	0	1	1	3	2
Belgium	2	0	0	2	0	4	0
USA qualified for the semi-finals.							

OLDEST TO SCORE A HAT-TRICK			
yrs/days			
29/329	Pedro Cea	URU	1930
29/95	Teófilo Cubillas	PER	1978
28/270	Preben Elkjaer	DEN	1986
Cubillas 2 penalties.			

Semi-finals

■ 26 July 1930 • Centenário, Montevideo •
72,886 • John Langenus (BEL)

▲ **ARGENTINA (1) 6**
Monti 20, Scopelli 56, Stábile 69, 87,
Peucelle 80, 85
USA (0) 1
Brown 89

● ARGENTINA *Juan Botasso, Della Torre, Paternóster,*
J. Evaristo, Monti, Orlandini, Peucelle, Alejandro
Scopelli, Stábile, Ferreira (c), M. Evaristo.
USA *Douglas, Wood, Moorhouse, Gallagher, Tracy,*
Gonsalves, Auld, Brown, Patenaude, Florie (c), McGhee.

The Americans found it harder to close down superior
ball players on a much larger pitch (134 yards by 100).
In the second half they had to do it without Tracy,
who'd broken a leg – and Douglas injured his knee.

Bossio, who'd kept goal in the group matches,
was known as 'the elastic marvel', which sounds like
an ad for a labour-saving appliance, but suggests he
was quite a keeper (he'd played in the Olympic
final). So why he was dropped isn't clear (there seems
to have been no word of an injury) – especially as it
meant replacing him with a player winning his first
cap. In the event, Botasso didn't have much to do, but
the Final would be a different matter.

The story goes that when the American trainer
Jack Coll came on to the pitch, he dropped a bottle
of chloroform from his bag and had to be led off in a
daze! The last ten minutes were just as much of a
farce, the Argentinian attack walking the ball past
exhausted opponents. Things might have been a little
different if Tracy hadn't begun his unhappy day by
missing two chances to open the score.

■ 27 July 1930 • Centenário, Montevideo •
79,867 • Gilberto de Almeida Rego (BRZ)

▲ **URUGUAY (3) 6**
Cea 18, 67, 72, Anselmo 20, 31, Iriarte 61
YUGOSLAVIA (1) 1
Vujadinovic 4

● URUGUAY *Ballestrero, Nasazzi (c), Mascheroni, Andrade,*
Fernández, Gestido, Dorado, Scarone, Anselmo, Cea, Iriarte.
YUGOSLAVIA *Jaksic, Ivkovic (c), Mihajlovic, Arsenijevic,*
Stevanovic, Dokic, Tirnanic, Marjanovic, Bek, Vujadinovic,
Sekulic.

The same deceptive scoreline. Yugoslavia took an early lead from a cross by Tirnanic, then had a goal controversially disallowed at 2-1 – and legend has it that Uruguay scored their third goal when the ball went out of play and was kicked back on by a policeman in uniform!

Nevertheless, as in the other semi-final, the right team won. With Nasazzi still giving no change at the back, the forwards cut through the middle at will. The equalizer, in a goalmouth scramble, was put in by Cea, toothy and skilful (the French player Laurent compared him with Platini). Anselmo scored with a header, Iriarte with a powerful low shot. Ultimately the Yugoslavs had little to offer except youthful spirit, although a lasting memory was the performance of Ivkovic, in every sense massive in defeat. He was killed by the Gestapo in 1943.

Scarone was winning his 50th cap. Old sources credited Sekulic with the opening goal.

Final

■ 30 July 1930 • Centenário, Montevideo •
68,346 • John Langenus (BEL)

▲ **URUGUAY (1) 4**
Dorado 12, Cea 57, Iriarte 68, Castro 89
ARGENTINA (2) 2
Peucelle 20, Stábile 37

● URUGUAY *Ballestrero, Nasazzi (c), Mascheroni, Andrade,*
Fernández, Gestido, Dorado, Scarone, Castro, Cea, Iriarte.
ARGENTINA *Botasso, Della Torre, Paternóster, J. Evaristo,*
Monti, Suárez, Peucelle, Varallo, Stábile, Ferreira (c),
M. Evaristo

If FIFA needed any reassurance about the decision to bring the tournament here, they got it just before the Final. Luis Monti received a death threat.

It proved the match mattered. Had it been held in Europe, how many spectators would have been locked out as they were here? Would they have been searched for weapons on the way in? How many European stadia needed a surrounding moat? The ground capacity was reduced for safety reasons.

Additional factors built tension: local derby; impending military dictatorship against Uruguayan coalition. Referee Langenus demanded guarantees of protection and planned a quick escape route to his ship. This isn't something invented by old wives; the official later admitted to feeling genuine fear.

On the day of the Final, he was put under extra pressure, both camps wanting to use a ball manufactured in their own country. Langenus ordered each half to be played with a different ball. Clad in his usual cap and plus-fours, he went out to play the part of gamekeeper.

Uruguay scored first. When Scarone's shot was

blocked by Paternóster, Castro, back in the team thanks to Anselmo's illness, pushed the loose ball wide to the right, where Dorado came in like a train to shoot under Botasso's body (some say between his legs) and past Juan Evaristo on the line.

Argentina responded with a picture goal. Juan Evaristo, conspicuous by his passing as well as his pale beret, took a return from Monti and found Ferreira, who sent Peucelle away up the right. The winger, one of the most dangerous forwards of his day, beat Gestido then left Ballestrero standing with a fierce shot high inside the right-hand post.

From this point until half-time, Argentina's emphasis on sheer skill seemed to win all arguments about how to play the game. Think of Brazil in 1982. Then add a decent striker. Monti's long ball drifted over Nasazzi for Stábile to score from close range with Andrade stranded. Nasazzi claimed offside, but the ball had been in the air a long time, and anyway he would wouldn't he? Argentina's flair was more

than holding its own. Then half-time came and changed everything.

Crudely put, Uruguay at last began to impose themselves physically. This isn't a euphemism for fouling; they simply remembered their legendary *garra,* akin to the Welsh *hwyl* and the Finnish *sisu* – a word to be pronounced through clenched teeth.

It's not a hereditary thing. The Germans, say, aren't genetically programmed to make famous comebacks in football matches – but because they've done it in the past, they believe it's there in them. Uruguay believed they were made of sterner stuff than the Argentinians and started acting on it, staying the course better despite a day less to recover from the semi-final.

And suddenly Argentina had no answer. The young Varallo, not fully recovered, was obliterated (*complètement neutralisé*) by Mascheroni. Monti, who seemed to have taken the death threat to

The Argentinian team that lost the Final. (l-r) standing: manager Olazar, J. Evaristo, Monti, Botasso, Paternóster, Suárez, Della Torre, coach Tramutola; kneeling: Peucelle, Varallo, Stábile, Ferreira, M. Evaristo, masseur.

The first goal in a World Cup Final. A shot by Dorado (out of picture) beats a grounded Botasso and Juan Evaristo on the line.

Peucelle (out of picture) equalizes for Argentina.

heart, wasn't his usual self (one of the reasons for his move to Italy was the reaction of the Argentinian press). The fight went out of them once and for all when Stábile, of all people, missed a chance to put them 3–1 ahead.

Now Gestido and Fernández were moving up to join the attack. The latter's free-kick reached Castro, who found Scarone with his back to goal six yards out. A clever overhead lob took out Della Torre and Paternóster, and Cea pushed a ground shot past Botasso's dive. Ten minutes later, Mascheroni robbed Varallo and brought the ball forward before passing

Stábile raises an arm after beating Andrade (left) and Ballestrero to put Argentina 2-1 ahead.

Cea (on his knees in the centre) brings Uruguay back into the game after half-time: 2-2.

Uruguay's winning goals. Above: a long range shot by Iriarte (out of picture). Below: a looping header from Castro (centre, hidden). The stump of his right arm is visible above the defender's shoulder.

to Iriarte, whose shot from outside the area surprised Botasso, who dived late.

Even then Argentina had one last chance, but Varallo's shot was cleared 'artistically' by Andrade, the first great black star. In the last minute, Dorado crossed for Castro to beat Della Torre in the air and send a looping header over Botasso's fingertips.

Langenus blew the last whistle and made his ship safely, Scarone fell into Castro's arms, seven of the Argentinians were never capped again.

The Evaristos were the first pair of brothers to play in a World Cup Final. The four matches in the tournament constituted Stábile's entire international career. He scored in each of them.

The Uruguay team who won the Final.

Nasazzi doesn't seem to have actually received the World Cup (Rimet handed it to Raúl Jude, president of the Uruguayan FA) but no-one deserved to get his hands on it more. Tall and grim-faced, he's invariably listed at No. 2, leading people to talk of his forceful full-back play, whereas in fact he was an early sweeper (already known as a 'broom back'). A natural leader, he was captain in every one of his 39 internationals spread over 13 years. From him, Uruguay drew the determination and drive to turn the Final round, winning the tournament for the same reason they staged it: they wanted it the most.

Naturally the day of the Final was declared a national holiday. Someone died in the celebrations, a mob stoned the Uruguayan embassy in Buenos Aires, and the two FAs broke off relations. It really did matter. Even the Europeans were about to believe it.

The Full Monti

Italy 1934

Having staged the first World Cup in the right place, FIFA now did the opposite. They handed the second tournament to Italy.

Over the years, Mussolini has been portrayed as something of a buffoon, and perhaps he was – but there was nothing very funny about the modern Fascist state, built on one-party rule, brownshirt gangs and informers, state torture and imprisonment without trial. And Mussolini was in power for a decade before Hitler. The World Cup would undoubtedly be a major propaganda tool.

Even FIFA must have had reservations; it took them eight meetings to make up their minds. Perhaps they eventually decided that human rights might have to be swept under the carpet for a while, but at least the tournament would run on time.

As for the actual football, again the hosts were expected to win, especially as Italy's coach was one of the great early man-managers and strategists. There had been some friction (the Italians called it 'rust') between his centre-half and centre-forward following a league match – so Pozzo made them share a room. He needed this kind of no-prisoners centre-half for his system of play, plus a pair of good wingers – and he knew where to find them, helping himself to a number of South American internationals, on the basis that if they could die for Italy (eligible for national service) they could play for Italy.

So in came Filó, capped by Brazil in 1925, and several high-class Argentinians: Demaría who'd played in the 1930 World Cup; Orsi who'd played in the last Olympic final; Guaita on the other wing; and Monti

The sign of the times. Germany give the Nazi salute before the match against Sweden. (l-r): Hohmann, Zielinski, Busch, Kobierski, Siffling, Conen, Lehner, Haringer, Gramlich, Kress, Szepan.

himself, a linchpin at Juventus (four league titles) once his weight problem was solved. After the tournament, Pozzo picked another 1930 Argentinian, Scopelli, as well as Mascheroni from Uruguay. They were all apparently ineligible, but FIFA turned a blind eye (a German publication uses the word 'collaboration').

There were home-grown stars too, especially the gracile centre-forward Peppino Meazza, whose hat-trick in Hungary had won the Dr Gero Cup, a forerunner of the European Championship.

Among the opposition, Hungary were improving, using the smooth Sárosi at centre-half as well as centre-forward. Czechoslovakia had Plánicka in goal, Nejedly and the forceful Puc up front. Spain had a great goalkeeper in Zamora.

Above all, Austria, managed by the passionate Jewish banker Hugo Meisl, had dominated the early 1930s *(das Wunderteam)*, beating Scotland 5-0, Germany 6-0 and 5-0, Switzerland 8-1. Playing the same old Scottish close-passing game as the other Danubians, they arrived in Italy without their fine goalkeeper Rudi Hiden, whom Arsenal tried to buy, but still had their share of world-class players: Smistik the attacking centre-half; the prolific Schall; two genuinely great forwards in Bican and the slender Sindelar. They were probably just past their peak (Meisl himself thought so) but had recently beaten Italy 4-2 in Turin.

Uruguay, however, stayed away, perhaps in revenge for being snubbed by the main European powers in 1930, or because their team needed rebuilding. Of the other absent friends, England lost in Hungary and Czechoslovakia just before the competition, and Meisl believed they wouldn't have reached the semi-finals.

The tournament had grown too big to be held in a single city, and there were enough entries to warrant a qualifying competition, in which even Italy had to take part, beating the weak Greeks 4-0 in Milan. Elsewhere, the big guns had no trouble with the likes of Luxembourg and the Baltic countries, and the USA had beaten Mexico 4-2 in Rome, all their goals coming from the Italian-born Donelli on his debut (he also missed a penalty). The problems of a knockout system began to show. Mexico had travelled 4,000 miles to play a single match and not even in the competition proper.

The Americans' next game was likely to be rather harder, especially as Il Duce himself, in the words of an Italian book, was 'bestowing the privilege of his presence, which would galvanise the two teams more than any other coefficient.' Should be a cracker.

Mean, moody and machiavellian. The first European team to win the World Cup. (l-r) standing: Combi, Monti, Ferraris, Allemandi, Guaita, Ferrari; kneeling: Schiavio, Meazza, Monzeglio, Bertolini, Orsi.

Round 1

■ 27 May 1934 • Nazionale del PNF, Rome • 25,000 • René Mercet (SWI)

▲ **ITALY (3) 7**
Schiavio 18, 29, 64, Orsi 20, 69,
Ferrari 63, Meazza 90
USA (0) 1
Donelli 57

● ITALY *Gianpiero Combi, Virginio Rosetta (c), Luigi Allemandi, Mario Pizziolo, Luis Monti, Luigi Bertolini, Amphilóquio 'Anfilogino' Guarisi, Giuseppe Meazza, Angelo Schiavio, Giovanni Ferrari, Raimundo Orsi. Vittorio Pozzo.*
USA *Julius Hjulian, Ed Czerkiewicz, George Moorhouse (c), Peter Pietras, Billy Gonsalves, Tom Florie, Francis Ryan, Werner Nilsen, Aldo Donelli, Walter Dick, Bill McLean.* Elmer Schroeder (coach David Gould).

The full name of the stadium, unsurprisingly, was the Stadio Nazionale del Partito Nazionale Fascista – and there was no shortage of straight-arm salutes before the match (from the referee and linesmen, too), while Mussolini sported a natty white sailing cap.

Schiavio opened the scoring from a pass by Meazza; the two of them made the second for Orsi; Guarisi hit the bar; and Schiavio's excellent shot from Ferrari's pass made it three by half-time.

The USA threw Gonsalves forward at the start of the second half. He forced Combi to a rare save, and Donelli scored a good individual goal, which helped persuade Napoli to buy him. But Ferrari converted Guarisi's corner, Schiavio headed the fifth (the 100th goal in World Cup finals), and Orsi knocked in the rebound when Hjulian punched clear. Meazza scored the last in injury-time. Then more salutes towards Benito's box.

Most sources spell Combi's first name Giampiero, but the *Almanacco Illustrato* insists on Gianpiero. Guarisi was known as 'Filó' in Brazil. Schroeder died a grim and bizarre death in 1953, strangled with the cord of his own window blind.

PLAYED FOR TWO COUNTRIES

Luis Monti	1930 ARG	1934 ITA
Atilio Demaría	1930 ARG	1934 ITA
José Santamaría	1954 URU	1962 SPA
Ferenc Puskás	1954 HUN	1962 SPA
José Altafini	1958 BRZ	1962 ITA

Altafini was known as 'Mazzola' in Brazil.

■ 27 May 1934 • Littorio, Trieste • 8,000 • John Langenus (BEL)

▲ **CZECHOSLOVAKIA (0) 2**
Puc 48, Nejedly 65
ROMANIA (1) 1
Dobay 11

● CZECHOSLOVAKIA *Frantisek Plánicka (c), Ladislav Zenísek, Josef Ctyroky, Josef Kostálek, Stefan Cambal, Rudolf Krcil, Frantisek Junek, Josef Silny, Jiri Sobotka, Oldrich Nejedly, Antonín Puc.* Karel Petru.
ROMANIA *William Zombori, Emerich Vogl (c), Gheorghe Albu, Vasile Deheleanu, Rudolf Kotormányi, Iosif Moravetz, Silviu Bindea, Nicolae Kovács, Gratian Sepi, Iuliu Bodola, Stefan Dobay.* Costel Radulescu, with Josef Uridil (AUT).

Czechoslovakia were heavy favourites but lucky to get through. Kovács and Sepi, attacking at speed, set up an excellent first goal for Dobay, and Bindea missed an open goal, the turning point.

Puc scored from Kostálek's free-kick, then Sepi missed another glaring chance before Czechoslovakia went ahead with a controversial goal. Deheleanu came off worse in a tackle, the decision went against Romania, and Nejedly scored from Sobotka's pass. Then Plánicka made several important saves, especially from Sepi's late thunderbolt.

Silny was winning his 50th and last cap. Many Romanian players of the time had Hungarian ancestry (Kovács and Bodola were capped by both countries), hence names like Kovács and Kotormányi, usually seen spelt in the Romanian fashion: Covaci and Cotormani.

■ 27 May 1934 • Giovanni Berta, Florence • 8,000 • Francesco Mattea (ITA)

▲ **GERMANY (1) 5**
Kobierski 28, Siffling 47, Conen 67, 70, 86
BELGIUM (2) 2
Voorhoof 32, 44

● GERMANY *Willibald Kress, Sigmund Haringer, Hans Schwartz, Paul Janes, Fritz Szepan (c), Paul Zielinski, Ernst Lehner, Karl Hohmann, Edmund Conen, Otto Siffling, Stanislaus Kobierski. Otto Nerz.*
BELGIUM *André Vandewijer, Philibert Smellinckx, Constant Joacim, Frans Peeraer, Félix Welkenhuysen (c), Jean Claessens, François De Vries, Bernard Voorhoof, Jean Capelle, Laurent Grimonprez, Albert Heremans. Hector Goetinck.*

The Nazis had just taken power and the German team came on to the pitch with a swastika on their flag. Ironically, in view of what was to come, their captain Szepan was of Polish extraction, original surname Sczepan.

A versatile player, he was at centre-half during this match, the Germans one of the very few continental sides playing with a genuine stopper. Much good it did them before half-time, even after Kobierski had put them ahead following some slick work by Conen and Siffling. The Belgian attack swarmed round their penalty area, scoring twice through the fair-haired Voorhoof, his second a header from Claessens' cross.

But the Belgians had exhausted themselves, and Siffling scored from a free-kick, Conen from crosses by Kobierski, Zielinski and Hohmann. A victory for Nerz's homework, many hours spent watching league and cup matches in England.

■ 27 May 1934 • Benito Mussolini, Turin • 15,000 • Joop van Moorsel (HOL)

▲ **AUSTRIA (1) (1) 3**
Sindelar 44, Schall 93, Bican 109
FRANCE (1) (1) 2
Nicolas 18, Verriest pen 115

● AUSTRIA *Peter Platzer, Franz Cisar, Karl Sesta, Franz Wagner, Josef (Pepi) Smistik (c), Hans Urbanek, Karl Zischek, Josef (Pepi) Bican, Matthias Sindelar, Anton Schall, Rudi Viertl. Hugo Meisl.*
FRANCE *Alexis Thépot (c), Jacques Mairesse, Étienne Mattler, Edmond Delfour, Georges Verriest, Noël Liétaer, Fritz Keller, Joseph Alcazar, Jean Nicolas, Roger Rio, Alfred (Freddy) Aston. Gaston Barreau (coach George Kimpton ENG).*

As in Montevideo, France gave the second favourites a scare but were unlucky. Nicolas' early head injury forced them to rearrange their forward line three times. Coming back on after treatment, he immediately took advantage of Cisar's blunder from Keller's cross – but it was understandably his last contribution. Platzer had already made an acrobatic save in the first minute.

Even with ten fit men, France held out well in the second half, Mattler playing in the middle to watch Sindelar. In extra-time, Schall put Austria ahead from a position that looked clearly offside to everyone (including Schall himself) except the referee. Bican shot the third, high to Thépot's right, and Verriest's penalty – for handball by Sesta – didn't matter.

This was the first World Cup match to go to extra-time. Kimpton was France's first ever national coach. Rio's son Patrice played in the 1978 finals.

■ 27 May 1934 • Luigi Ferraris, Genoa • 30,000 • Alfred Birlem (GER)

▲ **SPAIN (3) 3**
Iraragorri pen 17, Lángara 23, 28
BRAZIL (0) 1
Leônidas 52

● SPAIN *Ricardo Zamora (c), Ciriaco (Errasti), Jacinto Quincoces, Leonardo Cilaurren, José Muguerza, Martín Marculeta, Ramón de Lafuente, José Iraragorri, Isidoro Lángara, Simón Lecue, Guillermo Gorostiza.* Amadeo García de Salazar.
BRAZIL *Roberto Pedrosa, Sílvio Hoffmann, Luiz Luz, Alfredo Tinoco, Martim Silveira (c), Heitor Canalli, Luiz M. Oliveira, Waldemar de Britto, 'Armandinho' (Armando dos Santos), Leônidas (da Silva), 'Patesko' (Rodolfo Barteczko).* Luiz Vinhaes.

Again, as in 1930, Brazil scattered the pitch with new caps (a mere eight this time); again there was only one black player in the team (Leônidas); again the black player was their best, knocking in the rebound when Zamora pushed the ball out. But it was too late by then.

Spain scored from a penalty, a volley from Gorostiza's cross, and after a mix-up between Pedrosa and Luz. In the second half, Brazil scored, had a goal dis-allowed on the hour, and missed a penalty (Waldemar de Britto's nervous kick saved by Zamora) – but this is deceptive; Spain simply stopped attacking, conserving energy for the second round,

employing the bizarre tactic of deliberately giving away corners. Brazil had again looked skilful, but match reports emphasize a lack of cohesion, and they needed more than flashy touches to beat a goalkeeper like Zamora.

■ 27 May 1934 • San Siro, Milan • 35,000 • Ivan Eklind (SWE)

▲ **SWITZERLAND (2) 3**
Kielholz 6, 43, Abegglen 66
HOLLAND (1) 2
Smit 29, Vente 69

● SWITZERLAND *Frank Séchehaye, Severino Minelli (c), Walter Weiler, Albert Guinchard, Fernand Jaccard, Ernst Hufschmid, Willy von Känel, Raymond Passello, Leopold (Poldi) Kielholz, André 'Trello' Abegglen, Giuseppe Bossi.* Heinrich 'Henry' Müller.
HOLLAND *Gejus van der Meulen, Mauk Weber, Sjef van Run, Henk Pellikaan, Wim Anderiesen, Gerrit 'Puck' van Heel (c), Frank Wels, Leen Vente, Eberhard 'Bep' Bakhuys, Jaap 'Kick' Smit, Joop van Nellen.* Bob Glendenning (ENG).

Holland had some well-known players, but the Swiss were too quick and determined for them. Kielholz, who played in glasses, finished off a neat move involving Bossi and Abegglen, after which play was end-to-end for the rest of the first half. Smit scored from van Heel's free-kick and Kielholz put in Passello's cross from 20 yards.

In the second half, von Känel sprinted away to make an excellent volleyed goal for the bald and skilful Abegglen, one of three international brothers. Vente headed in another free-kick and Holland hit a post – but Switzerland's gritty display was typical of their performances in pre-war World Cups.

Authoritative sources list Bakhuys' first names as Eberhard Hendrik, but note that several call him

1934

Elyseus or Elisa (he was known as Elysée when he played in France).

■ 27 May 1934 • Littoriale, Bologna • 19,000 •
Eugen Braun (AUT)

▲ **SWEDEN (1) 3**
Jonasson 9, 67, Kroon 80
ARGENTINA (1) 2
Belis 3, Galateo 50

● SWEDEN *Anders Rydberg, Nils Axelsson, Sven Andersson, Rune Karlsson-Wamma, Nils Rosén (c), Ernst Andersson, Gösta Dunker, Ragnar Gustavsson, Sven Jonasson, Tore Keller, Knut Kroon.* József Nagy (HUN).
ARGENTINA *Héctor Luis Freschi, Juan Carlos Pedevilla, Ernesto Belis, José Nehín, Constantino Urbieta Sosa, Arcadio López, Francisco Rúa, Federico Wilde, Alfredo Devincenzi (c), Alberto Galateo, Roberto Luis Irañeta.* Felipe Pascucci (ITA).

A split in the Argentinian league led to their FA sending over a team of amateurs, of whom only Devincenzi had previously been capped. They provided some dazzling moments, Belis scoring with a 20-yard free-kick and Galateo scoring after a wonderful dribble (he'd earlier beaten five men and missed). But they were overtaken by defensive errors, Jonasson scoring in a scramble, then beating a hesitant Freschi to Rosén's long ball. It was Argentina's last World Cup match until 1957. None of the team won another cap.

The 1934 crop wasn't one of the richest for Italy to plunder (Devincenzi won a single B cap) – but the Argentinians were not averse to borrowing foreigners themselves; their coach was Italian and Urbieta Sosa had played for Paraguay.

■ 27 May 1934 • Giorgio Ascarelli, Naples •
8,000 • Rinaldo Barlassina (ITA)

▲ **HUNGARY (2) 4**
Teleki 11, Toldi 31, 61, Vincze 54
EGYPT (2) 2
Fawzi 39, 43

● HUNGARY *Antal Szabó, Gyula Futó, László Sternberg (c), István Palotás, György Szücs, Gyula Lázár, Imre Markos, Jenö Vincze, Pál Teleki, Géza Toldi, Gábor P. Szabó.* Ödön Nádas.
EGYPT *Mustafa Kamel Mansour, Ali Khaf, Hamidu (Sharli), Hassan El Far, Ismail Rafaat, Hassan Raghab, Mohammed Latif, Abdel Rahman Fawzi, Mahmoud Mokhtar (c), Mustafa Kamel Taha, Mohammed Hassan Helmy.* Jimmy McRea (SCO).

Egypt, who'd beaten Hungary 3-0 at the 1924 Olympics, had some skilful players, especially Mokhtar and the young goalkeeper. And the result might have been different if Mokhtar hadn't had a goal mysteriously disallowed after a fabulous dribble, and Fawzi hadn't missed an easy chance in the second minute. His two goals didn't quite compensate.

The hefty Toldi ('sturmtank') scored his first goal by charging the keeper over the line, Vincze intercepted a back-pass for the third, then Toldi sprinted in to convert Markos' cross. Victory for the more complete side, who had Sárosi ready to return for the local derby.

One publication says Hamidu's last name was Teles. Others give the half-time score as 2-1 (Fawzi scoring his second after 67 minutes). The goal times above come from several sources, including a Hungarian almanac and the official report on the tournament.

The captains shake hands before the quarter-final: Rosén of Sweden (left) and Szepan of Germany

Quarter-finals

■ 31 May 1934 • San Siro, Milan • 16,000 • Rinaldo Barlassina (ITA)

▲ **GERMANY (0) 2**
Hohmann 60, 62
SWEDEN (0) 1
Dunker 82

● GERMANY *Kress, Haringer, Willy Busch, Rudolf Gramlich, Szepan (c), Zielinski, Lehner, Hohmann, Conen, Siffling, Kobierski.*
SWEDEN *Rydberg, Axelsson, S. Andersson, Karlsson-Wamma, Rosén (c), E. Andersson, Dunker, Gustavsson, Jonasson, Keller, Kroon.*

The match turned on a weird accident 12 minutes into the second half, a clash of heads between Rosén and Ernst Andersson that forced them both off the pitch. Within five minutes, Hohmann put Germany two up.

Earlier, the tall and powerful Rosén had played a full part in contesting the midfield with his opposite number, the short blond Szepan. But it had been dull, the Germans earning a reputation for efficiency without flair that stayed with them for decades.

■ 31 May 1934 • Littoriale, Bologna • 14,000 • Francesco Mattea (ITA)

▲ **AUSTRIA (1) 2**
Horvath 5, Zischek 51
HUNGARY (0) 1
Sárosi pen 62

● AUSTRIA *Platzer, Cisar, Sesta, Wagner, Smistik, Urbanek, Zischek, Bican, Sindelar, Hans Horvath (c), Viertl.*
HUNGARY *Szabó, József Vágó, Sternberg (c), Palotás, Szücs, Antal Szalay, Markos, István Avar, György Sárosi, Toldi, Tibor Kemény.*
▼ SENT OFF: *Markos 63.*

■ 31 May 1934 • Giovanni Berta, Florence • 40,000 • Louis Baert (BEL)

▲ **ITALY (1) (1) 1**
Ferrari 45
SPAIN (1) (1) 1
Regueiro 31

● ITALY *Combi (c), Eraldo Monzeglio, Allemandi, Pizziolo, Monti, Armando Castellazzi, Enrique Guaita, Meazza, Schiavio, Ferrari, Orsi.*
SPAIN *Zamora (c), Ciriaco, Quincoces, Cilaurren, Muguerza, 'Fede' (Federico Sáiz), Lafuente, Iraragorri, Lángara, Luis Regueiro, Gorostiza.*

The anticipated display of limpid Middle European football turned into another World Cup brawl (there'd already been a few). Whereas Hungary brought back the tall and stylish Sárosi to add extra class to their attack, Horvath injected dash and aggression into Austria's. Short and craggy, he hammered in an early opening goal.

After that the game degenerated. Sesta, who'd conceded a penalty in the first round, did it again here, bringing down Kemény. Markos was sent off, Platzer and Wagner received knocks, and an injury to Avar reduced Hungary to nine men for the last 18 minutes.

One or two old sources mention Szabó saving two penalties after 52 and 56 minutes, but this seems unlikely and has been impossible to verify. Avar had earlier played for Romania under the name Stefan Auer. One leading source lists Vágó's first name as János, an error.

For the only time in their nine pre-war finals matches, Italy met a team who played a similar game, ready to trade sweat and studs. Pozzo knew it and made changes. He'd already left Umberto Caligaris out of his squad, after a record 59 caps, allowing the veteran only to carry the flag at the opening ceremony. Against the easy Americans,

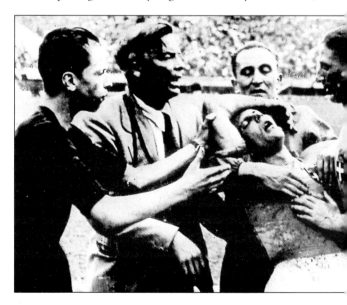

Spain weren't the only ones to suffer in the quarter-final. Meazza is helped off after being injured in the first match.

he'd given a last cap to Rosetta, the other full-back from that famous partnership. Now he recalled the rugged Monzeglio, a signal of intent.

The match was predictably rough and feebly refereed. Louis Baert refused Schiavio a penalty, disallowed a goal by Lafuente, gave Monti all the licence he needed, and above all did nothing to protect Zamora from the attentions of the Italian forwards.

After the romp against the USA, Italy seem to have decided a new tactic was needed. Pump in the crosses and pile into the keeper. It worked up to a point – Ferrari was able to head the equalizer only because Schiavio barged Zamora when he went up for Pizziolo's free-kick – but the Spanish captain played one of the games of his career, which was saying something.

In England, Zamora was remembered for a miserable display in Spain's 7-1 defeat at Highbury in 1931, but there's no doubt he was one of the greats – a brilliant shot-stopper and as brave as anyone in those days of the shoulder charge. In 46 internationals played in an attacking era, he conceded 42 goals. Here, in the only drawn game of the first two World Cup tournaments, he was so badly treated that he had to miss the replay.

MOST MATCHES 1930-38

9	Luis Monti	ARG/ITA	1930–34
9	Giuseppe Meazza	ITA	1934–38
8	Giovanni Ferrari	ITA	1934–38

LEADING GOALSCORERS 1934

5	Oldrich Nejedly	CZE
4	Edmund Conen	GER
4	Angelo Schiavio	ITA

REPLAY

■ 1 June 1934 • Giovanni Berta, Florence • 40,000 • René Mercet (SWI)

▲ **ITALY (1) 1**
Meazza 12
SPAIN (0) 0

● **ITALY** *Combi (c), Monzeglio, Allemandi, Attilio Ferraris, Monti, Bertolini, Guaita, Meazza, Felice Placido Borel, Atilio Demaría, Orsi.*
 SPAIN *Juan José Nogués, Ramón Zabalo, Quincoces (c), Cilaurren, Muguerza, Lecue, Martín Vantolrá, Regueiro, 'Campanal' (Marcelino González), 'Chacho' (Eduardo González), Crisanto Bosch.*

The rematch was held the following day, so both sides had to make changes. Pozzo picked a forward line with three Argentinians and Serie A's leading scorer Borel. He also recalled Bertolini and the combative Ferraris. Spain gave Nogués his only cap and feared for their health.

Sources disagree as to whether three or four Spaniards left the field with injuries, Mercet allowing so much latitude that he was suspended by his own federation. Italy's usual ploy brought them the only goal. Two forwards threw themselves at a corner from the left, Nogués was taken out, Meazza headed a spectacular goal. The rest was bruises.

Vantolrá's son José played for Mexico in the 1970 finals. The slight difference in the spelling of Ferraris' and Demaría's first name is correct.

The Italian team who won the quarter-final replay. (l-r) standing: coach Pozzo, Combi, Ferraris, Allemandi, Monti, Guaita; kneeling: Bertolini, Orsi, Monzeglio, Meazza, Borel, Demaría.

■ 31 May 1934 • Benito Mussolini, Turin • 9,000 • Alois Beranek (AUT)

▲ **CZECHOSLOVAKIA (1) 3**
Svoboda 23, Sobotka 49, Nejedly 83
SWITZERLAND (1) 2
Kielholz 18, Jäggi 80

● CZECHOSLOVAKIA *Plánicka (c), Zenísek, Ctyroky, Kostálek, Cambal, Krcil, Junek, Frantisek Svoboda, Sobotka, Nejedly, Puc.*
SWITZERLAND *Séchehaye, Minelli (c), Weiler, Guinchard, Jaccard, Hufschmid, von Känel, Willy Jäggi, Kielholz, Abegglen, Alfred Jaeck.*

In steady rain, the Swiss again battled to the wire, but Czechoslovakia were slightly too good. Needing more punch after the display against Romania, they replaced the silky Silny with Svoboda, who equalized from Sobotka's pass and hit a post early in the second half.

Kielholz had opened the scoring from a pass by Jäggi, who scored Switzerland's second with a shot that skidded through the mud. Some old sources credit Abegglen with the goal, an error. Not for the last time in the World Cup, he was the best player on the pitch – but Nejedly again poached the winner, and this time the Czechs deserved it.

Semi-finals

■ 3 June 1934 • San Siro, Milan • 45,000 • Ivan Eklind (SWE)

▲ **ITALY (1) 1**
Guaita 19
AUSTRIA (0) 0

● ITALY *Combi (c), Monzeglio, Allemandi, Ferraris, Monti, Bertolini, Guaita, Meazza, Schiavio, Ferrari, Orsi.*
AUSTRIA *Platzer, Cisar, Sesta, Wagner, Smistik (c), Urbanek, Zischek, Bican, Sindelar, Schall, Viertl.*

It's said that Austria didn't have a shot on goal in the first 40 minutes. If this is true, it's a startling statistic; they'd picked just about the strongest forward line in their history, and Italy had played a tough replay only two days earlier.

As in the other semi-final, two of the main European schools were in opposition. Reviewing Austria's gentle intricate game, an Italian publication referred to an *antico* dogma and a dose *di narcisismo*. The Italians seem to have taken almost personal offence to the Viennese habit of trying to walk the ball into the net, an indignation exemplified by the central duel of the match: Sindelar v Monti.

The Austrian was the nearest thing anyone could remember to the old England centre-forward G. O. Smith: similar ability to make the play from slightly behind the other forwards, similar paleness and spare physique, in Sindelar's case accentuated by a high forehead and limp smile. *Der Papierene*, the man made of paper. But there was nothing effete about his actual play, which looks sharp and even aggressive on film. He scored goals too, 27 in 43 internationals, including both in the win over Italy in 1932.

However, now 31, this was the only time he faced Monti in an international (Austria had recently won in Turin without him) and Monti, untroubled by death threats this time, had decided no more mister nice guy. Even older than Sindelar but never dependent on pace (his nickname was the rough equivalent of 'Stroller'), he was the most important player in the tournament – a thug but a great one, his long passes turning the Austrian full-backs, who couldn't cope with the Argentinian wingers. Meanwhile his other talents pushed Sindelar to the margins, the ghost of a vanished age.

For the third match in a row, Italy scored just a single goal, yet again in a goalmouth scramble, the opposition goalkeeper left injured on the deck with three Italians in the net. Meazza clattered Platzer, who recovered to dive after the ball but was beaten to it by Guaita virtually on the line.

Bican hit a post and Combi made good saves from Sesta and Zischek, but any losing team has moments like these, and anyway Platzer was more often in action. Italy, on a helpfully heavy pitch, bossed it. The only team to keep a clean sheet in the tournament, they did it twice. It was the closest Austria have ever come to reaching the Final. Sindelar gassed himself in 1939.

■ 3 June 1934 • Nazionale del PNF, Rome •
13,000 • Rinaldo Barlassina (ITA)

▲ **CZECHOSLOVAKIA (1) 3**
Nejedly 21, 69, 80
GERMANY (0) 1
Noack 59

● CZECHOSLOVAKIA *Plánicka (c), Jaroslav Burgr,
Ctyroky, Kostálek, Cambal, Krcil, Junek, Svoboda, Sobotka,
Nejedly, Puc.*
GERMANY *Kress, Haringer, Busch, Zielinski, Szepan,
Jakob Bender, Lehner, Siffling, Conen, Rudolf Noack,
Kobierski.*

The short-passing game was a style doomed to obsolescence, but not just yet. Czechoslovakia were slick up front and Plánicka had a much better game than Kress, who was blamed for two of the goals.

Plánicka himself made a hash of Noack's shot, but Czechoslovakia had the confidence to keep playing their game – and Nejedly was in the sort of form a hat-trick suggests. Similar to Sindelar and Meazza in being graceful but good in the air (two of his goals here came from headers), he was one of the great European matchwinners. Some old sources credit one of his goals to Krcil, an error he could afford. He scored 28 in 43 internationals. Burgr is no misprint.

3rd-place Final

■ 7 June 1934 • Giorgio Ascarelli, Naples •
7,000 • Albino Carraro (ITA)

▲ **GERMANY (3) 3**
Lehner 24 sec, 42, Conen 29
AUSTRIA (1) 2
Horvath 30, Sesta 55

● GERMANY *Jakob, Janes, Busch, Zielinski, Reinhold
Münzenberg, Bender, Lehner, Siffling, Conen, Szepan (c),
Matthias Heidemann.*
AUSTRIA *Platzer, Cisar, Sesta, Wagner, Smistik, Urbanek,
Zischek, Georg Braun, Bican, Horvath (c), Viertl.*

'It is of no purpose and should not exist.' So said Michel Hidalgo, manager of France, telling it like it is before the 3rd-place Final of 1982 – the biggest anticlimax in the game, unloved but apparently here to stay, someone squeezing out every last piece of silver. In 1934, perhaps Mussolini needed the gate receipts for his African empire.

Still, at least it was inaugurated with a flourish, Lehner leaping in to score right in front of Platzer after less than half a minute, the fastest World Cup goal until 1962. Conen volleyed Heidemann's cross just under the bar, Horvath pulled one back from Zischek's cross, but Lehner scored Germany's third with a ground shot.

Soon after half-time, Sesta lined up a free-kick 30 yards out. Small and hard, a former wrestler (he and Viertl look like a pair of dodgy brothers in team photos), he was the *Wunderteam's* one concession to the need for combat – appropriate, in a changing world, that he should provide its last gesture before it disappeared for ever. Jakob didn't move as the free-kick flew past him. Four years later, it wasn't just the Austrian football team that Germany would wipe off the map.

Final

- 10 June 1934 • Nazionale del PNF, Rome •
  50,000 • Ivan Eklind (SWE)

▲ **ITALY (0) (1) 2**
Orsi 81, Schiavio 95
CZECHOSLOVAKIA (0) (1) 1
Puc 71

● ITALY *Combi (c), Monzeglio, Allemandi, Ferraris, Monti,
Bertolini, Guaita, Meazza, Schiavio, Ferrari, Orsi.*
CZECHOSLOVAKIA *Plánicka (c), Zenísek, Ctyroky,
Kostálek, Cambal, Krcil, Junek, Svoboda, Sobotka,
Nejedly, Puc.*

*The goalkeeper captains shake hands: Combi (left) and Plánicka. Behind
them is Ivan Eklind, the youngest referee in any World Cup Final.*

Behind one of the stands in the stadium, in letters standing up over the horizon, ran the exhortation *Acquistate Prodotti Italiani*, 'Buy Italian'.

They weren't even buying Italian tickets. As with Italy's other matches, there were empty spaces in all parts of the ground. Either the Depression was pricing people out or they didn't have much enthusiasm for the event. Either way, it wasn't the image the Fascists wanted to project.

Still, there were enough spectators to provide an intimidating atmosphere. There was no moat here as in Montevideo, no running track, and the front row of the crowd came within ten yards of the pitch. Italian coach Pozzo spent the match squatting next to Plánicka's net, presumably for psychological reasons.

Hard to know if it worked. In the only Final with two goalkeeper captains, Plánicka was again the more prominent, catching everything the Italians threw at him. The first half was all attrition.

With 20 minutes left and tension all around, an amazing sequence took place. Ferraris crunched into Puc, who was carried to the sidelines, where a flask of ammonia was waved under his nose. Within two minutes, he was taking Nejedly's pass, breaking Monzeglio's tackle and beating Combi with a sliced shot low at the near post. The glorification of drug-taking!

Suddenly Italy fell apart, even in defence. Sobotka dribbled through but hit a post, Nejedly shot over the

*The referee and linesman give the Fascist salute before the Final. (l-r):
Louis Baert (BEL), Eklind (SWE), Mihály Iváncsics (HUN).*

Italy go 1-0 down as Puc's shot beats Combi at the near post.

As Plánicka gets to his feet in the goalmouth, Pozzo (extreme left) celebrates Italy's equalizer.

bar. The parallels with Sindelar were uncanny: both frail, both bullied by Monti and the gang. They even looked vaguely similar. Nejedly's missed chance was Czechoslovakia's last. Three minutes later, Italy scored their first really good goal in four games, though some say there was luck involved.

Orsi means 'bears' in English. No-one had a less appropriate name. Sleek-haired and very slim, he was a brilliant dribbler but 32 years old, drifting in and out of matches. Now he dummied Zenísek on the edge of the penalty area, shaped to shoot with his left foot, then hit the ball with the outside of his right.

Plánicka may have been at fault, though his reach probably had more to do with it (typical of the time, he was only 5′8″). The ball drifted beyond him as Pozzo jumped for joy on the goal line.

At the end of normal time, Pozzo effectively decided the match, telling Schiavio and Guaita to start switching positions. It may not sound much, but it was more than the other lot could manage. Petru was an organizer not a tactician, and anyway his tactics were set in stone; Czechoslovakia were still playing with an attacking centre-half (Cambal), essentially a sixth forward.

Five minutes into extra-time, he was nowhere to be seen as Meazza found Guaita, who ran into the penalty area and fed Schiavio unmarked on his right. The cross shot beat Plánicka from ten yards. Earlier in the move, Eklind had allowed Meazza to get away with a handball. Allegedly seen with Mussolini before the match, the referee was born on the same day as the winning goalscorer.

Pozzo was chaired off the pitch. The veteran Combi, recalled only because the flamboyant Carlo Ceresoli had broken an arm in training, received the Cup and retired from international football, as did Schiavio – a triumph for the hardworking man.

No doubt the Fascists used that in their brochures – but it had been a grim and gloomy tournament. Too many dirty matches, probably some dirty referees, the touch players stamped out. Visitors who'd come for the football glimpsed the reality of the regime: brutal, and smug with it; unsmiling; a heavy military presence. And that was just its centre-half.

The Judgment of Paris

France 1938

The World Cup was coming back to the land of its fathers, but any celebrations were tempered by events elsewhere. Austria, one of the great football powers, wasn't even a country any more, swallowed up by the *Anschlüss*. Others were soon to follow, including Czechoslovakia, where the Nazis had taken the Sudetenland without a peep from the West. There was civil war in Spain. And Italy, now firmly established as Germany's sidekick, were still strong on the football field.

Only the inside-forwards Meazza and Ferrari remained from the 1934 team. Three others came in from the side that had won the 1936 Olympics, and there was only one South American this time, the Uruguayan Andreolo in Monti's place. Above all, the latest centre-forward, Silvio Piola, was the best in Europe.

Czechoslovakia still had Plánicka, Nejedly and Puc. Brazil, as usual, hadn't played for more than a year. Hungary were full of goals, Sárosi scoring seven, no less, in an 8-3 win over Czechoslovakia, who had Plánicka in goal. The other goal came from the new young striker Zsengellér, who later scored five in the 11-1 qualifying win over Greece.

Uruguay again didn't turn up. Nor did Argentina, who'd won the Copa América the previous year (with Guaita back in the team). Meanwhile, a month before the tournament, England had won 6-3 in Germany and 4-2 in France, fielding players like Matthews, Bastin, Drake and Hapgood. Still outside FIFA, they apparently turned down an invitation to take Austria's place.

In October the Austrians beat lowly Latvia 2-1 to qualify. On 12 March, German troops crossed the border. On 12 April, the Austrian FA announced that it had ceased to exist. The Nazis had been welcomed by a surprising percentage of the population, keen on the idea of 'Greater Germany' and presumably proud when Austrian players were added to the German squad; seven in all, but not Matthias Sindelar, who was now required to wear a Star of David on his clothing.

One of the official posters for the tournament.

Round 1

■ 4 June 1938 • Parc des Princes, Paris • 27,152 •
John Langenus (BEL)

▲ **SWITZERLAND (1) (1) 1**
Abegglen 43
GERMANY (1) (1) 1
Gauchel 29

● SWITZERLAND *Willy Huber, Severino Minelli (c),
August Lehmann, Hermann Springer, Sirio Vernati, Ernest
Lörtscher, Lauro Amadò, Eugen Walaschek, Alfred (Fred)
Bickel, André 'Trello' Abegglen, Georges Aeby.* Karl
Rappan (AUT).
GERMANY *Rudolf Raftl, Paul Janes, Willibald Schmaus,
Andreas Kupfer, Hans Mock (c), Albin Kitzinger, Ernst
Lehner, Rudi Gellesch, Jupp Gauchel, Willi Hahnemann,
Hans Pesser.* Sepp Herberger.
▼ SENT OFF: *Pesser 96.*

A folkloric glow has settled on this one over the years. The brave little Swiss holding out against the might of the Nazis. The truth is rather more arithmetical. A week after the 6-3 win in Berlin, England had lost 2-1 in Switzerland, who were trying out an early form of *catenaccio* and were favourites here. Germany had won one of their last five matches – 2-1 against Luxembourg.

No surprise then, that their pragmatic new manager should seize the chance to pick five Austrian internationals (shades of Pozzo): Raftl, Mock, Hahnemann, Schmaus and Pesser, the last providing Gauchel with the opening goal then getting himself sent off for kicking Minelli. Abegglen headed the equalizer from a cross by Walaschek that came off Mock. Germany dominated the first half of extra-time but Vernati

and Walaschek were prominent in the second.

Unlike England in Berlin, the Swiss refused to give the Nazi salute before the match. The teams had five days to prepare for the replay – a leisure pursuit, alright.

REPLAY

■ 9 June 1938 • Parc des Princes, Paris • 20,025 •
Ivan Eklind (SWE)

▲ **SWITZERLAND (1) 4**
Walaschek 42, Bickel 64, Abegglen 75, 78
GERMANY (2) 2
Hahnemann 8, Lörtscher o.g. 22

● SWITZERLAND *Huber, Minelli (c), Lehmann, Springer,
Vernati, Lörtscher, Amadò, Walaschek, Bickel, Abegglen, Aeby.*
GERMANY *Raftl, Janes, Jakob Streitle, Kupfer, Ludwig
Goldbrunner, Stefan Skoumal, Lehner, Josef (Pepi) Stroh,
Hahnemann, Fritz Szepan (c), Leopold Neumer.*

Herberger added three more capped Austrians – Skoumal, Stroh and Neumer – and brought back the 1934 captain Szepan, but again the mix wasn't quite right (Germany hadn't had a quality schemer for years). They led 2-0, played against ten men for a while after an injury to Aeby, and still lost – to the rest of Europe's glee. Hahnemann gave them the lead from Lehner's pass after Huber had punched away Szepan's shot and Lörtscher scored an own goal when Neumer's drive came back off the right-hand post. But then Abegglen took over. His through-pass set up Walaschek for Switzerland's first, his cross was fisted out by Raftl for Bickel to shoot home, and he scored the last two goals himself, including the winner from Aeby's pass. Germany didn't play in another finals tournament until 1954, when Herberger would still be there.

1938

■ 5 June 1938 • Chapou, Toulouse • 6,707 •
Giuseppe Scarpi (ITA)

▲ **CUBA (1) (2) 3**
Socorro 44, 103, Magriña 69
ROMANIA (1) (2) 3
Bindea 35, Barátky 88, Dobay 105

● CUBA *Benito Carvajales, Jacinto Barquín, Manuel Chorens, Manuel Berges, José Rodríguez, Joaquín Arias, José Antonio Magriña, Tomás Fernández (c), Héctor Socorro, Juan Tuñas, Mario Sosa. José Tápia.*
ROMANIA *Dumitru Pavlovici, Rudolf Bürger, Vasile Chiroiu, Vintila (Cossini), Gheorghe Rasinaru, Ladislau Raffinsky, Silviu Bindea, Nicolae Kovács (c), Iuliu Barátky, Iuliu Bodola, Stefan Dobay. Alexandru Savulescu, with Costel Radulescu.*

REPLAY

■ 9 June 1938 • Chapou, Toulouse • 7,536 •
Alfred Birlem (GER)

▲ **CUBA (0) 2**
Socorro 51, Fernández 57
ROMANIA (1) 1
Dobay 35

● CUBA *Juan Ayra, Barquín, Chorens, Berges, Rodríguez, Arias, Magriña, Fernández (c), Socorro, Tuñas, Sosa.*
ROMANIA *Robert Sadowski, Bürger, Iacob Felecan, Andrei Barbulescu, Rasinaru, Raffinsky, Ion Bogdan, Ioachim Moldoveanu, Barátky, Iuliu Prassler, Dobay (c).*

Cuba arrived with little World Cup pedigree. They'd had to play Mexico three times in the 1934 qualifiers, losing the lot, and qualified this time only because the Mexicans dropped out. Yet they weren't short of confidence, announcing that they were here 'to win a match or two'.

Romania, who'd also qualified because their opponents withdrew, were surprised by the flair of the Cuban forwards, Socorro opening the scoring from Magriña's cross. The talented Kovács had played in the 1930 and 1934 tournaments. Some sources claim he scored the first goal, and there are various versions of the goal times, Cuban scorers and captain (one source says Rodríguez' brother Ignacio played). The details here are confirmed by the leading Cuban statistician and the press officer at the Romanian FA.

Vintila was one of the very few European players known by their first names. Alternative spellings: Rafinski, Baratki.

Although Carvajales had been a star of the first match, Cuba replaced him with the stocky little Ayra, who'd saved a penalty against Mexico in 1934 and was now their best player, 'a fantastic acrobat'. Fernández scored the winner (despite being flagged for offside by French linesman Georges Capdeville) to complete the first World Cup shock.

■ 5 June 1938 • Vélodrome, Rheims • 9,091 • Roger Conrié (FRA)

▲ **HUNGARY (4) 6**
Kohut 14, Toldi 16, Sárosi 25, 88, Zsengellér 30, 67
DUTCH EAST INDIES (0) 0

● HUNGARY *József Háda, Lajos Korányi, Sándor Biró, Gyula Lázár, József Turay, István Balogh, Ferenc Sas, Gyula Zsengellér, György Sárosi (c), Géza Toldi, Vilmos Kohut.* Károly Dietz (coach Alfréd Schaffer).
DUTCH EAST INDIES *Tan Mo Heng, Frans Hu Kom, Jack Samuels, Achmad Nawir (c), Frans Meeng, Anwar Sutan, Tan Hong Djien, Suvarte Sudarmadji, Hendrikus Zomers, Isaac (Tjak) Pattiwael, Hans Taihuttu.* Jan Mastenbroek (HOL).

The first real World Cup mismatch. Nine of the East Indians were winning their first caps, most of them were students (the captain was a doctor who played in glasses) and all of them were very small. 'Bien trop petits,' said a French reporter, who also thought their forwards 'très brilliants dribbleurs' but their defence lacking the rudiments: no marking, too many late tackles. Háda was surprisingly uncertain in goal, but the Hungarian inside-forward trio looked 'the equal of the Italians'. Zsengellér made the third goal for Sárosi and headed the fourth and they spent the second half practising their passing. The Tans were brothers. Zomers is also seen spelt Sommers. The stadium was later renamed Auguste Delaune.

■ 5 June 1938 • Olympique (Colombes), Paris • 30,454 • Hans Wüthrich (SWI)

▲ **FRANCE (2) 3**
Veinante 35 sec, Nicolas 11, 69
BELGIUM (1) 1
Isemborghs 19

● FRANCE *Laurent Di Lorto, Héctor Cazenave, Étienne Mattler (c), Jean Bastien, Gustave (Gusti) Jordan, Raoul Diagne, Alfred (Freddy) Aston, Oscar Heisserer, Jean Nicolas, Edmond Delfour, Émile Veinante.* Gaston Barreau.
BELGIUM *Arnold Badjou, Bob Paverick, Corneille Seys, John Van Alphen, Émile Stijnen (c), Alphonse De Winter, Charles Vanden Wouwer, Bernard Voorhoof, Henri Isemborghs, Raymond Braine, Fernand Buyle.* Jack Butler (ENG).

The hosts would have been very disappointed to lose this. Nicolas, avoiding injury this time, made the first goal with a shot Badjou couldn't hold, dribbled through for the second, then volleyed in Aston's short cross. Isemborghs scored from Voorhoof's free-kick. Butler had won a single England cap in 1924 – against Belgium, the country he later coached to their only win over England (1936).

CONSECUTIVE WINS		
7	Italy	1934–38
6	England	1966–70
6	Brazil	1970

■ 5 June 1938 • Cavée Verte, Le Havre • 10,550 • Lucien Leclercq (FRA)

▲ **CZECHOSLOVAKIA (0) (0) 3**
Kostálek 93, Zeman 111, Nejedly 118
HOLLAND (0) (0) 0

● CZECHOSLOVAKIA *Frantisek Plánicka (c), Jaroslav Burgr, Ferdinand Daucík, Josef Kostálek, Jaroslav Boucek, Vlasta Kopecky, Jan Ríha, Vladislav Simunek, Josef Zeman, Oldrich Nejedly, Oldrich Rulc. Jan Meissner (coach Josef Sedlácek).*
HOLLAND *Adri van Male, Mauk Weber, Bertus Caldenhove, Bas Paauwe, Wim Anderiesen, Gerrit 'Puck' van Heel (c), Frank Wels, Freek van der Veen, Jaap 'Kick' Smit, Leen Vente, Bertus de Harder. Bob Glendenning (ENG).*

Czechoslovakia should have had little trouble with a Dutch team deprived of its leading scorer Bakhuys and reduced to ten men by van der Veen's second-half injury. Instead their timing was out and Plánicka had to save a header and a fierce shot ('Bombenschuss') from the 18-year-old de Harder. In extra-time Kostálek scored from long range and at last the forwards began to combine well, Nejedly and Zeman making goals for each other.

LEADING GOALSCORERS 1938

7	Leônidas da Silva	BRZ
5	Gyula Zsengellér	HUN
5	György Sárosi	HUN
5	Silvio Piola	ITA

■ 5 June 1938 • De la Meinau, Strasbourg • 13,452 • Ivan Eklind (SWE)

▲ **BRAZIL (3) (4) 6**
Leônidas 18, 93, 104, Romeu 25, Perácio 44, 71
POLAND (1) (4) 5
Scherfke pen 23, Wilimowski 53, 59, 89, 118

● BRAZIL *'Batatais' (Algisto Lorenzato), Domingos (da Guia), Arthur Machado, José 'Zezé' Procópio, Martim Silveira (c), 'Afonsinho' (Afonso Guimarães), José Lopes, Romeu (Pellicciari), Leônidas (da Silva), José Perácio, Hércules (de Miranda). Adhemar Pimenta.*
POLAND *Edward Madejski, Wladyslaw Szczepaniak (c), Antoni Galecki, Wilhelm Góra, Erwin Nyc, Ewald Dytko, Ryszard Piec, Leonard Piontek, Fryderyk Scherfke, Ernest Wilimowski, Gerard Wodarz. Józef Kaluza.*

Brazil had lost the Copa América play-off to America only in extra-time but picked the usual crop of new caps (seven), plus Leônidas winning his first since 1934. Poland had just drawn with Switzerland and beaten the Republic of Ireland 6-0, and the 21-year-old Wilimowski was one of the sharpest strikers in Europe.

The muddy pitch persuaded Leônidas to play in his socks until Eklind made him put his boots back on (true story). Some of Poland's goals were down to bizarre Brazilian defending (the penalty was awarded for a copybook rugby tackle) but the forwards were better. The sturdy little Leônidas stood out with his pencil moustache and determination (though his ball skills on film don't quite match up to the legend). Old sources credit him with four goals, an error. In the first half, he and Romeu scored from close range high to the keeper's right.

Once Perácio had headed the third, Poland seemed to be out of it – but Wilimowski scored a second-half hat-trick. His fourth came too late to matter but made him the first player to score this many in a finals match. Not content with all their new Austrians, Germany later press-ganged him ('Ernst Willimowski') into scoring 13 goals for them during the War, which was started by the invasion of his own country. Dytko and Nyc were both later known as Edward, Piontek as Piatek.

■ 5 June 1938 • Vélodrome, Marseille • 18,826 • Alois Beranek (GER)

▲ **ITALY (1) (1) 2**
Ferraris 2, Piola 94
NORWAY (0) (1) 1
Brustad 83

● ITALY *Aldo Olivieri, Eraldo Monzeglio, Pietro Rava, Pietro Serantoni, Miguel Angel 'Michele' Andreolo, Ugo Locatelli, Piero Pasinati, Giuseppe Meazza (c), Silvio Piola, Giovanni Ferrari, Pietro Ferraris.* Vittorio Pozzo.
NORWAY *Henry Johansen, Rolf Johannesen, Øivind Holmsen, Kristian Henriksen, Nils Eriksen (c), Rolf Holmberg, Odd Frantzen, Reidar Kvammen, Knut Brynildsen, Magnar Isaksen, Arne Brustad.* Asbjørn Halvorsen.

The holders took the lead when Johansen couldn't stop Ferrari's shot and Ferraris poked it in. But in the Olympic Games two years earlier, Norway had lost only 2-1 to Italy after extra-time, Brustad scoring their equalizer, Italy going on to win the tournament. Surely it couldn't all happen again....

For virtually the whole 90 minutes, Italy were on the rack – Piola policed by Eriksen, the Italian wingers marked out of the game, the rangy Brynildsen a menace up front. Brustad, good enough to play for the Rest of Europe against England later in the year, dribbled half the length of the field to equalize, then had a second goal disallowed for offside.

Two players rescued Italy: Rava, tall and rugged (he'd been sent off in his first international) and the acrobatic Olivieri. In the last few minutes Brynildsen broke through on the right, Olivieri offered him a gap then saved the fierce shot, after which Brynildsen shook his hand. Relief was followed by Piola's winner when the experienced Johansen again failed to hold a shot, this time a trundler from Pasinati. A bad first day at the office for the new Italy, some of whom would lose their jobs.

Some English sources still persist in crediting the first goal to Ferrari, a definite error. Referee Beranek, listed as German, was yet another Austrian strong-armed by the Reich.

SWEDEN bye (Austria withdrew).

Quarter-finals

■ 12 June 1938 • Fort Carré, Antibes • 6,846 • Gustav Krist (CZE)

▲ **SWEDEN (4) 8**
H. Andersson 9, 81, 89, Wetterström 22, 37, 44, Keller 80, Nyberg 84
CUBA (0) 0

● SWEDEN *Henock Abrahamsson, Ivar Eriksson, Olle Källgren, Erik Almgren, Sven Jacobsson, Kurt Svanström, Arne Nyberg, Sven Jonasson, Harry Andersson, Tore Keller (c), Gustav Wetterström.* József Nagy (HUN).
CUBA *Carvajales, Barquín, Chorens, Berges, Rodríguez, Arias, Pedro Ferrer, Fernández (c), Socorro, Tuñas, Juan Alberto Alonso.*

Cuba recalled Carvajales, but the rest of the defence was taken apart. Wetterström, who'd proved himself a rabbit killer by scoring a hat-trick in 11 minutes in the qualifier against Estonia, got another here (hard to know why some sources credit him with four goals; the Swedes never have). Two of the other goals were headers by Andersson. Cuba were handicapped by an injury to Arias, who had to go off, and their last chance came and went when Abrahamsson saved a Fernández penalty. They left their mark on the tournament but haven't been back since.

■ 12 June 1938 • Victor Boucquey, Lille • 14,800 • Rinaldo Barlassina (ITA)

▲ **HUNGARY (1) 2**
Sárosi 42, Zsengellér 89
SWITZERLAND (0) 0

● HUNGARY *Szabó, Korányi, Biró, Antal Szalay, Turay, Lázár, Sas, Jenö Vincze, Sárosi (c), Zsengellér, Kohut.*
SWITZERLAND *Huber, Adolf Stelzer, Lehmann (c), Springer, Vernati, Lörtscher, Bickel, Abegglen, Amadò, Walaschek, Tullio Grassi.*

Two hard matches left the Swiss without Minelli and Aeby, and they had little chance once Sárosi had put Hungary ahead with Huber distracted by a heading duel between Lörtscher and Zsengellér, who scored the second from outside the area. Switzerland kept the score down with rigid defence, but couldn't get past Korányi and Biró, the best full-back pairing in the tournament.

■ 12 June 1938 • Olympique (Colombes), Paris • 58,455 • Louis Baert (BEL)

▲ **ITALY (1) 3**
Colaussi 9, Piola 52, 72
FRANCE (1) 1
Heisserer 10

● ITALY *Olivieri, Alfredo Foni, Rava, Serantoni, Andreolo, Locatelli, Amedeo Biavati, Meazza (c), Piola, Ferrari, Gino Colaussi.*
FRANCE *Di Lorto, Cazenave, Mattler (c), Bastien, Jordan, Diagne, Aston, Heisserer, Nicolas, Delfour, Veinante.*

Pozzo, reading the signs as well as ever, made three important changes: two new wingers, and Foni in place of Monzeglio, a lion of 1934 but now 32 years of age.

France allegedly paid the price for throwing themselves into attack in the second half, allowing Piola too much room – but perhaps it was always on the cards. Jordan had scored against England, but he was an attacking centre-half and his immediate opponent, Ted Drake, had scored twice.

Piola now did the same, the first time with a leaping header from Biavati's cross, the second with a low cross shot. Very tall and angular but mobile and confident, he scored 30 goals for Italy in only 34 games and wasn't particular how they went in: the following year he scored against England with his fist. What unleashed him in this World Cup was the arrival of the new wingers, especially the balding Biavati, whose foot-over-the-ball feint was the subject of diagrams. When Piola hit the ball out to the flanks, he now knew he'd get it back.

France scored a good equalizer – Delfour releasing Veinante, Heisserer putting in the cross – but Italy held their shape in front of a hostile crowd. Pozzo clearly believed they played better in adversity; he sent them out in a change strip of

Fascist black, a set of red rags to the many Italian anti-Fascists who'd escaped to Paris.

The French, though suffered the worst goalkeeping blunder in any World Cup with the first goal of the game, more glaring than Pat Bonner's in 1994 or anything by Kazadi. Surrounded by defenders on the left-hand corner of the penalty area, Colaussi looped a volley straight at Di Lorto, who hopped up for the easy catch then decided to push it away. Somehow he palmed it sideways, tried to follow it as it fell into the net, crashed into the goalpost, and kicked the ball away in disgust. A genuine masterpiece, and all his own work. He didn't play for France again; nor did the stylish Delfour, whose 41st cap was a national record.

The 31-year-old Veinante seems to have been the first player to appear in a finals match on his birthday. Foni was Switzerland's manager in the 1966 finals.

■ 12 June 1938 • Parc Lescure, Bordeaux •
22,021 • Paul von Hertzka (HUN)

▲ **BRAZIL (1) (1) 1**
Leônidas 30
CZECHOSLOVAKIA (0) (1) 1
Nejedly pen 65

● BRAZIL *Walter (de Souza), Domingos, Machado, Zezé Procópio, Martim Silveira (c), Afonsinho, Lopes, Romeu, Leônidas, Perácio, Hércules.*
CZECHOSLOVAKIA *Plánicka (c), Burgr, Daucík, Kostálek, Boucek, Kopecky, Ríha, Simunek, Nejedly, Josef Ludl, Antonín Puc.*
▼ SENT OFF: *Zezé Procópio 14, Machado 44, Ríha 44.*

There had been skirmishes before, even police on the pitch – but here was the first World Cup war, resulting in broken limbs for Plánicka (arm) and Nejedly (leg) which kept them out of the replay.

Brazil announced their intentions early, Zezé Procópio getting himself sent off for a wild tackle on Nejedly, who survived long enough to equalize from a penalty awarded for handball. Puc was also unfit for the replay and Plánicka didn't play for Czechoslovakia again, after a world record 73 caps. Leônidas was slowed by a bad foul seven minutes after opening the score from what looked an offside position.

The first name of von Hertkza, who was born on the Austrian side of the Austro-Hungarian Empire, is sometimes seen spelt the Hungarian way: Pál.

MOST SENDINGS-OFF IN A MATCH		
3	1938	Brazil v Czechoslovakia
3	1954	Brazil v Hungary

REPLAY

■ 14 June 1938 • Parc Lescure, Bordeaux •
18,141 • Georges Capdeville (FRA)

▲ **BRAZIL (0) 2**
Leônidas 57, Roberto 62
CZECHOSLOVAKIA (1) 1
Kopecky 25

● BRAZIL *Walter, 'Jaú' (Euclydes Barbosa), 'Nariz' (Alvaro Cançado Lopes), Hermínio de Britto, José Augusto Brandão, Argemiro (Pinheiro da Silva), Roberto (da Cunha), Luiz M. Oliveira, Leônidas (c), 'Tim' (Elba de Pádua Lima), 'Patesko' (Rodolfo Barteczko).*
CZECHOSLOVAKIA *Karel Burkert, Burgr (c), Daucík, Kostálek, Boucek, Ludl, Václav Horák, Karel Senecky, Vilém Kreuz, Kopecky, Rulc.*

A match awaited with bated breath – but Brazil made nine changes, the Czechs six, and that seemed to clear the air. The result turned on Walter's save from Senecky, the ball appearing to cross the line. Two minutes later Roberto headed the winner. Czechoslovakia were out and soon their prime minister would be sitting outside a room as the Allies voted to let Hitler take the rest of his country. Luiz M. Oliveira is sometimes referred to as 'Luisinho', but not in Brazil.

Semi-finals

■ 16 June 1938 • Parc des Princes, Paris • 20,155 • Lucien Leclercq (FRA)

▲ **HUNGARY (3) 5**
Jacobsson o.g. 19, Titkos 37, Zsengellér 39, 85, Sárosi 65
SWEDEN (1) 1
Nyberg 35 sec

● HUNGARY *Szabó, Korányi, Biró, Szalay, Turay, Lázár, Sas, Zsengellér, Sárosi (c), Toldi, Pál Titkos.*
SWEDEN *Abrahamsson, Eriksson, Källgren, Almgren, Jacobsson, Svanström, Wetterström, Keller (c), H. Andersson, Jonasson, Nyberg.*

Not so much that Sweden were found out, more that the Hungarian attack was irresistible (*Kombinationsmaschine*). Between them, the two main strikers eventually scored 74 goals in 100 internationals, Zsengellér inventive and a natural finisher, Sárosi one of the great all-round players, a withdrawn centre-forward who scored more often than most of his type. Here he headed the fourth after making two of the first three. Once Zsengellér's deflected shot had equalized their very early goal, Sweden had no answer.

■ 16 June 1938 • Vélodrome, Marseille • 33,000 • Hans Wüthrich (SWI)

▲ **ITALY (0) 2**
Colaussi 55, Meazza pen 60
BRAZIL (0) 1
Romeu 87

● ITALY *Olivieri, Foni, Rava, Serantoni, Andreolo, Locatelli, Biavati, Meazza (c), Piola, Ferrari, Colaussi.*
BRAZIL *Walter, Domingos, Machado, Zezé Procópio, Martim Silveira (c), Afonsinho, Lopes, Luiz M. Oliveira, Romeu, Perácio, Patesko.*

Italy, growing into their game, were generally expected to win, but it goes without saying that Brazil were dangerous, at least until Pimenta committed the worst selectorial blunder in any World Cup; he dropped Leônidas – to save him for the Final! Against the World Champions, with their formidable defence, it seemed complete lunacy – and sure enough....

Although a goalless first half suggests a tight match, Italy were biding their time, retreating to the edge of their area to suffocate Brazil's intricate passing. After half-time the counter-attacks bore fruit, first when Colaussi converted a right-wing cross, then when Domingos conceded a penalty.

Arguably the best defender in the tournament (admired by Pozzo), big and static but a famous reader of the ball, Domingos took a battering when Piola 'began to work with his elbows'. An exasperated foul led to the penalty. Meazza dipped his shoulder, scored high to his left, then went to the touchline to change his shorts; the elastic had snapped as he bent to put the ball on the spot. Coolness itself! Romeu scored from Perácio's corner after Olivieri had saved from Luiz Oliveira, but it was far too late.

3rd-place Final

■ 19 June 1938 • Parc Lescure, Bordeaux •
12,500 • John Langenus (BEL)

▲ **BRAZIL (1) 4**
Romeu 44, Leônidas 63, 74, Perácio 80
SWEDEN (2) 2
Jonasson 28, Nyberg 38

● BRAZIL *Batatais, Domingos, Machado, Zezé Procópio, Brandão, Afonsinho, Roberto, Romeu, Leônidas (c), Perácio, Patesko.*
SWEDEN *Abrahamsson, Eriksson, Erik Nilsson, Almgren, Arne Linderholm, Svanström (c), Nyberg, Erik Persson, H. Andersson, Jonasson, Åke Andersson.*

This was Leônidas' match. Back in the team, as captain, he scored twice to finish as the tournament's top scorer, a minor consolation. Jonasson's shot went in off a post and the keeper's body, and Sweden held their unlikely lead until half-time, but the interpassing of the Brazilian forwards was too much for them in the end. Twelve minutes from time a foul by Nilsson on Roberto led to a penalty which Patesko put over the bar (deliberately, it's said).

Pimenta, who resigned as manager after the match, was reappointed in 1942 – and immediately dropped Leônidas again. 'Lillis' Persson was one of three Erik Perssons capped in the 1930s.

Final

■ 19 June 1938 • Olympique (Colombes), Paris •
45,124 • Georges Capdeville (FRA)

▲ **ITALY (3) 4**
Colaussi 6, 35, Piola 16, 82
HUNGARY (1) 2
Titkos 7, Sárosi 69

● ITALY *Olivieri, Foni, Rava, Serantoni, Andreolo, Locatelli, Biavati, Meazza (c), Piola, Ferrari, Colaussi.*
HUNGARY *Szabó, Gyula Polgár, Biró, Szalay, György Szücs, Lázár, Sas, Vincze, Sárosi (c), Zsengellér, Titkos.*

Much the same story as in 1934; Italian ramparts keeping out the Danube. But this was a brighter, more athletic Italian team, with the pace and fitness to keep turning defence into attack – and the last thing Hungary needed was the injury that forced them to replace the hard-tackling Korányi with Polgár, who'd first been capped as a forward.

In fact the entire Hungarian defence was hardly worthy of the name. When Piola crossed from the right, after Biavati had beaten Biró, Colaussi was completely unmarked – and that barely begins to describe it; there wasn't a single Hungarian in that half of the penalty area. With goalkeepers still tending to stay on their lines, Colaussi was able to prod home from close range.

An immediate equalizer raised false hopes, a cross from the right finding Titkos, who lashed in a high shot at the near post. Crucially, Sárosi was being successfully marked by Andreolo – but his real problem was the pace at which Italy played, rushing his decisions. Only the Hungarian wingers carried any threat, and they didn't see enough of the ball.

And there was always Piola. After making the first

goal, he was first to a loose ball, hitting the post with a powerful left-footer. Then Ferrari, seven yards out with only the keeper in front of him, moved the ball to the right instead of shooting, Meazza laid it back – and Piola put an end to the pussyfooting by thumping a right-footed drive high inside the near post. Szabó didn't move. Colaussi walked in the third from the same position as his first, this time with a defender's arm round his waist.

Italy sat back after half-time, rode Sárosi's close-range goal, and sealed everything with a classic counter. Ferrari's crossfield ball found Piola, who sent Biavati away on the right, then met the low return with an uncompromising ground shot. Meazza received the trophy with a Fascist salute and not a Brylcreemed hair out of place, and the team were received by Mussolini, bareheaded this time while they wore the sailor hats. Pozzo is the only manager to have won the World Cup twice.

'How shall we play this game?' asked the French critic Jean Eskenazi. 'Do we make love, or catch a bus?' The Mid-Europeans' technique was known for its finesse, but Pozzo had finally found the right No. 9 to go with his Ferrari.

Italians kept winning in Paris in the summer of 1938. The great Gino Bartali finished first in the

Goalmouth action from the Final. (l-r): Olivieri, Locatelli, Sárosi, Foni, Andreolo.

Tour de France, and even their animals were dominant, Nearco taking the Grand Prix de Paris ahead of the winners of the French and English Derbies. But others would be conquering France soon and there wouldn't be another World Cup until 1950. Right across Europe, the beasts were taking over.

The winning team joined by extras from a Godfather film. (l-r) standing (players and coach only): Biavati, Pozzo, Piola, Ferrari, Colaussi; kneeling: Locatelli, Meazza, Foni, Olivieri, Rava, Andreolo; receiving Meazza's blessing: Serantoni.

The Weight of Shadows

Brazil 1950

The first truly peacetime World Cup in 20 years had its parallels with the previous one: only 13 teams taking part; a league system; a strong host team.

This time the idea of four mini-leagues was in place from the start, presumably because FIFA decided knockout matches were an arbitrary way of deciding the best in the world. To emphasize their thinking, the four group winners would qualify for yet another group, the champions to be decided on points. There was no provision for an actual Final – but one materialized all the same, and perhaps the most eviscerating of all.

Several things had happened in 1949 which seemed sure to affect the result of the tournament. Brazil won the Copa América, also held at home, also on a league basis, with scores of 9-1, 10-1, 5-0, 7-1 and 5-1 (v Uruguay) before thrashing Paraguay 7-0 in the play-off, the inside-forward trio of Zizinho, Ademir and Jair providing some startling action. In Italy, an air crash wiped out the entire Torino squad, the backbone of the national team. Sweden, strong Olympic champions in 1948, lost their best players to Italian clubs.

Of the other South Americans, Uruguay were back in the fold but having a mixed year, and Argentina pulled out yet again. Yugoslavia looked the strongest of the Europeans, Olympic runners-up and packed with world-class players – but the most intriguing entry was from the mother country, taking part for the first time.

The 1950 World Cup came a few years too late for England, who'd lost Frank Swift, Tommy Lawton and the incomparable Raich Carter from their team of the immediate post-war years. But Tom Finney was still there, with Billy Wright and Stan Mortensen and (eventually) Stanley Matthews. At the very least, they were expected to qualify for the final pool.

Places had been left open for the top two teams in the Home Championship, but Scotland decided they'd go as champions or not at all. They lost 1-0 to England at Hampden, where Willie Bauld hit the bar, and stayed behind – a mystery to this day.

Instead of re-drawing the competition after a rash of late withdrawals, the organizers left things as they stood. So while four teams played each other in two of the groups, Uruguay had only Bolivia to beat. And there was no zoning, which forced teams in the same group to travel hundreds of miles between cities.

Brazil had built a new stadium, the biggest in history, with twice the capacity of Wembley. On the first day of the tournament, it still wasn't ready. But the Brazilian public didn't mind too much. Their team seemed to be.

1950

Group 1

Brazil, Mexico, Switzerland, Yugoslavia

■ 24 June 1950 • Maracanã, Rio de Janeiro • 81,649 • George Reader (ENG)

▲ **BRAZIL (1) 4**
Ademir 31, 79, Jair 65, Baltazar 71
MEXICO (0) 0

● BRAZIL *Moacyr Barbosa, Augusto (da Costa) (c), Juvenal (Amarijo), Ely (do Amparo), Danilo (Alvim), 'Bigode' (João Ferreira), 'Maneca' (Manuel Marinho), Ademir (Menezes), 'Baltazar' (Oswaldo da Silva), Jair (Rosa Pinto), Albino Friaça.* Flávio Costa.
MEXICO *Antonio Carbajal, Felipe Zetter, Alfonso Montemayor (c), Rodrigo Ruiz, Mario Ochoa, José Antonio Roca, Carlos Septién, Héctor Ortiz, Horacio Casarín, Mario Pérez snr, Guadalupe (Lupe) Velázquez.* Octavio Vial.

Unusual for a stadium's capacity to be halved for an opening ceremony, but it was just as well. Along with the fireworks and 5,000 pigeons, there was a 21-gun salute, which the new edifice, its plaster still drying, didn't like very much. English referee Arthur Ellis and others in the stand 'were peppered with a shower of concrete, fortunately none of it in huge blocks!' Then when Brazil scored, 15 radio commentators and dozens of reporters ran on to the pitch for on-the-spot interviews (it still happens now).

Reader had the field cleared without fuss and Brazil resumed their bombardment. Carbajal, winning his first cap, was described as 'magnifico' and Brazil hit the woodwork five times. Mexico gave away six free-kicks in the first five minutes, Jair hit a post after six, then Ademir touched the ball past the advancing Carbajal, who began picking smoking

fireworks out of his goalmouth.

In the second half, Ademir switched to centre-forward, Baltazar moving to the wing. Friaça, Jair (twice) and Baltazar hit the bar, Jair scored with a cross-shot of 'optimum style', Baltazar headed the third from a corner, and Ademir drove in Jair's short pass. All this from a team who hadn't decided on their best forward line.

Mario Pérez was the brother of Luis (1930) who was 20 years older, and father of Mario junior (1970). The Maracanã was known as the Municipal at the time and later as the Mário Filho (it's in the Maracanã district of Rio).

■ 25 June 1950 • Independencia, Belo Horizonte • 7,336 • Giovanni Galeati (ITA)

▲ **YUGOSLAVIA (0) 3**
Mitic 58, Tomasevic 78, Ognjanov 84
SWITZERLAND (0) 0

● YUGOSLAVIA *Srdan Mrkusic, Ivan Horvat, Branko Stankovic, Zlatko Cajkovski, Miodrag Jovanovic, Predrag Dajic, Tihomir Ognjanov, Rajko Mitic (c), Kosta Tomasevic, Stjepan Bobek, Bernard Vukas.* Milorad Arsenijevic, with Ljubisa Brocic.
SWITZERLAND *Georges Stuber, André Neury, Roger Bocquet, Gerhard Lusenti, Olivier Eggimann, Roger Quinche, Alfred (Fred) Bickel (c), Charly Antenen, Jean Tamini, René Bader, Jacky Fatton.* Franco Andreoli.

By now the Swiss had perfected the *verrou*, their 'bolt' defence, but can't have been surprised by the result; they'd lost 4-0 at home to Yugoslavia two weeks earlier. Here, after the giant Horvat had defused an early crisis, 'el dominio de Yugoslavia es total'. Stuber made two brilliant saves from Bobek, who eventually sent Mitic in to score. Tomasevic headed the second and Ognjanov finished off a move involving the entire forward line by knocking in a pass by Jovanovic.

This was the first finals match in which floodlights were switched on. It started 20 minutes late while corner flags were found and a line of chairs moved from right next to one of the touchlines. Bickel was one of only two players (with Erik Nilsson of Sweden) to play in the finals before and after the War.

■ 28 June 1950 • Eucaliptos, Pôrto Alegre • 11,078 • Reg Leafe (ENG)

▲ **YUGOSLAVIA (2) 4**
Bobek 19, Zeljko Cajkovski 23, 51, Tomasevic 81
MEXICO (0) 1
Ortiz pen 87

● YUGOSLAVIA *Mrkusic, Horvat (c), Stankovic, Zlatko Cajkovski, Jovanovic, Dajic, Prvoslav Mihajlovic, Mitic, Tomasevic, Bobek, Zeljko Cajkovski.*
MEXICO *Carbajal, Manuel Gutiérrez, Samuel Cuburu, Gregorio Gómez, Ortiz, Roca, Septién, José Naranjo, Casarín (c), Pérez, Velázquez.*

Bobek drove in Mihajlovic's cross, Zlatko Cajkovski, a tenacious half-back, made a goal for his brother, who scored his second with a *violentissimo* shot. Tomasevic scored the fourth with a shot Carbajal couldn't hold. Mexico were on the defensive throughout, breaking out only when the match had been decided. The penalty was given for a foul on Velázquez.

■ 28 June 1950 • Pacaembu, São Paulo • 42,032 • Ramón Azon (SPA)

▲ **BRAZIL (2) 2**
Alfredo 3, Baltazar 32
SWITZERLAND (1) 2
Fatton 17, 88

● BRAZIL *Barbosa, Augusto (c), Juvenal, José Carlos Bauer, Rui (Campos), Alfredo Noronha, Alfredo (dos Santos), Maneca, Baltazar, Ademir, Friaça.*
SWITZERLAND *Stuber, Neury, Bocquet, Lusenti, Eggimann, Quinche, Tamini, Bickel (c), Hans Peter Friedländer, Bader, Fatton.*

Flávio Costa, reported as calling Switzerland 'contenders without importance', brought in a number of players from São Paulo clubs, presumably to please the crowd – who nearly lynched him for it. Alfredo scored with an excellent shot after Ademir's cut-back seemed to have gone out of play, Baltazar headed in Friaça's cross following a corner, Stuber made a marvellous save from Ademir and was knocked out by a shot from Baltazar – but the Swiss wouldn't lie down.

The dangerous little Fatton sped past Augusto to score their first, then tapped in from three yards after Bickel got away late in the game. The result left Yugoslavia needing only a draw with Brazil to qualify and the police had to save Costa from indignant fans. One plus for Brazil was the form of the statuesque Bauer, a tremendous all-rounder, who was here to stay.

Chilean linesman Sergio Bustamante was the youngest official in any finals match: 26 years 65 days.

■ 1 July 1950 • Maracanã, Rio de Janeiro • 142,429 • Mervyn Griffiths (WAL)

▲ **BRAZIL (1) 2**
Ademir 3, Zizinho 69
YUGOSLAVIA (0) 0

● BRAZIL *Barbosa, Augusto (c), Juvenal, Bauer, Danilo, Bigode, Maneca, 'Zizinho' (Thomaz Soares da Silva), Ademir, Jair, 'Chico' (Francisco Aramburu).*
YUGOSLAVIA *Mrkusic, Horvat, Stankovic, Zlatko Cajkovski (c), Jovanovic, Dajic, Vukas, Mitic, Tomasevic, Bobek, Zeljko Cajkovski.*

■ 2 July 1950 • Eucaliptos, Pôrto Alegre • 3,580 • Ivan Eklind (SWE)

▲ **SWITZERLAND (2) 2**
Bader 12, Antenen 44
MEXICO (0) 1
Casarín 75

● SWITZERLAND *Adolphe Hug, Neury, Bocquet (c), Lusenti, Eggimann, Quinche, Tamini, Antenen, Friedländer, Bader, Fatton.*
MEXICO *Carbajal, Gutiérrez, Gómez, Roca, Ortiz, Ochoa, Antonio Flóres, Naranjo, Casarín (c), José Luis Borbolla, Velázquez.*

There was an 'extraordinaria tensión' in Rio before the match, and many thought Costa had blundered again by leaving out Baltazar, so good in the air. But he'd got it right this time, restoring the great inside-forward trio, and Brazil had a slice of luck to set them on their way. In the changing room before the match, Mitic (a contemporary source says Zlatko Cajkovski) found out just how unfinished the stadium was, cutting his head on an exposed girder. The referee refused to delay the start and by the time Mitic came on, Brazil were ahead, Ademir heading in Maneca's cross.

Then Mitic (or Zlatko Cajkovski) joined in and Yugoslavia matched Brazil for skill and opportunities, Tomasevic blasting over the bar, Barbosa saving from Mitic. It took half an hour for the referee to order Mrkusic to change his jersey because it was the same colour as Brazil's all-white strip.

In the second half, Zizinho had a goal disallowed and Zeljko Cajkovski missed two chances. Then Ademir found Zizinho, who beat two men and shot low past Mrkusic. The hosts were through to their appointed place but by the skin of their opponents' brow.

In between their goals, Switzerland missed good chances through Bader and Tamini. In the second half, Hug saved twice from Casarín, who finally had his reward with a fierce cross shot.

Hug's first name is also seen spelt Adolf. Roca was Mexico's manager in the 1978 finals.

GROUP 1	P	W	D	L	F	A	PTS
Brazil	3	2	1	0	8	2	5
Yugoslavia	3	2	0	1	7	3	4
Switzerland	3	1	1	1	4	6	3
Mexico	3	0	0	3	2	10	0

Brazil qualified for the final pool.

Group 2

Chile, England, Spain, USA

■ 25 June 1950 • Maracanã, Rio de Janeiro •
29,703 • Karel van der Meer (HOL)

▲ **ENGLAND (1) 2**
Mortensen 39, Mannion 51
CHILE (0) 0

● CHILE *Sergio Livingstone (c), Arturo Farías, Fernando Roldán, Manuel Alvarez, Miguel Busquets, Hernán Carvallo, Lindorfo Mayanés, Atilio Cremaschi, Jorge Robledo, Manuel Muñoz, Guillermo Díaz Zambrano.* Alberto Buccicardi.
ENGLAND *Bert Williams, Alf Ramsey, Johnny Aston, Billy Wright (c), Laurie Hughes, Jimmy Dickinson, Tom Finney, Wilf Mannion, Roy Bentley, Stan Mortensen, Jimmy Mullen.* Walter Winterbottom.

This was Chile's first match against European opposition since the 1930 World Cup, and their press called it the most difficult match in their history – but they'd beaten Uruguay in their last match before the tournament and were now reinforced by 'George' Robledo, who played for Newcastle United (he scored the only goal of the 1952 FA Cup Final) and was the main danger to England, especially as they had a problem at centre-half.

Two months earlier the classy Neil Franklin had gone to look for El Dorado, or at least a living wage, in Colombia, leaving a gap in defence that wasn't fully filled for four years. Without him, England still beat Portugal 5-3 and Belgium 4-1, but both the opposition centre-forwards scored twice and Bill Jones was discarded. Like Robledo, the tall Laurie Hughes would be making his debut.

He did well enough, but the defence were regularly surprised by the trickery of the Chileans, Robledo hitting the post with a free-kick, Carvallo hitting the bar. The England forwards were praised for their precision but had trouble with 'the vigorous methods of the Chilean defenders' and the whole team found the humid conditions difficult, taking oxygen at half-time (Billy Wright 'gave it a test but found it of little use').

Mortensen headed in Mullen's cross then sent Finney away for a centre which Mannion steered neatly inside Livingstone's right-hand post – but no-one was unduly impressed. Wright's ghost-writer again: 'I personally did not feel elated.'

Mortensen (on the ground) watches the ball drop down the other side of the Chilean net. Note the sparse crowd for England's belated entry into the World Cup arena.

■ 25 June 1950 • Durival de Brito, Curitiba •
9,511 • Mario Vianna (BRZ)

▲ **SPAIN (0) 3**
Igoa 80, Basora 82, Zarra 85
USA (1) 1
Pariani 17

● SPAIN *Ignacio Eizaguirre (c), Gabriel Alonso, Francisco
(Paco) Antúnez, Mariano Gonzalvo, José Gonzalvo, Antonio
Puchades, Estanislao Basora, Rosendo Hernández, 'Zarra'
(Telmo Zarraonandia), Silvestre Igoa, Agustin 'Piru'
Gainza. Guillermo Eizaguirre, with Benito Díaz.*
USA *Frank Borghi, Harry Keough (c), Joe Maca, Ed
McIlvenny, Charlie Colombo, Walter Bahr, Adam Wolanin,
Virginio (Gino) Pariani, Joe Gaetjens, John Souza, Frank
Valcenti 'Wallace'. Walter Giesler, with coach Bill
Jeffrey (SCO).*

The Americans had qualified despite losing 6-0 and
6-2 to Mexico, but showed unsuspected stamina and
ball skills here, reinforced by Maca from Belgium,
Gaetjens from Haiti, and the Scotsman McIlvenny,
who later signed for Manchester United. Colombo
invited comment by playing in gloves. Zarra had a
goal disallowed, then at last the famous Spanish *furia*
struck – Igoa with a spectacular header, Basora an
'indefensible' shot, Zarra from close range.

Some English sources still credit J. Souza with the
US goal, but American publications agree that
Pariani 'tallied against Spain with a shot that
handcuffed one of the world's greatest goaltenders
Eizaguirre'. Official sources wrongly list Bob
Craddock in place of Wolanin. The Gonzalvos were
brothers. Bahr's sons Chris and Matt kicked goals in
various Superbowls.

*England's Mannion (centre) watches Bentley (left) and Mortensen challenge for a high ball
against Chile.*

■ 29 June 1950 • Maracanã, Rio de Janeiro •
19,790 • Alberto da Gama Malcher (BRZ)

▲ **SPAIN (2) 2**
Basora 17, Zarra 30
CHILE (0) 0

● SPAIN *Antonio Ramallets, Alonso, José Parra, M. Gonzalvo, J. Gonzalvo, Puchades, Basora, Igoa, Zarra, José Luis Panizo, Gainza (c).*
CHILE *Livingstone (c), Farías, Roldán, Alvarez, Busquets, Carvallo, Andrés Prieto, Cremaschi, Robledo, Muñoz, Díaz Zambrano.*

Sergio Livingstone, Chile's goalkeeper and captain.

Spain gave a first cap to Ramallets, who would remain their No. 1 for ten years and started with a *meravigliosa* save from Cremaschi. Livingstone saved from Zarra, but then Roldán gave the ball straight to Basora, who scored easily, and Zarra blasted the second from 12 yards. In the second half, he had a goal disallowed. Easy for the Spanish, who were suddenly being talked up as genuine threats. Prieto's brother Ignacio played in the 1966 finals.

■ 29 June 1950 • Independencia, Belo Horizonte •
10,151 • Generoso Dattilo (ITA)

▲ **USA (1) 1**
Gaetjens 38
ENGLAND (0) 0

● USA *Borghi, Keough, Maca, McIlvenny (c), Colombo, Bahr, Wallace, Pariani, Gaetjens, J. Souza, Ed Souza.*
ENGLAND *Williams, Ramsey, Aston, Wright (c), Hughes, Dickinson, Finney, Mannion, Bentley, Mortensen, Mullen.*

Were the USA really taken so lightly? They did remarkably well against Spain and lost only 1-0 to a strong English FA XI just before the tournament. Perhaps people took more notice of the defeats by Mexico, the 5-0 loss to Turkish club Besiktas, and the Americans' own dismissal of their chances, which now sounds like a smokescreen.

English reports of the match have tended to be little more than a catalogue of missed chances, Borghi acrobatics, eccentric refereeing – almost as if the writers thought this was what must have happened. In fact there was much more cut and thrust than that and the US goal was much better than we've been led to believe. The story goes that a mishit clearance from Bahr went in off Gaetjens' ear (Alf Ramsey said he 'ducked to avoid the ball'), but Bahr himself was scathing: 'What would I be doing, clearing the ball near the England goal?' He admitted his cross may have started life as a shot, but was adamant that Gaetjens' contribution was a deliberate, and brilliant, diving header. 'Joe regularly scored goals like that in the league.'

After half-time, England moved Mortensen to centre-forward and Bentley out to the wing, but made little headway. Match reports recount chances missed, but usually the same three: Mortensen's shot possibly crossing the line; Mullen's header from Ramsey's free-kick doing the same; Mortensen breaking through to be rugby-tackled by the Italian Colombo (puns on the Italian referee's first name). On the other side of the ledger, Pariani missed a chance and forced a fine save from Williams, and Ramsey had to kick the ball off the line near the end. Wallace: 'If I'd hit the ball harder, he'd never have touched it.'

The only American reporter at the game was the immortal Dent McSkimming of the St Louis Post-Despatch who was in Brazil on holiday – and an editor in London thought the scoreline was a misprint for 10-1. It was a remarkable match; not quite the great shock it appears, but an upset all the same.

These colonials were becoming real pests. On the same day, England's cricketers lost at home to the West Indies for the first time. One or two sources claim Borghi saved a penalty from Mortensen, a baffling fantasy. The crowd apparently swelled to c. 40,000 by the end. Gaetjens was murdered in 1964 by the Tontons Macoute, Duvalier's vicious secret police.

Despite previous captions, this isn't a picture of the US goal, but it's not far off. Williams and Gaetjens watch the ball slip down the back of the England net.

Aston watches Williams gather the ball against the USA. The American players, Gaetjens (18) and Wallace, were among the first to wear squad numbers in the World Cup.

■ 2 July 1950 • Maracanã, Rio de Janeiro • 74,462 • Giovanni Galeati (ITA)

▲ **SPAIN (0) 1**
Zarra 48
ENGLAND (0) 0

● SPAIN *Ramallets, Parra, Alonso, M. Gonzalvo, J. Gonzalvo, Puchades, Basora, Igoa, Zarra, Panizo, Gainza (c).*
ENGLAND *Williams, Ramsey, Bill Eckersley, Wright (c), Hughes, Dickinson, Stanley Matthews, Mortensen, Jackie Milburn, Eddie Baily, Finney.*

■ 2 July 1950 • Ilha do Retiro, Recife • 8,501 • Mario Gardelli (BRZ)

▲ **CHILE (2) 5**
Robledo 16, Cremaschi 32, 61, 82, Prieto 54
USA (0) 2
Wallace 47, Maca pen 48

● CHILE *Livingstone (c), Manuel Machuca, Alvarez, Busquets, Farías, Carlos Rojas, Fernando Riera, Cremaschi, Robledo, Prieto, Carlos Ibáñez.*
USA *Borghi, Keough, Maca, McIlvenny, Colombo, Bahr (c), Wallace, Pariani, Gaetjens, J. Souza, E. Souza.*

Winterbottom – or rather the sole selector Arthur Drewry – at last made changes, bringing in the speedy Milburn, new caps Eckersley and Baily, and Matthews at last. There was some definite improvement – but the England players later complained of continual bodychecking and handball. Spain persistently booted the ball into the crowd and Milburn had a goal contentiously disallowed after 14 minutes.

But there were too many excuses on this trip. Spain, who needed only a draw and deserved at least that, had some quality players: Ramallets, Panizo, the two wingers, and Zarra who scored 20 goals in 20 internationals, including this one, after Hughes (who wasn't capped again) missed Basora's cross. Once again the England forwards were criticized as too slow.

The bottom line? A teamsheet that reads like a Who's Who of the best in the Football League just wasn't good enough away from home. Someone really should have buried the hatchet with FIFA 20 years earlier. Matthews was the oldest player in this tournament and the next.

Again Robledo was the best Chilean forward, leading the line and scoring the first goal after Cremaschi had beaten a man. Riera crossed for Cremaschi to sprint in and smash home the second.

Immediately after half-time, Wallace scored with a header and Farías conceded a penalty by fouling Gaetjens – but Cremaschi drove in Robledo's pass, Prieto beat Maca and put in a shot Borghi might have saved, and Riera got away again to find Cremaschi, short and moustachioed, right in front of goal.

There's genuine confusion over Cremaschi's hat-trick. Old sources credit him with all three, but various publications say only two, with Riera scoring the other. However, the match report in Santiago's *El Mercurio* says three, and we'll go along with that. Early sources list Muñoz in place of Rojas, an error.

Some publications also say J. Souza scored the USA's first goal and Pariani took the penalty, more errors. *Soccer News* lists Wallace and Maca (pen) as the scorers, while another American source refers to Wallace scoring 'a beautiful headed goal'. The USA appointed a different captain for each match: Keough v Spain because he spoke Spanish, McIlvenny v

England because he was British, Bahr v Chile 'because he was the real captain'!

GROUP 2	P	W	D	L	F	A	PTS
Spain	3	3	0	0	6	1	6
England	3	1	0	2	2	2	2
Chile	3	1	0	2	5	6	2
USA	3	1	0	2	4	8	2

Spain qualified for the final pool.

Group 3

Italy, Paraguay, Sweden

■ 25 June 1950 • Pacaembu, São Paulo • 56,502 • Jean Lutz (SWI)

▲ **SWEDEN (2) 3**
Jeppson 25, 68, Andersson 33
ITALY (1) 2
Carapellese 7, Muccinelli 75

● SWEDEN *Kalle Svensson, Lennart Samuelsson, Erik Nilsson (c), Sune Andersson, Knut Nordahl, Ingvar Gärd, Stig Sundkvist, Karl-Erik Palmér, Hasse Jeppson, Lennart 'Nacka' Skoglund, Stellan Nilsson.* George Raynor (ENG).
ITALY *Lucidio Sentimenti, Attilio Giovannini, Zeffiro Furiassi, Carlo Annovazzi, Carlo Parola, Augusto Magli, Ermes Muccinelli, Giampiero Boniperti, Gino Cappello, Aldo Campatelli, Riccardo Carapellese (c).* Ferruccio Novo.

Both sides had been rebuilt, but Sweden shouldn't have had to. It's true that Milan had signed their great 'Grenoli' inside-forward trio (Gren-Nordahl-Liedholm), but they were kept out of the finals by the Swedish FA's refusal to pick players with foreign clubs. If they'd played, Sweden would have been the European team most likely to mount a challenge. As it was, Raynor had another chance to prove his ability to identify new talent – but it remains a case of what might have been.

After the Turin air disaster, Italy travelled by ship, to be met by thousands of Italian expatriates, who made up the bulk of the crowd in a stadium that sported a statue of Michelangelo's David. Home from home – but injury sidelined their main striker Benito Lorenzi (christened in different times) and there was no love lost among their selectors. Carapellese's clever early goal, from a pass by Cappello, gave false hope.

Parola was a genuinely world-class stopper, a master of the overhead clearance kick, but Jeppson emerged as 'un angelo sterminatore', or at least a bony nuisance. And the new midgets at inside-forward (Palmér weighed less than nine stone) were full of feints and dribbles, Raynor having stressed that 'we had to be light-footed'.

After Cappello had missed a clear chance to put Italy 2-0 up, Jeppson smashed in precise passes from Skoglund and Palmér, Andersson shooting the second in between.

Muccinelli pulled one back and Carapellese hit the bar, but the right team won.

This first defeat for any World Cup holders put an end to Italy's sequence of seven consecutive wins, still the finals record. Jeppson is the correct spelling, (not, say, Jepsson). Italian clubs promptly signed up almost the whole Sweden team.

■ 29 June 1950 • Durival de Brito, Curitiba • 7,903 • George Mitchell (SCO)

▲ **SWEDEN (2) 2**
Sundkvist 17, Palmér 25
PARAGUAY (1) 2
López 34, López Fretes 74

● SWEDEN *Svensson, Samuelsson, E. Nilsson (c), Andersson, Nordahl, Gärd, Egon Jönsson, Palmér, Jeppson, Skoglund, Sundkvist.*
PARAGUAY *Marcelino Vargas, 'Gonzalito' (Alberto González), Casiano Céspedes, Manuel Gavilán, Victoriano Leguizámon, Castor Sixto Cantero, Rafael Avalos, Atilio López, Dario Jara Saguier, César López Fretes (c), Leongino Unzain.* Manuel Fleitas Solich.

Paraguay were the Copa América runners-up, 'rapides et dynamiques', but the Swedes were better on the ball. They were also lucky that López Fretes missed an 'excellent probability' in the first ten minutes.

After that, Sundkvist scored from Jeppson's pass and Skoglund's long ball was put in by Palmér. Atilio López pulled one back after elegantly beating two men, then had a goal disallowed for handball. López Fretes scored from Jara's centre, but the latter was well marked by Nordahl.

Jönsson was a different player from Egon Johnsson (they played together in a qualifier against the Republic of Ireland). Another Rafael Avalos played for Mexico in the 1954 finals.

■ 2 July 1950 • Pacaembu, São Paulo • 25,811 • Arthur Ellis (ENG)

▲ **ITALY (1) 2**
Carapellese 12, Pandolfini 62
PARAGUAY (0) 0

● ITALY *Bepi Moro, Ivano Blason, Furiassi, Osvaldo Fattori, Leandro Remondini, Giacomo Mari, Muccinelli, Egisto Pandolfini, Amedeo Amadei, Cappello, Carapellese (c).*
PARAGUAY *Vargas, Gonzalito, Cespedes, Gavilán, Leguizámon, Cantero, Avalos, López, Jara Saguier, López Fretes (c), Unzain.*

Italy were in a decline that would last the decade, but at least little Carapellese scored another good goal, from Pandolfini's pass, returning the compliment in the second half. Seven Paraguayans were winning their last caps. As with Biavati in 1938, Amedeo is the correct spelling (not Amadeo).

GROUP 3	P	W	D	L	F	A	PTS
Sweden	2	1	1	0	5	4	3
Italy	2	1	0	1	4	3	2
Paraguay	2	0	1	1	1	4	1

Sweden qualified for the final pool. The group was reduced to three teams by the withdrawal of India. Legend has it they pulled out of the competition because FIFA insisted that they wear boots!

Group 4

Bolivia, Uruguay

■ 2 July 1950 • Independencia, Belo Horizonte • 5,284 • George Reader (ENG)

▲ **URUGUAY (4) 8**
Míguez 14, 40, 51, Vidal 18, Schiaffino 17, 53, Pérez 83, Ghiggia 87
BOLIVIA (0) 0

● URUGUAY *Roque Máspoli, Matias González, Eusebio Tejera, Juan Carlos González, Obdulio Varela (c), Victor Rodríguez Andrade, Alcide Ghiggia, Julio Pérez, Omar Míguez, Juan Schiaffino, Ernesto Vidal.* Juan López.
BOLIVIA *Eduardo Gutiérrez, Alberto de Achá, José Bustamante II (c), Antonio Grecco, Antonio Valencia, Leonardo Ferrel, Celestino Algarañáz, Victor Ugarte, Roberto Caparelli, Benigno Gutiérrez, Benjamin Maldonado.* Mario Pretto (ITA)

Bolivia made some confident noises beforehand, but once Uruguay had scored in their first attack, it turned into an embarrassment on a dustbowl. Bolivia, as bad as in 1930, had just lost 5-0 to Chile, and Uruguay unveiled some tremendous players: Máspoli in goal; Varela the attacking centre-half, first capped in 1939; Andrade, nephew of the great 1930s player; Schiaffino and Ghiggia both skinny and brilliant.

Míguez met Varela's cross with a 'potente impacto'; Schiaffino scored the second and sent Míguez dashing in for the fourth; Vidal finished off a three-man move; and Bolivia were handicapped by an injury to their centre-half Caparelli. In the second half, Míguez put in Ghiggia's pass; Schiaffino shot just inside a post; Pérez dribbled the keeper; and Ghiggia surprised Gutiérrez from long range. By staying at home, Scotland missed out on a victory over one of these

teams and a lesson from the other.

Some old publications list the scorers as Schiaffino 4, Míguez 2, Vidal, Ghiggia. One even credits Schiaffino with five – but all reliable sources (Uruguayan included) say only two.

GROUP 4	P	W	D	L	F	A	PTS
Uruguay	1	1	0	0	8	0	2
Bolivia	1	0	0	1	0	8	0

Uruguay qualified for the final pool. The number of teams in the group was halved by the withdrawal of Scotland, Turkey and the various countries invited to replace them.

Final Pool

Brazil, Spain, Sweden, Uruguay

■ 9 July 1950 • Pacaembu, São Paulo • 44,802 • Mervyn Griffiths (WAL)

▲ **URUGUAY (1) 2**
Ghiggia 27, Varela 72
SPAIN (2) 2
Basora 39, 41

● URUGUAY *Máspoli, M. González, Tejera, J. C. González, Varela (c), Rodríguez Andrade, Ghiggia, Pérez, Míguez, Schiaffino, Vidal.*
SPAIN *Ramallets, Alonso, Parra, M. Gonzalvo, J. Gonzalvo, Puchades, Basora, Igoa, Zarra, Luis Molowny, Gainza (c).*

Spain's rough-house tactics suddenly met their match. Andrade was compact and aggressive; Matias González dominated the rugged Zarra; Varela had the physique as well as the face of a bouncer.

Ghiggia, coming into tremendous form, sprinted in for the first goal, but Basora headed in Igoa's chip then converted a good pass from Molowny, and Uruguay were only saved when Varela came upfield and beat 'various adversaries' before scoring. A tough game, and two Uruguayans had to miss the next one.

■ 9 July 1950 • Maracanã, Rio de Janeiro • 138,886 • Arthur Ellis (ENG)

▲ **BRAZIL (3) 7**
Ademir 17, 37, 51, 59, Chico 39, 87, Maneca 85
SWEDEN (0) 1
Andersson pen 67

● BRAZIL *Barbosa, Augusto (c), Juvenal, Bauer, Danilo, Bigode, Maneca, Zizinho, Ademir, Jair, Chico.*
SWEDEN *Svensson, Samuelsson, E. Nilsson (c), Andersson, Nordahl, Gärd, Sundkvist, Palmér, Jeppson, Skoglund, S. Nilsson.*

After the uncertainties of the group matches, Brazil cut loose. It's tempting to wonder about the Swedish defence, but no other team in the tournament did this to them. Nilsson, Nordahl and the goalkeeper were international class, Gärd 'a great getter and tremendous fighter'. They'd simply never met inside-forwards of this standard before – and nor had anyone else.

All three had slim physiques and pencil moustaches, Jair a centre parting, Ademir blue eyes and a Jimmy Hill chin, Zizinho a strong resemblance to Little Richard. Their ball-control and inter-passing were beyond anything seen in Europe at the time and nobody was scoring goals like Ademir.

Tall and elegant, if slightly stiff-legged, he scored the best that referee Ellis had ever seen, a bicycle kick after flipping the ball up with his other foot. One source says he trapped the ball between his ankles and jumped over the keeper! If TV had been there (and if the reports are true), we wouldn't be talking about Pelé. Sweden's reply, a penalty awarded for handball by Juvenal, looks like a prize for turning up.

Ademir scored his first goal by running on to a first-time through-ball and flicking a half-volley wide of the advancing keeper; another by dummying to play a one-two before turning at speed and spearing a left-footed shot just inside the near post. He was good in the air too, happy to mix it with the beleaguered Svensson. Maneca converted Jair's pass from three yards out and Chico scored the last with a fierce shot. There might have been more if Brazil hadn't played exhibition football in the last half-hour.

■ 13 July 1950 • Pacaembu, São Paulo • 7,987 • Giovanni Galeati (ITA)

▲ **URUGUAY (1) 3**
Ghiggia 39, Míguez 77, 84
SWEDEN (2) 2
Palmér 4, Sundkvist 41

● URUGUAY *Anibal Paz, M. González, Tejera, Schubert Gambetta, Varela (c), Rodríguez Andrade, Ghiggia, Pérez, Míguez, Schiaffino, Vidal.*
SWEDEN *Svensson, Samuelsson, E. Nilsson (c), Andersson, Gunnar Johansson, Gärd, Jönsson, Bror Mellberg, Jeppson, Palmér, Sundkvist.*

Máspoli and J. C. González, injured against Spain, had to be replaced by Paz and the portly Gambetta, and Pérez had barely recovered. So Sweden were able to twice take the lead, showing great resilience after their humiliation. Palmér, a *gran figura* for such a tiny man, smacked in Mellberg's pass while surrounded by defenders, and Sundkvist scored the second from a narrow angle.

But their harder schedule caught up with them,

some of the Uruguayan tackling was barely legal (Jönsson had to go off for treatment), and although Palmér and the blond Skoglund were lionized by the South American press, Raynor later claimed they were 'good in ordinary internationals but not so good in World Cup matches'. Ghiggia had a goal disallowed for Andrade's foul on Palmér, then dribbled through for a shot that went in off Johansson, and the sturdy Míguez scored twice, the first from Ghiggia's cross. It was just enough to make Uruguay's last match a live one.

Gambetta wasn't the only Uruguayan with musical parents. Beethoven Javier played against England in 1977.

■ 13 July 1950 • Maracanã, Rio de Janeiro • 152,772 • Reg Leafe (ENG)

▲ **BRAZIL (3) 6**
Parra o.g. 15, Jair 21, Chico 29, 55, Ademir 57, Zizinho 74
SPAIN (0) 1
Igoa 70

● BRAZIL *Barbosa, Augusto (c), Juvenal, Bauer, Danilo, Bigode, Friaça, Zizinho, Ademir, Jair, Chico.*
SPAIN *Ramallets, Alonso, Parra, M. Gonzalvo, J. Gonzalvo, Puchades, Basora, Igoa, Zarra, Panizo, Gainza (c).*

One newspaper described Panizo as 'a remarkable strategist capable of highlighting the bad marking of the Brazilian defenders'. Ha. By now Brazil were unstoppable, inflicting a scoreline like this on a team which had beaten England. In the space of three minutes Ramallets saved from Chico and Zizinho but couldn't stop Jair's 'vigorous' 20-yarder going in off the bar. Then Friaça robbed the unfortunate Parra to make the third for Chico, who was hit by an

object from the celebrating crowd! Brazil protected their lead with a mixture of keep-ball and harsh tackling, Bigode fouling Basora, Bauer clattering Panizo, Danilo leaving Zarra needing attention.

After half-time Chico shot in a pass by Jair, Ademir scored the fifth (his name litters match reports) and set up Zizinho for the sixth. Zarra hit the bar and Panizo sent Basora away to make a consolation goal for Igoa.

There used to be genuine confusion as to how many goals Ademir scored in this match, affecting his total as top scorer in the tournament. Old English sources said none at all, more recent publications plumped for two, especially as the referee credited him with the first, heavily deflected by Parra. The main sources (including three from Brazil) now say one, and eight in total – but that own goal is a moot point.

■ 16 July 1950 • Pacaembu, São Paulo • 11,227 • Karel van der Meer (HOL)

▲ **SWEDEN (2) 3**
Sundkvist 15, Mellberg 34, Palmér 79
SPAIN (0) 1
Zarra 82

● SWEDEN *Svensson, Samuelsson, E Nilsson (c), Andersson, Johansson, Gärd, Jönsson, Mellberg, Ingvar Rydell, Palmér, Sundkvist.*
SPAIN *Eizaguirre, Vicente Asensi, Parra, Alonso, Alfonso Silva, Puchades, Basora, Hernández, Zarra (c), Panizo, José Juncosa.*

Spain couldn't get up for it and Sweden were already there. Sundkvist darted on to a marvellous pass from Palmér, Mellberg got the second when Ramallets was stranded outside his area, and Palmér shot the third. Basora and Zarra inter-passed through a packed defence to score. Coach George Raynor, who'd again worked minor miracles, even beat the Spanish officials at billiards!

■ 16 July 1950 • Maracanã, Rio de Janeiro • 205,000 • George Reader (ENG)

▲ **URUGUAY (0) 2**
Schiaffino 66, Ghiggia 79
BRAZIL (0) 1
Friaça 47

● URUGUAY *Máspoli, M. González, Tejera, Gambetta, Varela (c), Rodríguez Andrade, Ghiggia, Pérez, Míguez, Schiaffino, Rubén Morán.*
BRAZIL *Barbosa, Augusto (c), Juvenal, Bauer, Danilo, Bigode, Friaça, Zizinho, Ademir, Jair, Chico.*

Brazil were overwhelming favourites, needing only a draw in front of the biggest crowd ever to watch a football match – but there were signs and omens.

Uruguay, in an up-and-down season, had played Brazil three times, all in São Paulo or Rio, winning the first 4-3 before losing only 3-2 and 1-0. A year earlier, Brazil had gone into their last match needing just a draw to win the Copa América – and lost 2-1 to Paraguay before wreaking revenge in the play-off. This time there would be no second chances.

Thoroughly overshadowed by the great trio up front, the Brazilian defenders were adequate enough, especially the athletic Juvenal, but their diagonal formation left their wing-halves with no cover if the opposition wingers broke through. It simply hadn't mattered until now – you could afford to concede a goal through a weakness in your system if its strengths included scoring six or seven at the other end.

Against Uruguay, Brazil threatened to match those earlier scores (they had 30 shots at goal), but were frustrated by a wall of defenders. Every one of the Brazilian forwards was shadowed, the mighty

Varela staying back to help Tejera mark Ademir – and Máspoli played the game of his life.

After some typical interplay with Zizinho, Ademir's shot thumped into Máspoli, who then saved his 'impeccable' header and Chico's shot from Ademir's pass. The first goal didn't arrive until after half-time. With the Uruguayan defence drawn to the left, Ademir's reverse pass sent Friaça clear on the right. He held off Andrade and scored with a bobbling cross-shot that Máspoli should perhaps have stopped. Pandemonium ensued. Friaça had picked an interesting time to score his only goal for Brazil.

But it came too late to persuade Uruguay they were sacrificial lambs, rather than the men who'd played Brazil to a standstill three times in May. And they'd recovered from a goal down against Spain and Sweden. Varela began to emerge from defence and above all their outside-right had the Indian sign over Bigode.

So thin he made footballs look like medicine balls, moustachioed and aquiline, Ghiggia had a peculiar hunched style but also the classic tools of speed and elusiveness – and only one man to beat. Taking a pass from Varela, he dragged Bigode tight to the touchline, swayed over the ball, then scooted past on the outside before crossing to the near post. Schiaffino swept the ball high past Barbosa. Soon afterwards, Ghiggia repeated the move, but this time Schiaffino shot wide.

It's obvious with hindsight that someone should have dropped back to protect the hapless Bigode, especially once Brazil were in the lead – but it wasn't that kind of team. They went on going forward, Jair forcing yet another save from Máspoli, Andrade tackling Friaça close in – but the unsung Pérez played a one-two with Ghiggia that cut out Bigode, and the winger was away to angle his run towards the near post. With the defence struggling to get across and Barbosa expecting another centre, Ghiggia sent his shot bumbling in at the near post

---

from only a few yards out. When the final whistle blew, Máspoli was going up for a desperate high ball under Jair's challenge.

Bigode didn't play for Brazil again. Danilo was reported to have attempted suicide and one or two spectators were apparently more successful. A great *pesadumbre* fell over Rio, a despondency, a weight of shadows. Ademir would be remembered far longer than Gambetta or Tejera – but Uruguay still hadn't lost a World Cup match, and the trophy still hadn't been won by the more skilful side. And we think we invented defensive football.

Morán was the only player to win his first cap in a World Cup decider. The official crowd figure was 173,850. For once there's little doubt that it was an underestimate.

FINAL POOL	P	W	D	L	F	A	PTS
Uruguay	3	2	1	0	7	5	5
Brazil	3	2	0	1	14	4	4
Sweden	3	1	0	2	6	11	2
Spain	3	0	1	2	4	11	1

LEADING GOALSCORERS 1950

8	Ademir	BRZ
5	Omar Míguez	URU
4	Estanislao Basora	SPA
4	Chico	BRZ
4	Zarra	SPA
4	Alcide Ghiggia	URU

BIGGEST CROWDS

205,000	1950	BRZ	v	URU	Rio de Janeiro
152,772	1950	BRZ	v	SPA	Rio de Janeiro
142,429	1950	BRZ	v	YUG	Rio de Janeiro
138,886	1950	BRZ	v	SWE	Rio de Janeiro
114,600	1986	MEX	v	PAR	Mexico City
114,580	1986	MEX	v	BUL	Mexico City
114,580	1986	ARG	v	ENG	Mexico City
114,580	1986	ARG	v	WG	Mexico City

OLDEST REFEREES

yrs/days

53/236	George Reader	ENG	1950
51/284	Mario Vianna	BRZ	1954
50/140	Alfred Birlem	GER	1938
50/72	Jack Mowat	SCO	1958
50/34	Antonio Márquez	MEX	1986
50/03	Leo Lemesic	YUG	1958

Reader had been taken off the Football League list for being too old.

The Limping Major

Switzerland 1954

FIFA retained the mini-league system but couldn't resist a little tinkering. Instead of each team playing all the others in the group, two were seeded and would play only the two non-seeds – and any matches drawn after 90 minutes would go to extra-time. If the sides were still level after that, the result would stand. It was arbitrary and confusing.

Still, at least it was the first really representative World Cup – just at a time when it didn't seem necessary. No tournament has had a stronger favourite. The Hungarians were coming.

The statistics were impressive in themselves – unbeaten in 28 matches since 1950, Olympic champions – but it was the sheer number of goals they scored, and the way they scored them, that delighted and terrified the football world. They crushed even the good teams – Czechoslovakia 5-0 and 5-1, Italy 3-0, Sweden 6-0 – and their Wembley masterclass made them the first foreign country to win in England. Even that famous 6-3 scoreline doesn't tell the whole story: they led 6-2 before coasting the last half-hour. Later that season, in their last match before the World Cup, they inflicted England's record defeat, by the inhuman score of 7-1.

They brought with them genuine tactical innovations: the deep-lying centre-forward, so hard to mark; the near-post crosses later copied by Ron Greenwood; a system based on moving triangles.

They also introduced some of the best players in the world: Grosics in goal; the smooth Bozsik in midfield; Hidegkuti the centre-forward; Czibor on the wing; and the great front men – Kocsis so marvellous in the air, plus the incomparable Puskás – who scored 158 international goals between them. Switzerland wasn't a big enough stage.

No-one else seemed to come close, though Uruguay and Yugoslavia had several of their 1950 players and some skilful reinforcements. Brazil, their great forward trio gone, were over-compensating for their defensive frailties last time. Austria, supplanted as the best team in Europe, were in decline. West Germany had only just been allowed back into FIFA.

Meanwhile, Scotland deigned to take part this time but had just been well beaten at home by a shell-shocked England. Nothing had prepared them for what was coming.

Group 1

Brazil, France (seeded), Mexico, Yugoslavia

16 June 1954 • La Pontaise, Lausanne •
16,000 • Mervyn Griffiths (WAL)

YUGOSLAVIA (1) 1
Milutinovic 14
FRANCE (0) 0

YUGOSLAVIA *Vladimir Beara, Branko Stankovic, Tomislav Crnkovic, Zlatko Cajkovski, Ivan Horvat, Vujadin Boskov, Milos Milutinovic, Rajko Mitic (c), Bernard Vukas, Stjepan Bobek, Branko Zebec.* Aleksandar Tirnanic.
FRANCE *François Remetter, Lazare Gianessi, Raymond Kaelbel, Bob Jonquet (c), Jean-Jacques Marcel, Armand Penverne, René Dereuddre, Léon Glovacki, Raymond Kopaszewski (Kopa), André Strappe, Jean Vincent.* Gaston Barreau (coach Pierre Pibarot)

Hard to understand why France were seeded. They'd lost 3-1 to Yugoslavia earlier in the season and their opponents had some world-class new boys. The balletic Beara, Boskov, the versatile Zebec. Milutinovic scored from a pass by Mitic, then Zebec missed a magnificent opportunity after going round the keeper. Jonquet broke his nose six minutes from the end and Beara injured a hand. Revealingly, Yugoslavia had won each of their four qualifying matches 1-0 and beaten England by the same score just before the tournament.

Then, as now, the stadium was also known as the Olympic. Milutinovic's brother Bora later coached three different countries in the finals.

■ 16 June 1954 • Charmilles, Geneva • 13,000 •
Paul Wyssling (SWI)

▲ **BRAZIL (4) 5**
Baltazar 24, Didi 29, Pinga 34, 43, Julinho 69
MEXICO (0) 0

● BRAZIL *Carlos Castilho, Djalma Santos, Nílton Santos, José Carlos Bauer (c), João Carlos Pinheiro, 'Brandãozinho' (Antenor Lucas), 'Julinho' (Júlio Botelho), 'Didi' (Waldir Pereira), 'Baltazar' (Oswaldo da Silva), 'Pinga' (José Lázaro Robles), Francisco Rodrigues.* Alfredo 'Zezé' Moreira.
MEXICO *Salvador Mota, Narciso López, Juan Gómez González, Raúl Cárdenas, Jorge Romo, Rafael Avalos, Alfredo Torres, José Naranjo (c), José Luis Lamadrid, Tomás Balcázar, Raúl 'Piña' Arellano.* Antonio López Herranz (SPA).

After the dismay of Rio, Brazil had tilted the weight of their team towards the back, keeping the mighty Bauer and introducing a stern stopper (Pinheiro) and two great full-backs. There was still class up front – including the playmaker Didi and Julinho on the right wing – and some more pencil moustaches.

Again the Mexicans were purely sacrificial. Baltazar, who'd scored against them in 1950, did it with his foot this time, Didi curled in one of his speciality free-kicks, Pinga scored with a powerful header and dribbled through for his second. Mota, winning his only cap, made a marvellous save from Julinho, who later ran in to score the fifth. Zezé Moreira wasn't too impressed, however. The match, he said, 'showed our weak points'! Mota's brother Antonio, also a goalkeeper, was in the squads for the 1962 and 1970 finals.

1954

■ 19 June 1954 • Charmilles, Geneva • 19,000 • Manuel Asensi (SPA)

▲ **FRANCE (1) 3**
Vincent 19, Cárdenas o.g. 46, Kopa pen 88
MEXICO (0) 2
Lamadrid 54, Balcazar 85

● FRANCE *Remetter, Gianessi, Roger Marche (c), Kaelbel, Marcel, Abderrahman Mahjoub, Abdelaziz Ben Tifour, Dereuddre, Kopa, Strappe, Vincent.*
MEXICO *Antonio Carbajal, López, Romo, Saturnino Martínez, Cárdenas, Avalos, Torres, Naranjo (c), Lamadrid, Balcázar, Arellano.*

■ 19 June 1954 • La Pontaise, Lausanne • 25,000 • Charlie Faultless (SCO)

▲ **BRAZIL (0) (1) 1**
Didi 69
YUGOSLAVIA (0) (1) 1
Zebec 48

● BRAZIL *Castilho, D. Santos, N. Santos, Bauer (c), Pinheiro, Brandãozinho, Julinho, Didi, Baltazar, Pinga, Rodrigues.*
YUGOSLAVIA *Beara, Stankovic, Crnkovic, Cajkovski, Horvat, Boskov, Milutinovic, Mitic (c), Zebec, Vukas, Dionizije Dvornic.*

With only two matches per team, wooden spoons arrived early. Ben Tifour sent Vincent away for the first goal, Cárdenas turned in Dereuddre's cross-shot, and after Mexico had equalized, Romo's handball conceded the penalty.

One leading modern source lists Narciso as Avalos' first name, but there seems to be confusion with López. The official programme, the main Mexican football magazine, and leading French statisticians all confirm Rafael Avalos.

Like the 1950 match between the two, some high-class skills were on view. Both sides missed chances before a precise pass by Milutinovic set up Zebec for the opening goal. Brazil deservedly equalized when Nílton Santos found Didi, who turned inside the defensive cover before shooting. Cajkovski went off injured in extra-time, in which Brazil dominated the first half, Yugoslavia the second, forcing Castilho to make three good saves. Wyssling apart (see page 72), has there ever been a better name for a referee?

GROUP 1	P	W	D	L	F	A	PTS
Brazil	2	1	1	0	6	1	3
Yugoslavia	2	1	1	0	2	1	3
France	2	1	0	1	3	3	2
Mexico	2	0	0	2	2	8	0

Brazil and Yugoslavia qualified for the quarter-finals.

Group 2

Hungary, Turkey (seeded), South Korea, West Germany

■ 17 June 1954 • Hardturm, Zürich • 13,000 • Raymond Vincenti (FRA)

▲ **HUNGARY (4) 9**
Puskás 11, 89, Lantos 17, Kocsis 24, 35, 49, Czibor 58, Palotás 77, 84
SOUTH KOREA (0) 0

● HUNGARY *Gyula Grosics, Jenö Buzánszky, Mihály Lantos, József Bozsik, Gyula Lóránt, Ferenc Szojka, László Budai, Sándor Kocsis, Péter Palotás, Ferenc Puskás (c), Zoltán Czibor. Gusztáv Sebes (coach Gyula Mandi).*
S. KOREA *Hong Duck-yung, Park Kyu-chong, Kang Chang-gi, Min Byung-dae (c), Park Yae-seung, Chu Yung-kwang, Chung Nam-sik, Park Il-kap, Sung Nak-woon, Woo Sang-kwon, Choi Chung-min. Kim Yung-Sik.*

The biggest mismatch in any finals tournament. The most dominant team of all time against the absolute minnows, who were almost glad Hungary scored so many goals. Puskás said it allowed them to have a rest before kicking off! 'They were very weak and had had no training,' soon exhausted by chasing Hungary's quick-passing game.

Amazingly, the Koreans should have taken the lead, Sung Nak-woon missing a very early chance made by Woo Sang-kwon. But soon Czibor hit the bar and the ball came back off a defender into the path of Puskás, the player expected to make the tournament his own. Lantos fired in a typical free-kick, Kocsis chipped the ball over Hong and scored his second with a spectacular volley. When Palotás scored the seventh from Budai's pass, the 37-year-old

Chung Nam-sik sat down exhausted, whereupon Buzánszky gave him a leg massage. Mercy all round from the Hungarians. At the 1952 Olympics they'd beaten the same country (with Hong in goal) 12-0.

WINNING MARGINS				
9	Hungary	1954	v S. Korea	9-0
9	Yugoslavia	1974	v Zaire	9-0
9	Hungary	1982	v El Salvador	10-1
8	Sweden	1938	v Cuba	8-0
8	Uruguay	1950	v Bolivia	8-0

■ 17 June 1954 • Wankdorf, Berne • 28,000 • José da Costa (POR)

▲ **WEST GERMANY (1) 4**
Schäfer 12, Klodt 51, O. Walter 60, Morlock 84
TURKEY (1) 1
Suat 3

● W. GERMANY *Toni Turek, Fritz Laband, Werner Kohlmeyer, Horst Eckel, Jupp Posipal, Karl Mai, Bernhard Klodt, Max Morlock, Ottmar Walter, Fritz Walter (c), Hans Schäfer. Sepp Herberger.*
TURKEY *Turgay Seren (c), Ridvan Bolatli, Basri Dirimlili, Mustafa Ertan, Çetin Zeybek, Rober Eryol, Erol Keskin, Suat Mamat, Feridun Bugeker, Burhan Sargun, Lefter Küçükandonyadis. Sandro Puppo (ITA).*

Looking back, seeding the Turks seems laughable, but they'd qualified ahead of Spain (albeit on the toss of a coin after a play-off) – and the Germans were an unknown quantity. They had a famous midfield general in Fritz Walter, but he was a veteran by now (first capped in 1940) and Turek was even older. No great surprise when Suat's fierce shot gave Turkey an early lead.

But Posipal, 'the German crack', held the defence together and the attack was fit and smart. Turgay couldn't hold Schäfer's shot but made partial amends with a tremendous save from Morlock. The first half was as even as the scoreline says.

Afterwards Klodt scored from a pass by Ottmar Walter, who headed the third from his brother's cross then helped set up Morlock. The referee raised a jeer by accidentally barging one of the Turkish forwards off the ball.

West Germany were apparently the first finals team to use screw-in studs. Turkish players are almost invariably known by their first names. One source (not Turkish) lists Çetin's second name as Özkaynak.

■ 20 June 1954 • St Jakob, Basle • 53,000 • Bill Ling (ENG)

▲ **HUNGARY (3) 8**
Kocsis 3, 21, 69, 79, Puskás 17, Hidegkuti 52, 55, J. Tóth I 75
WEST GERMANY (1) 3
Pfaff 25, Rahn 78, Herrmann 84

● HUNGARY *Grosics, Buzánszky, Lantos, Bozsik, Lóránt, József Zakariás, József Tóth I, Kocsis, Nándor Hidegkuti, Puskás (c), Czibor.*
W. GERMANY *Heinz Kwiatkowski, Hans Bauer, Kohlmeyer, Posipal, Werner Liebrich, Paul Mebus, Helmut Rahn, Eckel, F. Walter (c), Alfred Pfaff, Richard Herrmann.*

What do we make of this? Received wisdom now has it that the wily Herberger sent out a skeleton team, concealing his best side while learning all about Hungary's, confident Germany would beat Turkey in the play-off. But why would he deliberately expose his players to an extra match, and what about the effect on their confidence? Being unconcerned about the result is one thing, but eight goals....

The truth is, throughout their history Hungarian national teams had invariably been ruthless against lesser opposition. This one, for instance, beat Albania 12-0, Finland 8-0 and Poland 6-0, not to mention England. And West Germany were hampered by an injury to Mebus, who limped on the right wing and wasn't capped again.

Kocsis scored almost nonchalantly from a corner and drove in the third after a typically brilliant combination with Puskás, who'd already beaten four men to score the second; simply the best. Pfaff ran through for a goal and had another disallowed. Kocsis became the first player to score hat-tricks in consecutive finals matches.

However, the really significant thing was the kick on the knee Puskás received from Liebrich, who was brought in for this match and changed places with Posipal during it. It was a clear foul (Liebrich was cautioned), committed long after the ball had gone. Earlier Puskás had been brought down three times 'so badly I thought we must surely be awarded penalties'. Hungary scored their last three goals without him, but the injury kept him out of the next two matches and mattered enormously in the one after that.

■ 20 June 1954 • Charmilles, Geneva • 2,000 •
Estéban Marino (URU)

▲ **TURKEY (4) 7**
Suat 10, 28, Lefter 24, Burhan 36, 64, 70, Erol 76
SOUTH KOREA (0) 0

● TURKEY *Turgay (c), Ridvan, Basri, Mustafa , Çetin, Rober, Erol, Suat, Necmi Onarici, Lefter, Burhan.*
S. KOREA *Hong Duck-yung, Park Kyu-chong (c), Kang Chang-gi, Han Chang-hwa, Lee Chong-kap, Kim Ji-sung, Choi Yung-keun, Lee Soo-nam, Lee Ki-joo, Woo Sang-kwon, Chung Kook-chin.*

GROUP 2	P	W	D	L	F	A	PTS
Hungary	2	2	0	0	17	3	4
W. Germany	2	1	0	1	7	9	2
Turkey	2	1	0	1	8	4	2
S. Korea	2	0	0	2	0	16	0

West Germany and Turkey played off to join Hungary in the quarter-finals.

MOST GOALS IN A GAME

12	1954	Austria	7	Switzerland	5
11	1938	Brazil	6	Poland	5
11	1954	Hungary	8	W. Germany	3
11	1982	Hungary	10	El Salvador	1
10	1958	France	7	Paraguay	3

MATCHES WON FROM 3 GOALS DOWN

1954	Austria	v Switzerland	7-5
1966	Portugal	v N. Korea	5-3

The Koreans really were cannon fodder, but with the play-off coming up the cannons needed it. Lefter scored with a precise shot from Necmi's pass, Burhan drove in his first two and headed the third. Soon after opening the scoring, Suat had a goal disallowed. The times of some of the goals are disputed; these come from a Turkish almanac.

2,000 spectators are underwhelmed as Suat scores his second goal for Turkey against South Korea.

*P*lay-off

■ 23 June 1954 • Hardturm, Zürich • 17,000 • Raymond Vincenti (FRA)

▲ **W. GERMANY (3) 7**
O. Walter 7, Schäfer 12, 79, Morlock 31, 62, 77, F. Walter 63
TURKEY (1) 2
Mustafa 17, Lefter 82,

● W. GERMANY *Turek, Laband, Bauer, Eckel, Posipal, Mai, Klodt, Morlock, O Walter, F Walter (c), Schäfer.*
TURKEY *Sükrü Ersoy, Ridvan, Basri, Naci Erdem, Çetin, Rober, Erol, Lefter (c), Necmi, Mustafa, Coskun.*

If Herberger's strategy really did point to this match, he was proved right. It helped his cause that Çetin went off injured and Turkey had to replace their *phantastischen* goalkeeper Turgay with Sükrü, who had a poor match. Again they made a game of it in the first half, Mustafa heading in a short cross, and Lefter showed why he's still regarded as Turkey's best player, dribbling through to score. But West Germany's attack, prompted by Fritz Walter, was increasingly impressive, especially for a team who'd qualified by beating Norway and The Saar.

*G*roup 3

Austria, Uruguay (seeded), Czechoslovakia, Scotland

■ 16 June 1954 • Hardturm, Zürich • 25,000 • Laurent Franken (BEL)

▲ **AUSTRIA (1) 1**
Probst 32
SCOTLAND (0) 0

● AUSTRIA *Kurt Schmied, Gerhard Hanappi, Ernst Happel, Leopold Barschandt, Ernst Ocwirk (c), Karl Koller, Robert Körner, Walter Schleger, Robert Dienst, Erich Probst, Alfred Körner.* Walter Nausch.
SCOTLAND *Fred Martin, Willie Cunningham (c), Jock Aird, Tommy Docherty, Jimmy Davidson, Doug Cowie, John Mackenzie, Willie Fernie, Neil Mochan, Allan Brown, Willie Ormond.* Andy Beattie.

Scotland made their bow with their first-ever team manager but a dearth of class players. No Billy Steel, no Bobby Johnstone or Bobby Evans, no natural captain once big George Young was left out. Faced with group matches against the World Champions and one of the strongest teams in Europe, they'd tuned up by playing Norway and Finland.

As it happened, they gave Austria a real contest. Ormond forced a save from Schmied after only 30 seconds and was stopped by Koller's last-ditch tackle; Mochan might have had a penalty after pushing the ball between Happel's legs and being obstructed as he went round him.

But Austria had some exceptional players: Happel himself, Hanappi who could play anywhere, the great Ocwirk. When Alfred Körner beat Aird yet again, Probst took the ball off his toes to score. Ocwirk and

Brown came to blows in the second half. The Körners were brothers. A different Willie Cunningham played for Northern Ireland in the 1958 finals.

■ 16 June 1954 • Wankdorf, Berne • 20,000 • Arthur Ellis (ENG)

▲ **URUGUAY (0) 2**
Míguez 71, Schiaffino 84
CZECHOSLOVAKIA (0) 0

● URUGUAY *Roque Máspoli, José Santamaría, William Martínez, Victor Rodríguez Andrade, Obdulio Varela (c), Luis Cruz, Julio César Abbadíe, Javier Ambrois, Omar Míguez, Juan Schiaffino, Carlos Borges. Juan López.*
CZECHOSLOVAKIA *Theodor Reimann, Frantisek Safránek, Jirí Hledík, Ladislav Novák (c), Jirí Trnka, Jan Hertl, Ladislav Hlavácek, Ota Hemele, Ladislav Kacáni, Emil Pazicky, Jirí Pesek. Jaroslav Cejp.*

If anything, the holders had an even stronger team than in 1950, Ghiggia had gone to Italy, but Abbadíe and Borges were explosive replacements. Santamaría, later a defensive pillar at Real Madrid, played for Spain in the 1962 finals.

Nevertheless, Uruguay had trouble with the heavy pitch and a Czech defence in which Hledík and Reimann had excellent games. Eventually Míguez scored from Varela's perfect pass and Schiaffino curled in a free-kick. Santamaría had to make a saving tackle from Hlavácek, but Uruguay were generally in charge, against a rather anonymous team.

Scotland 0 Uruguay 7 – and it could have been worse. Davidson and Martin close their eyes and their prayers are answered: Míguez heads over the bar.

■ 19 June 1954 • St Jakob, Basle • 34,000 • Vincenzo Orlandini (ITA)

▲ **URUGUAY (2) 7**
Borges 17, 48, 58, Míguez 31, 82, Abbadíe 55, 87
SCOTLAND (0) 0

● URUGUAY *Máspoli, Santamaría, Martínez, Rodríguez Andrade, Varela (c), Cruz, Abbadíe, Ambrois, Míguez, Schiaffino, Borges.*
SCOTLAND *Martin, Cunningham (c), Aird, Docherty, Davidson, Cowie, Mackenzie, Fernie, Mochan, Brown, Ormond.*

Any chance Scotland had of living up to their captain's bravado ('What's to stop us beating Uruguay?') probably disappeared when Andy Beattie resigned as manager after the Austria match – but it wouldn't have made much difference if he'd stayed; Scotland couldn't cope with the Uruguayan wingers, especially on such a hot day.

Abbadíe beat Aird and rolled the ball across the face of the goal for Borges to shoot home from 15 yards. Schiaffino, rather overshadowed by Ghiggia and the defence four years earlier, was now the complete inside-

forward: speed, vision, a fierce shot for someone so emaciated. According to Docherty, poor Cunningham developed 'a sunburned tongue' trying to contain him. Ghiggia brilliantly set up Míguez for the second goal.

After half-time, Borges beat Cunningham again and scored with a cross-shot, then from close range. Abbadíe, stocky and elusive, scored two more. Scottish embarrassment was completed in the last minute when Mackenzie shot feebly into Máspoli's hands from only a few yards out. The scale of this record defeat should have taught a few lessons in preparation and team selection, but four years later they still hadn't been learned.

GROUP 3	P	W	D	L	F	A	PTS
Uruguay	2	2	0	0	9	0	4
Austria	2	2	0	0	6	0	4
Czech	2	0	0	2	0	7	0
Scotland	2	0	0	2	0	8	0

Uruguay and Austria qualified for the quarter-finals.

Group 4

England, Italy (seeded), Belgium, Switzerland

■ 19 June 1954 • Hardturm, Zürich • 26,000 • Vasa Stefanovic (YUG)

▲ **AUSTRIA (4) 5**
Stojaspal 2, 65, Probst 4, 21, 24
CZECHOSLOVAKIA (0) 0

● AUSTRIA *Schmied, Hanappi, Happel, Barschandt, Ocwirk (c), Koller, R. Körner, Theo Wagner, Ernst Stojaspal, Probst, A. Körner.*
CZECHOSLOVAKIA *Imrich Stacho, Safránek, Svatopluk Pluskal, Novák (c), Trnka, Hertl, Hlavácek, Hemele, Kacáni, Pazicky, Tadeás Kraus.*

Those early goals settled it, of course. Probst volleyed the second after the Körner brothers had combined, beat three men to score the third, and hit the fourth from the edge of the area. Stojaspal ran on to a long pass to make it five. It wasn't until the 55th minute that Schmied had to make a meaningful save, from Hlavácek. The Körners had been impressive on the wings, but Ocwirk was again Austria's best player. Tall, dark and snub-nosed, operating from penalty area to penalty area (inevitably nicknamed 'Clockwork' in England), he was the last great attacking centre-half.

■ 17 June 1954 • St Jakob, Basle • 24,000 • Emil Schmetzer (WG)

▲ **BELGIUM (1) (3) 4**
Anoul 4, 74, Coppens 77, Dickinson o.g. 93
ENGLAND (2) (3) 4
Broadis 25, 62, Lofthouse 37, 91

● BELGIUM *Léopold Gernaey, Marcel Dries, Fons Van Brandt, Constant Huysmans, Louis Carré, Vic Mees, Jef Mermans (c), Denis Houf, Rik Coppens, Pol Anoul, Pieter 'Jeng' Vanden Bosch.* Dugald Livingstone (SCO).
ENGLAND *Gil Merrick, Ron Staniforth, Roger Byrne, Billy Wright (c), Syd Owen, Jimmy Dickinson, Stanley Matthews, Ivan Broadis, Nat Lofthouse, Tommy Taylor, Tom Finney.* Walter Winterbottom.

The trauma of Budapest was less than a month behind them, but at least England had never had any trouble with the Belgians, whom they'd beaten 5-2, 4-1 and 5-0 since the War. Here Belgium managed a very early goal, the bustling Anoul shooting high into the net, but were overhauled soon enough. Broadis squeezed in the equalizer before colliding with the onrushing Gernaey, then England scored one of the great World Cup goals, Finney beating his man on the wing, Lofthouse meeting his cross with an astounding diving header. In the second half, Broadis hit Matthews' deflected cross so hard it bent the keeper's wrist on the way in.

This was Matthews' first match against Belgium since 1947, when he'd made all five of England's goals. Now he pulled their defence inside out, preposterously quick and supple for a man of 39. But England still hadn't solved their old problem at centre-half, where Owen was now limping. Anoul ran past him to pull a goal back, then Merrick failed to hold a shot by the fiery Coppens.

In extra-time, Broadis' cross and Taylor's dummy set up Lofthouse for a 'crushing drive' that went in off the bar – but Dickinson headed in a Dries free-kick 'when no-one was anywhere near him'. England needed to win their last group match to qualify.

■ 17 June 1954 • La Pontaise, Lausanne • 43,000 • Mario Vianna (BRZ)

▲ **SWITZERLAND (1) 2**
Ballaman 18, Hügi 78
ITALY (1) 1
Boniperti 44

● SWITZERLAND *Eugène Parlier, André Neury, Roger Bocquet (c), Willy Kernen, Marcel Flückiger, Charles Casali, Robert Ballaman, Roger Vonlanthen, Josef Hügi, Eugen Meier, Jacky Fatton.* Karl Rappan (AUT).
ITALY *Giorgio Ghezzi, Guido Vincenzi, Giovanni Giacomazzi, Maino Neri, Omero Tognon, Fulvio Nesti, Ermes Muccinelli, Giampiero Boniperti (c), Carlo Galli, Egisto Pandolfini, Benito Lorenzi.* Lajos Czeizler (HUN).

Lorenzi was fit this time, and Italy deserved to be seeded – but again there were problems behind the scenes. They dominated possession in the first half but went behind when Fatton's headed pass was missed by Hügi but headed in by Ballaman. As always, the Swiss were defensive but good on the break.

Italy equalized from a Nesti free-kick headed on by Galli. Boniperti, who spent a decade not quite living up to a golden-boy tag, shot in at the near post despite an ankle swollen by Flückiger's tackle. Play became rough as both teams realized the balding Vianna was a bulldog without a bite. Galli hit a post and Lorenzi put in the rebound only to be given offside. Vianna had to push Italian players off with his hands and needed police protection from Lorenzi after the match. Hügi scored the winner from a cross by the inevitable Fatton.

■ 20 June 1954 • Cornaredo (Comunale), Lugano • 26,000 • Erich Steiner (AUT)

▲ **ITALY (1) 4**
Pandolfini pen 41, Galli 48, Frignani 58, Lorenzi 78
BELGIUM (0) 1
Anoul 81

● ITALY *Ghezzi, Ardico Magnini, Giacomazzi, Neri, Tognon, Nesti, Lorenzi, Pandolfini (c), Galli, Gino Cappello, Amleto Frignani.*
BELGIUM *Gernaey, Dries, Carré, Van Brandt, Huysmans, Mees, Mermans (c), Anoul, Coppens, Hippolyte Vanden Bosch, P. Vanden Bosch.*

Italy expected a harder time than this. Lorenzi, one of the personalities of the tournament, switched to centre-forward, beat two men and crossed for Galli to head in. Frignani chipped in the third then hit a free-kick which was glanced on by Galli for Lorenzi to score with a teasing header. Dries had fouled Frignani to concede the penalty.

The dramatic improvement may have had

something to do with the selection of a Hamlet (Frignani) as well as a Homer (Tognon). The Vanden Bosches were brothers.

■ 20 June 1954 • Wankdorf, Berne • 43,500 • István Zsolt (HUN)

▲ **ENGLAND (1) 2**
Mullen 44, Wilshaw 70
SWITZERLAND (0) 0

● ENGLAND *Merrick, Staniforth, Byrne, Bill McGarry, Wright (c), Dickinson, Finney, Broadis, Taylor, Dennis Wilshaw, Jimmy Mullen.*
SWITZERLAND *Parlier, Neury, Kernen, Olivier Eggimann, Bocquet (c), Heinz Bigler, Charly Antenen, Vonlanthen, Meier, Ballaman, Fatton.*

When Matthews pulled out with a bruised toe and Lofthouse with a throat infection, it looked as if somebody was trying to tell England something. But the various injuries cleared the deck a little. Taylor, unhappy in a double centre-forward formation, was now a single centre-forward of growing promise – and Mullen was an experienced winger. Above all, the solution to the centre-half problem had been there all along.

Billy Wright was one of the icons of post-war English football – but a very average wing-half. Now, at the age of 30, in his 60th international, he finally knew his place, staying in it for another five years despite being only 5'8".

At the other end, with England in dire need of a goal, Taylor headed the ball on, Mullen darted past his full-back, went round Parlier, and never played for England again. No surprise there. Wilshaw's goal was just as good, a dribble past three men after he 'suddenly remembered his body swerve'. But

England needed Matthews' toe to heal quickly: the reigning champions were lying in wait. Fatton was winning his 50th cap.

GROUP 4	P	W	D	L	F	A	PTS
England	2	1	1	0	6	4	3
Italy	2	1	0	1	5	3	2
Switzerland	2	1	0	1	2	3	2
Belgium	2	0	1	1	5	8	1

Italy and Switzerland played off to join England in the quarter-finals.

Play-off

■ 23 June 1954 • St Jakob, Basle • 30,000 • Mervyn Griffiths (WAL)

▲ **SWITZERLAND (1) 4**
Hügi 14, 85, Ballaman 48, Fatton 89
ITALY (0) 1
Nesti 67

● SWITZERLAND *Parlier, Neury, Bocquet (c), Kernen, Eggimann, Casali, Antenen, Vonlanthen, Hügi, Ballaman, Fatton.*
ITALY *Giovanni Viola, Magnini, Giacomazzi, Giacomo Mari, Tognon, Nesti, Muccinelli, Pandolfini (c), Lorenzi, Armando Segato, Frignani.*

It wasn't a defeat, said an Italian paper, it was a disaster. No excuses possible.

Early on, Italy looked over-confident but were probably just tired, allowing Switzerland to dictate from the moment Hügi scored after a bout of short passing. For the second match in a row, Lorenzi had a shot blocked on the line by a defender, then his powerful shot was superbly saved by Parlier. Soon after half-time, new cap Viola saved Ballaman's shot but couldn't stop him heading in the corner from two yards out.

Muccinelli's backheel spun up off a defender for Nesti to head in, but Vonlanthen was running things by then, making both the final goals. The Italians later complained of boredom at their training camp in Vevey, but that comes with the territory. Pozzo could have told them that, and he was still alive to ask.

Quarter-finals

Not content with the complications they'd arranged for the group matches, FIFA had decided on a free draw for the knock-out stage, with the possibility of the group winners playing each other in the quarter-finals instead of being rewarded with matches against the runners-up. And the two strongest teams could well meet in the semi-finals.

■ 26 June 1954 • St Jakob, Basle • 28,000 • Erich Steiner (AUT)

▲ **URUGUAY (2) 4**
Borges 5, Varela 38, Schiaffino 47, Ambrois 79
ENGLAND (1) 2
Lofthouse 15, Finney 66

● URUGUAY *Máspoli, Santamaría, Martínez, Rodríguez Andrade, Varela (c), Cruz, Abbadíe, Ambrois, Míguez, Schiaffino, Borges.*
ENGLAND *Merrick, Staniforth, Byrne, McGarry, Wright (c), Dickinson, Matthews, Broadis, Lofthouse, Wilshaw, Finney.*

Better go through the Uruguayan goals first, because Merrick was at fault with the last three and has generally been blamed for England's defeat (actually the Uruguayan manager said 'Gil Merrick estuvo magnifico,' which is stretching it a bit). He couldn't

Lofthouse (on the ground) equalizes for England against Uruguay.

do anything about the first. Schiaffino beat McGarry with a body swerve and Cruz backheeled to Borges, who lashed in Abbadíe's return pass. Uruguay went ahead for the second time when Dickinson headed away a free-kick and Varela returned it with a high curling shot from 25 yards which Merrick might have reached. Schiaffino 'rolled a slowish simple-looking shot ... Merrick seemed to turn his back and fall down facing his own goal'. Then he didn't get down to cover Ambrois' optimistic cross-shot.

But pointing the finger at goalkeepers is an old excuse. England played their best World Cup match so far – and it wasn't good enough to beat a team which ended the match with eight fit men after injuries to Andrade (bandaged thigh), Abbadíe and Varela. There had also been pre-match worries over Borges, Schiaffino and Míguez! And if Matthews hit the post, then Ambrois hit the bar. Uruguay were a great team and England did well to lose only 4-2.

They equalized when Matthews pushed the ball behind Varela to Wilshaw, whose reverse pass was put away by Lofthouse's cross-shot. Whatever limitations England may have had in the tournament, scoring exceptional goals wasn't one of them. Their second was poked in by Finney after two shots were blocked. But they fell into individualistic play in the second half, which played into the Uruguayans' hands. And the average age of the team was over 30. As Schiaffino said, if they could find some younger players....

Their oldest was still their best, and the match programme knew what it was doing when it listed him as St Matthews. Schiaffino was just as influential, dropping back into defence when the injuries began, and playing as well as ever. Two prodigious footballers.

Further down the scale, Merrick wasn't capped again after a season in which he conceded 30 goals in ten matches.

■ 26 June 1954 • La Pontaise, Lausanne • 32,000 • Charlie Faultless (SCO)

▲ **AUSTRIA (5) 7**
Wagner 25, 28, 54, A. Körner 26, 34, Ocwirk 32, Probst 77
SWITZERLAND (4) 5
Ballaman 16, 36, Hügi 17, 18, 60

● AUSTRIA *Schmied, Hanappi, Happel, Barschandt, Ocwirk (c), Koller, R. Körner, Wagner, Stojaspal, Probst, A. Körner.*
SWITZERLAND *Parlier, Neury, Bocquet (c), Kernen, Eggimann, Casali, Antenen, Vonlanthen, Hügi, Ballaman, Fatton.*

Whatever happened to the Swiss bolt? The Austrians thrust it aside with short passes, slowing down the play – but only after conceding those three goals in three minutes. An amazing scoreline, unthinkable nowadays – though it would have been even more eye-catching if Robert Körner hadn't missed a penalty three minutes before half-time!

A close call in front of the Uruguayan net. (l–r): Andrade, Finney, Santamaría, an acrobatic Lofthouse, and Máspoli.

Ballaman opened the scoring after a move involving three other players. Austria's brothers on the wing made all three of Wagner's goals (the last when Parlier dropped Alfred Körner's centre) and another for Ocwirk. Stojaspal was fouled for the penalty.

At half-time Schmied and Bocquet received medical attention for sunstroke. Hügi pulled a goal back with a shot deflected in by Hanappi, but Probst sealed things when Parlier couldn't hold his shot. With six minutes left, Neury made another saving tackle when Stojaspal seemed sure to score. As if it mattered by then!

■ 27 June 1954 • Charmilles, Geneva • 17,000 • István Zsolt (HUN)

▲ **WEST GERMANY (1) 2**
Horvat o.g. 9, Rahn 86
YUGOSLAVIA (0) 0

● W. GERMANY *Turek, Laband, Kohlmeyer, Eckel, Liebrich, Mai, Rahn, Morlock, O. Walter, F. Walter (c), Schäfer.*
YUGOSLAVIA *Beara, Stankovic, Crnkovic, Cajkovski, Horvat, Boskov, Milutinovic, Bobek, Mitic (c), Vukas, Zebec.*

After Horvat deflected in Schäfer's cross, Yugoslavia's chronic goalscoring problem finally caught up with them: six in eight matches. Mitic, winning his 50th cap, beat Liebrich and forced a save from Turek, and the unmarked Milutinovic shot just over. But Rahn made his first major contribution to the tournament. Very big but superb on the ball, he left Crnkovic needing attention after trying to tackle him, then beat six men (!) before scoring. This isn't an exaggeration or a fluke; ten minutes earlier he'd dribbled through the entire defence and the goalkeeper before Horvat kicked off the line.

■ 27 June 1954 • Wankdorf, Berne • 40,000 • Arthur Ellis (ENG)

▲ **HUNGARY (2) 4**
Hidegkuti 4, Kocsis 7, 88, Lantos pen 61
BRAZIL (1) 2
D. Santos pen 18, Julinho 66

● HUNGARY *Grosics, Buzánszky, Lantos, Bozsik (c), Lóránt, Zakariás, J. Tóth I, Kocsis, Hidegkuti, Czibor, Mihály Tóth.*
BRAZIL *Castilho, D. Santos, N. Santos, Bauer (c), Pinheiro, Brandãozinho, Julinho, Didi, Humberto Tozzi, 'Indio' (Aloísio da Luz), 'Maurinho' (Mauro Raphael).*
▼ SENT OFF: *Bozsik 71, N. Santos 71, Humberto 79.*

In the first World Cup to be televised, this was the first video nasty. It's been blamed on a clash of cultures and so on – but it was probably simpler than that. Hungary, for all their goals and brilliance, had some rather basic defenders (Lóránt a standard stopper, Lantos very big for a full-back) and strong characters; likewise Brazil. And with so much at stake, combustion was always possible. Ellis had to send someone off in an international for the first time. History has generally been kind to him, but he surely lost control here.

Brazil brought in three new forwards – but it was the defence that gave Hungary their flying start, Pinheiro trying to dribble out of his area and losing the ball to Hidegkuti, who blasted a shot from ten yards. Castilho made a wonderful save, then rushed across the goalmouth to block another shot – but was unlucky that the ball ran loose for Hidegkuti to smash high past the Santos full-backs at the near post. Then he replaced his shorts, ripped by a Brazilian, and crossed for Kocsis to head the second.

By the time Djalma Santos converted a penalty for a foul by Buzánszky on Indio, the match was

[Left] *Djalma Santos scores from the penalty spot against Hungary.*

[Below] *A symmetrical triangle amid the bloodletting between Brazil and Hungary. (l–r): Kocsis, Pinheiro, Castilho, J. Tóth, Bauer, Hidegkuti.*

becoming increasingly rough. Ellis broke up a general fracas in midfield, József Tóth went off injured, and the mood darkened further when Ellis gave a penalty for a foul on Kocsis that few others noticed.

Bauer brought down Bozsik, who needed treatment and came back infuriated. A smooth midfield general, one of the all-time greats, no-one knew he had a dander, let alone one that could get up. Yet here he was, sent off for tangling with Nílton Santos, who went with him. Czibor was chased by Djalma Santos, someone to be avoided in dark alleys, Hidegkuti pushed Indio to the ground and stamped on his calves, and the police had to order photographers off the pitch when Didi exacted revenge!

Julinho lightened things briefly with one of the great goals, beating Czibor, Lantos and Lóránt before firing in from 20 yards. Rather a forgotten figure by now, superseded by Garrincha, he looked an unlikely footballer – hollow-cheeked and very slim – but he was one of Brazil's best, which means something. This was his last international for five years; recalled against England, he scored within two minutes.

Humberto Tozzi was sent off for jumping on Kocsis ('one tremendous leap'), who headed

Hungary's fourth. As the teams left the pitch, a free-for-all broke out, a photographer attacking the police. Two separate sources say Puskás split open Pinheiro's head with a bottle. In the Hungarian changing room, the lights suddenly went out and some retaliatory glass came flying in. When order was restored ten minutes later, a doctor was administering treatment to one of the Tóths and there was bad blood everywhere. A classic of its kind. M. Tóth had played for Romania in 1946.

Semi-finals

■ 30 June 1954 • St Jakob, Basle • 57,000 •
Vincenzo Orlandini (ITA)

▲ **WEST GERMANY (1) 6**
Schäfer 31, Morlock 47, F. Walter pen 56,
pen 65, O. Walter 62, 88
AUSTRIA (0) 1
Probst 52

● W. GERMANY *Turek, Posipal, Kohlmeyer, Eckel,
Liebrich, Mai, Rahn, Morlock, O. Walter, F. Walter (c),
Schäfer.*
AUSTRIA *Walter Zeman, Hanappi, Happel, Schleger,
Ocwirk (c), Koller, R. Körner, Wagner, Stojaspal, Probst, A.
Körner.*

had scored from a penalty awarded for a foul on a
player 'not identified in the tumult'. Even the
Hungarians would be sitting up and taking notice.

■ 30 June 1954 • La Pontaise, Lausanne •
45,000 • Mervyn Griffiths (WAL)

▲ **HUNGARY (1) (2) 4**
Czibor 12, Hidegkuti 47, Kocsis 109, 116
URUGUAY (0) (2) 2
Hohberg 76, 87

● HUNGARY *Grosics, Buzánszky, Lantos, Bozsik (c),
Lóránt, Zakariás, Budai, Kocsis, Palotás, Hidegkuti, Czibor.*
URUGUAY *Máspoli, Santamaría, Martínez (c), Rodríguez
Andrade, Néstor Carballo, Cruz, Rafael Souto, Ambrois,
Schiaffino, Juan Eduardo Hohberg, Borges.*

Schmied hadn't recovered from his sunstroke, but it
didn't seem to matter. Zeman, whose international
career lasted from 1945 to 1960, was one of the best
goalkeepers in Europe.

Unfortunately he chose the wrong day to have his
worst match for Austria, slow to get down for shots, a
headless chicken in the second half. Things might
have been different if the prolific Probst hadn't missed
two early chances, the first made by Ocwirk.

West Germany took the lead when Fritz Walter
appeared on the right wing and Schäfer tapped in his
cross. Later Morlock headed in his corner. Turek
gifted Probst a goal by dropping his first shot, but
Happel brought down Schäfer in the area and the
Germans ran away with it after that, their forwards
pouring through a half-back line doomed to keep
going forward. When it came after all these years, the
demolition of the Viennese school wasn't pretty. The
underrated Ottmar Walter knocked in 'the loveliest
back-header' then headed the sixth after his brother

A leading candidate for greatest international match
of all time, it might have been really outstanding if
both teams had been at full strength. Hungary had
shown there was life after Puskás, but Uruguay were
without Varela (whose great international career was
over), Abbadíe and Míguez.

The Hungarians tried to take advantage with all-
out attack, Palotás forcing a save from Máspoli,
Hidegkuti and Bozsik shooting just wide, Czibor
scoring with a cross-shot from the left. Uruguay's
first real chance didn't come until the 39th minute,
when Schiaffino went round Grosics but couldn't
keep his balance. Just after half-time, Budai beat
Cruz and crossed for Hidegkuti to score with a
marvellous diving header right under Máspoli's
nose. The goalkeeper, a hero of 1950 but now 36 and
looking rather heavy, was slow to get across.

It looked all over, especially as Uruguay were
hampered by the wet conditions (they beat Scotland
and England in sunshine) – but true to the history
they'd made for themselves, they came back into it.

Kocsis watches Hidegkuti head a spectacular goal in the great semi-final against Uruguay.

Hohberg, their naturalized Argentinian, held off Buzánszky and scored with a low cross-shot. With time running out, the incredible Schiaffino beat two men and put Hohberg through again, to bundle in the rebound after Grosics saved his first shot.

In extra-time Hohberg was in once more but this time hit the post. Two minutes later the unheralded Budai made another goal, crossing for Kocsis to head in. By now Schiaffino and Andrade were feeling their earlier injuries and Kocsis headed the fourth from Bozsik's centre; a fitting end to a great game.

It's doubtful if anyone ever headed a ball like Sándor Kocsis, certainly no-one else who stood only 5'9". Quite slim with it, he had a neck so thick it looked deformed, and TV footage confirms the power of those headers, some from around the penalty spot, so it wasn't just the stuff of legend. Almost as good on the ground, he scored 75 goals in only 68 matches before the 1956 revolution cut short his international career. He scored in ten consecutive games for Hungary 1951–52 but not in the Olympic final. Now he'd scored 13 in the last five with only the Final to come.

3rd-place Final

■ 3 July 1954 • Hardturm, Zürich • 32,000 • Paul Wyssling (SWI)

▲ **AUSTRIA (1) 3**
Stojaspal pen 15, Cruz o.g. 59, Ocwirk 78
URUGUAY (1) 1
Hohberg 21

● AUSTRIA   *Schmied, Hanappi, Walter Kollmann, Barschandt, Ocwirk (c), Koller, R. Körner, Wagner, Dienst, Stojaspal, Probst.*
URUGUAY   *Máspoli, Santamaría, Martínez (c), Rodríguez Andrade, Carballo, Cruz, Abbadie, Hohberg, Omar Méndez, Schiaffino, Borges.*

This was the 100th World Cup finals match, for what it's worth. Stojaspal thumped in a penalty for a foul on Dienst, and Koerner's shot was deflected in by Cruz, who'd kicked lumps out of Finney in Montevideo the previous year. As always, Schiaffino and Ocwirk were the best on view, the former dribbling through before setting up Hohberg for the equalizer, then beating the whole defence and shooting wide. Ocwirk, a reminder of an era that was gone forever, shot into the corner of the net with Máspoli standing still and claiming offside.

Final

■ 4 July 1954 • Wankdorf, Berne • 62,472 • Bill Ling (ENG)

▲ **WEST GERMANY (2) 3**
Morlock 10, Rahn 19, 85
HUNGARY (2) 2
Puskás 6, Czibor 8

● W. GERMANY *Turek, Posipal, Kohlmeyer, Eckel, Liebrich, Mai, Rahn, Morlock, O. Walter, F. Walter (c), Schäfer*
HUNGARY *Grosics, Buzánszky, Lantos, Bozsik, Lóránt, Zakariás, Czibor, Kocsis, Hidegkuti, Puskás (c), M. Tóth.*

In the days leading up, all the talk was of Puskás, who surely couldn't be brought back now. He's only half fit, they said (he often was), he looks rather thick round the middle (ditto), the team has shown it doesn't need him (hmm).

He was also the most extravagantly talented and inspirational player of his day, famously one-footed but with a left foot that juggled the soap in the showers at Real Madrid. The nickname Galloping Major, which refers to his ersatz rank in the army, doesn't paint the right picture. And Hungary were always better with him than without.

So he came back, and things immediately happened around him. Bozsik sent Kocsis into the German penalty area, the ball ran loose after a challenge from Liebrich, and Puskás pushed it into an empty net. Two minutes later, Bozsik tried to find Hidegkuti, Turek spilled Kohlmeyer's back pass, Czibor kicked it in. What was that score in the group match?

Germany were saved by their unity (six players from Kaiserslautern) and instant comeback. Rahn crossed from the left, Buzánszky tried a back pass but Morlock slid in to divert it low past Grosics' right hand. Then Fritz Walter took a corner, Grosics lost the ball in Schäfer's challenge, and Rahn volleyed through a small gap.

The rest of the match is usually described as a Hungarian onslaught, kept at bay by Turek and slices of luck. But Hungary were at last facing opponents who weren't intimidated by them. Although Hidegkuti hit the post with a snap shot and a Kocsis header ran along the bar, West Germany were on the attack at the end. There were subsequent rumblings about drug-taking, especially when some of the German team went down with jaundice – but it's more likely that Hungary's hard matches with the South Americans caught up with them. With five minutes left, Schäfer shoved Bozsik off the ball and crossed, Lantos could only head the ball into the path of Rahn, and the shot went in low past Grosics' right hand.

In the dying minutes Puskás ran on to Tóth's pass to slide the ball under Turek, only for Mervyn Griffiths, the authoritarian, high-profile Welsh linesman, to leave his mark on the match as he was perhaps always likely to do. Offside. Thirty seconds from the end, Czibor, who'd switched back to the left after looking unhappy on the right, put everything into a powerful shot, but Turek, tremendously agile for a man of 35, turned it away.

It was the end of Hungary's run of 32 matches without defeat, a world record at the time. They had strong claims to that unwanted title: best team never to win the World Cup. Seven years later, Czibor again played for the hot favourites (Barcelona) in a major final (the European Cup) on the same ground. Again he scored in a 3-2 defeat. But this was worse, the end of the world.

Watched by Ottmar Walter (far left) and Lóránt, Morlock stretches to score West Germany's first goal in the Final.

LEADING GOALSCORERS 1954

11	Sándor Kocsis	HUN
6	Josef Hügi	SWI
6	Erich Probst	AUT
6	Max Morlock	WG

MOST GOALS IN A TOURNAMENT

27	Hungary	1954
25	W. Germany	1954
23	France	1958

WON TOURNAMENT AFTER LOSING A MATCH

1954	West Germany
1974	West Germany
1978	Argentina

The expressions say it all as Puskás congratulates Fritz Walter after the Final.

The West German team who won the Final. (l–r): F. Walter, Turek, Eckel, Rahn, O. Walter, Liebrich, Posipal, Schäfer, Kohlmeyer, Mai, Morlock.

Teenage Kicks

Sweden 1958

For the first time in the World Cup finals there was no outright favourite – and no certainty that a great team was going to emerge.

The hosts had as good a chance as anyone once they recalled Raynor as coach and broke with tradition by picking players with Italian clubs. Liedholm, Skoglund, Hamrin and Gustavsson were some of the greatest players of all time. But it was an elderly team (Gren 37, Liedholm 35, Svensson 32) and home support might not be enough.

The 1956 revolution, crushed by Moscow, deprived Hungary of Puskás, Kocsis and Czibor, while Hidegkuti and Bozsik were past their best. The Soviets themselves, entering for the first time, were Olympic champions and had the famous Yashin in goal. West Germany had Rahn and Schäfer, a dynamic young centre-forward in Seeler and two new heavies in Erhardt and Szymaniak, but were still relying on Fritz Walter, now 37, as playmaker.

Brazil had an unsatisfactory European tour in 1956 and their two qualifying games against Peru ended 1-1 and 1-0, but their new 4-4-2 formation was still being bedded down. Uruguay were out, beaten 5-0 in Paraguay. Argentina, back at long last, had won the 1957 Copa América with some scintillating football, scoring 25 goals in six matches – but yet again the Italians had swooped, taking away their brilliant inside-forward trio of Sivori-Maschio-Angelillo, all later capped by Italy. It was another virtual reserve team that came to Sweden.

For the first and only time, all four home countries were there, three of them affected by the Munich air crash which killed so many of the Manchester United squad and cost Scotland their part-time manager Matt Busby, who was badly injured.

Northern Ireland had beaten an Italian team which reverted to its old ruse of picking South Americans, in this case Schiaffino and Ghiggia, the latter getting himself sent off in Belfast. The Munich disaster deprived the Irish of their fine centre-half Jackie Blanchflower, their captain's brother.

Wales, eliminated by Czechoslovakia, were given a second chance when FIFA decided that Israel, blacklisted then as now by the Asian countries, couldn't be allowed to take part without playing any qualifying matches. Wales came out of the hat, won both legs 2-0, and persuaded the Italian FA to release their best-known player, giant John Charles, at the eleventh hour.

England lost three players in the air crash, none of them easily replaced: left-back Roger Byrne, Tommy Taylor up front, and the strapping young Duncan Edwards. Without them, they lost 5-0 in Belgrade to a team which hit the bar and had three goals disallowed. Things looked bleak, especially as their group included two of the fancied teams. But for Munich, England would have been one of them.

Group 1

Argentina, Czechoslovakia, Northern Ireland, West Germany

■ 8 June 1958 • Malmö Stadion • 31,156 • Reg Leafe (ENG)

▲ **WEST GERMANY (2) 3**
Rahn 32, 79, Seeler 42
ARGENTINA (1) 1
Corbatta 3

● W. GERMANY *Fritz Herkenrath, Georg Stollenwerk, Erich Juskowiak, Horst Eckel, Herbert Erhardt, Horst Szymaniak, Helmut Rahn, Fritz Walter, Uwe Seeler, Alfred Schmidt, Hans Schäfer (c).* Sepp Herberger.
ARGENTINA *Amadeo Carrizo, Pedro Dellacha (c), Federico Vairo, Francisco Lombardo, Néstor Rossi, José Varacka, Orestes Corbatta, Eliséo Prado, Norberto Menéndez, Alfredo Rojas, Osvaldo Cruz.* Guillermo Stábile.

The holders came through strongly in the end, but Argentina gave them an early scare, little Corbatta sprinting clear on the right wing to whip in a high shot at the near post. After that, Rahn stole the show. Recalled when Herberger persuaded him to lose weight by reducing his lager intake, he carried on where he left off last time by scoring twice, first with his left foot from 25 yards, then with his right from 20, a heavily sliced ground shot that made Carrizo look foolish and spoiled Dellacha's 32nd birthday. The new German defence lost nothing in comparison with 1954.

Pluskal, Dougan and Bingham watch as Cush beats Masopust to the ball and heads the only goal of the game.

■ 8 June 1958 • Orjans Vall, Halmstad • 10,647 • Fritz Seipelt (AUT)

▲ **NORTHERN IRELAND (1) 1**
Cush 21
CZECHOSLOVAKIA (0) 0

● N. IRELAND *Harry Gregg, Dick Keith, Alf McMichael, Danny Blanchflower (c), Willie Cunningham, Bertie Peacock, Billy Bingham, Wilbur Cush, Derek Dougan, Jimmy McIlroy, Peter McParland.* Peter Doherty.
CZECHOSLOVAKIA *Bretislav Dolejsí, Gustav Mráz, Ladislav Novák (c), Svatopluk Pluskal, Jiří Cadek, Josef Masopust, Václav Hovorka, Milan Dvorák, Jaroslav Borovicka, Jan Hertl, Tadeás Kraus.* Karel Kolsky.

Regarded as a surprise, then and now – but there was a similar number of quality players on each side. An injury to Billy Simpson led to a first cap for the tall 20-year-old Dougan, but the winning header came from a man several inches shorter, after McParland's short corner was crossed by McIlroy. Cunningham did well as a makeshift centre-half.

■ 11 June 1958 • Orjans Vall, Halmstad •
14,174 • Sten Ahlner (SWE)

▲ **ARGENTINA (1) 3**
Corbatta pen 37, Menéndez 56, Avio 60
NORTHERN IRELAND (1) 1
McParland 4

● ARGENTINA *Carrizo, Dellacha (c), Vairo, Lombardo, Rossi, Varacka, Corbatta, Ludovico Avio, Menéndez, Angel Labruna, Norberto Boggio.*
　N. IRELAND *Gregg, Keith, McMichael, Blanchflower (c), Cunningham, Peacock, Bingham, Cush, Fay Coyle, McIlroy, McParland.*

Now this *was* a surprise. Argentina had brought back the 39-year-old Labruna – once a genuinely great player – and were heard whistling and singing before the match. They eventually dominated it after Bingham's cross from Blanchflower's backheel had been headed in by McParland. Menéndez put away a precise pass by Avio, who headed the third, but Keith was unlucky to concede the penalty when a cross by Avio came up off his thigh on to his hand. Ireland should have regained the lead when Cush cleverly stepped over McIlroy's centre only for Coyle to shoot 'dismally wide' from six yards. He 'had a couple of bad misses' and wasn't capped again. By the end, the Argentinians were taking the ball off each other to perform party tricks (both Gregg and McIlroy used the phrase 'taking the mickey').

■ 11 June 1958 • Olympia, Hälsingborg •
25,000 • Arthur Ellis (ENG)

▲ **CZECHOSLOVAKIA (2) 2**
Dvorák pen 24, Zikán 42
WEST GERMANY (0) 2
Schäfer 60, Rahn 71

● CZECHOSLOVAKIA *Dolejsí, Mráz, Novák (c), Pluskal, Ján Popluhár, Masopust, Hovorka, Dvorák, Pavol Molnár, Jirí Feureisl, Zdenek Zikán.*
　W. GERMANY *Herkenrath, Stollenwerk, Juskowiak, Karl-Heinz Schnellinger, Erhardt, Szymaniak, Rahn, Walter, Seeler, Schäfer (c), Bernhard Klodt.*

In a strange group, sometimes well-balanced, sometimes the opposite, the Germans made one of their famous comebacks but were grateful for a controversial goal, Schäfer barging Dolejsí over the line. The Czechs appealed against the appointment of Ellis for their next match, but were presumably happy enough after it.

Schäfer (11) has just barged Dolejsí over the line for West Germany's controversial first goal. Novák (4) prepares to show righteous indignation.

■ 15 June 1958 • Malmö Stadion • 21,990 • Joaquim Campos (POR)

▲ **NORTHERN IRELAND (1) 2**
McParland 18, 60
WEST GERMANY (1) 2
Rahn 20, Seeler 78

● N. IRELAND *Gregg, Keith, McMichael, Blanchflower (c), Cunningham, Peacock, Bingham, Cush, Tommy Casey, McIlroy, McParland.*
W. GERMANY *Herkenrath, Stollenwerk, Juskowiak, Eckel, Erhardt, Szymaniak, Rahn, Walter, Seeler, Schäfer (c), Klodt.*

■ 15 June 1958 • Olympia, Hälsingborg • 16,418 • Arthur Ellis (ENG)

▲ **CZECHOSLOVAKIA (3) 6**
Dvorák 8, Zikán 17, 39, Feureisl 68, Hovorka 81, 89
ARGENTINA (0) 1
Corbatta pen 64

● CZECHOSLOVAKIA *Dolejsí, Mráz, Novák (c), Dvorák, Popluhár, Masopust, Hovorka, Molnár, Feureisl, Borovicka, Zikán.*
ARGENTINA *Carrizo, Dellacha (c), Vairo, Lombardo, Rossi, Varacka, Corbatta, Avio, Menéndez, Labruna, Cruz.*

Everything, here and in Hälsingborg, pointed to the Irish going out – but they played their best game of the tournament, Gregg making 'half a dozen fabulous saves' despite hobbling throughout the match (his full-backs took the goal kicks). They went ahead when Cush challenged the goalkeeper, the ball went loose to the right, and McIlroy's cross reached the unmarked McParland. Rahn, showing a full range of skills for such a powerhouse, hit a beautiful chip over Gregg for the equalizer, McParland volleyed in after Bingham headed on Cush's corner, and Seeler at last got through with a massive 25-yarder. Even then, Ireland almost won it, McParland heading onto the top of the bar from Cunningham's free-kick. All honours even.

Keith (left), Gregg and Cunningham can't stop Rahn (white shirt) scoring his brilliant equalizer.

Argentina needed only a draw to force a play-off, but their slow ancient game was taken apart by pace and movement. Dvorák scored with a cross-shot from outside the area, then two terrible defensive errors presented the ball to Zikán, who also clipped in the third when Carrizo fumbled a gentle shot. Hovorka went round Carrizo for his first, then put away a low cross which cut out the keeper and defender. The defeat, Argentina's worst ever, put an end to Stábile's reign as manager, which had lasted since 1941.

GROUP 1	P	W	D	L	F	A	PTS
W. Germany	3	1	2	0	7	5	4
Czechoslovakia	3	1	1	1	8	4	3
N. Ireland	3	1	1	1	4	5	3
Argentina	3	1	0	2	5	10	2

Czechoslovakia and Northern Ireland played off to join West Germany in the quarter-finals.

*P*lay-off

■ 17 June 1958 • Malmö Stadion • 6,196 •
Maurice Guigue (FRA)

▲ **NORTHERN IRELAND (1) (1) 2**
McParland 44, 97
CZECHOSLOVAKIA (1) (1) 1
Zikán 18

● N. IRELAND *Norman Uprichard, Keith, McMichael, Blanchflower (c), Cunningham, Peacock, Bingham, Cush, Jackie Scott, McIlroy, McParland.*
CZECHOSLOVAKIA *Dolejsí, Mráz, Novák (c), Titus Buberník, Popluhár, Masopust, Dvorák, Molnár, Feureisl, Borovicka, Zikán.*
▼ SENT OFF: *Buberník 100.*

More heroics. The Irish had beaten this side before, but not with so many players injured: Gregg and Casey out; Uprichard breaking a bone in his left hand; Peacock and Cush limping. And there was another new cap (Scott) at centre-forward. They went a goal down when Borovicka nudged Keith off the ball, which bounced in the area and was headed in by Zikán – but McParland equalized at an important time, driving the ball in after Cush had three shots blocked.

In an extra-time the eight fit men could have done without, Blanchflower curled a cross just beyond the keeper to be volleyed home by McParland, the unexpected bombardier (the goals in this tournament were his first for Ireland since the two on his debut in 1954). Buberník was sent off for spitting at the referee and Scott had a goal disallowed near the end. Just about Northern Ireland's finest hour. Or two.

Group 2

France, Paraguay, Scotland, Yugoslavia

■ 8 June 1958 • Idrottsparken, Norrköping • 16,518 • Juan Gardeazábal (SPA)

▲ **FRANCE (2) 7**
Fontaine 24, 30, 68, Piantoni 51, Wisnieski 62, Kopa 70, Vincent 84
PARAGUAY (2) 3
Amarilla 20, pen 43, Romero 50

● FRANCE *François Remetter, Raymond Kaelbel, André Lerond, Armand Penverne, Bob Jonquet (c), Jean-Jacques Marcel, Maryan Wisnieski, Raymond Kopaszewski (Kopa), Just Fontaine, Roger Piantoni, Jean Vincent. Paul Nicolas, Albert Batteux.*
PARAGUAY *Ramón Mayeregger, Eldemiro Arevalo, Juan Vicente Lezcano, Agustin Miranda, Ignacio Achucarro, Salvador Villalba, Juan Bautista Aguero (c), José Parodi, Jorgelino Romero, Cayetano Ré, Florencio Amarilla. Aurelio González.*

France had scored a few goals in qualifying – 6-3, 8-3, 5-1 – but no-one expected anything like this, against the team who'd thumped Uruguay and led 3-2 here. Amarilla cracked a left-footed free-kick through a broken wall, and Romero put Paraguay back in front after holding off a challenge – but Fontaine twice ran on to through-balls to score, Piantoni equalized with a glorious lob-volley across the keeper, and Wisnieski converted a free-kick by Kopa, who made the seventh for Vincent and scored the sixth with his knee! Kopa was wasted on the wing at Real Madrid and Fontaine was only in the team because René Bliard was injured, but their partnership was about to become legendary.

Wisnieski was christened Wisniewski but the French took an inexplicable dislike to that second w.

■ 8 June 1958 • Arosvallen, Västeras • 9,591 • Paul Wyssling (SWI)

▲ **SCOTLAND (0) 1**
Murray 47
YUGOSLAVIA (1) 1
Petakovic 6

● SCOTLAND *Tommy Younger (c), Eric Caldow, John Hewie, Eddie Turnbull, Bobby Evans, Doug Cowie, Graham Leggat, Jimmy Murray, Jackie Mudie, Bobby Collins, Stewart Imlach. Dawson Walker.*
YUGOSLAVIA *Vladimir Beara, Vasilije Sijakovic, Tomislav Crnkovic, Dobrosav Krstic, Branko Zebec (c), Vujadin Boskov, Aleksandar Petakovic, Todor Veselinovic, Milos Milutinovic, Dragoslav Sekularac, Zdravko Rajkov. Aleksandar Tirnanic.*

Against expectations, the Scots survived an early goal from the player who'd scored a hat-trick against England, and were unlucky that Mudie had a goal disallowed when the ball went in off him after Beara had simply dropped it. Collins, stubby and skilful, was their best player.

■ 11 June 1958 • Idrottsparken, Norrköping •
11,665 • Vincenzo Orlandini (ITA)

▲ **PARAGUAY (2) 3**
Aguero 3, Ré 44,, Parodi 74
SCOTLAND (1) 2
Mudie 32, Collins 76

● PARAGUAY *Samuel Aguilar, Arevalo, Eligio Echagüe,
Villalba, Lezcano, Achucarro, Aguero (c), Parodi, Romero, Ré,
Amarilla.*
SCOTLAND *Younger (c), Alex Parker, Caldow, Turnbull,
Evans, Cowie, Leggat, Collins, Mudie, Archie Robertson,
Willie Fernie.*

■ 11 June 1958 • Arosvallen, Västeras • 12,217 •
Mervyn Griffiths (WAL)

▲ **YUGOSLAVIA (1) 3**
Petakovic 16, Veselinovic 63, 87
FRANCE (1) 2
Fontaine 4, 85

● YUGOSLAVIA *Beara, Novak Tomic, Crnkovic, Krstic,
Zebec (c), Boskov, Petakovic, Veselinovic, Milutinovic,
Sekularac, Rajkov.*
FRANCE *Remetter, Kaelbel, Roger Marche (c), Penverne,
Jonquet, Lerond, Wisnieski, Kopa, Fontaine, Piantoni,
Vincent.*

This time someone got it badly wrong beforehand. Two of the Scottish squad, Robertson and Tommy Docherty, were sent to watch Paraguay play, reporting back that they were 'rough and fit and good'. Despite this, Scotland left out the combative likes of Mackay, Baird and Docherty himself and picked a forward line made up of the slim and the small. The Paraguayans brushed them aside. The 35-year-old Turnbull didn't last the pace this time, and errors by Younger led to two of the goals and the end of his international career. Collins' goal was the 500th scored in the finals.

Again there was no stopping Fontaine, who lashed in Piantoni's cross from the left and delicately lobbed Beara – but the French gave all their opponents a chance. Petakovic flicked in a ground shot after a corner, a defensive error let Veselinovic in for his first, and he ran in to lunge home the winner, leaving France needing to draw with Scotland to qualify.

*Fontaine (just out of picture, right) opens
the scoring for France against Yugoslavia,
watched by Boskov (9), Kopa (18),
Zebec (6), Beara and Wisnieski (22).*

1958

■ 15 June 1958 • Tunavallen, Eskilstuna • 13,103 • Martin Macko (CZE)

▲ **YUGOSLAVIA (2) 3**
Ognjanovic 12, Veselinovic 28, Rajkov 73
PARAGUAY (1) 3
Parodi 20, Aguero 51, Romero 80

● YUGOSLAVIA *Beara, Tomic, Crnkovic, Krstic, Zebec (c), Boskov, Petakovic, Veselinovic, Rade Ognjanovic, Sekularac, Rajkov.*
PARAGUAY *Aguilar, Arevalo, Echagüe, Villalba, Lezcano, Achucarro, Aguero (c), Parodi, Romero, Ré, Amarilla.*

■ 15 June 1958 • Eyravallen, Örebro • 13,554 • Juan Brozzi (ARG)

▲ **FRANCE (2) 2**
Kopa 22, Fontaine 45
SCOTLAND (0) 1
Baird 65

● FRANCE *Claude Abbes, Kaelbel, Lerond, Penverne, Jonquet (c), Marcel, Wisnieski, Kopa, Fontaine, Piantoni, Vincent.*
SCOTLAND *Bill Brown, Caldow, Hewie, Turnbull, Evans (c), Dave Mackay, Collins, Murray, Mudie, Sammy Baird, Imlach.*

A win would have put Paraguay through and again they scored three goals – but their defence was caught too square too often. Ognjanovic put a left-wing cross into an empty net; Veselinovic drove in low from 20 yards; and the long-range shot that eliminated them was badly missed by Aguilar. For Paraguay, Parodi lived up to his name by scoring without meaning to, the ball hitting his leg as he fell; Aguero was tenacious after his first attempt was blocked by Beara and Romero poked a shot in off a post. End to end, but what a way to run a railroad.

At last Scotland picked the right team: Mackay and Baird, the pugnacious red-haired Evans, Brown winning his first cap after being Younger's reserve for the previous 24 internationals. And they had their chances, especially when Hewie, their tall South African full-back, smacked a penalty against the post after half an hour. But Fontaine hit the bar twice as well as scoring from a long ball and cutting the ball back for Kopa to sidefoot home. Baird replied with a good early shot from a straightforward through-pass, but again Scotland simply hadn't been good enough – and wouldn't be back in the finals for another 16 years.

LEADING GOALSCORERS 1958

13	Just Fontaine	FRA
6	Helmut Rahn	WG
6	Pelé	BRZ

GROUP 2	P	W	D	L	F	A	PTS
France	3	2	0	1	11	7	4
Yugoslavia	3	1	2	0	7	6	4
Paraguay	3	1	1	1	9	12	3
Scotland	3	0	1	2	4	6	1

France and Yugoslavia qualified for the quarter-finals.

Group 3

Hungary, Mexico, Sweden, Wales

■ 8 June 1958 • Rasunda, Solna, Stockholm • 34,107 • Nikolai Latyshev (USR)

▲ **SWEDEN (1) 3**
Simonsson 16, 64, Liedholm pen 57
MEXICO (0) 0

● SWEDEN *Karl Svensson, Orvar Bergmark, Sven Axbom, Nils Liedholm (c), Bengt 'Julle' Gustavsson, Sigvard Parling, Kurt Hamrin, Bror Mellberg, Agne Simonsson, Gunnar Gren, Lennart 'Nacka' Skoglund.* George Raynor (ENG).
MEXICO *Antonio Carbajal (c), Jesús del Muro, José Villegas, Alfonso Portugal, Jorge Romo, Francisco Flóres, Alfredo Hernández, Salvador Reyes, Carlos Calderón, Crescencio Gutiérrez, Enrique Sesma.* Antonio López Herranz (SPA), with Ignacio Trelles.

Sweden's turn to have the Mexicans as an easy opener, but they had problems with skilful opponents who hit the post early on. There was no doubt about the penalty and Simonsson coolly slid in Skoglund's cut-back for the third – but Sweden had played at a fearfully slow pace to accommodate their veterans.

Some sources list Hernández as captain, but it's clearly Carbajal on TV.

CONSECUTIVE DEFEATS

9	Mexico	1930–58
7	Switzerland	1954–66
6	El Salvador	1970–82

El Salvador have lost every game they've played.

■ 8 June 1958 • Jernvallen, Sandviken • 15,343 • José María Codesal (URU)

▲ **HUNGARY (1) 1**
Bozsik 4
WALES (1) 1
J. Charles 26

● HUNGARY *Gyula Grosics, Sándor Mátrai, László Sárosi, József Bozsik, Ferenc Sipos, Pál Berendi, Károly Sándor, Nándor Hidegkuti (c), Lajos Tichy, Deszõ Bundzsák, Máté Fenyvesi.* Lajos Baróti.
WALES *Jack Kelsey, Stuart Williams, Mel Hopkins, Derrick Sullivan, Mel Charles, Dave Bowen (c), Colin Webster, Terry Medwin, John Charles, Ivor Allchurch, Cliff Jones.* Jimmy Murphy.

Welsh resources were so thin that they had to use Medwin out of position, and it was just as well for them that Hidegkuti, now 36, had a dismal match. After Bozsik's shot had surprised Kelsey out of the shadows of the stand, John Charles climbed above the defence to head in a corner. But his massive presence was soon reduced by a series of fouls tolerated by Codesal, who also denied Allchurch a penalty. His son Edgardo, representing Mexico, refereed the 1990 Final. Mel and John Charles were brothers.

YOUNGEST PLAYERS IN A FINAL

yrs/days			
17/249	Pelé	BRZ	1958
18/201	Giuseppe Bergomi	ITA	1982
19/344	Rubén Morán	URU	1950

■ 11 June 1958 • Rasunda, Solna, Stockholm • 15,150 • Leo Lemesic (YUG)

▲ **MEXICO (0) 1**
Belmonte 89
WALES (1) 1
Allchurch 32

● MEXICO *Carbajal (c), Del Muro, Miguel Gutiérrez, Raúl Cárdenas, Romo, Flóres, Jaime Belmonte, Reyes, Carlos Blanco, Carlos González, Sesma.*
WALES *Kelsey, Williams, Hopkins, Colin Baker, M. Charles, Bowen (c), Webster, Medwin, J. Charles, Allchurch, Jones.*

In their tenth finals match, Mexico avoided defeat for the first time, but Wales should have wrapped this one up earlier. Their goal came from a mishit shot after Webster's corner, Mexico's from a diving header. The injured Sullivan was replaced by new cap Baker, his understudy at Cardiff City, who had a disappointing match, as did Jones, one of the fastest wingers in world football.

■ 12 June 1958 • Rasunda, Solna, Stockholm • 38,850 • Jack Mowat (SCO)

▲ **SWEDEN (1) 2**
Hamrin 34, 55
HUNGARY (0) 1
Tichy 76

● SWEDEN *Svensson, Bergmark, Axbom, Liedholm (c), Gustavsson, Parling, Hamrin, Mellberg, Simonsson, Gren, Skoglund.*
HUNGARY *Grosics, Mátrai, Sárosi, Ferenc Szojka, Sipos, Berendi, Sándor, Tichy, Bozsik (c), Bundzsák, Fenyvesi.*

It's now said that the hosts were rather lucky to win, after a shot by Tichy hit the bar and appeared to cross the line – but Svensson got a touch to it, and replays show the ball landing in front of the line. Besides, Sweden could even afford to miss a penalty, Liedholm shooting wide after 71 minutes. It's true, however, that both of Hamrin's goals were rather fortunate, the first from close range after two defenders had a chance to clear, the other with a lob that may have been put in by a defender's lunge. Tichy, whose physique belied his name, eventually got his goal with a marvellous drive into the top corner.

■ 15 June 1958 • Rasunda, Solna, Stockholm • 30,287 • Lucien Van Nuffel (BEL)

▲ **SWEDEN 0**
WALES 0

● SWEDEN *Svensson, Bergmark, Axbom, Reino Börjesson, Gustavsson (c), Parling, Bengt Berndtsson, Arne Selmosson, Henry Källgren, Gösta Löfgren, Skoglund.*
WALES *Kelsey, Williams, Hopkins, Sullivan, M. Charles, Bowen (c), Roy Vernon, Ron Hewitt, J. Charles, Allchurch, Jones.*

To Hungary's wry indignation, Sweden picked several reserves, including four forwards – but Wales were still lucky to survive. Skoglund missed four good chances and John Charles played too deep, either to avoid Gustavsson, whom he called 'the greatest centre-half I have ever seen', or to see some of the ball for a change. Kelsey was fast emerging as the best keeper in the competition.

CONSECUTIVE DRAWS		
3	Wales	1958
3	England	1958
3	Cameroon	1982

■ 15 June 1958 • Jernvallen, Sandviken • 13,310 • Arne Eriksson (FIN)

▲ **HUNGARY (1) 4**
Tichy 19, 46, Sándor 54, Bencsics 60
MEXICO (0) 0

● HUNGARY *István Ilku, Mátrai, Sárosi, Szojka, Sipos, Antal Kotász, László Budai, József Bencsics, Hidegkuti (c), Tichy, Sándor.*
MEXICO *Carbajal (c), Del Muro, M. Gutiérrez, Cárdenas, Guillermo Sepúlveda, Flóres, Belmonte, Reyes, Blanco, González, Sesma.*

Tichy was obviously getting a taste for it. First he beat a man, fed Sándor on the left and banged in the low cross, then dummied a defender before shooting marvellously across Carbajal from over 20 yards. Sándor blasted in from an indirect free-kick inside the penalty area, and it's impossible to be sure who got the last touch for the fourth, which was a real mess. Some call it a González own goal. Hungary were now warm favourites to win the play-off.

GROUP 3	P	W	D	L	F	A	PTS
Sweden	3	2	1	0	5	1	5
Hungary	3	1	1	1	6	3	3
Wales	3	0	3	0	2	2	3
Mexico	3	0	1	2	1	8	1

Hungary and Wales played off to join Sweden in the quarter-finals.

Play-off

■ 17 June 1958 • Rasunda, Solna, Stockholm • 2,823 • Nikolai Latyshev (USR)

▲ **WALES (0) 2**
Allchurch 55, Medwin 76
HUNGARY (1) 1
Tichy 33

● WALES *Kelsey, Williams, Hopkins, Sullivan, M. Charles, Bowen (c), Medwin, Hewitt, J. Charles, Allchurch, C. Jones.*
HUNGARY *Grosics, Mátrai, Sárosi, Bozsik (c), Sipos, Kotász, Budai, Bencsics, Bundzsák, Tichy, Fenyvesi.*
▼ SENT OFF: *Sipos 84.*

The day before, Imre Nagy, leader of the 1956 uprising, had been executed, and the match was played to an eerie background of Free Hungarian chanting and banners draped in black. The football, for what it mattered, was suitably sombre

The Hungary-Wales play-off, a picture emphasizing the size of a) John Charles and b) the Stockholm crowd.

and often brutal – the Hungarians continuing their assault on John Charles, with Kotász and Mátrai the chief culprits.

A cross by Budai, unmarked on the right, reached Tichy, unmarked on the left, and his confident volley beat Kelsey low at the near post. The Welsh replied with perhaps the greatest shot ever seen in the World Cup. When John Charles flicked on a pass to the left, the ball drifted high just inside the Hungarian penalty area. Allchurch lost his marker and met the ball with a full swing of his left foot, volleying it high just inside the far post – a picture goal, with the TV cameras right behind it, too.

Grosics, who gave the defender an ear-bashing, had only himself to blame for the winner, hitting a goal kick so slowly that Medwin was able to steal it from Sárosi and shoot home. Sipos was sent off for hacking down Hewitt, who was stretchered off, and the remains of the great Hungarian team made a graceless exit. Wales were in the quarter-finals, but the adventure would surely have to end there; the endless fouling had finally caught up with John Charles.

Group 4

Austria, Brazil, England, USSR

■ 8 June 1958 • Nya Ullevi, Gothenburg • 49,348 • István Zsolt (HUN)

▲ **ENGLAND (0) 2**
Kevan 66, Finney pen 85
USSR (1) 2
Simonian 13, A. Ivanov 56

● USSR *Lev Yashin, Vladimir Kessarev, Boris Kuznetsov, Yuri Voinov, Konstantin Krijevski, Viktor Tsarev, Aleksandr Ivanov, Valentin Ivanov, Nikita Simonian (c), Sergei Salnikov, Anatoly Ilyin. Gavril Katchalin.*
ENGLAND *Colin McDonald, Don Howe, Tommy Banks, Eddie Clamp, Billy Wright (c), Bill Slater, Bryan Douglas, Bobby Robson, Derek Kevan, Johnny Haynes, Tom Finney. Walter Winterbottom.*

Howe (right) can't stop Simonian (centre) scoring the USSR's first goal against England in their first match.

Winterbottom picked the same team which had been unlucky to draw in Moscow three weeks earlier, but they were second-best for most of this match. Aleksandr Ivanov, winning his first cap, crossed hard and low from the right, and McDonald could only push the ball out to Simonian. The second goal was started by Kessarev, who came up from the back and found Tsarev in space that should have been occupied by Clamp; a third pass put Aleksandr Ivanov clear. The Soviets protected their lead with some hard tackling on the England wingers.

Vittorio Pozzo is alleged to have described a goal by Kevan, the big

Finney equalizes with a late penalty against the USSR.

■ 8 June 1958 • Rimnersvallen, Uddevalla •
21,000 • Maurice Guigue (FRA)

▲ **BRAZIL (1) 3**
Mazzola 37, 85, Santos 50
AUSTRIA (0) 0

● BRAZIL *Gylmar (dos Santos), Nílton de Sordi, Nílton Santos, Dino Sani, Hideraldo Luiz Bellini (c), Orlando (Peçanha), Joel (Martins), 'Didi' (Waldir Pereira), 'Mazzola' (José Altafini), 'Dida' (Edivaldo Alves), Mário Zagallo.* Vicente Feola.
AUSTRIA *Rudi Szanwald, Paul Halla, Franz Swoboda, Gerhard Hanappi (c), Ernst Happel, Karl Koller, Walter Horak, Helmut Senekowitsch, Hans Buzek, Alfred Körner, Walter Schleger.* Josef Argauer, with Josef Molzer.

rawboned England centre-forward, as 'scored with the outside of his head' – but they all count, none more so than the one coming up. Wright's long straightforward free-kick was touched-on by Douglas and put in by the outside of Kevan's head, leaving the great goalkeeper in mid-air with legs splayed. Equally undignified was Yashin's reaction to the penalty, throwing the ball at the referee. The kick, awarded for a collision between Voinov and Haynes, was tucked just inside a post, but it was Finney's last contribution before an injured ankle forced him out of the tournament. Robson had a goal disallowed for a challenge on Yashin, but England were happy with the draw.

Despite the scoreline, Feola wasn't happy with his forwards, worried that the 19-year-old Mazzola was more concerned with an impending move to Italy. Nevertheless he scored twice here, including a marvellous full-blooded 20-yarder from Didi's through-ball. Nílton Santos got the first after winning a tackle and playing a one-two. If the team wasn't quite right, the outclassed Austrians didn't notice.

Mazzola, who went on to play for Italy in the 1962 finals, took his nickname from Valentino Mazzola, who died in the 1949 air crash and whose son Sandro played in three World Cups.

CAPTAIN IN MOST TOURNAMENTS			
3	Billy Wright	ENG	1950–54–58
3	Ladislav Novák	CZE	1954–58–62
3	Björn Nordqvist	SWE	1970–74–78
3	Diego Maradona	ARG	1986–90–94

■ 11 June 1958 • Nya Ullevi, Gothenburg •
40,895 • Albert Dusch (WG)

▲ **BRAZIL 0**
ENGLAND 0

● BRAZIL *Gylmar, de Sordi, Santos, Dino Sani, Bellini (c),
Orlando, Joel, Didi, 'Vavá' (Edvaldo Izídio Neto), Mazzola,
Zagallo.*
ENGLAND *McDonald, Howe, Banks, Clamp, Wright (c),
Slater, Douglas, Robson, Kevan, Haynes, Alan A'Court.*

■ 11 June 1958 • Ryeleven, Borås • 21,239 • Carl
Frederik Jørgensen (DEN)

▲ **USSR (1) 2**
A. Ivanov 15, V. Ivanov 62
AUSTRIA (0) 0

● USSR *Yashin, Kessarev, Kuznetsov, Voinov, Krijevski,
Tsarev, A. Ivanov, V. Ivanov, Simonian (c), Salnikov, Ilyin.*
AUSTRIA *Kurt Schmied, Ernst Kozlicek, Karl Stotz,
Swoboda, Hanappi (c), Koller, Horak, Paul Kozlicek,
Buzek, Körner, Senekowitsch.*

England approached this in a negative way, but
rightly so: Brazil had more ability. The Tottenham
coach Bill Nicholson, out here as Winterbottom's
assistant, identified Didi as the focal point of the
attack and set out to neutralize him.

Didi was 30 by now, but age didn't matter with
someone who rarely did anything at speed, loping
his way through three World Cups, using that rare
gift of finding space without dashing into it. In every
match, despite the great players who were to come,
he was the team's point of light.

But England played him well, using Slater as a
man-marker with Howe and Banks covering Wright
against Brazil's double spearhead. It worked, but only
just; Mazzola and Vavá hit the woodwork. At the
other end Kevan might have had a penalty when he
went down in Bellini's challenge. It was the first
goalless draw in the finals and the first time Brazil
failed to score in a World Cup match.

Comfortable for the Soviets, but they were grateful
to Yashin for saving young Buzek's penalty in the
55th minute. The Kozliceks were brothers.

■ 15 June 1958 • Ryeleven, Borås • 15,872 • Jan
Bronkhorst (HOL)

▲ **AUSTRIA (1) 2**
Koller 15, Körner 71
ENGLAND (0) 2
Haynes 56, Kevan 74

● AUSTRIA *Szanwald, Walter Kollmann, Swoboda,
Hanappi (c), Happel, Koller, E. Kozlicek, P. Kozlicek,
Buzek, Körner, Senekowitsch.*
ENGLAND *McDonald, Howe, Banks, Clamp, Wright (c),
Slater, Douglas, Robson, Kevan, Haynes, A'Court.*

Having drawn with the strong teams, England were
expected to beat the other one, but were
unfortunate that Austria's first goals of the
tournament were both scored from long range. On
another day, Koller's shot might have gone into the
crowd instead of the very top corner. Körner's left-
footer went in low off a post.

In between, Haynes smashed the ball in from two yards after Szanwald made an unbelievable hash of A'Court's simple shot. Kevan scored the second from Haynes' angled pass and Robson had a late goal disallowed when the ball went in off his hand. But again the attack hadn't been up to standard. Haynes and Douglas had just spent a season in the Second Division and A'Court was no substitute for Finney. The young Bobby Charlton, who'd scored three goals in his first two England matches that year, was again left out.

There used to be serious confusion as to who refereed this match. Some sources mention Aksel Asmussen (DEN) but most agree on Bronkhorst, including 'all Austrian publications' and the Dutch FA.

■ 15 June 1958 • Nya Ullevi, Gothenburg •
50,928 • Maurice Guigue (FRA)

▲ **BRAZIL (1) 2**
Vavá 3, 77
USSR (0) 0

● BRAZIL *Gylmar, de Sordi, Santos, 'Zito' (José Ely de Miranda), Bellini (c), Orlando, 'Garrincha' (Manoel Francisco dos Santos), Didi, Vavá, 'Pelé' (Édson Arantes do Nascimento), Zagallo.*
USSR *Yashin, Kessarev, Kuznetsov, Voinov, Krijevski, Tsarev, A. Ivanov, V. Ivanov, Simonian, Igor Netto (c), Ilyin.*

YOUNGEST TO SCORE A HAT-TRICK

yrs/days			
17/244	Pelé	BRZ	1958
19/197	Edmund Conen	GER	1934
20/255	Bert Patenaude	BRZ	1930
20/261	Flórián Albert	HUN	1962

Brazil had brought a psychiatrist with them, João Carvalhães. Feola, thinking of including two new players, asked him what he thought of them. The first, quoth the good doctor, was 'too young, too infantile', the other so unsophisticated that 'including him in the team would be a disaster'. Feola disagreed and picked them both. They were Pelé and Garrincha. Brazil had found their team.

Zito was another important replacement, a better tackler than Dino Sani – but Garrincha and Pelé made the difference up front. And how! Garrincha hit the bar in the first minute, Pelé in the second, Vavá hammered home Didi's flick in the third. The Soviets used Netto to mark Didi, but he hadn't fully recovered from injury and it didn't work. Vavá stabbed in a loose ball for the second.

Pelé missed two early chances but obviously had all the skills in the world, eerily assured for a boy of 17. The pantherine Garrincha was simply unplayable, taking the ball past defenders with legs strangely twisted from birth. Vavá, far less skilful than Mazzola, was a hammer up front. Even Yashin had to hold his hands up.

GROUP 4	P	W	D	L	F	A	PTS
Brazil	3	2	1	0	5	0	5
USSR	3	1	1	1	4	4	3
England	3	0	3	0	4	4	3
Austria	3	0	1	2	2	7	1

England and USSR played off to join Brazil in the quarter-finals.

Play-off

Winterbottom at last made changes, but they were unexpected – still no Charlton, but a return for Clayton, whose 'performance was just too bad to be true' in Belgrade, and first caps for Broadbent and the 20-year-old Brabrook.

Again England had no luck. Six minutes before half-time, Broadbent's low cross from the right found two England players unmarked in front of goal. The first, Brabrook, somehow managed to turn it back straight to Yashin. In the second half, he broke through a tackle and galloped in on goal, only for his shot to trundle against a post. Then he ran at the heart of the defence and hit the same post. Finally, he slammed the ball in after accidentally controlling it with his hand.

Almost inevitably, when the USSR hit a post, the ball went in. McDonald ruined his excellent tournament by hitting a goal kick straight to Falin, the ball eventually reaching the unmarked Ilyin, who scored with a low cross-shot. Tough to bear, but England hadn't looked like contenders. Again.

Quarter-finals

*Hamrin (left) heads the opening
goal past Yashin.*

Raynor, astute as ever, recognized that England's problems with the USSR stemmed from Voinov's domination of Haynes, their only creative source. So he turned the tables, setting Liedholm to mark the marker. Gren took over the task of making the play, and this time the Soviet luck deserted them. Hamrin broke clear on the right, his attempted square pass came back off a defender, and his header sent the ball spinning in crazily at the near post. Later he made the second for Simonsson. The three teams who took part in group play-offs couldn't manage a goal between them two days later.

■ 19 June 1958 • Idrottsparken, Norrköping • 11,800 • Juan Gardeazábal (SPA)

▲ **FRANCE (1) 4**
Wisnieski 44, Fontaine 56, 64, Piantoni 68
NORTHERN IRELAND (0) 0

● FRANCE *Abbes, Kaelbel, Lerond, Penverne, Jonquet (c), Marcel, Wisnieski, Kopa, Fontaine, Piantoni, Vincent.*
N. IRELAND *Gregg, Keith, McMichael, Blanchflower (c), Cunningham, Cush, Bingham, Casey, Scott, McIlroy, McParland.*

A game too far for the walking wounded. The hardworking Peacock was out, Uprichard's broken hand meant Gregg had to play even though he was using a walking stick around the team hotel, and Casey's leg wound re-opened during the match. But the Irish had only their management to blame for the ridiculous travel arrangements that made them spend 12 hours in a coach 48 hours earlier.

They held out almost to half-time, but then Wisnieski ran on to a loose ball on the right and Gregg couldn't rush out in time. The second half wasn't a contest. Fontaine headed in Piantoni's cross then went round a defender and cracked a low shot

across Gregg, before Piantoni broke through a tired challenge to score the fourth. The Irish, who'd suffered enough by then, had done themselves very proud. They were the only British team to win two matches in the tournament.

■ 19 June 1958 • Nya Ullevi, Gothenburg • 25,923 • Fritz Seipelt (AUT)

▲ **BRAZIL (0) 1**
Pelé 73
WALES (0) 0

● BRAZIL *Gylmar, de Sordi, Santos, Zito, Bellini (c), Orlando, Garrincha, Didi, Mazzola, Pelé, Zagallo.*
WALES *Kelsey, Williams, Hopkins, Sullivan, M. Charles, Bowen (c), Medwin, Hewitt, Webster, Allchurch, Jones.*

John Charles couldn't play and his replacement Webster missed Wales' only chance of the match, hitting an early cross into the side netting after Jones had beaten de Sordi. After that, it was Kelsey v the Brazilian attack, the courageous keeper beaten only when Pelé's shot was deflected by Williams.

But this makes it sound as if it was going wide until someone stuck a foot out. In fact Pelé took Didi's headed pass on his chest, flicked it away from a defender before it bounced, then shot hard from eight yards. Williams' tackle simply slowed the ball down on its way in. Pelé wasn't lucky, he was brilliant.

Meanwhile Mazzola's marvellous overhead kick from 16 yards was disallowed for no obvious reason. Fair-haired and quick, sometimes scintillating, he went on to score the goals that won the 1963 European Cup for Milan and a semi-final for Juventus in 1973. But the match against Wales was his last for Brazil, which was a shame because his partnership with Pelé, average age 18, should have been one of the greats.

Garrincha hadn't had it easy against Hopkins, and Kelsey and Bowen had been excellent throughout the tournament – but, unlike the Irish, Wales never found a goalscorer, leading to an excess of caution which didn't endear them. And of course they were lucky to be there in the first place.

YOUNGEST GOALSCORERS

yrs/days			
17/239	Pelé	BRZ	1958
18/93	Manuel Rosas	MEX	1930
18/197	Nicolae Kovács	ROM	1930

Pelé scored in two later matches in 1958. Both of Rosas' goals were from the penalty spot.

The great Garrincha goes past Hopkins in Wales' last finals match to date.

■ 19 June 1958 • Malmö Stadion • 20,055 • Paul Wyssling (SWI)

▲ **WEST GERMANY (1) 1**
Rahn 12
YUGOSLAVIA (0) 0

● W. GERMANY *Herkenrath, Stollenwerk, Juskowiak, Eckel, Erhardt, Szymaniak, Rahn, Walter, Seeler, Schmidt, Schäfer (c).*
YUGOSLAVIA *Srboljub Krivokuca, Crnkovic, Sijakovic, Boskov, Zebec (c), Krstic, Petakovic, Ognjanovic, Milutinovic, Veselinovic, Rajkov.*

Rather dull all round, the German minders muffling an attack that missed the promptings of the 20-year-old Sekularac – but at least it was won by a

magnificent goal, Rahn beating three men on the right before scoring with a low shot from almost on the goal line. With a winger like that, with defenders like those, anything was possible, especially against their ageing hosts.

Semi-finals

■ 24 June 1958 • Nya Ullevi, Gothenburg • 49,471 • István Zsolt (HUN)

▲ **SWEDEN (1) 3**
Skoglund 33, Gren 80, Hamrin 87
WEST GERMANY (1) 1
Schäfer 25

● SWEDEN *Svensson, Bergmark, Axbom, Börjesson, Gustavsson, Parling, Hamrin, Gren, Simonsson, Liedholm (c), Skoglund.*
   W. GERMANY *Herkenrath, Stollenwerk, Juskowiak, Eckel, Erhardt, Szymaniak, Rahn, Walter, Seeler, Schäfer (c), Hans Cieslarczyk.*
▼ SENT OFF: *Juskowiak 58.*

If the holders planned to overwhelm Sweden with youthful pace and energy, it would have helped if they'd chosen the right studs. Struggling to keep their feet, they nevertheless took the lead with a spectacular goal. Seeler, mobile and relentless, beat a man on the left, chased the ball to the corner flag, and did well to get in any kind of cross. Schäfer met it 12 yards out with a left-footed volley that flew high past Svensson. They changed their studs at half-time.

Walter and Gren, born on the same day in 1920, were cancelling each other out, but another veteran sneaked the equalizer. Liedholm clearly used his arm to intercept a German pass, the referee waved his arms like a windmill, and a tackle sent the ball out to Skoglund, free on the left. The shot went between a defender's legs and across the keeper. In a long international career (1950–64), Skoglund won only 11 caps and scored only this one goal.

The match turned on a crunching tackle by Parling that temporarily forced Walter off the field and ended his international career – and Juskowiak's sending-off for showing his new studs in retaliating against the sly Hamrin.

Everything was running Sweden's way in front of a crowd roused by cheerleaders led by a middle-aged gent with a Swedish flag. The Germans held out till near the end, then Gren collected Herkenrath's punched clearance and fired it back high into the net. Finally, Hamrin drifted along the right at walking pace as if in a world of his own, then suddenly dashed past two defenders along the goal line and scored at the near post. This was the kind of individualism he'd shown throughout the competition and it seemed to give Sweden a real chance in the Final.

■ 24 June 1958 • Rasunda, Solna, Stockholm • 27,100 • Mervyn Griffiths (WAL)

▲ **BRAZIL (2) 5**
Vavá 2, Didi 39, Pelé 52, 64, 75
FRANCE (1) 2
Fontaine 9, Piantoni 82

● BRAZIL *Gylmar, de Sordi, Santos, Zito, Bellini (c), Orlando, Garrincha, Didi, Vavá, Pelé, Zagallo.*
   FRANCE *Abbes, Kaelbel, Lerond, Penverne, Jonquet (c), Marcel, Wisnieski, Kopa, Fontaine, Piantoni, Vincent.*

Goals were never more inevitable, and the first two arrived quickly, showing up the relative weakness at the centre of each defence. First the elegant Jonquet gave the ball straight to Garrincha (a grenade against a trampoline if ever there was one). Jonquet made an excellent saving tackle, but it took him away to the left, which left Vavá free in the middle when Didi's cross came over. The volley bored a hole through Abbes.

The equalizer followed a well-worn route, Fontaine taking Kopa's perfect through-pass round Gylmar for the first goal Brazil conceded in the tournament. But after 26 minutes Vavá's dreadful foul left Jonquet limping on the wing for the rest of the match.

Brazil would probably have won anyway – France simply leaked too many goals – but they wouldn't have felt safe against Fontaine if the French had remained at full strength. As it was, two minutes after the injury, Didi's low shot from the left found its way in at the far post, and the rest was a mopping-up operation. Zagallo should have been awarded a goal when his shot hit the bar and came down over the line. Pelé tapped in from five yards when Abbes dropped a gentle cross, then slashed in a lucky rebound after Vavá missed his kick. He saved the best till last, running on to Didi's pass, lifting it up with his thigh, and volleying low to the keeper's right. But it was cruel by then, against a depleted team. Now France knew how the Irish felt.

3rd-place Final

■ 28 June 1958 • Nya Ullevi, Gothenburg • 32,483 • Juan Brozzi (ARG)

▲ **FRANCE (3) 6**
Fontaine 15, 36, 77, 89, Kopa pen 27, Douis 50
WEST GERMANY (1) 3
Cieslarczyk 17, Rahn 52, Schäfer 83

● FRANCE *Abbes, Kaelbel, Lerond, Penverne (c), Maurice Lafont, Marcel, Wisnieski, Yvon Douis, Fontaine, Kopa, Vincent.*
   W. GERMANY *Heinz Kwiatkowski, Stollenwerk, Schnellinger, Erhardt, Heinz Wewers, Szymaniak, Rahn, Hans Sturm, Alfred Kelbassa, Schäfer (c), Cieslarczyk.*

The first half of the Brazil v France semi-final belonged to Vavá. Here he smashes in the opening goal.

Vavá shows the power and aggression that forced Jonquet out of the match; Marcel feels the full force.

One that got away from Fontaine. Kopa scores from a penalty in the 3rd-place Final between France and West Germany.

With no tackles taking place in midfield, Fontaine only had to stay on his feet to score goals. He knocked in Kopa's cut-back from the right, pivoted to put in a rebound, ran at the defence to shoot from 17 yards, and sprinted from the halfway line for his fourth. These were easy pickings, but his credentials as a goalscorer stand up to any scrutiny: 30 in 21 internationals before two broken legs ended his career at the age of 28. There were no sweepers around in 1958, so the 4-4-2 defences were regularly caught square – but no-one else scored 13 goals against them. Fontaine was deadly in front of goal; especially in front of Kopa.

The latter, about to become European Footballer of the Year, converted a penalty for Erhardt's foul on Wisnieski, and Douis volleyed the fourth. For the Germans, Cieslarczyk turned inside a defender before shooting, Schäfer converted a knock-down from close in, and Rahn scored the best of the lot, selling an exaggerated dummy before cutting back to the goal line and thrashing in a high shot, signing off as only he could. A World Cup giant.

Kwiatkowski was also in goal against Hungary in 1954, conceding another four goals to another tournament top scorer. They were his only matches in the finals!

MOST GOALS IN A TOURNAMENT

13	Just Fontaine	FRA	1958	
11	Sándor Kocsis	HUN	1954	
10	Gerd Müller	WG	1970	1 pen.
9	Eusébio	POR	1966	4 pen.
8	Guillermo Stábile	ARG	1930	
8	Ademir	BRZ	1950	

SCORED IN MOST CONSECUTIVE MATCHES

6	Just Fontaine	FRA	1958
6	Jairzinho	BRZ	1970
5	Gerd Müller	WG	1970

Thirteen goals – Just like that. Fontaine is chaired off the pitch after the match with West Germany.

Vavá equalizes from a low cross by Garrincha, who's on the goal line behind the post.

Final

- 29 June 1958 • Rasunda, Solna • Stockholm • 49,737 • Maurice Guigue (FRA)

▲ **BRAZIL (2) 5**
Vavá 9, 32, Pelé 55, 90, Zagallo 68
SWEDEN (1) 2
Liedholm 4, Simonsson 79

● BRAZIL *Gylmar, Djalma Santos, N. Santos, Zito, Bellini (c), Orlando, Garrincha, Didi, Vavá, Pelé, Zagallo.*
SWEDEN *Svensson, Bergmark, Axbom, Börjesson, Gustavsson, Parling, Hamrin, Gren, Simonsson, Liedholm (c), Skoglund.*

As in the match between the two countries in 1950, Raynor hoped for an early goal, confident the Brazilians would 'panic all over the show'. This time he got it – and they didn't.

Sweden played the ball confidently out of defence and found Simonsson wide on the right. His square pass reached Liedholm just outside the penalty area. Liedholm turned past Orlando, then past Bellini, then shot. His thin legs made the white ball look too big for him, but the ground shot was just firm enough to go past Gilmar's right hand.

But Raynor already had 'the sneaking suspicion the game was already over. Instead of looking dejected, the Brazilians were calling for the ball to restart the game. If that was their attitude, we were heading for trouble.'

Pelé's brilliant goal puts Brazil 3-1 ahead. Others (l–r): Bergmark, Zagallo, Vavá, Svensson.

They reached it within minutes. Garrincha went past his marker but topped his low cross, which found its way through to Vavá, who lunged in to score from inside the six-yard box. Twenty minutes later, there was a virtual re-run, Garrincha this time getting the cross right: too fast for Svensson, turned in by Vavá.

Brazil were on top throughout, their game at last the right mix of the athletic and the artistic, 1950 and 1954 blended. They brushed aside the Swedish veterans, who had wonderful careers and nothing to be ashamed of now (except perhaps some severe

short-back-and-sides, either a sign of solidarity or done for a bet). Gren was 20 years older than Pelé and it showed.

In the first half, Pelé hit a post. In the second, he scored a marvellous goal, chesting Nílton Santos' cross past Parling, flipping the ball over Gustavsson with his thigh, volleying low past the keeper, who had no chance (or, as commentator Kenneth Wolstenholme put it, 'If I were Svensson, I wouldn't worry about this'). Then Zagallo beat Bergmark to the ball and squeezed it in at the near post.

The key, as always, was Didi. Raynor didn't man-mark him, which was probably a mistake, leaving the job to two different players in different parts of the field. Didi simply flitted in and out of those areas, leaving the defenders chasing shadows. 'It was impossible,' said Raynor. 'He was masterful.'

Meanwhile there was no sign of the Swedish wingers. If Raynor was shrewd, Feola was no fool himself. Once he'd identified the main threat, he didn't hesitate for sentimental reasons. Out went the luckless de Sordi, in came big Djalma for his first game of the tournament. Ruthless and right.

Near the end, Liedholm came through the middle unchallenged to make a goal for Simonsson,

Hamrin (far left) watches as Simonsson scores Sweden's irrelevant second. Nílton Santos makes a token protest.

who may have been slightly offside but deserved it nonetheless; a selfless centre-forward of all-round quality. But it was right that Pelé should apply the finishing touch. After backheeling the ball to Zagallo on the left, he trotted towards the centre to get between two defenders and knock a looping header just inside the post as Svensson wrapped himself round it. Modern football, more or less, had arrived, and with it its greatest player.

[Top] *Pelé gets between Axbom (left) and Parling to head the seventh goal of the match, the most in any Final.*

[Middle] *It's all too much for a 17-year-old Pelé, who leans on the experienced Gylmar in the company of Djalma Santos (left) and Didi. Orlando (right) shows his feelings in a different way.*

[Bottom] *Brazil win the World Cup at last, with one of their greatest teams. (l–r) standing: manager Feola, D. Santos, Zito, Bellini, N. Santos, Orlando, Gylmar; kneeling: Garrincha, Didi, Pelé, Vavá, Zagallo, trainer Paulo Amaral.*

The Sorcerer's Apprentice

Chile 1962

This long slim country had a population of less than eight million, only one stadium of any size, and the aftermath of a giant earthquake that occured two years earlier – a third of all buildings were damaged beyond repair. Yet the president of their FA, Carlos Dittborn, argued that they had to have the World Cup 'because we have nothing'. He died just before the tournament and the stadium in Arica was named after him.

Since 1958 the Brazilian team had broken up, then almost completely re-formed. Zagallo had reclaimed his place from the explosive Pepé, Vavá from the chubby-cheeked Coutinho, Pelé's supercharged partner at Santos. Didi was back from two wasted years at Real Madrid. Only the twin stoppers were missing and even they had been replaced by names from the past: Zózimo a reserve in 1958 and Mauro who'd won his first cap in 1949. The only question mark was one of age; six of the team were over 30. But Pelé was just 21 and firmly established as the best in the world. They were obvious favourites.

The USSR had won all three matches on a tour of South America the previous year but still looked rather functional. Argentina had a new manager and a more defensive style. Yugoslavia, who'd finally struck Olympic gold after losing the previous three Finals, had Sekularac at his best and dangerous strikers in Galic and Jerkovic. Czechoslovakia's famous half-backs had muscled their way past Scotland in a play-off.

Spain and Italy tried to find instant success by padding their teams with foreigners. Spain picked Martínez from Paraguay, Santamaría from Uruguay and none other than Puskás, who was now 36 but had just scored another hat-trick in a European Cup final. The great Argentinian Alfredo Di Stéfano was in the squad but apparently injured. Italy had Maschio and Sivori from Argentina and Altafini (of 1958 fame) and Sormani from Brazil, which should have added up to a dazzling forward line.

England had better players than in 1958: Armfield and Wilson arguably their best ever full-backs; Charlton and Greaves up front. In the 1960–61 season they'd beaten Scotland 9-3, Spain 4-2, Italy 3-2 away, and other teams by scores of 5-2, 9-0, 5-1 and 8-0 – but all the play still went through Haynes and the impetus seemed to have gone.

As for the hosts, they had several players of international class or thereabouts, just enough to make them respectable opposition, but only in partnership with the Santiago crowd, one of the stars of the tournament.

FIFA's latest rule change made sense in a competition where time was limited. From now on, teams level on points would be separated by goal average (later goal difference). The days of play-offs were over.

The great Yashin, goalkeeper in three finals tournaments.

Group 1

Colombia, Uruguay, USSR, Yugoslavia

■ 30 May 1962 • Carlos Dittborn, Arica • 7,908 • Andor Dorogi (HUN)

▲ **URUGUAY (0) 2**
Cubilla 57, Sasia 73
COLOMBIA (1) 1
Zuluaga pen 18

● URUGUAY *Roberto Sosa, Horacio Troche (c), Emilio Alvarez, Mario Méndez, Néstor Goncálvez, Eliséo Alvarez, Luis Cubilla, Pedro Rocha, Ronald Langón, José Sasia, Domingo Pérez.* Juan Carlos Corrazzo, Juan López.
COLOMBIA *Efrain 'Caimán' Sánchez, Francisco Zuluaga (c), Jaime González, Oscar López, Héctor Echeverry, Jaime Silva, Marcos Coll, Germán Aceros, Marino Klinger, Delio Gamboa, Jairo Arias.* Adolfo Pedernera (ARG).

Nothing was expected of the Colombians, appearing in the finals for the first time, but they were Uruguay's equals in the first half, their veteran captain giving them the lead and Coll hitting a post. Uruguayan frustration led to some harsh tackling which left Zuluaga limping and ended his international career. Eventually Cubilla took a pass from Goncálvez and scored from a tight angle and Sasia stole the winner in a scramble. Eliséo and Emilio Alvarez were brothers.

■ 31 May 1962 • Carlos Dittborn, Arica • 9,622 • Albert Dusch (WG)

▲ **USSR (0) 2**
Ivanov 53, Ponedelnik 85
YUGOSLAVIA (0) 0

● USSR *Lev Yashin, Eduard Dubinsky, Leonid Ostrovsky, Valery Voronin, Anatoly Masylonkin, Igor Netto (c), Slava Metreveli, Valentin Ivanov, Viktor Ponedelnik, Viktor Kanevsky, Mikhail Meskhi.* Gavril Katchalin.
YUGOSLAVIA *Milutin Soskic, Vladimir Durkovic, Fahrudin Jusufi, Zeljko Matus, Vladimir Markovic, Vladimir Popovic, Muhamed Mujic (c), Dragoslav Sekularac, Drazen Jerkovic, Milan Galic, Josip Skoblar.* Selection committee (coach Milovan Ciric).

A repeat of the 1960 European Nations Cup Final, with the same result. Yashin made fine saves from Sekularac (after a typical blazing dribble) and Galic, but Ivanov put in the rebound when Ponedelnik hit the post with a free-kick. Dubinsky was hospitalized with a broken leg after a bad foul by Mujic, who was sent home by his selectors but not sent off by the referee, who lost control to the point of doing nothing when Jerkovic struck him.

■ 2 June 1962 • Carlos Dittborn, Arica • 8,829 • Karol Galba (CZE)

▲ **YUGOSLAVIA (2) 3**
Skoblar pen 26, Galic 30, Jerkovic 49
URUGUAY (1) 1
Cabrera 19

● YUGOSLAVIA *Soskic, Durkovic, Jusufi, Petar Radakovic, Markovic, Popovic, Vojislav Melic, Sekularac, Jerkovic, Galic (c), Skoblar.*
URUGUAY *Sosa, Troche (c), Em. Alvarez, Méndez, Goncálvez, El. Alvarez, Rocha, Mario Bergara, Rubén Angel Cabrera, Sasia, Pérez.*
▼ SENT OFF: *Popovic 71, Cabrera 71.*

■ 3 June 1962 • Carlos Dittborn, Arica • 8,040 • João Etzel (BRZ)

▲ **COLOMBIA (1) 4**
Aceros 22, Coll 68, Rada 71, Klinger 76
USSR (3) 4
Ivanov 5, 13, Chislenko 11, Ponedelnik 57

● COLOMBIA *Sánchez (c), J. González, López, Echeverry, Anibal Alzate, Rolando Serrano, Coll, Aceros, Antonio Rada, Klinger, Héctor González.*
USSR *Yashin, Givi Chokeli, Ostrovsky, Voronin, Masylonkin, Netto (c), Igor Chislenko, Ivanov, Ponedelnik, Kanevsky, Meskhi.*

Uruguay missed a good early chance and hit the bar with a header; Cabrera headed in a cross from the right, and Yugoslavia seemed to be on their way out. But Sekularac began to run the show. Shortish and neat, apparently of gypsy blood, he had great flair and this time kept his temper in check. Jerkovic, leggy and very tall, was fouled by Emilio Alvarez for the penalty and finished things off with a header from a right-wing cross. When his shot was saved, Galic poached the rebound. In a free-for-all provoked by Sasia's late challenge on Soskic, faces were slapped, Cabrera and Popovic sent off, Sasia lucky to stay on.

Wow! When the USSR took that early 3-0 lead, the Colombians looked a shambles, even their veteran goalkeeper, once one of the world's best. Ivanov's low left-foot shot from 20 yards went under his body and he might have done better with Ivanov's second, an unexceptional ground shot. His defence let him down for the other goal, allowing the ball to run on until Chislenko slid it in. Aceros pulled one back with a good chip from a position that may have been offside, but then Ponedelnik went past Alzate and that was surely that.

Colombia's recovery began with a freak goal. Coll's corner, hit low and poorly to the near post, should have been cleared by a defender, who stood aside and ushered it in, to Yashin's almost comical indignation. Rada poked in the second from eight yards, Klinger stabbed in the loose ball after Yashin had dived at his feet, and the Soviets were hanging on at the end. But normal service was about to be resumed.

■ 6 June 1962 • Carlos Dittborn, Arica • 9,973 • Cesare Jonni (ITA)

▲ **USSR (1) 2**
Mamykin 38, Ivanov 89
URUGUAY (0) 1
Sasia 53

● USSR *Yashin, Chokeli, Ostrovsky, Voronin, Masylonkin, Netto (c), Chislenko, Ivanov, Ponedelnik, Alexei Mamykin, Galimzyan Khusainov.*
URUGUAY *Sosa, Troche (c), Em. Alvarez, Méndez, Goncálvez, El. Alvarez, Cubilla, Julio César Cortés, Cabrera, Sasia, Pérez.*

The USSR's recovery from their Colombian hangover was aided by an injury to Eliséo Alvarez which reduced Uruguay to ten men. Almost immediately the lively little Chislenko beat Pérez to make a goal for Mamykin, and a strong midfield did the rest, even after Sasia scored from a loose ball.

■ 7 June 1962 • Carlos Dittborn, Arica • 7,167 • Juan Carlos Robles (CHI)

▲ **YUGOSLAVIA (2) 5**
Galic 20, 63, Jerkovic 25, 88, Melic 73
COLOMBIA (0) 0

● YUGOSLAVIA *Soskic, Durkovic, Jusufi, Radakovic, Markovic, Popovic, Andrija Ankovic, Sekularac, Jerkovic, Galic (c), Melic.*
COLOMBIA *Sánchez (c), J. González, López, Echeverry, Alzate, Serrano, Coll, Aceros, Klinger, Rada, H. González.*

No surprises this time, Sánchez' long international career ending in a flurry of goals. Jerkovic ran through alone for the first, shot the second in off a post, then missed an easy chance. Some English

publications still insist on crediting him with the third goal, giving him not only a hat-trick but eventually five goals in the tournament, which would have made him outright leading scorer. All reliable sources, Yugoslavian included, credit it to Galic (although admittedly 'with the help of Jerkovic').

GROUP 1	P	W	D	L	F	A	PTS
USSR	3	2	1	0	8	5	5
Yugoslavia	3	2	0	1	8	3	4
Uruguay	3	1	0	2	4	6	2
Colombia	3	0	1	2	5	11	1

USSR and Yugoslavia qualified for the quarter-finals.

Group 2

Chile, Italy, Switzerland, West Germany

■ 30 May 1962 • Nacional, Santiago • 65,006 • Ken Aston (ENG)

▲ **CHILE (1) 3**
L. Sánchez 44, pen 54, Ramírez 51
SWITZERLAND (1) 1
Wüthrich 6

● CHILE *Misael Escuti, Luis Eyzaguirre, Sergio Navarro (c), Carlos Contreras, Raúl Sánchez, Eladio Rojas, Jaime Ramírez, Jorge Toro, Honorino Landa, Alberto Fouilloux, Leonel Sánchez. Fernando Riera.*
SWITZERLAND *Karl Elsener, Heinz Schneiter, Fritz Morf, André Grobéty, Ely Tacchella, Hans Weber, Charly Antenen (c), Rolf Wüthrich, Norbert Eschmann, Philippe Pottier, Toni Allemann. Karl Rappan (AUT).*

Switzerland had qualified by twice beating a declining Swedish team and were now expected to be purely sacrificial – but suddenly Wüthrich scored from 30 yards and the 35-year-old Escuti had to make two good saves. Chile responded with some grim tackling, a feature of this World Cup. Aston booked Eschmann then Rojas but should have sent both off when they came to blows a few minutes later.

Chile hit a post, Rojas had a long-range goal disallowed, then at last Leonel Sánchez scored, and two quick goals settled the second half, in which Switzerland didn't have a shot till the 66th minute. The police had to clear spectators off the pitch after the first goal, but it was just enthusiasm spilling over.

■ 31 May 1962 • Nacional, Santiago • 65,440 • Bobby Davidson (SCO)

▲ **ITALY 0**
WEST GERMANY 0

● ITALY *Renzo Buffon (c), Giacomo Losi, Enzo Robotti, Sandro Salvadore, Cesare Maldini, Gigi Radice, Giorgio Ferrini, Gianni Rivera, José Altafini, Omar Sivori, Giampaolo Menichelli. Giovanni Ferrari.*
W. GERMANY *Wolfgang Fahrian, Hans Nowak, Karl-Heinz Schnellinger, Willi Schulz, Herbert Erhardt, Horst Szymaniak, Hans Sturm, Helmut Haller, Uwe Seeler, Hans Schäfer (c), Albert Brülls. Sepp Herberger.*

The inclusion of Schnellinger and Schulz made the Germans more physical than in 1958 – if that was possible – especially with Szymaniak and Erhardt still there. Italy's defence was marshalled by Maldini, father of Paolo (they were Italy's manager and captain in the 1998 qualifiers), and the willowy 18-year-old Rivera showed his full promise. But the South Americans up front were a disappointment, Altafini unable to escape Erhardt and getting booked

in his frustration, Sivori blotted out by Schulz. Fahrian kept a clean sheet on his 21st birthday.

MOST TOURNAMENTS AS COACH

4	Sepp Herberger	WG	1938–54–58–62
4	Walter Winterbottom		
		ENG	1950–54–58–62
4	Helmut Schön	WG	1966–70–74–78
4	Lajos Baróti	HUN	1958–62–66–78

APPOINTED FOR FRANCE '98

4	Carlos Alberto Parreira		
		BRZ	1982–90–94–98
4	Bora Milutinovic	YUG	1986–90–94–98

■ 2 June 1962 • Nacional, Santiago • 66,057 • Ken Aston (ENG)

▲ **CHILE (0) 2**
Ramírez 74, Toro 88
ITALY (0) 0

● CHILE *Escuti, Eyzaguirre, Navarro (c), Contreras, R. Sánchez, Rojas, Ramírez, Toro, Landa, Fouilloux, L. Sánchez.*
ITALY *Carlo Mattrel, Mario David, Robotti, Paride Tumburus, Francesco Janich, Salvadore, Bruno Mora (c), Humberto Maschio, Altafini, Ferrini, Menichelli.*
▼ SENT OFF: *Ferrini 7, David 44.*

Italy had been jeered and whistled in their first match, but this was something else. Two Italian journalists, Antonio Ghirelli and Corrado Pizzinelli, had written a series of articles emphasizing the poverty of Santiago and the alleged nocturnal activities of its women. They left the country before the tournament started, so the Italian team had to

---

bear the brunt of local reaction. They later claimed the Chilean players were spitting in their faces from the start.

Reaction wasn't slow in coming. Aston, tall and jug-eared, took no action when Ferrini and Leonel Sánchez kicked each other, but sent off Ferrini for retaliation against Landa. Play was held up for eight minutes until the police shepherded Ferrini away. Soon afterwards, the worst (and worst refereed) moment of the competition. Leonel Sánchez responded to a series of kicks from David by flattening him with a punch. When Aston did nothing, David took things into his own hands, getting himself sent off for kicking the same Sánchez in the neck. Maschio had his nose broken in a clash with Rojas and Toro should have been sent off for raising his fists in the last minute.

Italy held out until Mattrel punched away a Leonel Sánchez free-kick and Ramirez headed over two defenders into the net. Toro's low 25-yarder brought down the curtain on a horror show, the last of the three great World Cup slugfests. The Italian players were later stoned at their training camp. Aston became a senior member of the refereeing committees at the 1966 and 1970 tournaments, but this was the last match he refereed in the finals.

Ken Aston summons reinforcements to help him send off Ferrini (head in hands in the background).

The Battle of Santiago and some of its casualties. Hostile forces surround the referee while two Chileans lie as if mortally wounded.

■ 3 June 1962 • Nacional, Santiago • 64,922 •
Leo Horn (HOL)

▲ **WEST GERMANY (1) 2**
Brülls 44, Seeler 60
SWITZERLAND (0) 1
Schneiter 75

● W. GERMANY *Fahrian, Nowak, Schnellinger, Schulz, Erhardt, Szymaniak, Willi Koslowski, Haller, Seeler, Schäfer (c), Brülls.*
SWITZERLAND *Elsener, Tacchella, Schneiter, Grobéty, Wüthrich, Weber, Antenen (c), Roger Vonlanthen, Allemann, Eschmann, Richard Dürr.*

Switzerland played the prettier football and were unlucky when Szymaniak's sliding tackle broke Eschmann's ankle early in the first half – but they lacked a goalscorer and Germany were always stronger. When a defender missed his tackle, Brülls collected the ball, turned inside a challenge, and shot low into the far corner. Seeler also beat a man to score the second, from Schäfer's long pass. Schneiter, a composed defender, shot into the roof of the net following a corner. Herberger and Rappan had opposed each other as coaches in the 1938 finals.

GROUP 2	P	W	D	L	F	A	PTS
W. Germany	3	2	1	0	4	1	5
Chile	3	2	0	1	5	3	4
Italy	3	1	1	1	3	2	3
Switzerland	3	0	0	3	2	8	0

West Germany and Chile qualified for the quarter-finals.

■ 6 June 1962 • Nacional, Santiago • 67,224 •
Bobby Davidson (SCO)

▲ **WEST GERMANY (1) 2**
Szymaniak pen 22, Seeler 82
CHILE (0) 0

● W. GERMANY *Fahrian, Nowak, Schnellinger, Schulz, Erhardt, Willi Giesemann, Engelbert Kraus, Szymaniak, Seeler, Schäfer (c), Brülls.*
CHILE *Escuti, Eyzaguirre, Navarro (c), Contreras, R. Sánchez, Rojas, Ramírez, Mario Moreno, Landa, Armando Tobar, L. Sánchez.*

Chile had already qualified and confidence was high, but Germany put a few things in perspective. Dropping Haller and defending all over the pitch, even using Schäfer to mark the menacing Rojas, they were rarely in danger. Seeler, fantastic in the air for someone so stocky, was elbowed off the ball for the penalty and headed a marvellous second from a cross by Brülls.

■ 7 June 1962 • Nacional, Santiago • 59,828 •
Nikolai Latyshev (USR)

▲ **ITALY (1) 3**
Mora 2, Bulgarelli 65, 67
SWITZERLAND (0) 0

● ITALY *Buffon (c), Losi, Robotti, Salvadore, Maldini, Radice, Mora, Giacomo Bulgarelli, Angelo Sormani, Sivori, Ezio Pascutti.*
SWITZERLAND *Elsener, Tacchella, Schneiter, Grobéty, Eugen Meier, Weber, Antenen (c), Vonlanthen, Wüthrich, Allemann, Dürr.*

Irrelevant but nice enough. Again the Swiss traced some pleasing patterns, but Italy took their chances, despite leaving out Rivera and bringing in two new caps, Sormani and Bulgarelli. One of the Italian forwards did the cause no harm by accidentally treading on Elsener's hand. Of the goalkeepers who didn't concede a goal in World Cup tournaments, only Buffon played in more than one match.

Group 3

Brazil, Czechoslovakia, Mexico, Spain

■ 30 May 1962 • El Tranque, Viña del Mar • 10,484 • Gottfried Dienst (SWI)

▲ **BRAZIL (0) 2**
Zagallo 56, Pelé 72
MEXICO (0) 0

● BRAZIL *Gylmar (dos Santos), Djalma Santos, Nílton Santos, 'Zito' (José Ely de Miranda), Mauro (Ramos de Oliveira) (c), Zózimo (Alves), 'Garrincha' (Manoel Francisco dos Santos), 'Didi' (Waldir Pereira), 'Vavá' (Edvaldo Izídio Neto), 'Pelé' (Édson Arantes do Nascimento), Mário Zagallo.* Aymoré Moreira.

MEXICO *Antonio Carbajal (c), Jesús del Muro, José Villegas, Raúl Cárdenas, Guillermo Sepúlveda, Pedro Nájera, Alfredo del Aguila, Salvador Reyes, Héctor Hernández, Antonio Jasso, Isidoro Díaz.* Alejandro Scopelli (ARG), with Ignacio Trelles.

Yet again Brazil met Mexico in their first match, but there was more defensive organization around by now. When the first goal finally came, it owed much to Pelé's tenacity as well as his talent; he beat two

men, lost the ball in a tackle, eventually won it back, and crossed for Zagallo to run in and score with a diving header.

The second goal was all Pelé's own work. Walking the ball along the right touchline, he nutmegged one player, went past three more, disentangled himself inside in the area, and shot left-footed into the bottom corner. A frightening mixture of skill and power. Especially for someone who was hiding the extent of a groin injury from the team doctor...

Moreira, who took over as coach when Feola fell ill, was the brother of Zezé Moreira, who was Brazil's manager in 1954. They were the only brothers to coach teams in the finals. The stadium was later known as the Sausalito.

■ 31 May 1962 • El Tranque, Viña del Mar • 12,700 • Erich Steiner (AUT)

▲ **CZECHOSLOVAKIA (0) 1**
Stibrányi 79
SPAIN (0) 0

● CZECHOSLOVAKIA *Viliam Schrojf, Jan Lála, Ladislav Novák (c), Svatopluk Pluskal, Ján Popluhár, Josef Masopust, Jozef Stibrányi, Adolf Scherer, Andrej Kvasnák, Jozef Adamec, Josef Jelínek.* Rudolf Vytlacil (AUT).

SPAIN *Carmelo (Cedrún), Feliciano Rivilla, Severino Reija, Juan Segarra (c), José Santamaría, Jesús Garay, Luis Del Sol, Ferenc Puskás, Eulogio Martínez, Luis Suárez, Francisco Gento.* Pablo Hernández Coronado, with coach Helenio Herrera (ARG).

Santamaría and Puskás had played in the 1954 finals and were still world-class – but Czechoslovakia wore them down. Schrojf was the busier keeper early on, saving from Puskás and Suárez and receiving treatment after a full-blooded challenge from

Martínez – but eventually the rugged Scherer beat Santamaría and put Stibrányi clear to chip over the diving keeper. Pluskal and the balding Popluhár erected a big solid barrier at the back.

Herrera had been on Italy's coaching staff in the qualifying rounds. Note the slight spelling differences in the first names of Masopust and Jelínek, and Stibrányi and Adamec.

■ 2 June 1962 • El Tranque, Viña del Mar • 14,903 • Pierre Schwinte (FRA)

▲ **BRAZIL 0**
CZECHOSLOVAKIA 0

● BRAZIL *Gylmar, D. Santos, N. Santos, Zito, Mauro (c), Zózimo, Garrincha, Didi, Vavá, Pelé, Zagallo.*
CZECHOSLOVAKIA *Schrojf, Lála, Novák (c), Pluskal, Popluhár, Masopust, Stibrányi, Scherer, Kvasnák, Adamec, Jelínek.*

Early on, Pelé took Garrincha's pass, went through the defence, and shot against a post. In hitting the rebound, he felt something give way in his groin.

Later he remembered the way Popluhár and Lála refused to go into hard tackles while he stood helpless on the wing, 'one of those things I shall always remember with emotion, and one of the finest things that happened in my entire football career'. But it was the last good memory he took from this World Cup; his tournament was over.

■ 3 June 1962 • El Tranque, Viña del Mar • 11,875 • Branko Tesanic (YUG)

▲ **SPAIN (0) 1**
Peiró 89
MEXICO (0) 0

● SPAIN *Carmelo, 'Rodri' (Francisco Rodríguez), Sigfrido Gracia, Martín Vergés, Santamaría, 'Pachín' (Enrique Pérez Díaz), Del Sol, Joaquín Peiró, Puskás, Suárez, Gento (c).*
MEXICO *Carbajal (c), Del Muro, Ignacio Jáuregui, Cárdenas, Sepúlveda, Nájera, Del Aguila, Reyes, H. Hernández, Jasso, Díaz.*

Hernández missed a couple of late chances but Mexico again spent most of the match in defence and were glad Carbajal had a splendid game, saving from Puskás, Peiró, Vergés – oh well, everybody. Ironic that the goal should come from his failure to hold a shot by Gento, leaving Peiró with an open goal and Carbajal on his knees apparently weeping. An English report on the tournament lists Suárez as captain, but a Spanish history of their national team says Gento.

Vavá (right) watches as a header from Amarildo (out of picture) gives Brazil victory over Spain.

■ 6 June 1962 • El Tranque, Viña del Mar • 18,715 • Sergio Bustamante (CHI)

▲ **BRAZIL (0) 2**
Amarildo 72, 86
SPAIN (1) 1
Adelardo 35

● BRAZIL *Gylmar, D. Santos, N. Santos, Zito, Mauro (c), Zózimo, Garrincha, Didi, Vavá, Amarildo (Tavares), Zagallo.*
SPAIN *José Araquistain, Rodri, Gracia, Vergés, Luis María Echeberría, Pachín, Enrique Collar (c), Adelardo (Rodríguez), Puskás, Peiró, Gento.*

Looking for extra pace and mobility, Herrera dropped Del Sol, Santamaría and Suárez (but kept the 36-year-old Puskás!) and the changes nearly paid off. Adelardo shot into the bottom corner from 20 yards and volleyed wide after Gento, very fast and direct, had sprinted away from an ageing Djalma.

But Pelé's replacement, the talented young Amarildo, turned the trick, volleying home Zagallo's centre. His first goal for Brazil was followed by a second, a header after Garrincha at last got it right, beating two men before crossing. Spain came desperately close, having a goal from an overhead kick controversially disallowed – but Brazil had found a replacement for Pelé and looked ready to move up a gear.

■ 7 June 1962 • El Tranque, Viña del Mar • 10,648 • Gottfried Dienst (SWI)

▲ **MEXICO (2) 3**
Díaz 13, Del Aguila 30, H. Hernández, pen 88
CZECHOSLOVAKIA (1) 1
Masek 15 sec

● MEXICO *Carbajal (c), Del Muro, Jáuregui, Cárdenas, Sepúlveda, Nájera, Del Aguila, Reyes, H. Hernández, Alfredo Hernández, Díaz.*
CZECHOSLOVAKIA *Schrojf, Lála, Novák (c), Pluskal, Popluhár, Masopust, Stibrányi, Scherer, Kvasnák, Adamec, Václav Masek.*

At the 14th attempt, on their captain's 33rd birthday, Mexico won a finals match for the first time – despite conceding the fastest goal in the competition's history. Mexico kicked off but gave the ball away, Masopust wandered through to set up the blond Masek on the left, and the shot rolled under Carbajal. All performed in a daze, a kind of slow-motion. But by the end, Czechoslovakia were grateful that they'd already qualified. Carbajal, playing in a record fourth World Cup tournament, announced his retirement after the match, having never kept a clean sheet in the finals. Yet.

GROUP 3	P	W	D	L	F	A	PTS
Brazil	3	2	1	0	4	1	5
Czechoslovakia	3	1	1	1	2	3	3
Mexico	3	1	0	2	3	4	2
Spain	3	1	0	2	2	3	2

Brazil and Czechoslovakia qualified for the quarter-finals.

FASTEST GOALS
secs

15	Václav Masek	CZE	1962	v MEX
24	Ernst Lehner	GER	1934	v AUT
27	Bryan Robson	ENG	1982	v FRA
35	Émile Veinante	FRA	1938	v BEL
35	Arne Nyberg	SWE	1938	v HUN
37	Bernard Lacombe	FRA	1978	v ITA

Group 4

Argentina, Bulgaria, England, Hungary

■ 30 May 1962 • Braden Copper, Rancagua • 7,134 • Juan Gardeazábal (SPA)

▲ **ARGENTINA (1) 1**
Facundo 4
BULGARIA (0) 0

● ARGENTINA *Antonio Roma, Rubén Navarro (c), Silvio Marzolini, Carlos Alberto Sáinz, Federico Sacchi, Raúl Páez, Héctor Facundo, Oscar Rossi, Marcello Pagani, José Sanfilippo, Raúl Belén. Juan Carlos Lorenzo.*
BULGARIA *Georgi Naidenov, Kiril Rakarov (c), Stojan Kitov, Dimitar Kostov, Ivan Dimitrov, Nikola Kovachev, Todor Diev, Petar Velitchkov, Christo Iliev, Dimitar Yakimov, Ivan Kolev. Georgi Patchedzhiev, with Christo Chakarov.*

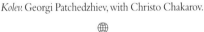

Marzolini, an attacking full-back of the highest class, a star in England four years later, showed his ability immediately, sprinting up the left to provide a cross which Pagani touched on to Facundo, who hit it first time. Promising.

But Argentina now had a hard edge, perhaps brought about by that 6-1 thrashing in 1958 and certainly instilled by their new coach, who went on to become one of the game's great bogeymen, manager of the Lazio team who attacked Arsenal in the street, Atlético Madrid when they had three men sent off against Celtic, and Boca Juniors when the national team coach refused to include any of their players in 1978. A real scary monster. He was also Argentina's manager in 1966....

Here he was still learning his trade, but the principle was already established: identify the opposition's main players, then stop them playing. Kolev was cut down time and again, Iliev and Diev were out injured for the rest of the tournament. They licked their wounds, Lorenzo his lips; Greaves, Charlton and Haynes were next.

■ 31 May 1962 • Braden Copper, Rancagua • 7,938 • Leo Horn (HOL)

▲ **HUNGARY (1) 2**
Tichy 16, Albert 70
ENGLAND (0) 1
Flowers pen 58

● HUNGARY *Gyula Grosics (c), Sándor Mátrai, László Sárosi, Ernö Solymosi, Kálmán Mészöly, Ferenc Sipos, Károly Sándor, Gyula Rákosi, Flórián Albert, Lajos Tichy, Máté Fenyvesi. Lajos Baróti.*
ENGLAND *Ron Springett, Jimmy Armfield, Ray Wilson, Bobby Moore, Maurice Norman, Ron Flowers, Bryan Douglas, Jimmy Greaves, Gerry Hitchens, Johnny Haynes (c), Bobby Charlton. Walter Winterbottom.*

England had given the 21-year-old Moore his first cap 11 days earlier, but he and Flowers were too similar: equally blond, equally defensive, unable to provide the creative help Haynes needed; 1958 all over again. Compare and contrast Hungary's ball-playing half-back Solymosi, or Argentina's Sacchi. The scoreline flattered England.

As the rain came down, Tichy scored a goal reminiscent of his performances in Sweden. Bringing the ball through the inside-left channel, he dummied Moore before thumping the ball high past Springett's right hand. Springett then saved well from Sándor and Albert missed from six yards. England were kept out by a packed defence in which the 20-year-old Mészöly was already looking a tremendous player – until Grosics lost the ball in a

---

challenge by Hitchens and Sárosi did remarkably well to stop Greaves' close-range shot with his hand. Flowers just beat Grosics with the penalty.

But when Flowers slipped on the wet pitch, Albert was clear on goal, taking the ball round Springett, who also lost his footing, and pushing it past the covering Wilson. Not for the first time in a World Cup, England were left needing a big improvement in their second match. This time perhaps they had the players to provide it.

[Top] Flowers equalizes from the penalty spot against Hungary.

■ 2 June 1962 • Braden Copper, Rancagua • 9,794 • Nikolai Latyshev (USR)

▲ **ENGLAND (2) 3**
Flowers pen 17, Charlton 42, Greaves 65
ARGENTINA (0) 1
Sanfilippo 78

● ENGLAND *Springett, Armfield, Wilson, Moore, Norman, Flowers, Douglas, Greaves, Alan Peacock, Haynes (c), Charlton.*
ARGENTINA *Roma, Vladislao Cap, Marzolini, Sacchi, Páez, Navarro (c), Antonio Rattin, Juan Carlos Oleniak, Sanfilippo, Rubén Sosa, Belén.*

The biters bit. After watching the horror show against Bulgaria, England 'were determined the same thing wasn't going to happen to us'. Winterbottom sent them out to 'bite in', and the Argentinians began behaving themselves. Charlton went past his man and crossed for the tall new cap Peacock to beat Roma with a header. Navarro handled on the line and Flowers didn't miss penalties while playing for England.

Charlton was already looking the best outside-left in the competition. When the defence backpedalled, waiting for another dart on the outside, he simply shot with his right foot, all the way along the ground just inside the far post. Greaves put in the loose ball when Roma saved from Douglas, and the much-vaunted Sanfilippo scored from a tight angle but didn't play for Argentina again.

■ 3 June 1962 • Braden Copper, Rancagua • 7,442 • Juan Gardeazábal (SPA)

▲ **HUNGARY (4) 6**
Albert 1, 6, 54, Tichy 8, 70, Solymosi 12
BULGARIA (0) 1
Sokolov 64

● HUNGARY *István Ilku, Mátrai, Sárosi (c), Solymosi, Mészöly, Sipos, Sándor, János Göröcs, Albert, Tichy, Fenyvesi.*
BULGARIA *Naidenov, Rakarov (c), Kitov, D. Kostov, Dimitrov, Kovachev, Georgi Sokolov, Velitchkov, Georgi Asparoukhov, Kolev, Dinko Dermendjiev.*

Hungary established themselves as one of the tournament favourites in the first 12 minutes of this one-way traffic, directed by Solymosi and driven home by Albert, who later re-invented himself as a deep-lying centre-forward in the Hidegkuti tradition, but was now still the immensely talented striker first capped at 17. He scored the first goal by cleverly diverting Fenyvesi's corner, the second when Naidenov pushed out a shot by Göröcs, his third when Göröcs ran through to set him up. Naidenov was also at fault with Tichy's first, rushing out and falling over the ball. Tichy went past three men to score the last. Sokolov's 20-yard shot beat Ilku, brought in when Grosics damaged a hand.

■ 6 June 1962 • Braden Copper, Rancagua • 7,945 • Arturo Yamasaki (PER)

▲ **ARGENTINA 0**
HUNGARY 0

● ARGENTINA *Rogelio Domínguez, José Manuel Ramos Delgado, Marzolini, Sáinz, Sacchi, Cap, Facundo, Martin Pando (c), Pagani, Oleniak, Alberto González.*
HUNGARY *Grosics (c), Mátrai, Sárosi, Solymosi, Mészöly, Sipos, Béla Kuharszki, Göröcs, Tichy, Tivadar Monostori, Rákosi.*

Hungary, already through, used three reserves up front and spent the game on the defensive. Grosics, still slim and agile at 36, made saves from Facundo, Pando and Sáinz, and Argentina were out unless Bulgaria could somehow beat England. Good riddance.

Quarter-finals

■ 7 June 1962 • Braden Copper, Rancagua • 5,700 • Arthur Blavier (BEL)

▲ **BULGARIA 0**
ENGLAND 0

● BULGARIA *Naidenov, Dimitar Dimov, D. Kostov, Dobromir Zhechev, Dimitrov, Kovachev (c), Aleksandar Kostov, Velitchkov, Asparoukhov, Kolev, Dermendjiev.*
ENGLAND *Springett, Armfield, Wilson, Moore, Norman, Flowers, Douglas, Greaves, Peacock, Haynes (c), Charlton.*

There was talk of Bulgaria being happy to see England through at the expense of Lorenzo & Co, but the truth is neither side had the inclination to make anything happen. Moore: 'We would have a dozen passes at our end then try and hit the ball up to our one forward. He was bound to lose it. So they had a dozen passes down their end. It was one of the worst internationals of all time.' No arguments here.

There used to be all kinds of confusion about the Bulgarian line-up. The one above comes from several sources including a Bulgarian match programme and the leading Bulgarian statistician.

■ 10 June 1962 • Carlos Dittborn, Arica • 17,268 • Leo Horn (HOL)

▲ **CHILE (2) 2**
L. Sánchez 11, Rojas 28
USSR (1) 1
Chislenko 26

● CHILE *Escuti, Eyzaguirre, Navarro (c), Contreras, R. Sánchez, Rojas, Ramírez, Toro, Landa, Tobar, L. Sánchez.*
USSR *Yashin, Chokeli, Ostrovsky, Voronin, Masylonkin, Netto (c), Chislenko, Ivanov, Ponedelnik, Mamykin, Meskhi.*

Yashin has been blamed for both the Chilean goals, scored from long range, but it's a harsh judgement. It's true that the first – a free-kick from wide on his right – surprised him at the near post (the USSR didn't form a wall), but Rojas' low shot was an excellent strike. Yashin later made an amazing one-handed save when Landa was clean through. Chislenko equalized

GROUP 4	P	W	D	L	F	A	PTS
Hungary	3	2	1	0	8	2	5
England	3	1	1	1	4	3	3
Argentina	3	1	1	1	2	3	3
Bulgaria	3	0	1	2	1	7	1

Hungary and England qualified for the quarter-finals.

Ramírez looks on as Rojas' long ground shot beats Yashin for Chile's winner in the quarter-final against the USSR.

when Escuti stopped Ponedelnik's shot, then Ivanov hit a post, but Chile pulled nine men back in defence and held out, backed by that full-throated crowd.

■ 10 June 1962 • Nacional, Santiago • 63,324 • Arturo Yamasaki (PER)

▲ **YUGOSLAVIA (0) 1**
Radakovic 85
WEST GERMANY (0) 0

● W. GERMANY *Fahrian, Nowak, Schnellinger, Schulz, Erhardt, Giesemann, Brülls, Haller, Seeler, Szymaniak, Schäfer (c).*
YUGOSLAVIA *Soskic, Durkovic, Jusufi, Radakovic, Markovic, Popovic, Vladimir Kovacevic, Sekularac, Jerkovic, Galic (c), Skoblar.*

For the third time in a row, Yugoslavia were faced with West Germany in the quarter-finals, but this time edged through in a fascinating match, full of personal duels with honours even: Sekularac v Szymaniak, Markovic v Seeler, both goalkeepers. Seeler hit the post with a low shot after running on to Haller's pass, Schnellinger kicked a shot off the line following a corner, and the only goal came when Galic pulled the ball back after working his way to the goal line. Radakovic, his head bandaged, lashed the ball high into the net from 12 yards. It was the end of the canny Herberger's reign as coach, which began before the 1938 finals.

■ 10 June 1962 • El Tranque, Viña del Mar • 17,736 • Pierre Schwinte (FRA)

▲ **BRAZIL (1) 3**
Garrincha 31, 59, Vavá 53
ENGLAND (1) 1
Hitchens 38

● BRAZIL *Gylmar, D. Santos, N. Santos, Zito, Mauro (c), Zózimo, Garrincha, Didi, Vavá, Amarildo, Zagallo.*
ENGLAND *Springett, Armfield, Wilson, Moore, Norman, Flowers, Douglas, Greaves, Hitchens, Haynes (c), Charlton.*

It was just a matter of time before Garrincha's outrageous individualism paid off. Only Maradona has ever left such a mark on a World Cup quarter- and semi-final.

Early on, he beat three men before Haynes tackled him near the goal line. Then, showing an unexpected side of his talent, he got in front of Norman at a Zagallo corner and headed past a stationary Springett and Armfield's desperate dive.

Hitchens, the only England player in the picture, equalizes against Brazil to the disappointment of Mauro (left), Zagallo, Nílton Santos and Zózimo.

England equalized when Greaves hit the bar with a looping header and Hitchens, back in the side because Peacock had pulled a groin muscle, banged in an instant shot. But the roof fell in on Springett soon after half-time. When Garrincha's free-kick blazed through the wall, he bent down and scooped it up for Vavá to head in. Then Garrincha took Amarildo's lay-off just outside the D and curled a marvellous shot into the top corner. A woolly black dog had strayed on to the pitch and avoided capture until Greaves got down on all fours and collared it. But it achieved the rare feat of sidestepping Garrincha.

If England hadn't qualified for the tournament, some might have wondered how this superannuated Brazil (average age of 30) would have fared against the likes of Charlton, Greaves, Moore, Haynes and Wilson. In the event, they emphasized the gulf between the two teams. Like Hitchens, Haynes wasn't capped again. The first £100-a-week man, he was a genuine class act, a fine passer of the ball, but not against World Cup defences.

Time for a little humility, perhaps. Since before the First World War, England hadn't been as good as they thought they were, and it was beginning to look as if the only way they were going to win this pesky competition was to stage it.

■ 10 June 1962 • Braden Copper, Rancagua • 11,690 • Nikolai Latyshev (USR)

▲ **CZECHOSLOVAKIA (1) 1**
Scherer 13
HUNGARY (0) 0

● CZECHOSLOVAKIA *Schrojf, Lála, Novák (c), Pluskal, Popluhár, Masopust, Tomás Pospíchal, Scherer, Josef Kadraba, Kvasnák, Jelínek.*
HUNGARY *Grosics (c), Mátrai, Sárosi, Solymosi, Mészöly, Sipos, Sándor, Rákosi, Albert, Tichy, Fenyvesi.*

Hungary were firm favourites but knocked themselves out on the Czech wall. A patchy pitch didn't help their passing, though Czechoslovakia had little trouble with it when their three half-backs interpassed and Masopust's through-ball cut out three defenders for Scherer to score. Schrojf, shortish and balding, made save after save, from Albert, Sándor, Solymosi and a Sipos thunderbolt. Tichy hit the bar as in 1958, and the utilitarians had won again.

Vavá punishes Springett's mistake by heading the ball past him to regain the lead for Brazil.

Semi-finals

■ 13 June 1962 • Nacional, Santiago • 76,594 • Arturo Yamasaki (PER)

▲ **BRAZIL (2) 4**
Garrincha 9, 32, Vavá 48, 78
CHILE (1) 2
Toro 42, L. Sánchez pen 62

● BRAZIL *Gylmar, D. Santos, N. Santos, Zito, Mauro (c), Zózimo, Garrincha, Didi, Vavá, Amarildo, Zagallo.*
CHILE *Escuti, Eyzaguirre, Manuel Rodríguez, Contreras, R. Sánchez, Rojas, Ramírez, Toro (c), Landa, Tobar, L. Sánchez.*
▼ SENT OFF: *Landa 80, Garrincha 84.*

Naturally this attracted the biggest attendance of the competition, but Brazil were too old to be affected by a crowd, and Chile were always playing catch-up. The powerful Rojas hit a post early on, but Brazil had an obvious penalty turned down and a goal disallowed for offside (the linesman didn't flag). Soon Zagallo hit a long cross, Vavá missed his overhead kick, and Garrincha cracked the loose ball into the top corner from 20 yards; right foot, head, now left foot. Pelé wasn't missed.

Later he proved his header against England wasn't just a one-off, hammering in another corner by Zagallo, whose lung power and underrated skills were transforming Brazil's 4-4-2 into a virtual 4-3-3. Toro gave Chile hope with a fabulous 25-yard free-kick and Zózimo's handball gave away the penalty (he'd done exactly the same – twice – at Wembley in 1956) – but Vavá headed in a corner and a cross. As the play grew rougher, two players were sent off, Garrincha having his head cut by a missile from the crowd. Brazil's background team immediately began strenuous negotiations to let the tournament's best player play in the Final.

■ 13 June 1962 • El Tranque, Viña del Mar • 5,890 • Gottfried Dienst (SWI)

▲ **CZECHOSLOVAKIA (0) 3**
Kadraba 48, Scherer 80, pen 84
YUGOSLAVIA (0) 1
Jerkovic 68

● CZECHOSLOVAKIA *Schrojf, Lála, Novák (c), Pluskal, Popluhár, Masopust, Pospíchal, Scherer, Kadraba, Kvasnák, Jelínek.*
YUGOSLAVIA *Soskic, Durkovic, Jusufi, Radakovic, Markovic, Popovic, Vasilije Sijakovic, Sekularac, Jerkovic, Galic (c), Skoblar.*

Didi, Amarildo and Zito parade with a Chilean flag after Brazil's win in the semi-final.

In front of another tiny crowd, Czechoslovakia again beat a more skilful side, relying on Schrojf to do his thing. After the Yugoslavs had missed two good chances in the first half, Kadraba headed in a rebound and the unmarked Scherer pushed a cross past the onrushing Soskic, then converted a penalty after Markovic had handled the ball a long way from goal. Jerkovic equalized with a backheader after beating Schrojf to a cross.

[Above] *Yugoslavia's equalizer in the semi-final. Pluskal (5) and Novák (4) look on as Popluhár's attempted overhead kick fails to keep the ball out of the net.*

[Right] *Czechoslovakia pose before their semi-final against Yugoslavia. (l–r) standing: Lála, Masopust, Popluhár, Schrojf, Pluskal, coach Vytlacil; kneeling: Pospíchal, Scherer, Kadraba, Jelínek, Kvasnák, Novák.*

3rd-place Final

■ 16 June 1962 • Nacional, Santiago • 66,697 • Juan Gardeazábal (SPA)

▲ **CHILE (0) 1**
Rojas 89
YUGOSLAVIA (0) 0

● CHILE *Adán Godoy, Eyzaguirre, Rodríguez, Humberto Cruz, R. Sánchez, Rojas, Ramírez, Toro (c), Carlos Campos, Tobar, L. Sánchez.*
YUGOSLAVIA *Soskic, Durkovic, Slavko Svinjarevic, Radakovic, Markovic, Popovic, Kovacevic, Sekularac, Jerkovic, Galic (c), Skoblar.*

With spectators like these, no match could be meaningless. It was decided by another long low shot from Rojas, possibly deflected. Chile's players had grown in stature during the tournament – Raúl Sánchez arguably its best stopper, Eyzaguirre now a cultured full-back, plus Rojas and Toro – and nobody begrudged the country its final placing.

Final

- ■ 17 June 1962 • Nacional, Santiago • 68 679 •
  Nikolai Latyshev (USR)

- ▲ **BRAZIL (1) 3**
  Amarildo 16, Zito 69, Vavá 78
  CZECHOSLOVAKIA (1) 1
  Masopust 14

- ● BRAZIL *Gylmar, D. Santos, N. Santos, Zito, Mauro (c), Zózimo, Garrincha, Didi, Vavá, Amarildo, Zagallo.*
  CZECHOSLOVAKIA *Schrojf, Jiří Tichy, Novák (c), Pluskal, Popluhár, Masopust, Pospíchal, Scherer, Kadraba, Kvasnák, Jelínek.*

Garrincha was allowed to play but made surprisingly little impact, stifled by the veteran Novák and his defence. Still, Brazil had enough firepower elsewhere. As against England, they did just enough to beat a good but not great European side. As in 1958, they won despite conceding an early goal, little Masopust running on to Scherer's clever pass to hit a low first-time shot before Zózimo could get to him. If Czechoslovakia, with their muscular defence, could hold the lead for any length of time....

Instead, within two minutes Amarildo received a throw-in, shrugged off Kvasnák, beat Pluskal near the left-hand goal line, and shot in at the near post where Schrojf, expecting a cross, had left a wide gap.

The Czech wingers played well after the interval, as did Masopust and the loping Kvasnák, and Czechoslovakia should have had a penalty when Djalma blocked a shot with his arms outstretched – but they were a pedestrian side, who had lacked a genuine finisher since Rudolf Kucera was injured before the tournament. And this was Amarildo's day. Zito sent him away on the left with a pass that convulsed Popluhár, Amarildo dummied to cross, cut back on to his right foot, and dinked a lob beyond Schrojf. Zito, short but unmarked, headed in.

Schrojf had redeemed himself with several good saves, but the magic was gone. When Brazil won a throw-in near the Czech penalty area, big Djalma came up, held off an opponent by turning his back, then spun and hit a hopeful hanging cross with his left foot. Schrojf came out, overran the ball as it dropped out of the sun, and let it slip out behind him as he fell. Almost as soon as it hit the ground, Vavá knocked it in, grinning like a shark.

It was the end of the international road for Zózimo and two of the greats, Didi and Nílton Santos, the strolling commander and the best left-back of all time. They had just enough left in the tank to survive the first stirrings of the new, more iron-clad football, but they belonged to another time. Nílton saw the change coming: unlike Didi and Zito, he'd shaved off the pencil moustache. Some of the other elders would still be there four years later, with results foreseen by Pelé.

LEADING GOALSCORERS 1962

4	Flórián Albert	HUN	
4	Valentin Ivanov	USR	
4	Garrincha	BRZ	
4	Leonel Sánchez	CHI	2 pen
4	Drazen Jerkovic	YUG	
4	Vavá	BRZ	

SCORED IN MOST FINALS

2	Vavá	BRZ	1958 & 1962
2	Pelé	BRZ	1958 & 1970
2	Paul Breitner	WG	1974 & 1982

MOST GOALS IN FINAL MATCHES

3	Vavá	BRZ	1958 & 1962
3	Geoff Hurst	ENG	1966
3	Pelé	BRZ	1958 & 1970

Schroff, a fallen hero by now, wishes the ground would open up after his error presents Vavá (9) with Brazil's third goal in the Final. Pluskal, hands on hips, knows it's not Czechoslovakia's day.

The Brazilian team who retained the Cup. (l–r, team only) standing: *coach Moreira, Djalma Santos, Zito, Gylmar, Zózimo, Nílton Santos, Mauro, team doctor Hílton Gosling;* kneeling: *trainer Mário Américo, Garrincha, Didi, Vavá, Amarildo, Zagallo.*

The Shadow of a Doubt

England 1966

Most certainly, said Alfred Ernest Ramsey – using that well-worn phrase of his – most certainly England will win the World Cup. The man with a legendary aversion to the press had provided them with their juiciest quote. Presumably he'd have taken it back, given the chance. But no, there it was on record, a rod for his own back.

Ramsey knew he hadn't been first choice to replace Winterbottom as manager, but no doubt thought he should have been. None of the other candidates could have achieved what he did in 1961–62, taking little Ipswich Town to the First Division title the season after bringing them out of the Second. Significantly, he achieved it by fitting journeyman players into a system that took the opposition by surprise. The new man had credentials – and more power. He took the job on condition that the selection committee which had so hindered poor Winterbottom was disbanded. All team decisions would be his, bringing England into the twentieth century.

There was also the little matter of home advantage, and enough good players to fortify Sir Alf's optimism, especially in a very open tournament. Bobby Moore, now the captain, was still making the occasional crass mistake, but had matured into probably the best defender in the world and the rest of the back four looked just as dependable: Ray Wilson still there and Jack Charlton winning his first cap at 30. Charlton's brother Bobby had moved into midfield, where he saw more of the ball but didn't quite look the part of playmaker. Greaves recovered well enough from hepatitis to score four goals in a warm-up match.

Just as importantly, Ramsey was in the process of making a revolutionary change to the shape of the team. The first three matches of the season had been a 0-0 draw with Wales, a 3-2 home defeat by Austria (Jimmy Hill: 'England won't win the World Cup. But don't blame Alf. No-one could win it with this lot.') and a late 2-1 win over Northern Ireland. So, on a freezing December night in Madrid, Ramsey sent out a team with (gasp) no wingers.

The 2-0 scoreline was a travesty. The Spanish full-backs, looking for someone to mark, were dragged out of position, Alan Ball and two mobile strikers filled the gaps, Moore came up to join the attack. A night when the term 'wingless wonders' wasn't used in derision. Spanish coach José Villalonga: 'They were phenomenal. Far superior in their experiment and in their players.'

This was the match that marked Ramsey as an international coach of the highest rank – yet he was wasn't quite ready to act on its findings. A full-back in his playing days, he knew the value of wingers; indeed he went on using them right up to the World Cup quarter-final. It took him a long time to accept there wasn't a stray Garrincha in the country.

While England were winning all four matches on a pre-tournament tour, the other home countries were wondering what might have been. Northern Ireland missed out on a play-off by being held to a draw in Albania and Wales beat the USSR at home but lost in Greece. Scotland lost 3-0 in Naples after injuries and the club managers in England (including well-known Scots like Busby and Shankly) had deprived them of a string of world-class players: Law, Baxter, Henderson, McNeill, Bill Brown. A frustrated Jock Stein resigned as manager.

Italy were devastating at home but far less convincing away. West Germany, who'd shown their mettle by winning in Sweden after drawing at home, had Seeler up front, new stars in midfield, and several players from the Borussia Dortmund team which had just beaten Liverpool in the Cup-Winners Cup Final. Argentina won the 'Little World Cup' in Brazil, beating the hosts (3-0), England and Portugal, then recalled the dreaded Lorenzo as manager. Portugal, heavily reliant on Benfica, had qualified for the first time by putting out the 1962 runners-up Czechoslovakia, the only goal in Bratislava scored by Eusébio, the European Footballer of the Year. The USSR were strong.

Meanwhile, Brazil seemed to believe the Cup was now theirs by right. All they needed was to resuscitate some of the veterans from 1962 and even 1958. So out went the young Carlos Alberto and Djalma Dias, back came Bellini (now 36) and Orlando. In stayed Djalma Santos (37), Gylmar (35), Zito (33) and an injury-prone Garrincha. There were some promising newcomers – Jairzinho, Gérson, Tostão, the 16-year-old Edu – but their time hadn't yet come. As in 1962, Pelé was the one great hope, still very much the best in the world – but there was no Amarildo to act as deputy; he'd been dropped too. 'There is only one way to describe Brazil's 1966 World Cup effort and that is to declare openly that from the beginning it was a total and unmitigated disaster.' Pelé's words – and England fans wanted to believe them.

In March, the World Cup trophy was stolen from the Stampex exhibition in Westminster. A week later a dog called Pickles discovered it under a hedge in south-east London and its owner handed it in, hoping he wouldn't be the last Englishman to pick it up that summer. Alf had promised as much, so it had to be true. Most certainly.

What it's all about, Alfie. Moore presents the trophy to Ramsey, who seems reluctant to be dragged away by a sabre-toothed Stiles.

Group 1

England, France, Mexico, Uruguay

■ 11 July 1966 • Wembley, London • 87,148 • István Zsolt (HUN)

▲ **ENGLAND 0**
URUGUAY 0

● ENGLAND *Gordon Banks, George Cohen, Ray Wilson, Nobby Stiles, Jack Charlton, Bobby Moore (c), Alan Ball, Jimmy Greaves, Bobby Charlton, Roger Hunt, John Connelly.* Alf Ramsey.
URUGUAY *Ladislao Mazurkiewicz, Luis Ubiña, Omar Caetano, Milton Viera, Jorge Manicera, Horacio Troche (c), Julio César Cortés, Néstor Goncálvez, Héctor Silva, Pedro Rocha, Domingo Pérez.* Ondino Viera.

If there was any deep optimism beforehand, much of it had drained away by the end of the day's proceedings. Uruguay used Troche as sweeper behind a back four, and everyone else in withdrawn positions, including their two most creative players, Rocha and Cortés – all in all, a web the England players rarely looked like breaking. When they did, bodychecks and knee-high tackles came into play, one of the worst (ironically) committed against Stiles, Ramsey's new terrier in midfield. Connelly was crowded out and the overlapping full-backs channelled into blind alleys. Draw the curtain across.

This was the only example of a coach picking his son to play in the World Cup finals. Early English sources spell the surname Ubinas, an error.

France equalize against Mexico, Hausser's shot beating Calderón and going in off a post.

■ 13 July 1966 • Wembley, London • 69,237 • Menachem Ashkenazi (ISR)

▲ **FRANCE (0) 1**
Hausser 61
MEXICO (0) 1
Borja 48

● FRANCE *Marcel Aubour, Robert Budzinski, Jean Djorkaeff, Marcel Artelesa (c), Bernard Bosquier, Gabriel De Michele, Joseph Bonnel, Roby Herbin, Néstor Combin, Philippe Gondet, Gérard Hausser.* Henri Guérin.
MEXICO *Ignacio Calderón, Arturo Chaires, Gustavo Peña (c), Gabriel Núñez, Guillermo Hernández, Isidoro Díaz, Salvador Reyes, Magdaleno Mercado, Enrique Borja, Javier Fragoso, Aarón Padilla.* Ignacio Trelles.

France were proud of their speed, but their ball-control and passing were lamentable (the highly touted Combin a particular failure) and they never came to terms with Borja, whose 32 goals make him Mexico's record scorer. When Aubour saved his shot, from Padilla's cross, he pushed the loose ball in from close range. France also scored from a rebound, Hausser's ground shot going in off a post, but the only people to take any pleasure were England and Uruguay.

■ 15 July 1966 • White City, London • 45,662 • Karol Galba (CZE)

▲ **URUGUAY (2) 2**
Rocha 27, Cortés 32
FRANCE (1) 1
De Bourgoing pen 16

● URUGUAY *Mazurkiewicz, Ubiña, Caetano, Viera, Manicera, Troche (c), Cortés, Goncálvez, José Sasia, Rocha, Pérez.*
FRANCE *Aubour, Djorkaeff, Budzinski, Artelesa (c), Bosquier, Yves Herbet, Bonnel, Héctor de Bourgoing, Jacky Simon, Gondet, Hausser.*

■ 16 July 1966 • Wembley, London • 92,570 • Concetto Lo Bello (ITA)

▲ **ENGLAND (1) 2**
R. Charlton 36, Hunt 76
MEXICO (0) 0

● ENGLAND *Banks, Cohen, Wilson, Stiles, J. Charlton, Moore (c), Terry Paine, Greaves, R. Charlton, Hunt, Martin Peters.*
MEXICO *Calderón, Chaires, Peña (c), Jesús del Muro, Núñez, Hernández, Díaz, Reyes, Ignacio Jáuregui, Borja, Padilla.*

Again the French were quick, Herbet taking a return pass at speed and hurtling towards the right-hand goal line, where Manicera pulled him back with a better sense of where the penalty area was than the referee. De Bourgoing, capped by Argentina in 1956 and 1957, made no mistake with the penalty but didn't play for France again.

Perhaps this shook the Uruguayans out of their defensive shell. At any rate they took over from then on, missing easy chances after scoring their two goals. First they kept possession interminably until Rocha shot home from the right, then Cortés smashed in a volley from a similar position.

England's first goal of the tournament was worth the wait. Taking Hunt's pass in the centre circle, Bobby Charlton set off towards the opposite penalty area. With the Mexicans holding off instead of challenging, he swerved to his right with a kind of hitch-kick before hitting one of his patented long-shots across the keeper at about chest height. One of the most famous Wembley goals.

He had a leading part in the second too, exchanging a series of passes on the left before sending Greaves in to shoot at Calderón, who could only push the ball straight to Hunt. Better from England, but still room for improvement against these packed defences. When Mexico kicked-off at the start of the match, Díaz banged the ball upfield while the rest of the team scuttled towards their own goal, a sign of what football was coming to. Again the solitary winger (Paine) couldn't get into the game, but England seemed sure to go through.

PLAYED IN MOST TOURNAMENTS

5	Antonio Carbajal MEX	1950–54–58–62–66
4	Pelé BRZ	1958–62–66–70
4	Karl-Heinz Schnellinger WG	1958–62–66–70
4	Uwe Seeler WG	1958–62–66–70
4	Gianni Rivera ITA	1962–66–70–74
4	Pedro Rocha URU	1962–66–70–74
4	Wladyslaw Zmuda POL	1974–78–82–86
4	Lothar Matthäus WG/GER	1982–86–90–94
4	Diego Maradona ARG	1982–86–90–94

LONGEST WORLD CUP PLAYING SPANS

yrs/days			
16/25	Antonio Carbajal	MEX	1950–66
16/17	Hugo Sánchez	MEX	1978–94
15/346	Elias Figueroa	CHI	1966–82

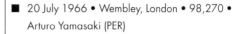

■ 19 July 1966 • Wembley, London • 35,000 •
Bertil Lööw (SWE)

▲ **MEXICO 0**
URUGUAY 0

● MEXICO *Antonio Carbajal, Chaires, Peña (c), Núñez, Hernández, Díaz, Mercado, Reyes, Ernesto Cisneros, Borja, Padilla.*
URUGUAY *Mazurkiewicz, Ubiña, Caetano, Viera, Manicera, Troche (c), Cortés, Goncálvez, Sasia, Rocha, Pérez.*

■ 20 July 1966 • Wembley, London • 98,270 •
Arturo Yamasaki (PER)

▲ **ENGLAND (1) 2**
Hunt 36, 76
FRANCE (0) 0

● ENGLAND *Banks, Cohen, Wilson, Stiles, J. Charlton, Moore (c), Ian Callaghan, Greaves, R. Charlton, Hunt, Peters.*
FRANCE *Aubour, Djorkaeff, Budzinski, Artelesa (c), Bosquier, Herbet, Bonnel, Herbin, Simon, Gondet, Hausser.*

Mexico needed to win by an unlikely two goals to qualify, and never stopped trying to get them, Cisneros hitting a post in the first half, Borja always a threat in the air. In the end, the match mattered most to the 37-year-old Carbajal, who was winning his last cap and appearing in his fifth World Cup finals. The official attendance figure was 61,112. Lööw is no misprint.

Against France, Roger Hunt scores one of his easiest goals for England after a header by Jack Charlton (in the background) comes back off the other post.

Even though France were weakened by an injury to Herbin after only eight minutes, they gave England another frustrating night, constantly catching Greaves and Hunt offside. In the end the latter celebrated his 28th birthday with two goals, though the second was a gift, Aubour palming a header from Callaghan's cross into the side of the net. Earlier, Hunt had put the loose ball in from very close in (inevitable cries of offside) after Jack Charlton had headed a cross by Greaves on to the post. England scored their goals at exactly the same times as against Mexico.

Stiles had a bad time all round, knocked down by the referee, booked for a foul, lucky to stay on the pitch after sliding in on Simon ('It was a bad, bad tackle. I got stick and deserved to get stick'). It's said that certain officials wanted him dropped from the team and only an ultimatum from Ramsey kept him in it. Whatever, he was lucky to have the manager's faith; his tackles had been wild and we don't usually talk about his passing. But at least the back four had again looked impregnable.

It really was the beginning of the end for wingers under Ramsey. Neither Connelly nor Paine was ever capped again, and Callaghan didn't return until 1977, a gap of 11 years 59 days, still the England record.

GROUP 1	P	W	D	L	F	A	PTS
England	3	2	1	0	4	0	5
Uruguay	3	1	2	0	2	1	4
Mexico	3	0	2	1	1	3	2
France	3	0	1	2	2	5	1

England and Uruguay qualified for the quarter-finals.

Group 2

Argentina, Spain, Switzerland, West Germany

■ 12 July 1966 • Hillsborough, Sheffield • 36,127 • Hugh Phillips (SCO)

▲ **WEST GERMANY (3) 5**
Held 16, Haller 21, pen 77, Beckenbauer 40, 62
SWITZERLAND (0) 0

● W. GERMANY *Hans Tilkowski, Horst-Dieter Höttges, Karl-Heinz Schnellinger, Franz Beckenbauer, Willi Schulz, Wolfgang Weber, Albert Brülls, Helmut Haller, Uwe Seeler (c), Wolfgang Overath, Sigi Held.* Helmut Schön.
SWITZERLAND *Karl Elsener, André Grobéty, Heinz Schneiter (c), Ely Tacchella, Hansrüdi Fuhrer, Heinz Bäni, Richard Dürr, Karl Odermatt, Fritz Künzli, Robert Hosp, Jean-Claude Schindelholz.* Alfredo Foni (ITA).

Switzerland had suspended two of their leading players, Kuhn and Leimgruber, for breaking curfew,

but even at full strength they wouldn't have been a match for this German team. And it wasn't just a case of brave part-timers being steam-rollered by Teutonic power (though there was some of that), West Germany were awesome, and awesomely talented. After Held put in the rebound when Seeler's shot was saved, they scored three of the best goals seen in a single World Cup match, Beckenbauer (twice) and Haller running through to finish with confidence and perfect technique. Seeler played a part in all three and was fouled for the penalty.

The running from midfield was wonderfully powerful, full of decisions made at speed, Overath distributing with his excellent left foot, Beckenbauer one of the most precocious players in Europe, Haller bulky but full of talent as well as himself. Tilkowski, on his 31st birthday, had little to do.

■ 13 July 1966 • Villa Park, Birmingham • 42,738 • Dimitar Rumenchev (BUL)

▲ **ARGENTINA (0) 2**
Artime 65, 77
SPAIN (0) 1
Roma o.g. 71

● ARGENTINA *Antonio Roma, Roberto Perfumo, Silvio Marzolini, Roberto Ferreiro, Rafael Albrecht, Antonio Rattin (c), Jorge Solari, Alberto González, Luis Artime, Ermindo Onega, Oscar Más.* Juan Carlos Lorenzo.
SPAIN *José Angel Iríbar, Manuel Sanchís snr, Eladio (Silvestre), 'Pirri' (José Martínez), 'Gallego' (Francisco Fernández), Ignacio Zoco, Luis Del Sol, Luis Suárez, José Armando Ufarte, Joaquin Peiró, Francisco Gento (c).* José Villalonga.

Argentina presented an unnerving sight, quite unlike any of their predecessors; almost European with their neat kit, short hair and severe sliding tackles in the rain – many of them directed at Suárez, Inter Milan's delicate playmaker. Contact sport apart, Argentina had as many world-class players as anyone in the tournament: Marzolini and Ferreiro; Onega and Más; the 6′3 Rattin a one-man half-back line; Artime a finisher who scored 24 goals in 25 internationals.

Here he converted González' low cross from the right and dragged Onega's pass past a defender before hitting a left-foot shot that drew applause from the St John's Ambulance men on the touchline. Every known source, Spanish and otherwise, credits Spain's equalizer to Pirri, but that's not how it looks on the screen. When a Suárez cross is headed almost straight up in the air, Pirri jumps for it with Roma, but it's clearly the goalkeeper's hand that dunks it in the net like a water polo player. Not the way he'd have chosen to celebrate his 34th birthday. Sanchís' son, Manuel junior, played in the 1990 finals.

■ 15 July 1966 • Hillsborough, Sheffield • 32,028 • Tofik Bakhramov (USR)

▲ **SPAIN (0) 2**
Sanchís 57, Amancio 75
SWITZERLAND (1) 1
Quentin 31

● SPAIN *Iríbar, Sanchís, Severino Reija, Pirri, Gallego, Zoco, Del Sol, Suárez, Amancio (Amaro), Peiró, Gento (c).*
SWITZERLAND *Elsener, Fuhrer, René Brodmann (c), Werner Leimgruber, Kurt Armbruster, Xavier Stierli, Bäni, Jakob (Köbi) Kuhn, Vittore Gottardi, Hosp, René-Pierre Quentin.*

This already had the look of a scrap between also-rans, and again Switzerland were unlikely to keep pace with the professionals. Nevertheless they took the lead, the reinstated Kuhn sending Gottardi away on the right, Quentin shooting home the cross. But

Sanchís had already served warning with a strong run through the middle, and now scored a sensational individual goal, beating man after man before hammering the ball into the roof of the net. Short and slight, he'd made his debut in the recent defeat by England, but this was a better day.

Remarkably, Spain's winner was almost as good, Gento going on a long run down the left that recalled his prime, Amancio diving to head in the cross. The Germans, next up, would have taken note.

■ 16 July 1966 • Villa Park, Birmingham • 46,587 • Konstantin Zecevic (YUG)

▲ **ARGENTINA 0**
WEST GERMANY 0

● ARGENTINA *Roma, Perfumo, Marzolini, Ferreiro, Albrecht, Rattin (c), Solari, González, Artime, Onega, Más.*
W. GERMANY *Tilkowski, Höttges, Schnellinger, Beckenbauer, Schulz, Weber, Brülls, Haller, Seeler (c), Overath, Held.*
▼ SENT OFF: *Albrecht 66.*

The irresistible force met the immovable object, but it was hard to be sure which was which. When the Germans attacked, they were stopped by bodychecks and sly trips followed by practised gestures of innocence. When Argentina ventured upfield, they were hit by tackles they clearly thought were illegal and may well have been; the likes of Schnellinger and Schulz knew how to take man and ball and take them very hard. With so many talented forwards on either side, neither midfield felt free to commit itself to going forward. For Argentina this was a normal state of affairs, but it was odd to see Haller hanging back, Beckenbauer fouling Ferreiro and Overath flattening González.

Eventually, after more than one wild tackle,

Albrecht was sent off for kneeing Weber in the groin, which must have been a formidable part of his anatomy; Albrecht was limping as he left the field. Perfumo twice headed against his own bar. Germany were no angels, but it was Lorenzo's mob who received a warning from FIFA.

■ 19 July 1966 • Hillsborough, Sheffield • 32,127 • Joaquim Campos (POR)

▲ **ARGENTINA (0) 2**
Artime 52, Onega 79
SWITZERLAND (0) 0

● ARGENTINA *Roma, Perfumo, Marzolini, Ferreiro, Oscar Calics, Rattin (c), Solari, González, Artime, Onega, Más.*
SWITZERLAND *Leo Eichmann, Brodmann (c), Fuhrer, Armbruster, Stierli, Bäni, Kuhn, Gottardi, Künzli, Hosp, Quentin.*

Even against clearly inferior opposition, Argentina were still happy to play out a barren first half and wait for the goals. Artime shot in off a post after the Swiss had given the ball away; Onega ran on to a return pass from González and lobbed the keeper as Eichmann and Fuhrer collided. It was the first time Argentina had qualified for the second phase since 1930 and Switzerland's last appearance in the finals until 1994.

GROUP 2	P	W	D	L	F	A	PTS
W. Germany	3	2	1	0	7	1	5
Argentina	3	2	1	0	4	1	5
Spain	3	1	0	2	4	5	2
Switzerland	3	0	0	3	1	9	0

West Germany and Argentina qualified for the quarter-finals.

■ 20 July 1966 • Villa Park, Birmingham • 45,187 • Armando Marques (BRZ)

▲ **WEST GERMANY (1) 2**
Emmerich 39, Seeler 84
SPAIN (1) 1
Fusté 23

● W. GERMANY *Tilkowski, Höttges, Schnellinger, Beckenbauer, Schulz, Weber, Werner Krämer, Held, Seeler (c), Overath, Lothar Emmerich.*
SPAIN *Iríbar, Sanchís, Reija, Jesús Glaría, Gallego, Zoco (c), Adelardo (Rodríguez), José María Fusté, Amancio, Marcelino (Martínez), Carlos Lapetra.*

Spain, needing a win to qualify, seemed to have little chance of achieving it without their three best-known players – Suárez and Del Sol out through injury, Gento dropped for loss of pace. Yet they took the lead when Fusté ran on to Marcelino's lob.

West Germany woke up after that. They'd added balance to their side by moving Held back inside from the wing where his left foot had let him down, and bringing in the naturally left-sided Emmerich, his beefy partner at Borussia Dortmund. The latter equalized with a staggering goal, chasing a loose ball to the left-hand goal line and battering it into the roof of the net from an impossible angle. It happened so fast and so implausibly that one of the Spaniards cleared the ball upfield like a boy hoping teacher hadn't noticed.

Then Held went back to the left, beat Sanchís, and hit a low cross which Seeler controlled and pushed home. Even under pressure, West Germany had again looked the part.

Group 3

Brazil, Bulgaria, Hungary, Portugal

■ 12 July 1966 • Goodison Park, Liverpool • 47,308 • Kurt Tschenscher (WG)

▲ **BRAZIL (1) 2**
Pelé 13, Garrincha 63
BULGARIA (0) 0

● BRAZIL *Gylmar (dos Santos), Djalma Santos, Paulo Henrique (Souza), Denílson (Machado), Hideraldo Luiz Bellini (c), Altair (Gomes), 'Garrincha' (Manoel Francisco dos Santos), Antônio Lima, Alcindo (de Freitas), 'Pelé' (Édson Arantes do Nascimento), 'Jairzinho' (Jair Ventura).* Vicente Feola.
BULGARIA *Georgi Naidenov, Aleksandar Shalamanov, Dimitar Penev, Ivan Vutzov, Boris Gaganelov (c), Stojan Kitov, Dobromir Zhechev, Dinko Dermendjiev, Georgi Asparoukhov, Dimitar Yakimov, Ivan Kolev.* Rudolf Vytlacil (AUT).

With all his reservations about Brazil's preparation, Pelé set out to win the match on his own, and just about succeeded, even though Bulgaria man-marked him ruthlessly. 'My legs ached as a result of Zhechev's constant tripping and kicking.' In the end the referee had to separate them and wag a finger, which is as tough as they ever got in those days. In the debates about footballers from different eras, it's worth remembering the relative protection ball-players get nowadays. Zhechev was booked but would have been sent off before half-time today.

Not that Pelé was particularly intimidated. He was too well-built for a start, a brick powerhouse with genius. How else do you stop that except by fouling? When Bulgaria did it yet again, with only 13 minutes gone, the great man exacted appropriate

revenge. With none of the bending and curling commonly associated with Brazilian free-kicks, this one (hit with anger?) blazed through the wall and yorked Naidenov. The first goal of the tournament.

Ironically, the free-kick had been given away by Yakimov, Bulgaria's most accomplished player. If the team had given him more support, if the talented Asparoukhov had shaken off an ankle injury, who knows what tremors might have been caused in that creaking Brazilian defence? As it was, the 35-year-old Kolev, first capped in 1952, was a peripheral figure. Until, that is, he committed a rather sheepish foul just outside the area. Garrincha picked himself up and smashed the ball into the top near corner with the outside of his right foot. Those deformed legs, bending in at the knee from the side, looked almost made for shots like this.

Brazil had played well in fits and starts but looked a one-man army. Late in the game, Pelé put his head down and went on an angled run reminiscent of a famous televised goal by George Best, ending in a shot which Naidenov did well to turn over the bar. Magnificent – but Pelé's legs had taken so much stick that he was rested for the next match. Vytlacil's last finals match as coach had also been against Brazil, the 1962 Final.

CONSECUTIVE MATCHES UNBEATEN		
13	Brazil	1958–66
11	Uruguay	1930–54
11	Brazil	1970–74
11	Brazil	1978–82
11	WG/Germany	1990–94
10	Italy	1982–86

■ 13 July 1966 • Old Trafford, Manchester •
29,886 • Leo Callaghan (WAL)

▲ **PORTUGAL (1) 3**
José Augusto 2, 65, Torres 88
HUNGARY (0) 1
Bene 60

● PORTUGAL *Joaquim Carvalho, João Morais, Alexandre Baptista, Vicente (Lucas), Hilário (da Conceição), Jaime Graça, Mário Coluna (c), José Augusto (de Almeida), José Torres, Eusébio (Ferreira), Antônio Simões.* Otto Glória (BRZ).
HUNGARY *Antal Szentmihályi, Sándor Mátrai, Benö Káposzta, Kálmán Mészöly, Ferenc Sipos (c), Kálmán Sóvári, Ferenc Bene, István Nagy, Flórián Albert, Gyula Rákosi, János Farkas.* Lajos Baróti.

Two of the best teams in the tournament, in their contrasting styles, produced a fascinating match and a distorted scoreline. Portugal, marvellous going forward, had a so-so back line. Hungary, with a packed and talented defence, were – well, marvellous going forward, but atrocious goalkeeping and missed chances destroyed them.

Talk beforehand centred round Eusébio and his credentials as the 'European Pelé' (actually the African Pelé: like Coluna, he was born in Mozambique). No-one was disappointed. Showing his intent in the very first minute, he beat Sóvári and Káposzta to force a corner, which José Augusto headed in while the 6′4″ Torres concentrated defenders' minds.

Hungary, forced to come out at once, dominated the next hour, Albert comfortable in his withdrawn role, Farkas streaming past Vicente, Nagy making the great Coluna lose his rag. But they needed a reciprocal goalkeeping error for their equalizer, Carvalho losing the ball in Albert's challenge to leave Bene with an open goal.

Within five minutes, they were back where they started, Szentmihályi letting an easy cross from Torres bounce off his chest for José Augusto to head in again. Mátrai, the masterly grey-haired sweeper, lay on the ground in despair. At the very end Torres headed in Eusébio's corner. By then Szentmihályi was all a-tremble and Hungary were one of those teams who look too good to go down but usually do.

■ 15 July 1966 • Goodison Park, Liverpool •
51,387 • Ken Dagnall (ENG)

▲ **HUNGARY (1) 3**
Bene 3, Farkas 64, Mészöly pen 72
BRAZIL (1) 1
Tostão 15

● HUNGARY *József Gelei, Mátrai, Káposzta, Mészöly, Sipos (c), Gusztáv Szepesi, Bene, Imre Mathesz, Albert, Rákosi, Farkas.*
BRAZIL *Gylmar, Santos, Paulo Henrique, Lima, Bellini (c), Altair, Garrincha, Gérson (de Oliveira), Alcindo, 'Tostão' (Eduardo Gonçalves), Jairzinho.*

Two Hungarian defenders prostrate themselves before the power and dynamism of Eusébio.

Brazil's old guard succumb to the shock of the new. Bellini (extreme left) can't reach Bene's cross and Farkas leaves Djalma Santos in his wake as he smashes in his famous goal.

One of the most vivid matches of all time, and the subject of regular repeats, it would have been a classic if one side hadn't been so dominant, and you can call them that even though the scores were level for almost an hour.

Hungary lit the touchpaper early. Sipos pushed the ball out to Bene on the right, the winger jagged inside to stop Altair in his tracks, left him on his backside by beating him on the outside, cut inside Bellini, and scored with a low left-footer inside the near post. A little jewel, and just the start Hungary needed.

Brazil's two goals so far had come from free-kicks, as did their third, the ball deflecting through to the 19-year-old Tostão, whose left foot struck it high to Gelei's left. Hungary didn't lose their nerve, and a superb sequence of play nearly put them back in front. Rákosi's cross-field pass was volleyed back by Mathesz to Mészöly, then Bene played a headed one-two with Albert only for Gylmar to make the save. Seven touches in all, without letting the ball hit the ground.

By now Albert was running the match, socks around his ankles, ball tied to his feet. In the second half, he played Bene in behind the full-back, Farkas volleying the low cross wide of the near post. Bene put his head in his hands, Rákosi remonstrated with all his heart, Farkas snapped back. It looks comical now, but the last thing Hungary needed was another missed chance; as things stood, they were out.

But the same three players produced an almost exact repeat for one of the great World Cup goals. Albert clipped a first-time pass up the right wing. Instead of beating his man, Bene looked up and hit a cross which dropped just above the penalty spot. Farkas, running full pelt, caught it with his instep just above the ground and a fraction behind him. The shot nearly holed the net behind a stationary Gylmar.

Brazil were broken then, missing Pelé like a lost limb. The killer third goal began with a fair but very firm tackle by Szepesi that left Garrincha limping. An inside pass reached Albert, who accelerated between two players in midfield and sent the ball out to Bene yet again. He beat Altair and was brought down by Paulo Henrique for the penalty. It was Brazil's first World Cup defeat since 1954, and by the same country.

If Albert was the conductor, Bene was a wonderful second string. Like Albert, he began as a centre-forward first capped at 17, soon scoring all the goals in a 6-0 win over Morocco at the 1964 Olympics. But his size and close control made him perfectly suited to life out on the wing. He scored in every match in these finals, played a part in all the other goals, and was still playing for Hungary in 1979.

1966

In sad contrast, another brilliant winger wasn't capped again. This was the great Garrincha's 50th and last international, and no-one else has been so indispensable; it was the only time he finished on the losing side.

■ 16 July 1966 • Old Trafford, Manchester • 25,438 • José María Codesal (URU)

▲ **PORTUGAL (2) 3**
Vutzov o.g. 7, Eusébio 38, Torres 82
BULGARIA (0) 0

● PORTUGAL *José Pereira, Alberto Festa, Vicente, Hilário, Germano (de Figueiredo), Graça, Coluna (c), José Augusto, Torres, Eusébio, Simões.*
BULGARIA *Naidenov, Shalamanov, Penev, Vutzov, Gaganelov (c), Zhechev, Dermendjiev, Petar Zhekov, Asparoukhov, Yakimov, Aleksandar Kostov.*

Much as expected. Torres, very mobile for such a human goalpost, sent in a high cross which Vutzov headed past his own goalkeeper. Torres and Zhekov both hit the bar, then Simões sent Eusébio in to open his account in the tournament with a shot that went in off Naidenov and the post. Torres ended the scoring by following Gaganelov's feeble back-pass into the net. Eusébio generally played within himself, happy to test out his long-range shooting. Uncomfortable viewing for Brazil. Common spelling variations: Chalamanov, Jetchev, Jekov.

Torres (on the ground for once) watches Eusébio rise above Orlando's challenge to head Portugal's second goal against Brazil.

■ 19 July 1966 • Goodison Park, Liverpool • 58,479 • George McCabe (ENG)

▲ **PORTUGAL (2) 3**
Simões 15, Eusébio 24, 85
BRAZIL (0) 1
Rildo 71

● PORTUGAL *Pereira, Morais, Baptista, Vicente, Hilário, Graça, Coluna (c), José Augusto, Torres, Eusébio, Simões.*
BRAZIL *'Manga' (Aílton Corrêa), José Maria Fidélis, Hércules de Brito, Denílson, Orlando (Peçanha) (c), Rildo (da Costa), Jairzinho, Lima, Walter da Silva, Pelé, 'Paraná' (Adhemir de Barros).*

Pelé had to be brought back, but the contest with Eusébio was horribly unequal. Pelé hadn't fully recovered, and the Portuguese defenders made sure he didn't get a chance to, a wild early tackle cutting his knees from under him without so much as a booking. Before long Morais finished the demolition job with a murderous double foul on the edge of the penalty area. Either tackle was worth a sending-off, but again there was no booking; spineless refereeing

from McCabe. Pelé was carried off by the team doctor and masseur, taking Brazil's chances with him.

In truth, they hadn't been worth much from the moment their team-sheet showed nine changes, including the return of Orlando to mark Eusébio. Pelé thought 'it would have been ridiculous in a junior league. In the World Cup, against one of the strongest teams of the tournament, it was suicidal.'

Manga and the tiny Fidélis had a particularly unhappy time. The goalkeeper, whose pockmarked face earned him the nickname Frankenstein from his kindly peers, looked nervous from the start, and Eusébio soon gave him good reason to be, beating his man on the left and putting over a near-post cross which Manga was a little unlucky to bat straight onto the head of Simões. The second goal was utterly predictable. Coluna took a free-kick deep on the right, Torres soared to head it back from the far post, Eusébio headed almost through Manga, flattening Orlando in the process. Rildo pulled one back with a stern ground shot, but Brazil really needed to win, and Eusébio extinguished their chances with one of the great power goals of the World Cup.

After Manga had saved his shot he touched the corner short to Simões, whose cross was aimed at Torres as usual. The ball bounced back towards the right, where Eusébio met it with a terrifying shin-high volley that left Manga on his knees. David Coleman: 'Oh my word! Have you ever seen anything like that?' Orlando, who pulled out of the tackle, didn't play for Brazil again.

That goal was an abiding memory of the tournament, but no more so than the sight of Pelé walking off with a coat around his shoulders and his knee heavily bandaged, vowing never to play in the World Cup again. The whole Brazilian approach had been a monument to complacency. Pelé again: 'I suppose our directors put their faith in the old dictum that "God is a Brazilian", forgetting that God also helps those who help themselves.'

■ 20 July 1966 • Old Trafford, Manchester • 24,129 • Roberto Goicoechea (ARG)

▲ **HUNGARY (2) 3**
Davidov o.g. 42, Mészöly 44, Bene 53
BULGARIA (1) 1
Asparoukhov 15

● HUNGARY *Gelei, Mátrai, Káposzta, Mészöly, Sipos (c), Szepesi, Bene, Mathesz, Albert, Farkas, Rákosi.*
BULGARIA *Simeon Simeonov, Dimitar Largov, Penev, Vutzov, Gaganelov (c), Zhechev, Ivan Davidov, Kolev, Asparoukhov, Yakimov, Nikola Kotkov.*

No reprieve for Brazil, although Asparoukhov did give Bulgaria the lead when Gelei ran out in a flap. Earlier Yakimov had hit a post, and it was nearly half-time when Mészöly hammered a half-volley into the top corner. Bene headed the third, but the goal that effectively eliminated Brazil was an own goal from Davidov on his international debut.

Asparoukhov and Kotkov died in the same car crash in 1971.

GROUP 3	P	W	D	L	F	A	PTS
Portugal	3	3	0	0	9	2	6
Hungary	3	2	0	1	7	5	4
Brazil	3	1	0	2	4	6	2
Bulgaria	3	0	0	3	1	8	0

Portugal and Hungary qualified for the quarter-finals.

1966

Group 4

Chile, Italy, North Korea, USSR

■ 12 July 1966 • Ayresome Park, Middlesbrough •
23,006 • Juan Gardeazábal (SPA)

▲ **USSR (2) 3**
Malofeyev 30, 88, Banishevsky 31
NORTH KOREA (0) 0

● USSR *Anzor Kavazashvili, Vladimir Ponomaryev, Leonid Ostrovsky, Georgy Sichinava, Murtaz Khurtsilava, Albert Shesternev (c), Igor Chislenko, Iosif Sabo, Anatoly Banishevsky, Eduard Malofeyev, Galimzyan Khusainov.* Nikolai Morozov.
N. KOREA *Lee Chan-myung, Park Lee-sup, Shin Yung-kyoo, Kang Bong-chil, Lim Zoong-sun, Im Seung-hwi, Park Seung-jin (c), Han Bong-jin, Park Doo-ik, Kang Ryong-woon, Kim Seung-kil.* Myung Rye-hyun.

When FIFA refused to guarantee Africa its own qualifier, the entire continent withdrew, along with most of Asia, leaving only two countries to represent two billion people or so. North Korea's 9-2 aggregate win over Australia didn't incite terror among the big names, but many were intrigued by their two years of monastic existence and training in barracks. Fitness, a big failing of the last Korean team to reach the finals, probably wouldn't be a factor.

Size, however, was. The USSR, big men in any company, looked virtually twice the height and bulk of the Koreans, none of whom stood higher than 5'8", including the 19-year-old goalkeeper, the youngest in any finals tournament.

He did well throughout it, but there was no stopping these Soviet goliaths. The fair-haired Banishevsky made a goal for Malofeyev and headed in Chislenko's free-kick, then Malofeyev scored the best of the day, running on to Sabo's chip, chesting down and half-volleying in. There should have been others; the USSR seemed reluctant to make the most of their pace and physique. For the Koreans, apparently nothing but more hard labour ahead. Sabo was of Hungarian extraction, real name József Szabó.

■ 13 July 1966 • Roker Park, Sunderland •
27,199 • Gottfried Dienst (SWI)

▲ **ITALY (1) 2**
Mazzola 9, Barison 88
CHILE (0) 0

● ITALY *Enrico Albertosi, Tarcisio Burgnich, Giacinto Facchetti, Giovanni Lodetti, Roberto Rosato, Sandro Salvadore (c), Marino Perani, Giacomo Bulgarelli, Sandro Mazzola, Gianni Rivera, Paolo Barison.* Edmondo Fabbri.
CHILE *Juan Olivares, Luis Eyzaguirre, Hugo Villanueva (c), Humberto Cruz, Elias Figueroa, Rubén Marcos, Pedro Araya, Ignacio Prieto, Armando Tobar, Alberto Fouilloux, Leonel Sánchez.* Luis Alamos.

No-one really expected a repeat of the 1962 street fight; there was even a steady drizzle to cool things down. Instead the match was thoroughly tepid, frustratingly so after Italy's upbeat start. Bulgarelli sent a perfect pass inside Eyzaguirre for the hefty Barison to thump in a shot. Olivares saved it, Mazzola slid in to score.

Mazzola would later move back into midfield, skilfully but not quite convincingly. For the moment, he was still the wiry and gifted striker who'd helped Inter win two European Cups. Bulgarelli and Rivera were smoothness itself in the middle, Burgnich and Facchetti already famous full-backs. But Bulgarelli had to come off for treatment, Rivera was having one of his regular off-days and the whole team seemed obsessed with defence away from home, even against a team reduced to ten men when Tobar went off after an hour. Barison scored a spectacular goal, going past Eyzaguirre again to thrash the ball in from a narrow angle, but this didn't look like the side which had beaten Bulgaria 6-1 and Argentina 3-0 in June. Still, with two such weak teams in the group, they were surely already through.

■ 15 July 1966 • Ayresome Park, Middlesbrough • 13,792 • Ali Kandil (EGY)

▲ **CHILE (1) 1**
Marcos pen 27
NORTH KOREA (0) 1
Park Seung-jin 88

● CHILE *Olivares, Alberto Valentini, Villanueva (c), Cruz, Figueroa, Marcos, Araya, Prieto, Honorino Landa, Fouilloux, Sánchez.*
N. KOREA *Lee Chan-myung, Park Lee-sup, Shin Yung-kyoo, Lim Zoong-sun, Oh Yoon-kyung, Park Seung-jin (c), Im Seung-hwi, Han Bong-jin, Park Doo-ik, Lee Dong-woon, Kim Seung-il.*

The Koreans were almost unnaturally slim, but also nimble and young (average age 22) and their fitness came into its own this time, culminating in Park Seung-jin's fierce low volley after a defensive header dropped to him on the edge of the box. The Chileans had tried to muscle them out of it but couldn't. Marcos, who thumped in the penalty awarded for a foul by Oh Yoon-Kyung on Araya, was probably the worst offender, booked by the referee and booed by the crowd. A tall spectator in full sailor's costume joined in the celebrations at the end, hugging assorted Koreans, some of whom (probably not for this reason) left the pitch in tears.

Marcos of Chile scores from a penalty against North Korea.

■ 16 July 1966 • Roker Park, Sunderland • 27,793 • Rudolf Kreitlein (WG)

▲ **USSR (0) 1**
Chislenko 57
ITALY (0) 0

● ITALY *Albertosi, Burgnich, Facchetti, Lodetti, Rosato, Salvadore (c), Gianfranco Leoncini, Luigi Meroni, Bulgarelli, Mazzola, Ezio Pascutti.*
USSR *Lev Yashin, Ponomaryev, Vasily Danilov, Sabo, Khurtsilava, Shesternev (c), Chislenko, Valery Voronin, Banishevsky, Malofeyev, Khusainov.*

With both teams apparently certain to qualify, this looked the most obvious draw on the schedule and neither side took many risks. There were giants on either side. Facchetti, who stood taller than his goalkeeper, was a fast attacking full-back for Inter but now stayed back to watch Chislenko. Shesternev, similarly broad and wide, was stopper and sweeper in one. He had the better of it today, Chislenko going past Facchetti to score with a fierce rising left-footer. Earlier, Mazzola of all people had missed when clean through on goal, but there again Yashin was as intimidating as Shesternev.

■ 19 July 1966 • Ayresome Park, Middlesbrough •
17,829 • Pierre Schwinte (FRA)

▲ **NORTH KOREA (1) 1**
Park Doo-ik 42
ITALY (0) 0

● N. KOREA *Lee Chan-myung, Shin Yung-kyoo, Lim Zoong-sun, Ha Jung-won, Oh Yoon-kyung, Park Seung-jin (c), Im Seung-hwi, Han Bong-jin, Park Doo-ik, Kim Bong-hwan, Yang Sung-kook.*
ITALY *Albertosi, Spartaco Landini, Facchetti, Romano Fogli, Aristide Guarneri, Francesco Janich, Perani, Bulgarelli (c), Mazzola, Rivera, Barison.*

Ferruccio Valcareggi, Fabbri's assistant, was soon to take over as No. 1 and lead Italy to the European Championship – which redeemed his reputation somewhat. Sent to watch North Korea's matches, he returned with the opinion that they were 'una squadra di Ridolini', the Italian name for Charlie Chaplin. They weren't the ones looking like little tramps at the end.

Rivera came back, and played well enough – but Italy were a man down for the last hour (people forget this) after Bulgarelli aggravated his knee injury in a late tackle on Park Seung-jin. Soon afterwards came the famous goal. An Italian clearance was headed back towards their area and Park Doo-ik let it run into his stride before hitting a ground shot across Albertosi, who might have done better. Earlier Lee Chan-myung had made a fantastic save from Perani's close-range volley.

North Korea outlasted the ten men in the second half, making a mess of at least two good chances. Fabbri was sacked, Janich, Perani and Barison weren't capped again, and the Italians returned to the traditional reception of tomatoes and other missiles. An astounding result, perhaps the most popular in any World Cup. Park Doo-ik later became a dentist. Quips on a postcard.

Janich arrives too late and the tall Facchetti can only watch from afar as Park Doo-ik (far right) scores the most traumatic goal in Italian football history.

■ 20 July 1966 • Roker Park, Sunderland • 16,027 • John Adair (NIR)

▲ **USSR (1) 2**
Porkujan 29, 87
CHILE (1) 1
Marcos 33

● USSR *Kavazashvili, Viktor Getmanov, Alexei Korneyev, Ostrovsky, Shesternev (c), Valentin Afonin, Slava Metreveli, Voronin, Viktor Serebrianikov, Eduard Markarov, Valery Porkujan.*
CHILE *Olivares, Valentini, Villanueva (c), Cruz, Figueroa, Marcos, Araya, Prieto, Landa, Guillermo Yavar, Sánchez.*

The USSR, already through, sent out their reserves, one of whom stayed in the team after scoring twice. Porkujan drove in a rebound then lobbed Olivares after the injured Marcos had equalized in a scramble. Chile played with spirit but were worn down by superior ground forces. Story of the tournament.

GROUP 4	P	W	D	L	F	A	PTS
USSR	3	3	0	0	6	1	6
N. Korea	3	1	1	1	2	4	3
Italy	3	1	0	2	2	2	2
Chile	3	0	1	2	2	5	1

USSR and North Korea qualified for the quarter-finals.

LEADING GOALSCORERS 1966

9	Eusébio	POR	4 pen
6	Helmut Haller	WG	1 pen
4	Ferenc Bene	HUN	
4	Franz Beckenbauer	WG	
4	Valery Porkujan	USR	
4	Geoff Hurst	ENG	

Quarter-finals

■ 23 July 1966 • Wembley, London • 90,584 • Rudolf Kreitlein (WG)

▲ **ENGLAND (0) 1**
Hurst 77
ARGENTINA (0) 0

● ENGLAND *Banks, Cohen, Wilson, Stiles, J. Charlton, Moore (c), Ball, Geoff Hurst, R. Charlton, Hunt, Peters.*
ARGENTINA *Roma, Ferreiro, Marzolini, Albrecht, Rattín (c), Solari, Perfumo, González, Artime, Onega, Más.*
▼ SENT OFF: *Rattín 36.*

Jimmy Greaves was one of England's most prolific strikers (44 goals in 57 internationals) but not in the World Cup (one in seven). Again strangely out of sorts, he'd now had his leg gashed open by the French. Ramsey replaced him with Hurst and recalled Ball for his fighting qualities. 'Well, gentlemen, you know the kind of game you have on your hands this afternoon.'

It's hard to get a balanced view on this match. Virtually all the testimony in England naturally comes from the England players and English journalists and apparently England committed as many fouls as Argentina. The trouble probably grew out of mutual suspicion. Pelé wasn't the only one to hear the rumour ('and I firmly believe it') that FIFA president Stanley Rous had instructed the referees to go easy on the 'virile' European style of play. Pelé was fouled out of the tournament, an Argentinian sent off against West Germany, and there were dismissals in both the quarter-finals involving South American teams, refereed by a German and an Englishman. Meanwhile Moore & Co. had watched Argentina play West Germany: 'We accepted in our guts it was

The taller they are … Rattin (left) contemplates the touchline as Kreitlein sends him off.

From a cross by Peters (in the distance), Hurst gets in front of Perfumo to head his first goal for England.

going to be hard. Maybe brutal.'

In the end, you probably have to take the England players' word for it; it sounds so grimly plausible. Hurst, for example, felt as if he'd walked down a dark alley in a strange town: 'At any moment, for no reason, you thought you might be attacked from behind.' Twice, when he was nowhere near the ball, he was kicked in the ankle, each time 'I swung round and there was a ring of blank faces'. Moore claimed 'they did tug your hair, spit at you, poke you in the eyes and kick you when the ball was miles away and no-one was looking'. Meanwhile Stiles put his own perspective on things: 'Apart from the violence, I came through with no problems.'

Kreitlein's patience was thin from the start (five bookings) and cracked within half an hour, during which Rattin had spat in front of him, disputed every decision that went against Argentina, and fouled anyone that came within range. Kreitlein, who'd already cautioned him, sent him off – and all hell broke loose.

Rattin refused to go. His excuse: that he'd merely been asking for an interpreter, which doesn't tally with anything he'd done beforehand (and who goes around asking for interpreters during a football match?). Albrecht signalled the rest of the team to go with him. Some of them, reinforced by various officials, mobbed Kreitlein. After eight minutes that seemed an eternity, Rattin allowed himself to be led off, tried to sit on the touchlines, was talked out of it by the police and took the scenic route back to the changing

Please do not clothe the animals. Ramsey stops Cohen exchanging shirts with González after the match.

he made his notorious speech comparing the Argentinian team to animals, which many felt was unfair to animals. Somehow, in all the mayhem, even Bobby Charlton was booked.

Lorenzo moved on to ply his trade in Europe, and Argentinian clubs began to wreak havoc in the World Club Cup. Two years later, for example, Stiles was sent off and Bobby Charlton had his shin cut to the bone. Jimmy Johnstone had to wash the spittle out of his hair against Racing, Cruyff's ankle was severely damaged by Independiente and three Estudiantes players were jailed by their own president! Sir Alf, for a period of about eight years, was right.

room, stopping from time to time to observe the play, villain of the piece in England, martyr back home. A shame, because he'd been the hub of the side, tall and unhurried, always finding a team-mate with his passes. Their chances were naturally reduced without him, although it took England a fearfully long time to make the extra man tell.

The violence didn't end with Rattin's departure. Hurst hurt Ferreiro with a high tackle, Jack Charlton came up for a corner and was barged from behind by Albrecht while in mid-air, a really dangerous challenge. Eventually, after Roma had made a solid save from Hurst, England scored a very good goal. From wide on the left, Peters hit a kind of brisk lob which left Roma in two minds, and Hurst came in to glance his header across the keeper and inside the far post. A small boy ran on to offer congratulations and had his ear clipped – boo hiss – by Más.

In the aftermath, while Kreitlein was being escorted off the pitch by the police and Ken Aston (who knew the feeling), Ramsey forcibly stopped Cohen from exchanging shirts with González. Later

---

■ 23 July 1966 • Hillsborough, Sheffield • 40,007 • Jim Finney (ENG)

▲ **WEST GERMANY (1) 4**
Haller 11, 84, Beckenbauer 70, Seeler 77
URUGUAY (0) 0

● W. GERMANY *Tilkowski, Höttges, Schnellinger, Beckenbauer, Schulz, Weber, Held, Haller, Seeler (c), Overath, Emmerich.*
URUGUAY *Mazurkiewicz, Ubiña, Caetano, Héctor Salva, Manicera, Troche (c), Cortés, Goncálvez, Silva, Rocha, Pérez.*
▼ SENT OFF: *Troche 50, Silva 55.*

Further north, a carbon-copy game was emerging. Again there were two schools of violence and ways of reacting to it; again the South Americans felt aggrieved. While the German tackles were going right through people, whenever they themselves were challenged they rolled around as if in mortal agony, only to rise from the dead seconds after the free-kick had been awarded. Haller was the best at this, and when he flukily diverted Held's shot to open the score, Uruguay must have felt there was no justice, certainly not from an English referee who'd waved play on when Schnellinger clearly handled the ball under his own crossbar.

Even so, some of the Uruguayan habits weren't whiter than white. Troche was sent off for kicking Emmerich in the stomach, slapping Seeler's face as he left. Silva, a dead ringer for Uri Geller with a similar influence on football matches, kicked Schulz as Tilkowski collected the ball, then kicked the ball as Tilkowski held it on the ground, and finally joined forces with Caetano for a violent double attack on Haller, grinding his studs in the German's leg as he received treatment. Another police escort was required.

A goal down with only nine men, Uruguay left great gaps at the back. Beckenbauer repeated one of his runs against Switzerland, taking Seeler's return pass round the keeper. Emmerich charged up the left in oceans of space before passing inside to Held; his square pass went behind Seeler, who calmly re-gathered it before blasting into the top corner from 18 yards. Cue pitch invasion by fan with German

flag and lederhosen. Finally Manicera's slip let Haller take Seeler's return chip and push it past the exposed keeper. Merciless, and all adding to the South Americans' sense of grievance.

■ 23 July 1966 • Goodison Park, Liverpool • 40,248 • Menachem Ashkenazi (ISR)

▲ **PORTUGAL (2) 5**
Eusébio 26, pen 43, 57, pen 60, José Augusto 80
NORTH KOREA (3) 3
Park Seung-jin 1, Lee Dong-woon 20, Yang Sung-kook 24

● PORTUGAL *Pereira, Morais, Baptista, Graça, Vicente, Hilário, José Augusto, Coluna (c), Torres, Eusébio, Simões.* N. KOREA *Lee Chan-myung, Shin Yung-kyoo, Lim Zoong-sun, Ha Jung-won, Oh Yoon-kyung, Park Seung-jin (c), Im Seung-hwi, Han Bong-jin, Park Doo-ik, Lee Dong-woon, Yang Sung-kook.*

A unique match. Certainly no other had such a gobsmacking start. Whereas Brazil had seemed petrified of the Portuguese attack, the Koreans attacked the Portuguese defence, which was weaker. Logical, really.

They were a goal up in less than a minute. Han Bong-jin rolled the ball square from the right and Park Seung-jin struck it cleanly with the outside of his left foot into the top left-hand corner. Then Han Bong-jin's cross from the right went all the way through to Yang Sung-kook on the left-hand goal line; his instant cross was turned into the empty net by Lee Dong-woon. The crowd had just started chanting 'We want three' when they got it. Park Doo-ik's shot fell to Yang Sung-kook, who kept his cool to take it round a defender and leave Pereira standing with a ground shot. Portuguese and crowd alike were rubbing their eyes.

Eusébio of Portugal converts one of his penalties against North Korea.

Common consensus has it that North Korea lost the match by maintaining all-out attack instead of protecting their lead, but there's too much condescension in that. They were always going to be under threat as soon as Eusébio got into his stride. First he cracked home José Augusto's through-ball then hit both penalties hard to the keeper's right, the first when Torres was fouled by a man half his height, the other when his own forceful run down the left was ended by a sliding tackle. His other goal was similar to his first, shooting without breaking stride. He made the fifth too, his corner being headed back across goal by the inevitable Torres for José Augusto to head in unopposed. It was Eusébio's match, but he had to share it with some of the little people.

■ 23 July 1966 • Roker Park, Sunderland • 22,103 • Juan Gardeazábal (SPA)

▲ **USSR (1) 2**
Chislenko 5, Porkujan 48
HUNGARY (0) 1
Bene 58

● USSR *Yashin, Ponomaryev, Danilov, Voronin, Shesternev (c), Sabo, Khusainov, Chislenko, Banishevsky, Malofeyev, Porkujan.*
HUNGARY *Gelei, Mátrai, Káposzta, Mészöly, Sipos (c), Szepesi, Bene, Nagy, Albert, Farkas, Rákosi.*

Hungary appeared to have everything necessary for success in the modern game. Massed defence, fast-breaking midfield, slick forwards. But the Soviets simply brutalized them.

Close-marking Bene, Albert and Farkas, thumping home their tackles, they also took advantage of defensive slips, especially an early goalkeeping blunder. Porkujan took a short corner on the left and hit the return low to the near post, where Gelei gathered it comfortably then let it loose behind him. Chislenko got to it before Banishevsky. Gelei, turning out to be no better than Szentmihályi, knelt and wrung his hands, which wasn't the part his team-mates had in mind. Then Khusainov's free-kick from the left reached Porkujan absurdly unmarked at the far post.

Mészöly pushed forward in the second half and burst through a tackle to set up a goal for Bene, but Rákosi missed the ball completely from three yards out, and Yashin, still an acrobat at 36, dived to save a Sipos free-kick. Hungary's defeat was everyone's loss, but the USSR got through on sheer strength; of mind, too.

Semi-finals

■ 25 July 1966 • Goodison Park, Liverpool • 38,273 • Concetto Lo Bello (ITA)

▲ **WEST GERMANY (1) 2**
Haller 43, Beckenbauer 68
USSR (0) 1
Porkujan 87

● W. GERMANY *Tilkowski, Friedel Lutz, Schnellinger, Beckenbauer, Schulz, Weber, Held, Haller, Seeler (c), Overath, Emmerich.*
USSR *Yashin, Ponomaryev, Shesternev (c), Danilov, Voronin, Sabo, Khusainov, Chislenko, Banishevsky, Malofeyev, Porkujan.*
▼ SENT OFF: *Chislenko 44.*

If you liked your meat raw, this was the place to be, with one side built like bull calves and the other more hammer than sickle. It all came down to who had more men standing at the end.

Germany were ahead on that count almost at

Bobby Charlton at his explosive best, thrashing in a pass by Hurst (centre) for his second goal in the semi-final against Portugal.

once, Sabo twisting an ankle trying to foul Beckenbauer and needing a painkilling injection at half-time. Near the end of the first half, Schnellinger went into a typical tackle on Chislenko, who was about half his size and weight. He took ball and man, leaving Chislenko clutching his ankle, then showed the other side of his game by running powerfully upfield before hitting a pass to the right-hand side of the penalty area, where it was met by Haller's diagonal run and strong shot. Immediately after the kick-off, a limping Chislenko lost the ball to Held and gave him a clip on the back of the ankle. By the standards of this tournament, it was an innocuous foul, but Lo Bello sent him off.

Beckenbauer scored the second goal by drifting outside a pack of players on the edge of the area before shooting left-footed just inside the left-hand post. Yashin, who stood and watched, was either unsighted or thought the ball was going wide. Porkujan scored when Tilkowski dropped the ball under pressure from Malofeyev, and Banishevsky headed over the bar – but even on an off day the

Germans had shown what they were made of, and Chislenko knew what that felt like.

There was some disappointment that England didn't play their semi-final up here, but it was always in the rules of the competition that they'd stay at Wembley if they won their group.

■ 26 July 1966 • Wembley, London • 94,493 • Pierre Schwinte (FRA)

▲ **ENGLAND (1) 2**
R. Charlton 30, 79
PORTUGAL (0) 1
Eusébio pen 82

● ENGLAND *Banks, Cohen, Wilson, Stiles, J. Charlton, Moore (c), Ball, Hurst, R. Charlton, Hunt, Peters.*
PORTUGAL *Pereira, Festa, Baptista, Graça, José Carlos (da Silva), Hilário, José Augusto, Coluna (c), Torres, Eusébio, Simões.*

Of all the teams in the tournament, Portugal had perhaps the most identifiable strengths and weaknesses. There were five Benfica players in the team – the entire forward line. The defence was drawn from four other clubs and played like strangers. If the great Germano and Costa Pereira hadn't been past their prime, things might have been different. Instead Portugal had to make do with José Carlos and José Pereira (no relation, no comparison). Bobby Moore looked forward to it 'the way many League clubs thought about playing West Ham: it would be a good game but not a hard fight, and we would probably win in the end.'

The Portuguese were almost preposterously genteel. No-one to mark Bobby Charlton, no fouls in the first 20 minutes. They'd even dropped Vicente and Morais, who'd kicked pieces out of Pelé. When Charlton scored his second goal, José Augusto shook his hand. Nothing wrong with that, but not something Stiles would have done.

Moore again: 'Eusébio didn't have the stomach for Nobby Stiles,' which seems to be the prevailing view over the years but must be too simplistic by half. Stiles didn't man-mark Eusébio and hardly ever fouled him. The England defence simply retreated rather than diving in and playing to his strengths. As for Eusébio's implied lack of courage, we're back to the question of different eras of refereeing. In the European Cup final two years later, Stiles bodychecked Eusébio three times in quick succession without so much as a booking. Only one of them would have been a star today.

England's opening goal stemmed from a long pass by Wilson into the path of Hunt, who cleverly touched the ball to one side of José Carlos and ran round the other. Pereira rushed out, made a sliding tackle instead of diving at Hunt's feet, and the ball reached Bobby Charlton, who sidefooted it back between goalkeeper and defender into the net.

The other full-back and front runner laid the groundwork for his second goal, Hurst chasing Cohen's long ball to the right-hand goal line. José Carlos should have won the ball but lost it, and Hurst rolled it back for Charlton to smash in one of the famous England goals. He hit the ball quite low but so hard it appeared to hit a pocket of air and rise sharply, although perhaps (heresy, this) it took a slight deflection.

Portugal didn't give up. If Eusébio was being tamed and Simôes getting little change out of Cohen, Coluna was still a force in midfield, built like a welterweight but with all the skills, and not even Big Jack could conquer Mount Torres. Simôes, forced to switch wings, hit a high ball to the far post, Banks came out and missed it, Torres headed goalwards, Jack Charlton handled. Eusébio thumped his penalty in the

Banks goes the wrong way for Eusébio's penalty and concedes his first goal in a World Cup match.

usual place, which annoyed Banks, who'd intended to dive that way but then saw various team-mates reminding him of it: 'for some reason they kept pointing me in that direction ... Coluna went and whispered in Eusébio's ear, enough to convince me he was going to change the direction of his kick. I could have cried.' It was the first goal England had conceded in seven matches, still the national record.

There was still time for Torres to beat Charlton in the air again and knock the ball down for Simões to nudge it wide as Banks rushed out. The earlier error was a rare one for Banks, rapidly proving himself Yashin's successor. He showed it at the death here, making an excellent save when Coluna sidestepped a tackle and put everything into a shot just under the bar. The chance had been set up by Eusébio, lest we forget him, but it was Bobby Charlton's day.

3rd-place Final

■ 28 July 1966 • Wembley, London • 87,696 •
Ken Dagnall (ENG)

▲ **PORTUGAL (1) 2**
Eusébio pen 13, Torres 88
USSR (1) 1
Malofeyev 44

● PORTUGAL *Pereira, Festa, Baptista, Graça, José Carlos, Hilário, José Augusto, Coluna (c), Torres, Eusébio, Simões.*
USSR *Yashin (c), Ponomaryev, Korneyev, Sichinava, Khurtsilava, Danilov, Serebrianikov, Voronin, Banishevsky, Malofeyev, Metreveli.*

Portugal were the better side and people wanted them to win, but it was dull as well as pointless. Khurtsilava, terrified of Torres, committed an unnecessary handball for the penalty. Pereira fumbled Metreveli's

long shot for Malofeyev to put in the rebound and we were spared extra-time when Torres won the ball in the air for the thousandth time and José Augusto chipped it back to him. The volley was touched gently past Yashin, whose days came quietly to an end. The actual attendance was probably c.70,000.

Final

■ 30 July 1966 • Wembley, London • 93,802 •
Gottfried Dienst (SWI)

▲ **ENGLAND (1) (2) 4**
Hurst 19, 100, 119, Peters 78
WEST GERMANY (1) (2) 2
Haller 13, Weber 89

● ENGLAND *Banks, Cohen, Wilson, Stiles, J. Charlton, Moore (c), Ball, Hurst, R. Charlton, Hunt, Peters.*
W. GERMANY *Tilkowski, Höttges, Schnellinger, Beckenbauer, Schulz, Weber, Held, Haller, Seeler (c), Overath, Emmerich.*

The first goal in the 1966 World Cup Final. (l–r): Banks, Jack Charlton, Wilson, the scorer Haller, Emmerich.

As with Puskás in 1954, the whispers began: was Greaves coming back? It was never a straight choice between him and Hunt, who'd been his partner at the start ('A lot of people still say it was me who took Jimmy's place, but it was Geoff Hurst'). Hurst had scored the winner in the quarter-final and made the winner in the semi. Greaves had barely recovered. No contest in Ramsey's mind.

If Greaves' absence left England short of charm, they were nevertheless the only team to make West Germany change their game plan. Bobby Charlton's performance against Portugal persuaded Schön to put a man on him. His midfield didn't have a natural marker, so Beckenbauer would have to do. Do well enough, too – he and Charlton cancelled each other out – but the loss was probably Germany's. If Schön really wanted a minder, he had Klaus-Dieter Sieloff in his squad. All he had to do was drop Emmerich. After that freakish goal against Spain, the big winger had done very little and looked clumsy on the ball, out of place in a passing team. But this had been his big season, especially in the Cup-Winners' Cup: six goals in one match, two in each leg to beat the holders West Ham in the semi-final. That hammer of a left foot helped him to 115 goals in 183 *Bundesliga*

games. Schön decided he needed a matchwinner more than a ball winner and picked an unchanged front five.

West Germany made the better start, on a pitch greased by rain, and aided by an England error or three. From out on the left, Held hit a deep cross towards the far post, Banks shouted for Wilson to let it go, Wilson 'seemed to think I was shouting a warning' and went up too early for the header, knocking it down too close to goal. Haller reached back to collect it and shot, none too hard, along the ground past Jack Charlton and Banks ('we left it to each other'). England were already clinging to omens. In every World Cup Final since the War, the side who scored first had lost the match.

Moore later said that Haller 'shouldn't be the sort of player who scores against us and certainly isn't the class of player to win a World Cup Final' – but that's a comment with a lot of baggage. Haller was everything the English loved to hate about German footballers: strutting, snub-nosed and blond, an actor when he was fouled, a first name of Helmut. He was also a world-class player who helped Bologna and Juventus win the Italian league. Why did he deserve a goal in a World Cup Final any less than Hurst or Peters?

Perhaps fuelled by this indignation, Moore came up a long way on the left until Overath brought him down. Taking the free-kick before the referee's whistle, he clipped it in to coincide with Hurst's perfect run and downward header.

Hurst's header leaves Tilkowski standing and brings England level at 1-1, watched by Schulz (5), Beckenbauer (4) and Hunt (21, next to Hurst).

Another West Ham goal.

For the next hour, something of a stand-off punctuated with sporadic shots from behind the barricades. Both defences were in control, England superbly marshalled by Moore, Germany coagulating around Schulz, the underrated Höttges hitting his tackles hard.

Eventually Ball took a corner on the right, the ball reached Hurst on the edge of the area, he shot, optimistically and badly, a lunging block by Höttges sent the ball ballooning behind him, and Peters beat Jack Charlton to it on the way down. 'No I didn't feel cheated, I'm glad the bugger never came to me because I'd have kicked it over the bar.' Peters drove it in from seven yards past Tilkowski and Schnellinger, who both ended up sitting on the goal line.

That should have put an end to it. The England players believed they should have been able to hold out for 12 minutes, and would have done so if the referee hadn't awarded a free-kick against Jack Charlton for leaning on Held, who may have been making a back for him. Emmerich, scenting last-minute redemption, hit the free-kick hard, there were assorted ricochets, Moore appealed for handball by Schnellinger (Banks: 'There's no way it was deliberate'), the ball finally squeezed out to the right, where Weber scooped it over Wilson's leg and Banks' hands. Extra-time in a Final for the first time since 1934.

England must have been crushed, but according to Moore 'Alf was unbelievably good,' making his 'you've won it once, now go and win it again' speech with very little time for rehearsal. In extra-time, Ball set about obeying the instruction. He was up against Schnellinger ('and there's no way that was your birthday') but simply ran the big man ragged. Chasing a long pass from Stiles out to the right-hand corner flag, he hit it first time. Hurst got in front of some shoddy marking by Schulz to control the ball and crash it against the underside of the bar. When it

bounced down, Hunt appealed instead of following in ('I wouldn't have got to the ball') and Weber headed it over the bar for a corner. But Dienst, surely passing the buck, went to his linesman Tofik Bakhramov, who was a long way off. The England players have watched the ball hit the line. They think it's all over. It is now, the linesman says he's seen it.

It's still the most controversial moment in any World Cup Final, mainly because it simply wasn't a goal. There's no discussion about it (though there's been some). Photographs prove that when the ball meets its shadow, the whole thing clearly isn't over the line.

That was the beginning of the end for this strong and talented German team. In the last minute, Moore chested down a cross in his penalty area, drove Big Jack mad by not kicking it into Neasden, and hit a cool long pass to Hurst just inside the opposition half. He ran on, puffed his cheeks, and smashed his shot high inside the near post. He was the only player to score three goals in a World Cup Final, although he needed extra-time and a little help to do so. He scored with his head and each foot.

At the final whistle, Jack Charlton knelt with his face in his hands, Stiles jumped on Cohen's back ('It looked like copulation. I don't know what he was

doing but I didn't enjoy it very much!') and Ramsey sat impassively on the bench while the world jumped around him, basking in being proved right. London could start calling itself the capital of the world: Swinging Sixties, Jagger and Richards, Norbert Peter Stiles. But if God was now an Englishman, the old devil with the flag was Azerbaijani. The main football ground in Baku is the Tofik Bakhramov Stadium.

[Right] *Peters (far right) blasts the ball past Schnellinger and Tilkowski on the line. Jack Charlton breathes a sigh of relief that the chance didn't fall to him.*

[Opposite] *The trademark puff of the cheeks as Hurst blasts the goal that completes his unique hat-trick. Overath, whose brave pursuit was admired by Ramsey, had his reward eight years later.*

[Below] *Movement and assorted emotions are frozen in time as Weber (far left) equalizes in the last minute, watched by Seeler, a grounded Cohen, Wilson, an appealing Moore, Schnellinger, Banks, Jack Charlton and Held. One of the great World Cup photographs.*

England's disputed winning goal. Schulz (5) and Hurst are on the ground, Höttges (2) and Schnellinger (3) hope the linesman sees things their way.

The contribution of the three West Ham players (the captain and both goalscorers) is matched by Sir Nobby's celebrated Wembley jig.

The Height of Brilliance: 7,000 Feet

Mexico 1970

In the four years between World Cups, Ramsey's England lost just four out of 35 matches, only against very good teams and never by more than one goal. But there were ten draws in that time, and some very dreary performances; England were difficult to beat but just as hard to watch. Still, this may be carping too much; the squad for Mexico looked as good as in 1966. Banks, Moore, Ball, Hurst, Peters and the Charltons were still there, and Stiles had been replaced by Mullery, who was better on the ball and almost as spiky off it. There was a dynamic new winger in Lee and an excellent crop of attacking full-backs, increasingly necessary in a wingless team. Preparation had included several matches at altitude, and there was no shortage of confidence. Moore: 'We believed we had the best squad in England's history. We believed we were going to win it again.'

But they weren't the favourites. Brazil had done enough, admittedly in a weak qualifying group, to serve notice that 1966 was firmly behind them, winning all six matches and scoring 23 goals, including ten from Tostão, whose promise was now being fulfilled in a rich partnership with a rejuvenated Pelé, who scored six himself. Carlos Alberto, Gérson and Jairzinho were coming into their prime, and there was some bright new blood in Clodoaldo and Rivelino. They even picked the right manager. Twice.

João Saldanha, a journalist, had been such a vehement critic of the national team that eventually the patience of the powers that be snapped and he was made national coach! What sounds like something done for a bet – a disaster – was an instant success. Saldanha built the team round the Santos club, kept the same squad throughout, and they cut a swathe through the qualifying matches.

Soon, however, his famously short fuse began getting in the way. Pelé said that 'whenever we saw a group in one corner of the pitch, we knew João had invited someone there to settle things with fists'. But it wasn't the fists that provided the last straw; Saldanha was discovered at the house of a particularly vociferous critic – brandishing a revolver! Zagallo, infinitely calmer, a star of 1958 and 1962, took the squad to Mexico.

Intriguingly, a year earlier Brazil had recovered from 1-0 down to score two late goals against England at home, a scoring sequence that gave hope to both camps, who were drawn in the same World Cup group.

Elsewhere, West Germany added the great goalscoring talents of Gerd Müller to their 1966 squad but scraped through 3-2 against Scotland. Italy, who'd recovered from their Korean trauma to win the European Championship, looked strong in qualifying, Luigi Riva scoring seven of their ten goals. Argentina, more violent than ever, were eliminated by Peru despite almost unlimited injury-time in the deciding match. The USSR put out a Northern Ireland team denied the services of George Best. And Mexico's position as hosts allowed another Central American country to take part, El Salvador qualifying after three matches with neighbouring Honduras, which sparked off a war that had more to do with immigration than football (we hope). Three thousand people died.

Another two hundred had been shot dead two years earlier, when armed police opened fire on peaceful demonstrators before the Olympics held in Mexico City. FIFA turned a blind eye, to that and to the enormous problems of heat and altitude which had left European competitors needing oxygen at the Games. Indeed, they added to them by arranging matches at noon to accommodate European television schedules. While FIFA fiddled, players burned, losing ten pounds in fluid during a single game or being sent home with heatstroke. The tournament produced some exhilarating football, and one of the greatest forward lines, but the price, in human terms, was a rip-off.

$Group$ 1

Belgium, El Salvador, Mexico, USSR

■ 31 May 1970 • Azteca, Mexico City • 107,160 • Kurt Tschenscher (WG)

▲ **MEXICO 0**
USSR 0

● MEXICO *Ignacio Calderón, Gustavo Peña (c), Mario Pérez jnr, Guillermo Hernández, Horacio López, José Vantolrá, Javier Guzmán, Héctor Pulido, Mario Velarde [Antonio Munguía 67], Javier Valdivia, Javier Fragoso.* Raúl Cárdenas.
USSR *Anzor Kavazashvili, Vladimir Kaplichny, Evgeny Lovchev, Gennady Logofet, Albert Shesternev (c), Kakhi Asatiani, Vladimir Muntian, Viktor Serebrianikov [Anatoly Puzach HT], Anatoly Byshovets, Gennady Evriuzhikin, Givi Nodia [Vitaly Khmelnitsky 66].* Gavril Katchalin.

As grim a start as everyone feared (altitude and heated tackles) but one with surprisingly pleasing repercussions. Some blamed Tschenscher for booking five players, but the referees had been given strict instructions and were clearly going to follow them; dirty play was never a feature of the tournament. López missed a couple of chances, but the football in this match was secondary. Puzach was the first substitute in a finals match.

■ 3 June 1970 • Azteca, Mexico City • 30,000 • Andrei Radulescu (ROM)

▲ **BELGIUM (1) 3**
Van Moer 8, 54, Lambert pen 79
EL SALVADOR (0) 0

● BELGIUM *Christian Piot, Georges Heylens, Jean Thissen, Nico Dewalque, Jean Dockx, Léon Semmeling, Wilfried Van Moer, Johan Devrindt, Paul Van Himst (c), Wilfried Puis, Raoul Lambert [Odilon Polleunis 81].* Raymond Goethals.
EL SALVADOR *Raúl Magaña, Roberto Rivas, Salvador Mariona (c), Saturnino Osorio, Mauricio Manzano [Santiago Cortés 67], Antonio Quintanilla, Jorge Vásquez, Salvador Cabezas, Mauricio 'Pipo' Rodríguez [Genaro Sermeño 79], Ramón Martínez, Ernesto Aparicio.* Hernán Carrasco (CHI).

El Salvador were as weak as predicted and Belgium should have scored more. But the famous Van Himst had a terrible time in the thin air, missing easy chances, and only little Van Moer stood out, hammering the first goal from 30 yards and converting a cross from Semmeling, who was fouled for the penalty. Aparicio wasted a good chance when clean through. The official attendance figure was 92,205!

■ 6 June 1970 • Azteca, Mexico City • 95,261 •
Rudi Scheurer (SWI)

▲ **USSR (1) 4**
Byshovets 14, 63, Asatiani 57, Khmelnitsky 75
BELGIUM (0) 1
Lambert 86

● USSR *Kavazashvili, Kaplichny [Lovchev 43], Valentin Afonin, Revaz Dzodzuashvili [Nikolai Kiselev 65], Murtaz Khurtsilava, Shesternev (c), Asatiani, Muntian, Evriuzhikin, Byshovets, Khmelnitsky.*
BELGIUM *Piot, Heylens, Thissen, Dewalque, Dockx, Léon Jeck, Semmeling, Van Moer, Van Himst (c), Puis, Lambert.*

■ 7 June 1970 • Azteca, Mexico City • 103,058 •
Ali Kandil (EGY)

▲ **MEXICO (1) 4**
Valdivia 44, 47, Fragoso 58, Basaguren 83
EL SALVADOR (0) 0

● MEXICO *Calderón, Peña (c), Pérez, Munguía, Enrique Borja [López HT, Juan Ignacio Basaguren 75], Aarón Padilla, Vantolrá, Guzmán, José Luis González, Valdivia, Fragoso.*
EL SALVADOR *Magaña, Rivas, Mariona (c), Osorio, Cortés [Mario Monge 66], Quintanilla, Rodríguez, Vásquez, Martínez, Cabezas, Aparicio [Sergio Méndez 56].*

Billed as an exciting Belgian forward line versus the plodding Soviets, the match was turned on its head when Kavazashvili saved a header from Van Moer, who hit the bar from the rebound. The USSR immediately went down the other end and scored the first of their four tremendous goals, Byshovets hammering home from 30 yards. Despite the conditions, Goethals didn't use any substitutes as the scoreline mounted. Asatiani turned Heylens and shot in off the far post. Shesternev, massively impassable as ever, intercepted a pass and fed Byshovets, who cut inside Jeck and Dockx and scored with a screaming left-footed drive. Khmelnitsky's subterranean header from Evriuzhikin's dinked cross made it four, and Lambert's goal, after Van Moer hit a post, went almost unnoticed. Overwhelming.

Mexico were so poor that the minnows would have held out into the second half but for a mighty refereeing controversy. El Salvador, who thought Kandil had awarded them a throw or a free-kick, stood still as he waved away their protests when Mexico took the kick. Padilla crossed, Borja missed an open goal but Valdivia didn't.

Pandemonium. The Salvadoreans surrounded Kandil, turning their backs so he could see their numbers to book them, jostling Bermudan linesman Keith Dunstan, kicking the ball into the crowd. In the second half, they did little except try and kick as many Mexicans as possible, conceding goals to Valdivia (a cross shot after beating a man), Fragoso (from a López header) and Basaguren, the first substitute to score in a World Cup tournament. TV replays of the main incident are inconclusive (El Salvador may simply have misunderstood) but Kandil never refereed another finals match.

■ 10 June 1970 • Azteca, Mexico City • 25,000 •
Rafael Hormazábal (CHI)

▲ **USSR (0) 2**
Byshovets 51, 73
EL SALVADOR (0) 0

● USSR *Kavazashvili, Shesternev (c), Dzodzuashvili, Khurtsilava, Afonin, Serebrianikov, Kiselev [Asatiani 79], Muntian, Puzach [Evriuzhikin HT], Byshovets, Khmelnitsky.*
EL SALVADOR *Magaña, Rivas, Mariona (c), Osorio, Cabezas [Aparicio 79], Vásquez, Monge, Jaime Portillo, Rodríguez [Sermeño 85], Guillermo Castro, Méndez.*

Yet again El Salvador did their best, especially their eccentric goalkeeper, but the chunky and sure-footed Byshovets put away a through-pass from Serebrianikov and shot the second after Muntian had beaten three men. Rodríguez missed a golden chance and El Salvador would have to wait 12 years for their first goal in the finals. Many were disappointed that the Soviets hadn't selected Yashin, in the squad at the age of 40. The official attendance figure was 89,979.

■ 11 June 1970 • Azteca, Mexico City • 108,192 •
Norberto Angel Coerezza (ARG)

▲ **MEXICO (1) 1**
Peña pen 15
BELGIUM (0) 0

● MEXICO *Calderón, Peña (c), Vantolrá, Guzmán, Pérez, Pulido, González, Munguía, Valdivia [Basaguren HT], Fragoso, Padilla.*
BELGIUM *Piot, Heylens, Thissen, Dewalque, Dockx, Jeck, Semmeling, Polleunis [Devrindt 65], Van Moer, Van Himst (c), Puis.*

Another match in the Azteca, another slice of helpful refereeing. Van Moer mistimed a clearance, Jeck kicked it away, and Valdivia fell over his leg. Penalty, followed by the time-honoured scene of players mobbing the referee, who threw an air punch to fend them off. Valdivia hit a post and Mexico were in the next round for the first time. Hardly surprising with 12 men.

GROUP 1	P	W	D	L	F	A	PTS
USSR	3	2	1	0	6	1	5
Mexico	3	2	1	0	5	0	5
Belgium	3	1	0	2	4	5	2
El Salvador	3	0	0	3	0	9	0

USSR and Mexico qualified for the quarter-finals.

(opposite page) Hellström lets the ball slip under his body for Italy's only goal of the qualifying group.

Group 2

Israel, Italy, Sweden, Uruguay

■ 2 June 1970 • Cuauhtemoc, Puebla • 20,654 • Bobby Davidson (SCO)

▲ **URUGUAY (1) 2**
Maneiro 22, Mujica 51
ISRAEL (0) 0

● URUGUAY *Ladislao Mazurkiewicz, Atilio Ancheta, Juan Mújica, Julio Montero Castillo, Roberto Matosas, Luis Ubiña, Luis Cubilla, Pedro Rocha (c) [Julio César Cortés 13], Victor Espárrago, Ildo Maneiro, Julio Losada.* Juan Eduardo Hohberg.
ISRAEL *Yitzak Visoker, Yeshayahu Schwager, David Primo, Daniel Rom [Yohanan Vollach 57], Zvi Rosen, Shmuel Rosenthal, Gyora Spiegel, Mordechai Spiegler (c), Yitzak Shum, Yoshua Feygenbaum, Rachamin Talbi [Shraga Bar HT].* Emmanuel Schaeffer.

If any team were equipped to handle Mexican conditions it was Uruguay, compact and cautious, doing only just enough – an approach cemented by the injury which put their stylish playmaker Rocha out of the tournament. They were still far too good for the Israeli amateurs. Mújica overlapped on the left and put in a basic cross which bounced in front of a hesitant Visoker for Maneiro to dart in and head home. Mújica scored the second himself, driving in the rebound when Visoker saved from Maneiro. Cubilla, tubby but tricky, one of the characters of the tournament, shot against the bar. Spiegler, who later interested West Ham, was Israel's best player.

Rom's original name was Szmulewicz (or Schmolwitch). Vollach's is also written Wallach. Espárrago means 'asparagus' in English.

■ 3 June 1970 • Luis Gutiérrez Dosal, Toluca • 13,433 • Jack Taylor (ENG)

▲ **ITALY (1) 1**
Domenghini 11
SWEDEN (0) 0

●

ITALY *Enrico Albertosi, Tarcisio Burgnich, Giacinto Facchetti (c), Mario Bertini, Comunardo Niccolai [Roberto Rosato 37], Pierluigi Cera, Angelo Domenghini, Sandro Mazzola, Roberto Boninsegna, Giancarlo 'Picchio' De Sisti, Luigi Riva.* Ferruccio Valcareggi.
SWEDEN *Ronnie Hellström, Jan Olsson I, Kurt Axelsson, Bo Larsson [Göran Nicklasson 77], Roland Grip, Björn Nordqvist (c), Tommy Svensson, Ove Grahn, Ove Kindvall, Claes Cronqvist, Leif Eriksson [Inge Ejderstedt 57].* Orvar Bergmark.

Toluca lies 8,744 feet above sea-level, the highest in the competition – and both teams felt it, notably Riva and Kindvall, who'd scored 13 goals between them in the qualifying rounds. But if Riva had difficulties with the altitude, the Swedish defence had an equally hard time with him. Lean and craggy,

with rough edges to his play, he impressed with his acceleration and ability to get in a shot from unpromising positions. In the first few minutes, he turned the ball against a post with his thigh. All he needed was luck.

Italy had some early on. Domenghini pushed a corner on the left to Facchetti, took the return, and shot from outside the area. Hellström, going down at his near post, tried to cup the ball to his chest but let it in under his body. He went on to become Sweden's best-ever keeper, a star of the 1974 and 1978 finals, but this was his last match in Mexico.

A different Jan Olsson played in the 1974 tournament. The stadium was commonly known as La Bombonera, the chocolate box. Picchio means 'woodpecker' in English.

■ 6 June 1970 • Cuauhtemoc, Puebla • 29,968 • Rudi Glöckner (EG)

▲ **ITALY 0**
URUGUAY 0

● ITALY *Albertosi, Burgnich, Facchetti (c), Bertini, Rosato, Cera, Domenghini [Giuseppe Furino HT], Mazzola, Boninsegna, De Sisti, Riva.*
URUGUAY *Mazurkiewicz, Ubiña (c), Mújica, Montero Castillo, Ancheta, Matosas, Cubilla, Cortés, Espárrago, Maneiro, Rubén Bareño [Oscar Zubía 70].*

Probably the most predictable of all goalless draws. Cubilla went round Facchetti, Riva sprinted clear of Ancheta to hit the side netting. That's all, folks. The one talking point was Rivera's continued absence, this time even from the subs' bench. The Mazzola–Rivera question occupies minds to this day. It's a little surprising that they couldn't be accommodated in the same midfield, though it's not easy to see who could have been left out. Valcareggi would soon arrive at a solution, but even that wasn't wholly convincing.

■ 7 June 1970 • Luis Gutiérrez Dosal, Toluca • 9,624 • Seyoum Tarekegn (ETH)

▲ **ISRAEL (0) 1**
Spiegler 57
SWEDEN (0) 1
Turesson 54

● ISRAEL *Visoker, Bar, Primo, Vollach [Aaron Shuruk 60], Rosen, Schwager, Rosenthal, Shum, Spiegler (c), Spiegel, Feygenbaum.*
SWEDEN *Sven-Gunnar Larsson, Axelsson, Hans Selander, Grip, Svensson (c), B. Larsson, Kindvall, Örjan Persson (Sten Pålsson 75], Thomas Nordahl, Tom Turesson, Olsson.*

Kindvall played better against inferior opposition but was still struggling for breath. At his best he was one of Europe's sharpest strikers; a month earlier, he'd scored the winner for Feyenoord against Celtic in the European Cup final. Selander's cross from the right was sidefooted in by Turesson, but Israel's spirit compensated for their shortcomings, and they equalized when Spiegler fired in from 20 yards.

Nordahl's uncle Knut played in the 1950 finals. His father Gunnar and another uncle, Bertil, were also capped by Sweden.

■ 10 June 1970 • Cuauhtemoc, Puebla • 18,163 • Heinrich (Henry) Landauer (USA)

▲ **SWEDEN (0) 1**
Grahn 89
URUGUAY (0) 0

● SWEDEN *S-G. Larsson, Axelsson, Selander, Nordqvist (c), Grip, Svensson, B. Larsson, Nicklasson [Grahn 84], Eriksson, Kindvall (Turesson 57), Persson.*
URUGUAY *Mazurkiewicz, Ancheta, Matosas, Ubiña (c), Montero Castillo, Mújica, Cortés, Maneiro, Zubía, Espárrago [Dagoberto Fontes 60], Losada.*

There was a whiff of scandal before the match, a rumour that the original referee De Moraes had asked for money to favour Uruguay. FIFA investigated, decided he had no case to answer, switched him to the Israel-Italy match, and waved away Uruguayan counter-claims about a plot to discredit them. Meanwhile, back in the real world....

Sweden needed to win by two goals, and the Uruguayans weren't remotely unhappy to lose by one, though they might have been stirred out of mass defence if Eriksson's first-minute shot had gone in instead of hitting a post. Young Ancheta again looked a fine centre-half and Mazurkiewicz made a good save from Kindvall. Eventually, too late, Grahn headed in Persson's cross. Would the Uruguayan coach have enjoyed being a spectator at his team's matches? It wasn't his business, he said, to think like the crowd. This from the man who scored twice in the great Hungary-Uruguay match of 1954.

■ 11 June 1970 • Luis Gutiérrez Dosal, Toluca • 9,860 • Aírton Vieira de Moraes (BRZ)

▲ **ISRAEL 0**
ITALY 0

● ISRAEL *Visoker, Bar, Primo, Schwager, Rosenthal, Rosen, Menachem Bello, Shum, Spiegler (c), Spiegel, Feygenbaum [Rom HT].*
ITALY *Albertosi, Burgnich, Facchetti (c), Bertini, Rosato, Cera, Domenghini [Gianni Rivera HT], Mazzola, Boninsegna, De Sisti, Riva.*

It looks embarrassing on paper (it wasn't much better on the pitch), but Riva was unlucky to have a goal disallowed and a penalty appeal turned down. Rivera came on as substitute, but if this was the answer, the question seemed to need re-phrasing. He had a very quiet second half.

GROUP 2	P	W	D	L	F	A	PTS
Italy	3	1	2	0	1	0	4
Uruguay	3	1	1	1	2	1	3
Sweden	3	1	1	1	2	2	3
Israel	3	0	2	1	1	3	1

Italy and Uruguay qualified for the quarter-finals. Italy set a record by winning their group despite scoring only a single goal.

Group 3

Brazil, Czechoslovakia, England, Romania

If England were to retain the trophy, they would have to overcome some unnecessary and bizarre obstacles; which is one way of introducing the Bogotá Affair.

On 18 May, England were in Colombia to play the first of two warm-up matches at altitude. In the foyer of the Tequendama hotel, Moore and Bobby Charlton wandered into the Fuego Verde (Green Fire) jewellery shop to kill time. When they left, they were accused of stealing a bracelet. Ramsey smoothed things over, England beat Colombia 4-0 and flew on to play in Ecuador. Their return flight included a stop-over back in Bogotá, in fact at the same hotel, returning to the scene of someone's crime.

To cut the sordid story short, Moore was held for four days before a judge decided there was insufficient evidence for a trial. Alvaro Suárez, the witness who was suddenly unearthed while England were in Ecuador, turned out to be a jewellery dealer not an innocent passer-by (touring teams in Colombia had been subjected to this kind of thing for years). Moore's chief accuser, shop assistant Clara Padilla, fled to the USA, and shop owner Danilo Rojas (who'd asked for £6,000 damages for a £600 bracelet) had to close down. The case wasn't officially dropped for another five years, during which Moore had to endure jibes in the street and the feeling that if he walked into a jewellery shop 'I have to keep my hands behind my back and point with my nose'. The affair underlined his dignity under pressure and only added to people's admiration, but he and the England camp could have done without it. Mind you, according to Nobby Stiles they'd chosen the right

victim: 'If it had been me in that shop, they'd have hung me without a trial!'

Other pressures stemmed from Ramsey's prickliness in press conferences, giving the impression of a Little Englander mentality. The result: a hostile press, plus Mexican fans camped round the team hotel night after night, sounding their car horns and banging on the bodywork. And, of course, a hostile crowd at every match – but this England team had been there and seen that, they could handle it, especially their ice man of a captain.

■ 2 June 1970 • Jalisco, Guadalajara • 50,560 • Vital Loraux (BEL)

▲ **ENGLAND (0) 1**
Hurst 64
ROMANIA (0) 0

● ENGLAND *Gordon Banks, Keith Newton [Tommy Wright 52], Terry Cooper, Alan Mullery, Brian Labone, Bobby Moore (c), Francis Lee [Peter Osgood 77], Alan Ball, Bobby Charlton, Geoff Hurst, Martin Peters.* Alf Ramsey.
ROMANIA *Stere Adamache, Lajos Satmareanu, Mihai Mocanu, Ion Dumitru, Nicolae Lupescu, Cornel Dinu, Radu Nunweiller, Emerich Dembrowski, Gheorghe Tataru [Alexandru Neagu 74], Florea Dumitrache, Mircea Lucescu (c).* Angelo Niculescu.

The creative midfielder Nicolae Dobrin was out of the tournament with heatstroke, but Romania would probably have been just as defensive if he'd played. They nearly took a very early lead – Cooper standing and watching as Dembrowski prodded the ball just wide from Dumitrache's cross – but Lee soon hit the bar with a header.

The Romanian tackling became vicious and then some. Dumitru didn't hold back but Mocanu was something else. First he kicked Newton's knee so badly he had to go off, then he took Lee's legs, then went after Newton's replacement Wright ('I thought my leg had snapped, my eyes watered like they've never done before'). Lee felt 'he must have created a new tackle, leaving identical bootprints on each knee'. Any one of those fouls would have earned a red card today, but Loraux didn't even book him. The debutant Tataru tried hard but Dumitrache, who'd scored in the 1-1 draw at Wembley in 1969 and boasted he'd get another two here, was still feeling an ankle injury.

England scored when Ball's cross from the right seemed to clip Lee's head on its way to Hurst, who turned past Satmareanu and shot left-footed – 'he told me later he topped it' – and the ball went between Adamache's legs. England's 'slow sodium' pills had seen them through the worst and Alan Ball enjoyed reminding Dumitrache about his two goals.

Satmareanu was generally known as Ludovic, the 'official' Romanian version of his first name. Similarly, Dembrowski was often spelt Dembrovschi.

■ 3 June 1970 • Jalisco, Guadalajara • 52,897 • Ramón Barreto (URU)

▲ **BRAZIL (1) 4**
Rivelino 24, Pelé 59, Jairzinho 64, 82
CZECHOSLOVAKIA (1) 1
Petrás 11

● BRAZIL *Félix (Mielli), Carlos Alberto (Torres) (c), Everaldo (Marques), Clodoaldo (Tavares), Hércules de Brito, Wilson Piazza, 'Jairzinho' (Jair Ventura), Gérson (de Oliveira) [Paulo César (Lima) 73], 'Tostão' (Eduardo Gonçalves), 'Pelé' (Édson Arantes do Nascimento), Roberto Rivelino.* Mário Zagallo.
CZECHOSLOVAKIA *Ivo Viktor, Karol Dobias, Alexander Horváth (c), Václav Migas, Vladimír Hagara, Ivan Hrdlicka [Andrej Kvasnák HT], Ladislav Kuna, Frantisek Vesely [Bohumil Vesely 75], Ladislav Petrás, Jozef Adamec, Karol Jokl.* Jozef Marko.

🌐

Hurst, all in white, carries on where he left off in 1966 by scoring England's goal against Romania.

Horváth (left) can't stop Pelé planting the ball beyond Viktor to put Brazil ahead against Czechoslovakia.

Doubts as well as excitement surrounded the entry of the Brazilians. Had Tostão fully recovered from an operation on a detached retina? Would the late change of manager affect morale? Could Gérson at last influence matches away from home (he'd been invisible in 1966)?

The problems in defence were still there. Clodoaldo held on too long and lost the ball to Petrás, a blond firebrand in only his second international (he'd been sent off in the first!). After stop-starting to confuse Brito, Petrás dragged the ball past him and clipped it beyond Félix for a splendid individual goal. Soon afterwards, Adamec should have punished Carlos Alberto's bad pass.

But Brazil had already served notice. Rivelino, bristling with talent, sold an exaggerated dummy before firing in a low cross which deflected off a defender and was put over an open goal by Pelé, of all people. Then Rivelino went one better, his left foot aiming a cobra of a free-kick straight at Jairzinho on the end of the wall. When Jairzinho got out of the way, Viktor did well to touch the shot on its way in.

On the stroke of half-time, Pelé's sudden shot from inside his own half drifted just wide of the right-hand post, one of the seminal World Cup moments. They're all trying it nowadays, the Beckhams even succeed at times, but it took the master to mark their card.

As Czechoslovakia began to tire, Brazil went ahead with another marvellous goal. Gérson, whose left foot was the equal of Rivelino's, hit a perfect aerial ball which dropped just over Horváth for Pelé to chest down and push the volley across the keeper. Then another Gérson pass was in the air long enough for Jairzinho to look offside as he ran on. Flipping the ball over the onrushing Viktor, he slammed it into the empty net.

Before that, Czechoslovakia had missed their one big chance. The tall Kvasnák, who came on at half-time, had done well in the 1962 Final but was now a ghost at the feast. When Hagara's cross reached him five yards out, he blasted it over the bar. Jairzinho completed the scoring with a superb individual goal, resisting two sliding tackles in that inelegant but oddly skilful way of his, before finishing with a low cross-shot.

David Coleman's comment about Brazil, made immediately after they went a goal down, turned out to be right ('All we ever knew about them has come true') but not in the way he meant – and Alan Ball's confidence ('We'll beat these') was looking positively unnatural. Note the slight spelling difference in the first names of Dobias and Jokl. Paulo César is now known as Paulo César Caju in Brazil.

■ 6 June 1970 • Jalisco, Guadalajara • 56,818 • Diego de Leo (MEX)

▲ **ROMANIA (0) 2**
Neagu 53, Dumitrache pen 78
CZECHOSLOVAKIA (1) 1 Petrás 3

● ROMANIA *Adamache, Satmareanu, Mocanu, Dumitru [László Gergely 81], Lupescu, Dinu, Neagu, Dembrowski, Nunweiller, Dumitrache, Lucescu (c) [Tataru 69].*
CZECHOSLOVAKIA *Alex Vencel, Dobias, Horváth (c), Migas, Ján Zlocha, Kuna, Kvasnák, B. Vesely, Josef Jurkanin [Adamec HT], Petrás, Jokl [F. Vesely 74].*

Again Petrás scored an early goal, a sharp header from Bohumil Vesely's cross, again Czechoslovakia faded badly in the second half. Neagu beat Migas before shooting the equalizer and was fouled by Zlocha for the penalty. Kvasnák wasn't capped again. Gergely, of Hungarian extraction, was usually known by the 'official' version of his names: Vasile Ghergheli.

■ 7 June 1970 • Jalisco, Guadalajara • 70,950 •
Avraham Klein (ISR)

▲ **BRAZIL (0) 1**
Jairzinho 62
ENGLAND (0) 0

● BRAZIL *Félix, Carlos Alberto (c), Everaldo, Clodoaldo,
Brito, Piazza, Jairzinho, Paulo César, Tostão [Roberto
(Miranda) 68], Pelé, Rivelino.*
ENGLAND *Banks, Wright, Cooper, Mullery, Labone,
Moore (c), Lee [Jeff Astle 64], Ball, R. Charlton [Colin
Bell 64], Hurst, Peters.*

For England fans, there was the nagging feeling that
they were hanging in there a little, against better
players – but this doesn't prevent it being one of the
great matches. The same few incidents have been
shown so often that we know them by heart, and it's
never enough.

First up: That Save. Carlos Alberto hit a brilliant
pass that skidded low inside then outside Cooper
into the path of the galloping Jairzinho, who
stumbled to the England goal line and got in a cross
just before the ball went out of play. At the far post,
Pelé outjumped Wright to head down and surely in,
only for Banks to dive to his right and fingertip the
ball over the bar. In our heart of hearts we think the
unthinkable, that it wasn't that great (Banks: 'I'm sure
I've equalled that save in League games') but it
certainly kept England in the match, and Tostão
thought it was pretty good. He spent several seconds
with his hands up in disbelief.

Mullery, confident enough to leave Pelé alone for
a while, chipped a pass out to the right-hand corner
flag, where Wright put over an equally good cross.
Hurst jumped and missed but barged his man, and
Lee came in at speed. He intended a volley, caught his

studs in the long grass, and connected with a flying
header that brought an unexpectedly good save from
the dreadful Félix. Looking for a loose ball, Lee
caught the goalkeeper and was booked.

All over the pitch, people were having excellent
games, none more so than Moore, showing no ill-
effects from the heat, altitude or Colombian shysters.
One copybook tackle took the ball off Jairzinho's toes
in the penalty area when the slightest mistiming would
have brought a penalty. When Jairzinho repeated his
trick of joining the wall at a Rivelino free-kick, Moore
solved the puzzle by standing behind him. The kick
seared through, he stopped it and brought the ball
upfield. You almost wished he *had* filched that bracelet:
it might have proved he was human.

On the hour, Tostão's work-rate and awareness
brought the only goal. When his first shot on the
edge of the area was blocked by Labone, he chased
back ten yards to regather, took a return pass from
Paulo César, elbowed Ball in the face, took a
rebound from Moore's shins, beat Wright, and finally
(phew) crossed from the left in the general direction
of the penalty spot. Unfortunately for England, Pelé
was there to trap it and push it short to his right all in
one movement, taking out two defenders. Jairzinho,
unmarked because Cooper had come inside to see to

Tostão and Mullery watch as Banks makes his famous save from Pelé.

Pelé, hammered the ball across Banks from six yards. England were back there in numbers and did nothing wrong, but Brazil still got through. That was the difference between the teams.

But England came desperately close. Moore's perfect tackle on Jairzinho led to Cooper's long cross from the left, which was hilariously miskicked by Everaldo deep in his own area, the ball squirting straight to Astle, so good in the air but less so on the deck. With the same left foot that scored a screaming winner in an FA Cup Final, he hit the ball firmly but past the far post, one of the famous misses. Then Ball, picking his spot, was unlucky to clip the top of the bar. England deserved a draw but no more, and Brazil were without their midfield general Gérson – but if defeat was ever glorious, this was it.

■ 10 June 1970 • Jalisco, Guadalajara • 50,804 • Ferdinand Marschall (AUT)

▲ **BRAZIL (2) 3**
Pelé 19, 66, Jairzinho 21
ROMANIA (1) 2
Dumitrache 33, Dembrowski 82

● BRAZIL *Félix, Carlos Alberto (c), Everaldo [Marco Antônio (Feliciano) 56], Piazza, Brito, José Fontana, Jairzinho, Clodoaldo ['Edu' (Eduardo Américo 73], Tostão, Pelé, Paulo César.*
ROMANIA *Adamache [Necula Raducanu 28], Satmareanu, Mocanu, Dumitru, Lupescu, Dinu, Neagu, Dembrowski, Nunweiller, Dumitrache [Tataru 71], Lucescu (c).*

There was a rumour that Brazil might deliberately lose to make qualification more difficult for England. Instead they played some of the best football of the tournament. Pelé smashed in the first goal (again no frills with a free-kick) and toe-poked the third, Jairzinho scored at the near post after Paulo César

beat Satmareanu. For Romania, Dumitrache stabbed in a rebound after an attempted dribble went wrong, and Dembrowski headed in Satmareanu's cross.

■ 11 June 1970 • Jalisco, Guadalajara • 35,000 • Roger Machin (FRA)

▲ **ENGLAND (0) 1**
Clarke pen 48
CZECHOSLOVAKIA (0) 0

● ENGLAND *Banks, Newton, Cooper, Mullery, Jack Charlton, Moore (c), Bell, R. Charlton [Ball 65], Astle [Peter Osgood 60], Allan Clarke, Peters.*
CZECHOSLOVAKIA *Viktor (c), Dobias, Vladimír Hrivnák, Migas, Hagara, Kuna, Ján Capkovic [Jokl 70], Jaroslav Pollák, Adamec, Petrás, F. Vesely.*

As usual, the crowd gave England the bird, with some justification this time; a poor performance to mark Bobby Charlton's 105th cap, which equalled Billy Wright's world record. His brother, now 35, and Astle weren't capped again. Dobias hit the bar from long range and England were given a goal by the referee, when Kuna tangled with Bell and fell on the ball with his hand. Clarke, typically cool in the heat, scored on his England debut. It was his wife's birthday, their wedding anniversary, and the anniversary of his transfer from Fulham to Leicester! The official attendance figure was 49,292.

GROUP 3	P	W	D	L	F	A	PTS
Brazil	3	3	0	0	8	3	6
England	3	2	0	1	2	1	4
Romania	3	1	0	2	4	5	2
Czechoslovakia	3	0	0	3	2	7	0
Brazil and England qualified for the quarter-finals.							

Group 4

Bulgaria, Morocco, Peru, West Germany

■ 2 June 1970 • Guanajuato, León • 13,765 •
Antonio Sbardella (ITA)

▲ **PERU (0) 3**
Gallardo 51, Chumpitáz 56, Cubillas 74
BULGARIA (1) 2
Dermendjiev 13, Bonev 49

● PERU *Luis Rubiños, Eloy Campos [Javier González 27],
Nicolas Fuentes, Roberto Challe, Orlando De la Torre,
Héctor Chumpitáz (c), Julio Baylón [Hugo Sotil 50],
Ramón Mifflin, Pedro 'Perico' León, Teófilo Cubillas, Alberto
Gallardo. 'Didi' (Waldir Pereira) (BRZ).*

BULGARIA *Simeon Simeonov, Aleksandar Shalamanov,
Stefan Aladjov, Ivan Davidov, Dimitar Penev, Ivan
Dimitrov (c), Dinko Dermendjiev, Christo Bonev [Georgi
Asparoukhov 83], Petar Zhekov, Dimitar Yakimov, Georgi
Popov [Dimitar Marashliev 59]. Stefan Bozhkov.*

Before the match, both sides observed a minute's silence for the victims of Peru's recent earthquake – then Bulgaria caught their opponents cold with a clever free-kick. Dermendjiev ran past the left-hand edge of the Peruvian wall, the ball went to the other side and was touched into his path by a team-mate; he drove in Bulgaria's first goal of the tournament on his 29th birthday. Peru missed chances through some wild shooting, especially by Gallardo, then Bulgaria made the most of another free-kick. Bonev, lean and all-purpose, scored a record 47 goals for Bulgaria, but this was just about the softest, his kick full of spin but straight at Rubiños, who fumbled it in.

Peru had no choice but to keep attacking, and eventually one of Gallardo's thunderbolts crashed into the roof of the net. Then three Peruvians stood in the end of the wall at a free-kick, Chumpitáz shot straight at them and scored with a ground shot, and Cubillas played a one-two with Mifflin before beating a man and shooting an excellent goal. Peru, rampant by now, had two more goals disallowed.

■ 3 June 1970 • Guanajuato, León • 12,942 •
Laurens van Ravens (HOL)

▲ **WEST GERMANY (0) 2**
Seeler 56, Müller 78
MOROCCO (1) 1
Houmane 22

● W. GERMANY *Sepp Maier, Berti Vogts, Horst-Dieter
Höttges [Hannes Löhr 75], Franz Beckenbauer, Klaus
Fichtel, Willi Schulz, Helmut Haller [Jürgen Grabowski
HT], Uwe Seeler (c), Gerd Müller, Wolfgang Overath, Sigi
Held. Helmut Schön.*

MOROCCO *Allal Ben Kassou, Abdullah Lamrani,
Boujemaa Benkhrif, Kacem Slimani, Moulay Driss
Khanoussi, Mohammed Maaroufi, Saïd Ghandi, Mouhoub
Ghazouani [Abdelkader El Khyati 55], Driss Bamous (c)
[Ahmed Faras 70], Houmane Jarir, Mohammed El Filali.
Blagoje Vidinic (YUG).*

How would Schön accommodate Seeler and Müller in the same team? By simply withdrawing Seeler into midfield, where he showed what an adaptable player he was, one of the World Cup's most redoubtable figures. Before the partnership began to flourish, West Germany were threatened with one of the great shock results. Morocco had qualified under a French coach called Cluseau, but there was nothing comical about their efforts in the finals. Houmane knocked in a bad defensive header by Höttges, and Kassou had a fine game in goal, but eventually Seeler scored in a scramble and Müller put in the rebound when the ball came back off the bar. Some of the Moroccans were known by their first names.

SCORED IN MOST TOURNAMENTS

4	Uwe Seeler WG	1958–62–66–70
4	Pelé BRZ	1958–62–66–70
3	Joe Jordan SCO	1974–78–82
3	Grzegorz Lato POL	1974–78–82
3	Andrzej Szarmach POL	1974–78–82
3	Dominique Rocheteau FRA	1978–82–86
3	Michel Platini FRA	1978–82–86
3	Julio Salinas SPA	1986–90–94
3	Diego Maradona ARG	1982–86–94
3	Rüdi Völler WG/GER	1986–90–94
3	Lothar Matthäus WG/GER	1986–90–94

■ 6 June 1970 • Guanajuato, León • 7,000 •
Tofik Bakhramov (USR)

▲ **PERU (0) 3**
Cubillas 65, 76, Challe 69
MOROCCO (0) 0

● PERU *Rubiños, Pedro González, Fuentes, Challe, De la Torre, Chumpitáz (c), Sotil, Mifflin [Luis Cruzado 55], León, Cubillas, Gallardo [Osvaldo Ramírez 75].*
MOROCCO *Ben Kassou, Lamrani, Boujemaa [Jilali Fadili 65], Slimani, Moulay Driss, Maaroufi, El Filali, Saïd [Ahmed Allaoui 80], Bamous (c), Ghazouani, Houmane.*

Again Kassou played well, but his error led to the first goal, León's weak shot coming back off his legs for Cubillas to drive into an empty net. The official attendance figure was 13,537.

Müller scores from the penalty spot against Bulgaria.

■ 7 June 1970 • Guanajuato, León • 12,710 •
José María Ortíz de Mendibil (SPA)

▲ **WEST GERMANY (2) 5**
Libuda 19, Müller 27, pen 52, 88, Seeler 69
BULGARIA (1) 2
Nikodimov 12, Kolev 89

● W. GERMANY *Maier, Vogts, Höttges, Beckenbauer [Wolfgang Weber 73], Fichtel, Karl-Heinz Schnellinger, Reinhard Libuda, Seeler (c), Müller, Overath, Löhr [Grabowski 58].*
BULGARIA *Simeonov, Milko Gaydarski, Dobromir Zhechev, Penev, Boris Gaganelov (c) [Shalamanov 57], Todor Kolev, Bonev, Asparoukh Nikodimov, Dermendjiev [Vasil Mitkov HT], Asparoukhov, Marashliev.*

Again West Germany conceded an early goal, again Bulgaria scored from a free-kick, again the result was the same for both sides. Schön brought in Libuda, a snaky winger who'd scored the goal that knocked out Scotland, and he dominated the match, especially the Bulgarian captain, who wasn't capped again. First he beat Gaganelov to Seeler's through-pass and jabbed a low cross into the six-yard area, where Simeonov let it

slip under him and just over the line. Libuda is credited with it, but it was clearly an own goal. Next he scuttled through a gap, slipped, got up and dribbled past Nikodimov to make an open goal for Müller. Then Gaganelov fouled him for the penalty. Seeler arrived at the far post to meet a low cross from Müller, who headed the fifth from a free-kick, excellent in the air for someone so short and swarthy.

Kolev's brother Ivan played in the '62 and '66 finals.

■ 10 June 1970 • Guanajuato, León • 17,875 • Abel Aguilar (MEX)

▲ **WEST GERMANY (3) 3**
Müller 19, 26, 38
PERU (1) 1
Cubillas 44

● W. GERMANY *Maier, Vogts, Höttges [Bernd Patzke HT], Beckenbauer, Fichtel, Schnellinger, Libuda [Grabowski 74], Seeler (c), Müller, Overath, Löhr.*
PERU *Rubiños, P. González, Fuentes, Challe [Cruzado 70], De la Torre, Chumpitáz (c), Sotil, Mifflin, León [Ramírez 51], Cubillas, Gallardo.*

Again Schön got it right, planning to stop Peru playing their little one-twos and to hit them with high crosses from the wings. One from Libuda drifted over the

entire defence for Müller to chest down and push home. Then Löhr beat González and made Müller's second, and Seeler's cross was put in with a cleverly placed looping header. Cubillas scored with a deflected free-kick, but the Peruvian defence had been shown up and would now have to face the full glare of Brazil.

■ 11 June 1970 • Guanajuato, León • 12,299 • Antônio Saldanha (POR)

▲ **BULGARIA (1) 1**
Zhechev 39
MOROCCO (0) 1
Ghazouani 59

● BULGARIA *Stoyan Yordanov, Zhechev, Shalamanov (c), Penev [Dimitrov 42], Gaydarski, Nikodimov, Kolev, Yakimov [Bonev 62], Asparoukhov, Popov, Mitkov.*
MOROCCO *Mohammed Hazzaz, Fadili, Moulay Driss, Slimani, Boujemaa, Maaroufi, Bamous (c) [Mustafa Choukri HT], Saïd, Allaoui [Faras 73], Filali, Ghazouani.*

Meaningless except for the teams involved. It appeared to be Bulgaria's best chance of winning a finals match for the first time, but they hit the woodwork twice and still couldn't cope with the heat, allowing Morocco to become the first African country to avoid defeat in the finals. The crowd may have been as small as 4,000.

GROUP 4	P	W	D	L	F	A	PTS
W. Germany	3	3	0	0	10	4	6
Peru	3	2	0	1	7	5	4
Bulgaria	3	0	1	2	5	9	1
Morocco	3	0	1	2	2	6	1
West Germany and Peru qualified for the quarter-finals.							

Müller, super cool close to goal, slips the ball past Rubiños for his first goal against Peru.

Quarter-finals

■ 14 June 1970 • Azteca, Mexico City • 96,085 • Laurens van Ravens (HOL)

▲ **URUGUAY (0) (0) 1**
Espárrago 117
USSR (0) (0) 0

● URUGUAY *Mazurkiewicz, Ancheta, Matosas, Montero Castillo, Ubiña (c), Mújica, Cubilla, Cortés, Maneiro, Julio César Morales [Alberto Gómez 96], Fontes [Espárrago 103].*
USSR *Kavazashvili, Shesternev (c), Dzodzuashvili, Kaplichny, Khurtsilava [Logofet 83], Afonin, Asatiani [Kiselev 71], Muntian, Byshovets, Evriuzhikin, Khmelnitsky.*

In a dreary, rough match (70 fouls), Uruguay stopped Byshovets by fair means and otherwise, and won because they kept playing to the end. Ancheta, up for one final attack, glanced a header towards the Soviet goal line on the left, Afonin shielded it with his body, only for Cubilla to steal it between his legs from behind and dig up a near-post cross which beat Kavazashvili and was headed in by Espárrago. The USSR surrounded the referee, but TV replays show conclusively that the ball didn't go out of play. One source puts the attendance at around 45,000.

■ 14 June 1970 • Luis Gutiérrez Dosal, Toluca • 26,851 • Rudi Scheurer (SWI)

▲ **ITALY (1) 4**
Guzmán o.g. 25, Riva 63, 76, Rivera 70
MEXICO (1) 1
● González 13

ITALY *Albertosi, Burgnich, Facchetti (c), Bertini, Rosato, Cera, Domenghini [Sergio Gori 84], Mazzola [Rivera HT], Boninsegna, De Sisti, Riva.*
MEXICO *Calderón, Peña (c), Vantolrá, Guzmán, Pérez, Pulido, González [Borja 67], Munguía [Isidoro Díaz 59], Valdivia, Fragoso, Padilla.*

Mexico's goal was a good one, González slicing in Valdivia's flicked pass – but there were no refereeing handouts this time and Italy were soon in control. Early sources credit the own goal (from Domenghini's right-wing cross) to Guzmán, and in this case they're right. More recent publications, Italian included, cite Peña, but it's clearly No. 14 on the replay (Peña was No. 3). Rivera came on again at half-time and this time formed a matchwinning partnership with Riva, who'd stayed upbeat despite his lack of goals.

Riva's first of the tournament came from his famous left foot, a low cross-shot that Calderón should have reached. His second was prodded in off Guzmán after Calderón saved his first shot. In between, Rivera shot home after he'd gone round the keeper and assorted shots had been blocked. The Mazzola-Rivera *staffetta* (relay) seemed to be here to stay. Facchetti was winning his 50th cap.

■ 14 June 1970 • Jalisco, Guadalajara • 54,233 •
Vital Loraux (BEL)

▲ **BRAZIL (2) 4**
Rivelino 11, Tostão 15, 52, Jairzinho 75
PERU (1) 2
Gallardo 27, Cubillas 69

● BRAZIL *Félix, Carlos Alberto (c), Marco Antônio, Clodoaldo, Brito, Piazza, Jairzinho [Roberto 80], Gérson [Paulo César 67], Tostão, Pelé, Rivelino.*
PERU *Rubiños, Campos, Fuentes, Challe, José Fernández, Chumpitáz (c), Baylón [Sotil 53], Mifflin, León [Eladio Reyes 61], Cubillas, Gallardo.*

Gérson was back and Peru's fate was sealed, their tactic of marking space absurdly vulnerable against a front line as mobile and intelligent as Brazil's. And goals were always likely against the two worst keepers in the tournament.

Pelé hit a post early on then crossed from the right. Campos slipped and chested the ball straight to Tostão, who immediately pushed it to Rivelino, whose shot went in off the bottom of the far post. Next Tostão took a short corner on the left, ran round a defender to get to the goal line, and hit Rivelino's return pass straight at Campos, who let it in at the near post as Fernández put his face in his hands.

Peru kept trying. Gallardo, tall and powerful, beat Carlos Alberto down the left and hit his shot at Félix, who returned Campos' compliment by letting the ball in off his thigh. But the Peruvian defenders, in their white shirts with a red sash across the chest, were standing around like so many Red Stripe cans. After Rubiños had fumbled Pelé's shot on to a post, Jairzinho put Pelé clear on the right, a defender deflected his gentle cross over the diving Rubiños into the path of Tostão, who knocked it in then put his hand over one ear to cut out the roar of the crowd. Cubillas met a clearance with a low volley from the edge of the area, but Jairzinho went past the hapless Rubiños to score the fourth.

Jairzinho (centre) and Rubiños (on the ground, right) hold up their arms for different reasons as Tostão (extreme right, half hidden by the referee) scores Brazil's second goal against Peru.

■ 14 June 1970 • Guanajuato, León • 23,357 •
Angel Norberto Coerezza (ARG)

▲ **WEST GERMANY (0) (2) 3**
Beckenbauer 67, Seeler 82, Müller 109
ENGLAND (1) (2) 2
Mullery 32, Peters 50

● W. GERMANY *Maier, Vogts, Höttges [Schulz HT],
Beckenbauer, Fichtel, Schnellinger, Libuda [Grabowski 57],
Seeler (c), Müller, Overath, Löhr.*
ENGLAND *Peter Bonetti, Newton, Cooper, Mullery,
Labone, Moore (c), Lee, Ball, R. Charlton [Bell 69], Hurst,
Peters [Norman Hunter 80].*

🌐

had just played brilliantly to help Chelsea win the FA Cup Final, and in his six England appearances he'd been on the winning side every time while conceding just a single goal. Here in León, he was hardly needed in a first hour that belied both teams' form in the tournament so far, England at last looking every inch the World Champions.

Bonetti's face expresses the full horror of seeing a header from Seeler (on the ground) drop in for the equalizer. Mullery tries to will it over the bar.

Their first goal was started and finished by the impressive Mullery. After exchanging passes with Lee, he found Newton overlapping on the right, ran for the return at the near post ('I kept expecting to be clattered any second') and scooped it high past Maier. It was the only goal he scored in 35 internationals, but an exceptional one. Early in the second half Newton put in another cross, this time to the far post, where Peters made

A model defender. Schnellinger strikes an artistic pose as Fichtel and Lee chase the ball.

At the last moment, Banks went down with food poisoning ('Montezuma's Revenge') but his replacement came highly recommended. Bonetti

his only contribution to the tournament by forcing the ball in off Maier's dive. That was enough for some English journalists to shout 'Auf Wiedersehen' at the German supporters. They were right, but not in the way anyone expected.

As well as coming forward on the left, Cooper had done a complete job by shutting out Libuda, but the replacement Grabowski was fresh and dangerous. And West Germany were let back in by a goal that according to Moore 'cut into our confidence at the back'. Beckenbauer beat Mullery on the right-hand corner of the England area and shot immediately; the ball seemed to surprise Bonetti for pace and went in under his body. 'From that moment it was one-way traffic towards our goal, a total turnabout.'

Seeler's equalizer owed something to luck. His back-header was aimed towards Müller (if it was aimed at all) but drifted over Bonetti. And England should have gone 3-1 up when Hurst met Bell's right-wing cross with a marvellous diving header that crept just wide as Lee waited for it to come back off the far post. But Ramsey's dependence on wing-backs was beginning to count against him. In extra-time Grabowski went past a tiring Cooper to the goal line, his high cross was headed back from beyond the far post by Löhr, and Müller at last came to life by getting behind Labone to volley home while in mid-air. Again, Bonetti might have done better.

British prime minister Harold Wilson blamed the result for his defeat in the General Election and he may not have been joking. Ramsey was later criticized for the timing of his substitutions, but they made sense enough, and in Germany it's seen as a glorious comeback, not something England threw away. But those guys had all the luck. After Müller's goal, Lee beat Schnellinger and pulled the ball back for Hurst, whose goal was mysteriously disallowed by the dreaded Coerezza. It was a tough way to go for Moore, the heroic Hurst and the exhausted and underrated Newton, who didn't play for England again; nor did Labone, Charlton or the unhappy Bonetti, forever remembered for this one overcrowded hour.

Bonetti has to hold up his hands for England's surrender of the trophy. Müller leaps to volley the winner.

Semi-finals

■ 17 June 1970 • Jalisco, Guadalajara • 51,261 •
José María Ortíz de Mendibil (SPA)

▲ **BRAZIL (1) 3**
Clodoaldo 44, Jairzinho 69, Rivelino 89
URUGUAY (1) 1
Cubilla 17

● BRAZIL *Félix, Carlos Alberto (c), Everaldo, Clodoaldo, Brito, Piazza, Jairzinho Gérson, Tostão, Pelé, Rivelino.*
URUGUAY *Mazurkiewicz, Ancheta, Matosas, Montero Castillo, Ubiña (c), Mújica, Cubilla, Cortés, Maneiro [Espárrago 74], Morales, Fontes.*

Perhaps Brazil were still carrying scars from 1950. At any rate, they needed a half-time rocket from Zagallo to raise their game. They fell behind to a ludicrous goal, Brito giving the ball straight to Morales, whose chip found Cubilla running into the penalty area on the right. He controlled the ball on his thigh before lifting it across the six-yard box, where Félix let it bounce inside the far post then knelt in despair.

Brazil struggled for the rest of the half, but their equalizer arrived at the right time and was beautifully made and finished. Clodoaldo knocked a short ball to Tostão on the left wing then sprinted for the return pass, which he thrashed first time past the keeper's left hand. The other goals also took a while coming but were almost as good. Pelé's touch to Tostão was followed by a pass out to Jairzinho, who cleverly beat Matosas before scoring with a low cross-shot. Finally Pelé rolled the ball back for Rivelino's left foot to do the rest, though Mazurkiewicz bravely got a touch.

Uruguay had had an excellent tournament, making light of Rocha's injury – but the better side won. They still had time for the most imaginative move in any World Cup; Pelé sprinting on to an angled through-ball from Tostão and dummying past Mazurkiewicz, beating a world-class goalkeeper without actually touching the ball. The shot rolled just past the far post, which was just as well; if it had gone in, they'd have had to close the sport down. There'd have been nothing left to aim for.

Ancheta turns to see the ball fly between the keeper's head and the post as Clodoaldo (extreme left) scores Brazil's superb equalizer against Uruguay.

■ 17 June 1970 • Azteca, Mexico City •
102,444 • Arturo Yamasaki (MEX)

▲ **ITALY (1) (1) 4**
Boninsegna 8, Burgnich 98, Riva 104, Rivera 111
WEST GERMANY (0) (1) 3
Schnellinger 90, Müller 94, 110

● ITALY *Albertosi, Burgnich, Facchetti (c), Bertini, Rosato [Fabrizio Poletti 91], Cera, Domenghini Mazzola [Rivera HT], Boninsegna, De Sisti, Riva.*
W. GERMANY *Maier, Vogts, Patzke [Held 65], Beckenbauer, Schnellinger, Schulz, Grabowski, Seeler (c), Müller, Overath, Löhr [Libuda 51].*

A match that rose to the heights despite itself, though the conditions had something to do with it; they weren't made for extra-time.

After the willing Boninsegna had despatched a rebound from the edge of the area, Italy set out their stall to hold out. Overath hit the bar with a mighty left-footer and Albertosi recovered to kick clear from Müller after his attempted clearance hit Grabowski and rebounded on to the goal line. Eventually, in injury-time, Grabowski held off two tackles on the left and crossed for Schnellinger to arrive unmarked and leap at the ball with feet splayed, volleying in with his right. Cue the great 30-minute rollercoaster.

Albertosi remonstrates with Rivera, who drapes himself round the post after failing to stop the header by Müller (getting up) which brought West Germany level at 3-3. Burgnich, hands on hips, awaits the next twist in the tale.

Italy's downhill spiral continued when Poletti ran back towards his own goal and chested the ball towards Albertosi, Müller getting in to touch the ball just over the line. Rivera, who'd been bypassed in the urgency of the game, chipped a free-kick without a run-up but hit it too far. What Held was doing in his own area isn't clear, especially as it brought his marker back with him. He let the ball bounce off him straight to Burgnich, who banged the ball in with his left foot to score his second and last goal in an eventual 66 internationals.

Riva beat Schnellinger with an exaggerated turn and scored with a confident low cross-shot. Seeler climbed to head on a corner, the ball barely brushed Müller's head, and Rivera seemed to usher it past, only to see it bounce in. He wrapped himself round the post as Albertosi held his hands out in supplication.

But Rivera redeemed himself soon enough. Straight from the kick-off Boninsegna beat the veteran Schulz on the left and Rivera met his low cross with excruciating calmness, sidefooting the ball into the middle of the goal as Maier was forced to dash to his left. With Beckenbauer's arm strapped and everyone's chest heaving, Italy held out till the end.

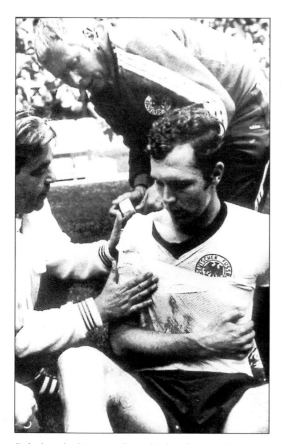

Beckenbauer has his arm taped across his chest, the injury that helped decide the semi-final between Italy and West Germany.

3rd-place Final

■ 20 June 1970 • Azteca, Mexico City •
104,403 • Antonio Sbardella (ITA)

▲ **WEST GERMANY (1) 1**
Overath 26
URUGUAY (0) 0

● W. GERMANY *Horst Wolter, Vogts, Schnellinger [Max Lorenz HT], Patzke, Fichtel, Weber, Libuda [Löhr 73], Seeler (c), Müller, Overath, Held.*
URUGUAY *Mazurkiewicz, Ancheta, Matosas, Montero Castillo, Ubiña (c), Mújica, Cubilla, Cortés, Maneiro [Rodolfo Sandoval 67], Morales, Fontes [Espárrago HT].*

Müller needed three goals to equal Fontaine's 13 in a tournament, but it was never very likely. Instead, freed from competitive tensions, Uruguay came out to attack, but had no luck. Overath scored with a low shot after Müller laid the ball back, and Seeler hit the bar – but Uruguay might have had three or four. Wolter, in a nervy last international, made a tremendous save from Ancheta's late header. The real attendance figure has been variously estimated as 32,000 and 85,000!

Top coaches called it a basketball match and it wasn't a compliment – but fans have always disagreed. It's recently been voted the best World Cup match of all time. Yamasaki represented Peru when he refereed in the 1962 and 1966 tournaments.

MOST MATCHES

21	Uwe Seeler WG	1958–70
21	Wladyslaw Zmuda POL	1974–86
21	Diego Maradona ARG	1982–94
21	Lothar Matthäus WG/GER	1982–94
20	Grzegorz Lato POL	1974–82
19	Wolfgang Overath WG	1966–74
19	Berti Vogts WG	1970–78
19	Karl-Heinz Rummenigge WG	1978–86
BRITISH		
17	Peter Shilton ENG	1982–90

Final

■ 21 June 1970 • Azteca, Mexico City •
107,412 • Rudi Glöckner (EG)

▲ **BRAZIL (1) 4**
Pelé 18, Gérson 66, Jairzinho 71, Carlos Alberto 86
ITALY (1) 1
Boninsegna 37

● **BRAZIL** *Félix, Carlos Alberto (c), Everaldo, Clodoaldo,
Brito, Piazza, Jairzinho, Gérson, Tostão, Pelé, Rivelino.*
ITALY *Albertosi, Burgnich, Facchetti (c), Bertini [Antonio
Juliano 74], Rosato, Cera, Domenghini, Mazzola, Boninsegna
[Rivera 84], De Sisti, Riva.*

Italy seemed to start where they left off in the semi-final. Riva took Mazzola's inside pass on the left wing and showed poor control but great self-belief and shooting power, forcing Félix to tip over from 25 yards. But defence was still the Italian womb, and they retreated immediately and in numbers, Brazil coming forward just as naturally.

From a throw-in on the left, Rivelino hooked over a volleyed cross, Pelé beat Burgnich easily in the air and headed down and in at the far post; Brazil's 100th goal in the finals. Italy were allowed back in by yet another of the slapdash goals Brazil gave away in this tournament, Clodoaldo attempting a lazy backheel, Boninsegna charging it down, Félix coming out much too soon. Boninsegna held off Brito's challenge and the ball ran free towards the left, where Riva was waiting but stood aside for Boninsegna to turn the ball into an empty net. However, the Brazilian menace was always there. Pelé had a goal disallowed only because the referee had

Pelé beats Burgnich to head Brazil's opening goal in the Final.

---

blown for half-time. And Rivelino (with his right foot of all things) thrashed a free-kick against the bar.

When Brazil's second goal finally arrived, it was very well struck but owed a little to luck. Jairzinho, who looks big and strong on the screen, now found a full-back he couldn't brush aside. Facchetti, who positively dwarfed him, had an excellent match, showing all his concentration and surprising speed. Here he tackled Jairzinho only for the ball to go straight to Gérson, who stepped away from a challenge and scored with a crisp cross-shot just before another tackle came in, the ball beating Albertosi to his left. Within minutes, Gérson hit another of his tremendous long crosses deep to the left-hand side of the Italian penalty area. Pelé was marked by Burgnich, one of the great defensive

right-backs but never likely to match him in the air. Pelé headed across goal, for once Facchetti gave Jairzinho too much room, and the winger miskicked the ball in from close range. He emulated Ghiggia (1950) by scoring in every round of a World Cup tournament including the Final.

For some reason Italy didn't man-mark Gérson and had no contingency plan when he began to turn the screw, which he did only in the second half, giving the Italians no chance to change things at half-time. His patience, as well as that remarkable left foot, was probably the determining factor in the Final.

This time Rivera didn't come on at half-time, mainly because Mazzola was playing too well, with great courage as well as intimate control. When Rivera did arrive, it was a ludicrous sop; six minutes,

Facchetti can't stop Jairzinho from scoring in every round of the tournament.

with the match already lost. Meanwhile Juliano, the first substitute in a Final, did little.

The last, celebratory goal showed all the Brazilian skills. Clodoaldo held off several Italian players deep in his half before feeding Jairzinho on the left. He rushed inside but again Facchetti wouldn't let him pass, so the ball was transferred to Pelé, who repeated the simple square passes which had killed off England and Uruguay. This time Carlos Alberto came charging up on the right and the ball bobbled at the last second, sitting up for the shot which crashed low past Albertosi's right hand. The president's goal, they called it, because the president of Brazil, General Medici, had predicted they'd score four. A reminder that one of the reasons for the removal of Saldanha as coach had been his political opinions, and that winning the World Cup did Brazil's brutal military government no harm.

But what a front five! The equal of the 1958 forwards. Whether they would have succeeded in a tournament held in a different climate is debatable, whether it's important is another. Gérson's lack of fitness (it's said he smoked three packs a day) had been exposed in 1966, and that defence and goalkeeper would have been under greater pressure if the European teams had been able to play their natural game. But the other side of the coin includes the great intelligence and economy of Tostão, Pelé's Indian summer, all those dazzling goals. Was that worth some burning Bulgarian lungs, some exhausted Belgians and Englishmen? A definite maybe.

LEADING GOALSCORERS 1970

10	Gerd Müller	WG	1 pen
7	Jairzinho	BRZ	
5	Teófilo Cubillas	PER	

WORLD CUP WINNER AS PLAYER AND COACH

Mário Zagallo BRZ	1958–62	1970
Franz Beckenbauer WG	1974	1990

Beckenbauer was also a losing finalist as a player (1966) and coach (1986).

The pinnacle of the greatest career. Pelé celebrates his goal in the Final.

Orange is not the Only Fruit

West Germany 1974

Brazil lost the World Cup almost as soon as they regained it. The Jules Rimet Trophy, theirs to keep after they'd won it for the third time, was stolen and never seen again. Their 1970 team melted away too, Pelé retiring too early at 31 and three important players dropping out injured: Carlos Alberto, Clodoaldo and especially Tostão, whose eye problem had resurfaced. In their absence, Zagallo put together a far more physical side, in the belief that the old skills wouldn't survive against European athleticism.

No-one seemed to epitomize this more than the hosts and favourites, who'd won the 1972 European Championship with some masterly all-round football, outclassing England at Wembley before winning the final 3-0 at a canter. Three of the team finished 1-2-3 in the European Footballer of the Year poll and there were world-class players in every department: Maier in goal; Vogts and the new discovery Breitner at full-back; the incomparable Beckenbauer, now the world's first great attacking sweeper; the imperious blond Netzer in midfield; Müller ever more unstoppable up front. Seven of the squad came from Bayern Munich, who had recently won the European Cup for the first time. The most intriguing match of an easy first round group would be a first meeting with neighbours East Germany.

Italy were as defensive as ever and apparently even more impregnable. Zoff had just completed 12 consecutive internationals without conceding a goal. But they were an ageing team, short of goalscoring power. England were out, after a frantic emotional night against the Poles at Wembley, but Scotland were back for the first time since 1958, good in parts but lacking a genuine midfield general. Holland still hadn't harnessed the brilliance of their Ajax players, who'd just been beaten in the European

Cup after winning it three years in a row. Only a very late goal in Norway sent them through at the expense of Belgium, against whom they'd played two goalless draws.

The USSR, required to play off against Chile, were disqualified for refusing to appear in the National Stadium in Santiago, which had been used as a concentration camp for political prisoners after the overthrow of Salvador Allende's elected government. Chile kicked off against non-existent opponents (shades of Scotland v Estonia in 1996) and put the ball into an empty net. The Soviet protest might have attracted more sympathy if they'd refused to play Chile before the first leg instead of waiting until they'd been held 0-0 at home.

Yet again FIFA couldn't leave well alone. Although the format of the last three tournaments had been generally acceptable, they insisted on trying to give the event more of the appearance of a league and making the successful teams play an extra match, as if that would give the winners more credibility as world champions. All it succeeded in doing was tiring the players even more and depriving spectators of two knock-out rounds, all for a few dollars more.

1974

Group 1

Australia, Chile, East Germany, West Germany

■ 14 June 1974 • Olympia, West Berlin • 83,168 • Dogan Babaçan (TUR)

▲ **WEST GERMANY (1) 1**
Breitner 18
CHILE (0) 0

● W. GERMANY *Sepp Maier, Berti Vogts, Paul Breitner, Bernd Cullmann, Georg Schwarzenbeck, Franz Beckenbauer (c), Jürgen Grabowski, Uli Hoeness, Gerd Müller, Wolfgang Overath [Bernd Hölzenbein 75], Jupp Heynckes. Helmut Schön.*
CHILE *Leopoldo Vallejos, Rolando García, Alberto Quintano, Antonio Arias, Elias Figueroa, Juan Rodríguez [Alfonso Lara 83], Carlos Caszely, Francisco Valdez (c) [Leonardo Véliz 76], Sergio Ahumada, Carlos Reinoso, Guillermo Páez. Luis Alamos.*
▼ SENT OFF: *Caszely 67.*

The term Total Football, coined during this tournament, wasn't used to describe West Germany's play – but their goal here fitted the bill. A confident passing movement reached the bushy-haired Breitner, a Marxist with Harpo tendencies, whose 25-yarder was touched by Vallejos on its way into the top corner. A left-back scoring with his right foot from inside-right. After that came delusion. Netzer, after injury and a poor season with Real Madrid, was badly missed, and the team were whistled off at the end. The skilful Caszely was sent off for a foul.

■ 14 June 1974 • Volkspark, Hamburg • 18,180 • Youssou Ndiaye (SEN)

▲ **EAST GERMANY (0) 2**
Curran o.g. 58, Streich 72
AUSTRALIA (0) 0

● E. GERMANY *Jürgen Croy, Bernd Bransch (c), Gerd Kische, Konrad Weise, Siegmar Wätzlich, Jürgen Pommerenke, Harald Irmscher, Jürgen Sparwasser, Wolfram Löwe [Martin Hoffmann 55], Joachim Streich, Eberhard Vogel. Georg Buschner.*
AUSTRALIA *Jack Reilly, Dragan 'Doug' Utjesenovic, Peter Wilson (c), Manfred Schaefer, Col Curran, Ray Richards, Jimmy Rooney, Jimmy Mackay, John Warren, Adrian Alston, Branko Buljevic. Rale Rasic (YUG).*

East Germany were rugged and defensive, grouping round their captain, a sweeper who always stayed back. Australia, willing but limited, couldn't stretch them. Curran slid in for an own goal and the dynamic blond Streich scored with a fierce high shot.

■ 18 June 1974 • Volkspark, Hamburg • 52,000 • Mahmoud Mustafa Kamel (EGY)

▲ **WEST GERMANY (2) 3**
Overath 12, Cullmann 34, Müller 53
AUSTRALIA (0) 0

● W. GERMANY *Maier, Vogts, Breitner, Cullmann [Herbert Wimmer 68], Schwarzenbeck, Beckenbauer (c), Grabowski, Hoeness, Müller, Overath, Heynckes [Hölzenbein HT].*
AUSTRALIA *Reilly, Utjesenovic, Wilson (c), Schaefer, Curran, Richards, Rooney, Mackay, Ernie Campbell [Attila Abonyi HT], Alston, Buljevic [Peter Ollerton 62].*

Overath scored from long range, Cullmann from a right-wing cross, Müller with a near-post header – but the mix still wasn't right. Abonyi hit a post in the second half.

■ 18 June 1974 • Olympia, West Berlin • 27,000 • Aurelio Angonese (ITA)

▲ **CHILE (0) 1**
Ahumada 69
EAST GERMANY (0) 1
Hoffmann 55

● CHILE *Vallejos, García, Quintano, Arias, Figueroa, Páez, Valdez (c) [Guillermo Yavar HT], Reinoso, Jorge Socias [Rogelio Farías 67], Ahumada, Véliz.*
E. GERMANY *Croy, Kische, Bransch (c), Weise, Wätzlich, Irmscher, Wolfgang Seguin [Hans-Jürgen Kreische 73], Sparwasser, Hoffmann, Streich, Vogel [Peter Ducke 30].*

With that severe defence, East Germany looked safe once they'd taken the lead through the 19-year-old Hoffmann, who'd been in the Magdeburg team which had just won East Germany's only European club title, the Cup-Winners' Cup. But Ahumada's equalizer left them vulnerable.

■ 22 June 1974 • Volkspark, Hamburg • 58,900 • Ramón Barreto (URU)

▲ **EAST GERMANY (0) 1**
Sparwasser 77
WEST GERMANY (0) 0

● E. GERMANY *Croy, Lothar Kurbjuweit, Bransch (c), Weise, Wätzlich, Reinhard Lauck, Kreische, Irmscher [Erich Hamann 65], Sparwasser, Kische, Hoffmann.*
W. GERMANY *Maier, Vogts, Breitner, Cullmann, Schwarzenbeck [Horst-Dieter Höttges 68], Beckenbauer (c), Grabowski, Hoeness, Müller, Overath [Günter Netzer 69], Heinz Flohe.*

The East put up more of a wall than ever but broke dangerously from the back. Although Müller hit a post, Kreische missed an open goal from a short left-wing cross, then Sparwasser chased a long ball into the D, cleverly headed the ball away from Schwarzenbeck, sold Maier half a dummy, and drove high into the net. Croy was surrounded by photographers at the end, but East Germany had condemned themselves to the harder second-round group. Netzer appeared for just 20 minutes in the finals, a great player reduced to a footnote. This was the only match ever played between the two Germanys.

Giant steps for mankind? The two Germanys walk out for their only match together.

Group 2

Brazil, Scotland, Yugoslavia, Zaire

■ 22 June 1974 • Olympia, West Berlin • 16,100 • Jafar Namdar (IRN)

▲ **AUSTRALIA 0**
CHILE 0

● **AUSTRALIA** *Reilly, Utjesenovic, Wilson (c), Schaefer, Curran [Harry Williams 82], Richards, Rooney, Mackay, Abonyi, Alston, [Ollerton 65], Buljevic.*
CHILE *Vallejos, García, Quintano, Arias, Figueroa, Páez, Valdez (c) [Farías 57], Reinoso, Caszely, Ahumada, Véliz [Yavar 72].*
▼ SENT OFF: *Richards 83.*

The right result between two unexceptional teams. Chile drew two matches and lost the other by a single goal but were very unimpressive. The next time they reached the finals, eight years later, General Pinochet would still be in power, after murdering and 'disappearing' his own people.

GROUP 1	P	W	D	L	F	A	PTS
E. Germany	3	2	1	0	4	1	5
W. Germany	3	2	0	1	4	1	4
Chile	3	0	2	1	1	2	2
Australia	3	0	1	2	0	5	1

East Germany and West Germany qualified for the second round.

■ 13 June 1974 • Waldstadion, Frankfurt • 61,500 • Rudi Scheurer (SWI)

▲ **BRAZIL 0**
YUGOSLAVIA 0

● **BRAZIL** *Emerson Leão, 'Nelinho' (Manoel Rezende de Matos), Francisco Marinho Chagas, Wilson Piazza (c), Luís Pereira, Mário (Marinho) Peres, Valdomiro (Vaz), 'Jairzinho' (Jair Ventura), 'Leivinha' (João Leiva), Roberto Rivelino, Paulo César (Lima). Mário Zagallo.*
YUGOSLAVIA *Enver Maric, Ivan Buljan, Drazen Muzinic, Enver Hadziabdic, Josip Katalinski, Vladislav Bogicevic, Branko Oblak, Jovan Acimovic, Ilija Petkovic, Ivo Surjak, Dragan Dzajic (c). Miljan Miljanic.*

Zagallo's apprehensive approach brought its first result, another opening match with no goals – though in fact both teams made chances. A shortage of quality led to Jairzinho playing in the middle up

Lorimer volleys Scotland's first goal in the finals since 1958.

front, where he was unrecognizable, and not just for his new afro. English sources refer to Marinho Peres as Mario Marinho, which means nothing in Brazil.

■ 14 June 1974 • Westfalen, Dortmund •
25,800 • Gerd Schulenburg (WG)

▲ **SCOTLAND (2) 2**
Lorimer 26, Jordan 34
ZAIRE (0) 0

● SCOTLAND *David Harvey, William 'Sandy' Jardine, Danny McGrain, Davie Hay, Jim Holton, John Blackley, Kenny Dalglish [Tommy Hutchison 75], Billy Bremner (c), Joe Jordan, Denis Law, Peter Lorimer.* Willie Ormond.
ZAIRE *Kazadi Mwamba, Mwepu Ilunga, Mukombo Mwanza, Bwanga Tshimen, Lobilo Boba, Kilasu Masamba, Mayanga Maku [Kembo Uba Kembo 64], Mana Mambwene, Ndaye Mulamba, Kidumu Mantantu (c) [Kibonge Mafu 75], Kakoko Etepe.* Blagoje Vidinic (YUG).

Easy as expected for Scotland, but they didn't make enough of the opportunity. Zaire showed some skilful touches but were all over the place at the back, leaving Jordan horribly unmarked when he headed Bremner's free-kick straight at Kazadi, who stood transfixed and let the ball in under his armpit. Earlier, Lorimer had scored with a typically glorious volley from Jordan's knock-down. The two goals seemed to satisfy the Scots, who spent too much time passing the ball around in midfield. Law, once a great player but now 34, was a forlorn figure in his last international.

The Zaire players were known by their first names. Bwanga and Kazadi were cousins. Vidinic had coached Morocco in the 1970 finals.

■ 18 June 1974 • Waldstadion, Frankfurt •
60,000 • Arie van Gemert (HOL)

▲ **BRAZIL 0**
SCOTLAND 0

● BRAZIL *Leão, Nelinho, Marinho Chagas, Piazza (c), Pereira, Marinho Peres, Jairzinho, 'Mirandinha' (Sebastião Miranda), Leivinha [Paulo César Carpegiani 65], Rivelino, Paulo César.*
SCOTLAND *Harvey, Jardine, McGrain, Hay, Holton, Martin Buchan, Willie Morgan, Bremner (c), Dalglish, Jordan, Lorimer.*

It's now been rewritten as Scotland's Braveheart draw with the World Champions, Bremner unlucky to see the ball rebound off his shins just past the post – but these were two pedestrian teams and goalless was about right. Jairzinho moved back to the right wing, but the Mirandinha-Leivinha partnership was cumbersome and Paulo César an enormous let-down. At least the defence was much better than in 1970: Leão consistent in goal; Pereira a dominating stopper; the blond Marinho Chagas a glamorous attacking left-back. Zagallo was probably satisfied as well as relieved, but it made difficult viewing.

Bremner (4) agonizes as the ball bounces off his legs and just past the post. Rivelino (left) and Leão have different ways of showing their relief.

■ 18 June 1974 • Parkstadion, Gelsenkirchen • 30,500 • Omar Delgado (COL)

▲ **YUGOSLAVIA (6) 9**
Bajevic 8, 30, 81, Dzajic 14, Surjak 18, Katalinski 22, Bogicevic 35, Oblak 61, Petkovic 65
ZAIRE (0) 0

● YUGOSLAVIA *Maric, Buljan, Hadziabdic, Katalinski, Bogicevic, Petkovic, Oblak, Acimovic, Surjak, Dusan Bajevic, Dzajic (c).*
ZAIRE *Kazadi [Tubilandu Dimbi 21], Mwepu, Mukombo, Bwanga, Lobilo, Kilasu, Ndaye, Mana, Kembo, Kidumu (c), Kakoko [Mayanga HT].*
▼ SENT OFF: *Ndaye 23.*

■ 22 June 1974 • Waldstadion, Frankfurt • 54,000 • Alfonso Archundia (MEX)

▲ **SCOTLAND (0) 1**
Jordan 88
YUGOSLAVIA (0) 1
Karasi 81

● YUGOSLAVIA *Maric, Buljan, Hadziabdic, Oblak, Katalinski, Bogicevic, Petkovic, Acimovic, Surjak, Bajevic [Stanislav Karasi 70], Dzajic (c).*
SCOTLAND *Harvey, Jardine, McGrain, Hay, Holton, Buchan, Morgan, Bremner (c), Dalglish [Hutchison 65], Jordan, Lorimer.*

Yugoslavia's talented forwards put Scotland's performance in perspective. Bajevic, a rabbit killer who'd once scored five against Venezuela, thrashed in a close-range hat-trick and Dzajic curled in a free-kick. Vidinic took off Kazadi as soon as he'd conceded more goals in 18 minutes than in 90 against Scotland. His substitute's first task was to pick the ball out of the net, put there by Katalinski with two other Yugoslavs in the six-yard box; Ndaye was sent off for protesting too much. Bogicevic headed the fifth over a defender and Oblak's free-kick was badly fumbled by Tubilandu, who conceded more goals, pro rata, than any other World Cup goalkeeper. Yugoslavia's seven scorers in one match set another record.

Dzajic, wandering to the right wing, turned inside and crossed for Karasi to head home, and Jordan's goal came too late, volleyed in at the far post after the long-legged Hutchison had beaten his man and crossed low from the left. He should have been in the team from the start, in place of the dreadfully disappointing Dalglish ('I was frightened to try things in case they didn't come off'). Meanwhile the sight of the red-haired Bremner, essentially a ball winner, taking the ball from his goalkeeper showed how little was coming from the midfield. Scotland were the only unbeaten team in the tournament and the first ever to be eliminated without losing a match, but these were mere statistics.

Jardine (white shirt) can only watch as Karasi (on the ground) heads the goal that eliminates Scotland from the tournament.

■ 22 June 1974 • Parkstadion, Gelsenkirchen •
35,000 • Nicolae Rainea (ROM)

▲ **BRAZIL (1) 3**
Jairzinho 12, Rivelino 66, Valdomiro 79
ZAIRE (0) 0

● BRAZIL *Leão, Nelinho, Marinho Chagas, Piazza (c)*
[Mirandinha 59], Pereira, Marinho Peres, 'Edu' (Eduardo
Américo), Jairzinho, Leivinha [Valdomiro 10], Rivelino,
Carpegiani.
ZAIRE *Kazadi, Mwepu, Mukombo, Bwanga, Lobilo,*
Kibonge, Tshinabu Kamunda [Kembo 62], Mana, Ntumba
Kalala, Kidumu (c) [Kilasu 61], Mayanga.

At last Brazil scored some goals, but the first was scrappy and the second took its time. When it arrived it was wasted on a team like Zaire, Jairzinho laying the ball back for Rivelino to hit it so hard that it rebounded yards out off the netting. But the third goal, which sent them through, was a joke. Valdomiro hit a low cross-cum-shot from almost on the right-hand goal line, Kazadi fumbling it in at the near post as he tried to clutch it to his chest. Earlier he'd made a very good one-handed save from Pereira, no consolation to him or the Scots. Mwepu was booked for charging out of the wall at a free-kick and kicking the ball away – but it was probably something he'd seen the professionals do. It was about the only thing Zaire learned from their embarrassing three games, which were used to denigrate black African football for years.

GROUP 2	P	W	D	L	F	A	PTS
Yugoslavia	3	1	2	0	10	1	4
Brazil	3	1	2	0	3	0	4
Scotland	3	1	2	0	3	1	4
Zaire	3	0	0	3	0	14	0

Yugoslavia and Brazil qualified for the second round.

Group 3

Bulgaria, Holland, Sweden, Uruguay

■ 15 June 1974 • Niedersachsen, Hanover •
53,700 • Károly Palotai (HUN)

▲ **HOLLAND (1) 2**
Rep 9, 86
URUGUAY (0) 0

● HOLLAND *Jan Jongbloed, Wim Suurbier, Ruud Krol,*
Wim Jansen, Wim Rijsbergen, Arie Haan, Johan Neeskens,
Wim van Hanegem, Johnny Rep, Johan Cruyff (c), Rob
Rensenbrink. Rinus Michels.
URUGUAY *Ladislao Mazurkiewicz, Baudilio Jáuregui,*
Juan Masnik (c), Pablo Forlán, Ricardo Pavoni, Victor
Espárrago, Julio Montero Castillo, Pedro Rocha, Luis Cubilla
[Denis Milar 64], Fernando Morena, Walter Mantegazza.
Roberto Porta.
▼ SENT OFF: *Montero Castillo 69.*

Rocha was back, Cubilla still there at 34, Morena the most prolific scorer in Uruguayan club history – but it didn't add up to much against the almost casually brilliant Dutch, who looked disinterested at times but won very easily against a brutal and discredited team. Montero Castillo, swarthy and sideburned, was sent off for kicking Rensenbrink, but others might have gone with him. Forlán, for instance, kicked Neeskens as he went in for a header. The fair-haired Rep headed the first goal and slotted the second after Rensenbrink's pass from the left gave him an open goal. Jansen had earlier hit a post. The quicksilver Cruyff was well established as the greatest attacking player in Europe. Palotai was one of that very rare breed, an international footballer (1964 Olympics) turned international referee.

1974

■ 15 June 1974 • Rheinstadion, Düsseldorf •
22,500 • Edison Pérez (PER)

▲ BULGARIA 0
SWEDEN 0

● BULGARIA *Rumentscho Goranov, Zonyo Vasiliev, Kiril Ivkov, Stefan Velichkov, Bojil Kolev, Dimitar Penev, Voin Voinov [Atanas Mikhailov 73], Christo Bonev (c), Georgi Denev, Pavel Panov [Mladen Vasiliev 75], Asparoukh Nikodimov. Christo Mladenov.*
SWEDEN *Ronnie Hellström, Jan Olsson II, Kent Karlsson, Bo Larsson (c), Björn Andersson, Ove Grahn, Staffan Tapper, Ove Kindvall [Benno Magnusson 73], Ralf Edström, Conny Torstensson, Roland Sandberg. Georg 'Åby' Ericsson.*

Sweden were very defensive, despite Kindvall and the 6'4" Edström up front. Bonev did his best but there was little happening in front of him.

■ 19 June 1974 • Westfalen, Dortmund •
52,500 • Werner Winsemann (CAN)

▲ HOLLAND 0
SWEDEN 0

● HOLLAND *Jongbloed, Suurbier, Krol, Jansen, Rijsbergen, Haan, Neeskens, van Hanegem [Theo de Jong 73], Cruyff (c), Rep, Piet Keizer.*
SWEDEN *Hellström, J. Olsson II [Roland Grip 75], Andersson, Karlsson, Björn Nordqvist, Larsson (c), Inge Ejderstedt, Tapper [Örjan Persson 61], Edström, Grahn, Sandberg.*

Same again from the Swedes, but Holland were perfectly happy to go along with it, taking their cue from Ajax, whose great European Cup record was sprinkled with 0-0 draws. Here, they made light of the

loss of Barrie Hulshoff by moving Haan back to join the impressive young Rijsbergen. In May they'd replaced their injured first choice goalkeeper with the 33-year-old Jongbloed whose only previous cap had been as a substitute 11 years earlier. The slow-moving beetle-browed van Hanegem was a marvellous playmaker, the brilliant Keizer used as a reserve.

■ 19 June 1974 • Niedersachsen, Hanover •
13,400 • Jack Taylor (ENG)

▲ BULGARIA (0) 1
Bonev 75
URUGUAY (0) 1
Pavoni 87

● BULGARIA *Goranov, Velichkov, Ivkov, Kolev, Vasiliev, Penev, Voinov, Bonev (c), Denev, Panov, Nikodimov [Mikhailov 59].*
URUGUAY *Mazurkiewicz (c), Jáuregui, Forlán, Pavoni, Espárrago, Morena, Rocha, Luis Garisto [Masnik 73], Mantegazza [Alberto Cardaccio 62], Milar, Romeo Corbo.*

A rough match between two poor teams. Again Bonev was a one-man attack, but the veteran Pavoni headed a late equalizer.

■ 23 June 1974 • Westfalen, Dortmund •
52,100 • Tony Boskovic (AUS)

▲ **HOLLAND (2) 4**
Neeskens pen 5, pen 44, Rep 71, de Jong 88
BULGARIA (0) 1
Krol o.g. 78

● HOLLAND *Jongbloed, Suurbier, Krol, Jansen, Rijsbergen, Haan, Neeskens [Theo de Jong 78], van Hanegem [Rinus Israël HT], Cruyff (c), Rep, Rensenbrink.*
BULGARIA *Stefan Staykov, Velichkov, Ivkov, Vasiliev, Penev, Ivan Stoyanov [Mikhailov HT], Bonev (c), Kolev, Voinov, Panov [Krasimir Borisov 55], Denev.*

It was as if Holland came to life just because they decided to, swarming around the Bulgarian goal. Both the penalties were indisputable, for crude fouls on Cruyff and Jansen. Neeskens, who took both kicks with tremendous power, also hit a post. Vasiliev's header back across his own penalty area was met by Rep's fierce instinctive volley, and de Jong's diving header finished off a centre by Cruyff, who'd again been kingly throughout. Krol turned a cross past Jongbloed but it was the merest blip.

It was about now that people started referring to Total Football, every player able to attack and defend with equal facility. It wasn't strictly accurate (impossible to imagine Krol and van Hanegem interchanging positions, or Rijsbergen and Cruyff) but you get the gist. This was a game never quite seen before among national teams, introduced by the same coach who'd led Ajax to their first European title. The defenders weren't just hard (something Zagallo misunderstood) but good on the ball. And the team was more than attractively functional; Cruyff's much-televised piece of genius against Sweden, beating a man tight to the left-hand goal line by turning the ball behind his own leg, was the undying image of the tournament.

■ 23 June 1974 • Rheinstadion, Düsseldorf •
28,300 • Erich Linemayr (AUT)

▲ **SWEDEN (0) 3**
Edström 46, 77, Sandberg 74
URUGUAY (0) 0

● SWEDEN *Hellström, Andersson, Grip, Karlsson, Nordqvist, Larsson (c), Grahn, Kindvall [Torstensson 76], Edström, Magnusson [Thomas Ahlström 60], Sandberg.*
URUGUAY *Mazurkiewicz (c), Jáuregui, Forlán, Pavoni, Garisto [Masnik HT], Espárrago, Morena, Rocha, Mantegazza, Milar, Corbo [Cubilla 43].*

The Swedes kept their heads down for yet another 45 minutes, then peeked over the ramparts and this time saw nothing threatening. Straight from the second kick-off, Edström was left unmarked at the far post to flip the ball up and score with a crushing left-foot volley. Sandberg ran round a defender's back to score off the bottom of the post then turned a somersault in delight, and Hellström put his 1970 experience behind him with an excellent first half. Sweden, growing in stature, were deservedly through. Uruguay didn't reach the finals for another 12 years and nobody missed them.

GROUP 3	P	W	D	L	F	A	PTS
Holland	3	2	1	0	6	1	5
Sweden	3	1	2	0	3	0	4
Bulgaria	3	0	2	1	2	5	2
Uruguay	3	0	1	2	1	6	1

Holland and Sweden qualified for the second round.

Group 4

Argentina, Haiti, Italy, Poland

■ 15 June 1974 • Olympia, Munich • 51,100 • Vicente Llobregat (VEN)

▲ **ITALY (0) 3**
Rivera 52, Auguste o.g. 64, Anastasi 78
HAITI (0) 1
Sanon 46

● ITALY *Dino Zoff, Luciano Spinosi, Giacinto Facchetti (c), Romeo Benetti, Francesco Morini, Tarcisio Burgnich, Fabio Capello, Sandro Mazzola, Giorgio Chinaglia [Pietro Anastasi 69], Gianni Rivera, Luigi Riva. Ferruccio Valcareggi.*
HAITI *Henri Francillon, Pierre Bayonne, Arsène Auguste, Guy François, Wilner Nazaire (c), Ernst Jean-Joseph, Philippe Vorbe, Eddy Antoine, Emmanuel Sanon, Jean-Claude Désir, Guy Saint-Vil [Claude Barthélemy HT]. Antoine Tassy.*

Before the match, the Haitian camp had been playing up their 'secret weapon', voodoo, and for nearly an hour it didn't seem tongue-in-cheek. Italy had virtually all the play but were dreadful up front: Riva past his best; Chinaglia heavy-footed and overrated. Just after half-time, Sanon outsprinted Spinosi and went round Zoff. Haiti had reached the finals only because the qualifying tournament was held at home, and they'd won their last match 2-1 after Trinidad had four goals disallowed in front of Duvalier and his thugs. Now, of all teams, they were the ones to end Zoff's run of 1,143 minutes without conceding a goal, still the world record.

Italy camped round the Haitian penalty area and scored all three goals through a packed defence, Benetti's shot deflecting in off a defender – but they'd made very heavy weather of a simple task. Chinaglia later sounded off about being substituted, adding to the disquiet in the camp. Jean-Joseph, the first player to be caught taking drugs in a finals tournament, was sent home to face Papa Doc and his gentle friends.

The voodoo that you do so well. Sanon goes past Spinosi and Zoff to provide the biggest surprise in the tournament and end Italy's world record.

■ 15 June 1974 • Neckar, Stuttgart • 31,500 • Clive Thomas (WAL)

▲ **POLAND (2) 3**
Lato 7, 62, Szarmach 8
ARGENTINA (0) 2
Heredia 60, Babington 66

● POLAND *Jan Tomaszewski, Antoni Szymanowski, Adam Musial, Zygmunt Maszczyk, Jerzy Gorgon, Wladyslaw Zmuda, Grzegorz Lato, Henryk Kasperczak, Andrzej Szarmach [Jan Domarski 70], Kazimierz Deyna (c), Robert Gadocha [Leslaw Cmikiewicz 85].* Kazimierz Górski, with Jacek Gmoch.
ARGENTINA *Daniel Carnevali, Roberto Perfumo (c), Enrique Wolff, Ramón Heredia, Francisco Sa, Angel Hugo Bargas [Roberto Telch 67], Rubén Ayala, Carlos Babington, Mario Kempes, Miguel Angel Brindisi [René Houseman HT], Agustin Balbuena.* Vladislao Cap.

Górski had promised that Poland would play 'offensive football', which raised a grim smile among those who remembered Poland's brutality in their home qualifiers against England and Wales. But here they were a pleasant surprise. Wlodek Lubanski's injury against England led them to adopt West Germany's successful system of two fast wingers and a single central striker, too much for an Argentinian team infinitely less violent, and formidable, than in recent World Cups.

It wasn't helped by an appalling start. Carnevali, under no challenge, dropped Gadocha's left-wing corner straight to Lato, who then made the second by picking up a shocking Argentinian pass and finding the sharp new centre-forward Szarmach, whose long hair, moustache and nose gave him the look of Vlad the Impaler. He later hit a post. Heredia finished a slick move with an excellent curling shot – but Carnevali, one of the worst

goalkeepers in the tournament, undid the good work by throwing the ball the width of his penalty area for Lato to run on and shoot past him. Babington pulled another one back after four other shots had been blocked, but Poland suddenly looked an exciting and dangerous side.

■ 19 June 1974 • Neckar, Stuttgart • 68,900 • Pavel Kasakov (USR)

▲ **ARGENTINA (1) 1**
Houseman 20
ITALY (1) 1
Perfumo o.g. 35

● ITALY *Zoff, Spinosi, Facchetti (c), Benetti, Morini [Giuseppe Wilson 66], Burgnich, Capello, Mazzola, Anastasi, Rivera [Franco Causio 66], Riva.*
ARGENTINA *Carnevali, Wolff [Rubén Glaría 64], Sa, Telch, Heredia, Perfumo (c), Ayala, Babington, Héctor Yazalde [Enrique Chazarreta 78], Houseman, Kempes.*

Argentina really were lightweight; they should have beaten this lumpen Italian side. They did score the goal of the tournament, the dynamic little Houseman running on to Babington's tremendous through-ball to shoot high past Zoff. But the own goal – Perfumo turning in a low cross – seemed to inhibit them. Italy were now likely to qualify but again looked very poor, Burgnich incongruous as a 35-year-old sweeper, Rivera on his last legs.

■ 19 June 1974 • Olympia, Munich • 25,400 •
Govindasamy Suppiah (SNG)

▲ **POLAND (5) 7**
Lato 17, 87, Deyna 18, Szarmach 30, 34, 50,
Gorgon 31
HAITI (0) 0

● POLAND *Tomaszewski, Szymanowski, Musial [Zbigniew Gut 71], Maszczyk [Cmikiewicz 65], Gorgon, Zmuda, Lato, Kasperczak, Szarmach, Deyna (c), Gadocha.*
HAITI *Francillon, Bayonne, Auguste, Vorbe, Nazaire (c), Antoine, Fritz André [Bathélemy 37], François, Roger Saint-Vil [Serge Racine HT], Désir, Sanon.*

■ 23 June 1974 • Olympia, Munich • 24,000 •
Pablo Sánchez Ibáñez (SPA)

▲ **ARGENTINA (2) 4**
Yazalde 15, 68, Houseman 18, Ayala 55
HAITI (0) 1
Sanon 63

● ARGENTINA *Carnevali, Wolff, Heredia, Perfumo (c), Sa, Telch, Ayala, Babington, Yazalde, Kempes [Balbuena 52], Houseman [Brindisi 57].*
HAITI *Francillon, Serge Ducoste, Bayonne, Vorbe, Désir, Antoine, G. Saint-Vil [Fritz Léandre 52], Racine, Nazaire (c) [Joseph-Marion Léandre 25], Sanon, Wilfried Louis.*

Like Zaire in their second match, Haiti were shown up by the most talented forwards in the group. Szarmach's hat-trick was a cheap one, but he took all the goals well and only the bravery of Francillon, later signed by 1860 Munich, kept the score below double figures. Even the gigantic blond Gorgon scored with a thumping free-kick (only Daniel Killer of Argentina had a better name for a central defender). Roger Saint-Vil was the brother of Guy Saint-Vil who played against Italy and Argentina.

Argentina, who needed to win by three goals and hope Italy lost, fulfilled their part of the equation but Babington, their talented fair-haired playmaker, would miss the next match after committing two daft handballs which earned him a booking for the third match in a row. Sanon, Francillon and the slim Vorbe were the only Haitians not to look out of place, the Léandres the only brothers to come on as substitutes in a finals match.

GROUP 4	P	W	D	L	F	A	PTS
Poland	3	3	0	0	12	3	6
Argentina	3	1	1	1	7	5	3
Italy	3	1	1	1	5	4	3
Haiti	3	0	0	3	2	14	0

Poland and Argentina qualified for the second round.

1974

■ 23 June 1974 • Neckar, Stuttgart • 68,900 • Hans-Joachim Weyland (WG)

▲ **POLAND (2) 2**
Szarmach 38, Deyna 44
ITALY (0) 1
Capello 85

● POLAND *Tomaszewski, Szymanowski, Musial, Maszczyk, Gorgon, Zmuda, Lato, Kasperczak, Szarmach [Cmikiewicz 77], Deyna (c), Gadocha.*
ITALY *Zoff, Spinosi, Facchetti (c), Benetti, Morini, Burgnich [Wilson 31], Causio, Capello, Chinaglia [Roberto Boninsegna HT], Mazzola, Anastasi.*

Italy needed only a draw and might well have got it if there'd been any justice early on. Straight from the kick-off, Tomaszewski missed a right-wing cross and Anastasi would have turned the ball into the empty net if Szymanowski hadn't taken his legs from behind. No penalty.

After that, the modern athleticism of the Poles showed up Italy's old-fashioned defensiveness. Without needing to, they scored two excellent goals, Szarmach's head and Deyna's fierce right foot converting short crosses from Kasperczak, Deyna's able lieutenant in midfield. Several sources, Italian as well as Polish, claim that the Poles were offered bribes on the pitch, but they weren't having any of it, allowing only a late close-range goal. Italy hit a post and Tomaszewski made a fine save, but Chinaglia had another bad match and only the great Mazzola, still fit and determined, sold himself dearly. Along with other world-class players like Riva, Rivera and Burgnich, he didn't play for Italy again.

Lato, the tournament's top scorer, in action against Italy.

1974

2nd Round
Group A

Argentina, Brazil, East Germany, Holland

■ 26 June 1974 • Niedersachsen, Hanover • 58,463 • Clive Thomas (WAL)

▲ **BRAZIL (0) 1**
Rivelino 60
EAST GERMANY (0) 0

● BRAZIL *Leão, 'Zé Maria' (José Maria Rodrigues), Marinho Chagas, Carpegiani, Pereira, Marinho Peres (c), Valdomiro, Paulo César, Jairzinho, Rivelino, Dirceu (Guimarães).*
E. GERMANY *Croy, Kurbjuweit, Bransch (c), Weise, Wätzlich, Lauck [Löwe 64], Sparwasser, Hamann [Irmscher HT], Streich, Kische, Hoffmann.*

A match between two harsh teams was decided by yet another fearsome Rivelino free-kick. The East Germans, who apparently hadn't watched replays of Mexico 1970, allowed Jairzinho to stand in the middle of their wall, he ducked when Rivelino aimed at him,

the ball skidded in low to Croy's left. The powerful Zé María did well, but East Germany offered little up front.

■ 26 June 1974 • Parkstadion, Gelsenkirchen • 55,348 • Bobby Davidson (SCO)

▲ **HOLLAND (2) 4**
Cruyff 11, 90, Krol 25, Rep 73
ARGENTINA (0) 0

● HOLLAND *Jongbloed, Suurbier [Israël 84], Krol, Jansen, Rijsbergen, Haan, Neeskens, van Hanegem, Rep, Cruyff (c), Rensenbrink.*
ARGENTINA *Carnevali, Wolff [Glaría HT], Heredia, Perfumo (c), Sa, Telch, Ayala, Balbuena, Yazalde, Carlos Squeo, Houseman [Kempes HT].*

Having developed the taste for translating their superiority into goals, the Dutch scored when they felt like it, keeping their feet in a rain-soaked second half. Cruyff went round the keeper for the first and put in the fourth from a tight angle after Carnevali made a good save. Krol's ferocious shot pinballed through a packed area, Rep headed in Cruyff's pinpoint cross, and Neeskens had a goal narrowly disallowed. What really made itself felt, especially on some of the Argentinians, was Holland's severity in the tackle. The first goal followed Rijsbergen's brusque challenge from behind on Yazalde, and Wolff was left writhing on the touchline by a tackle of incredible power from Krol, whose blend of skill and ruthlessness epitomized the whole team. The future looked orange.

Rivelino (centre, near the referee) turns away after scoring with a typical free-kick against East Germany in the 2nd round.

■ 30 June 1974 • Parkstadion, Gelsenkirchen •
67,148 • Rudi Scheurer (SWI)

▲ **HOLLAND (1) 2**
Neeskens 7, Rensenbrink 59
EAST GERMANY (0) 0

● HOLLAND *Jongbloed, Suurbier, Krol, Jansen, Rijsbergen, Haan, Neeskens, van Hanegem, Rep, Cruyff (c), Rensenbrink.*
E. GERMANY *Croy, Kurbjuweit, Pommerenke, Rüdiger Schnuphase, Bransch (c), Weise, Kische, Lauck [Kreische 64], Löwe [Ducke 54], Sparwasser, Hoffmann.*

Croy and Pommerenke (7) remain upright but Neeskens is happier on the ground as he scores Holland's first goal against East Germany.

Back to taking it easy. After scoring the early goal that gave them command, the Dutch played their version of keep-ball while always looking a threat. Neeskens' fierce drive left Croy standing, and Rensenbrink, slightly underrated at the time, scored with a low cross shot. Cruyff was yet again the dominant personality; it's not too much of an exaggeration to say he put Holland on the map. Born in tough circumstances, he knew the value of hard currency (known as 'the Money Wolf' as well as 'Nose') and as a cigarette smoker he was in the Gérson class.

Cruyff, in the distance behind the keeper, crowns his regal performance against Argentina with his second goal and Holland's fourth.

■ 30 June 1974 • Niedersachsen, Hanover •
38,000 • Vital Loraux (BEL)

▲ **BRAZIL (1) 2**
Rivelino 32, Jairzinho 49
ARGENTINA (1) 1
Brindisi 35

● BRAZIL *Leão, Zé Maria, Marinho Chagas, Carpegiani, Pereira, Marinho Peres (c), Valdomiro, Paulo César, Jairzinho, Rivelino, Dirceu.*
ARGENTINA *Carnevali, Glaría, Heredia, Bargas, Sa [Jorge Carrascosa HT], Brindisi (c), Ayala, Squeo, Babington, Balbuena, Kempes [Houseman HT].*

They used to be giants, now it was sub-standard and untidy, although the goals were good. Rivelino unleashed a low drive from 20 yards, the last of his six goals in World Cup finals. No-one else scored so many with such power in one foot. Brindisi curled a free-kick in off the bar and Zé María won the ball and crossed from the goal line for Jairzinho to head into an empty net. But it's unlikely the Dutch were quaking in their boots.

■ 3 July 1974 • Parkstadion, Gelsenkirchen • 53,054 • Jack Taylor (ENG)

▲ **ARGENTINA (1) 1**
Houseman 20
EAST GERMANY (1) 1
Streich 14

● ARGENTINA *Ubaldo Fillol, Wolff (c), Heredia, Bargas, Carrascosa, Brindisi, Ayala, Telch, Kempes, Babington, Houseman.*
E. GERMANY *Croy, Kurbjuweit, Bransch (c), Pommerenke, Weise, Schnuphase, Löwe [Vogel 66], Streich [Ducke 81], Sparwasser, Kische, Hoffmann.*

Argentina at last dropped Carnevali, giving a first cap to Fillol, an important member of their 1978 side, and played their part in a pleasing match of no consequence. The goals were scored by the best forward on each side, Streich building up to a very impressive total of 55, which remained easily the East German record to the end. Houseman left thoughts of what might have been if the defence had matched his talents and those of Babington and the speedy Ayala, or if the 19-year-old Kempes had lived up to his billing. He, at least, would have another chance four years later.

GROUP A	P	W	D	L	F	A	PTS
Holland	3	3	0	0	8	0	6
Brazil	3	2	0	1	3	3	4
E. Germany	3	0	1	2	1	4	1
Argentina	3	0	1	2	2	7	1

Holland qualified for the Final, Brazil for the 3rd-Place Final.

■ 3 July 1974 • Westfalen, Dortmund • 52,500 • Kurt Tschenscher (WG)

▲ **HOLLAND (0) 2**
Neeskens 50, Cruyff 65
BRAZIL (0) 0

● HOLLAND *Jongbloed, Suurbier, Krol, Jansen, Rijsbergen, Haan, Neeskens [Israël 84], van Hanegem, Rep, Cruyff (c), Rensenbrink [de Jong 67].*
BRAZIL *Leão, Zé Maria, Marinho Chagas, Carpegiani, Pereira, Marinho Peres (c), Valdomiro, Paulo César [Mirandinha 61], Jairzinho, Rivelino, Dirceu.*
▼ SENT OFF: *Pereira 84.*

Holland were expected to stroll it, but no Brazilian team is completely without flair, and they should have taken an early lead when Paulo César shot past the far post. A reasonable reserve in 1970 but dreadful here, he had the misfortune to be touted as the first 'new Pelé'. Jairzinho also missed an early chance, but Leão had to make a fantastic close-range save when Zé María let a cross bounce off him straight to Cruyff.

Neeskens, as good as any player in the tournament according to Alf Ramsey, was talented but provocative. When Marinho Peres knocked him cold, his reward was a shin gashed from knee to ankle. When Pereira had enough and hacked him down spectacularly from behind, he was sent off. But the match had been decided by then.

Van Hanegem sent a quickly taken free-kick up to Neeskens who scooped Cruyff's return cross over Leão, two attackers taking out three defenders. Then Krol overlapped on the left, Cruyff volleyed in unchallenged from close range, and Holland stood in the place that Brazil had recently occupied. Some sources list Pereira as captain, but Marinho Peres is wearing the armband on the video.

Group B

Poland, Sweden, West Germany, Yugoslavia

■ 26 June 1974 • Rheinstadion, Düsseldorf • 66,085 • Armando Marques (BRZ)

▲ **WEST GERMANY (1) 2**
Breitner 39, Müller 82
YUGOSLAVIA (0) 0

● W. GERMANY *Maier, Vogts, Breitner, Rainer Bonhof, Schwarzenbeck, Beckenbauer (c), Hölzenbein [Flohe 78], Wimmer [Hoeness 73], Müller, Overath, Dieter Herzog.*
YUGOSLAVIA *Maric, Buljan, Hadziabdic, Muzinic, Katalinski, Oblak [Jure Jerkovic 84], Danilo Popivoda, Acimovic, Surjak, Karasi, Dzajic (c) [Petkovic 84].*

The hosts were kick-started by another Breitner long-range shot, but this time they were far more convincing. There was talk of Schön allowing a cabal led by Beckenbauer to pick the team, but if it was true it didn't do any harm. The strong-running Bonhof galvanized the midfield and Beckenbauer was back to his imperious best ('Der Kaiser'). Müller, also getting there, slid in a cross from close range.

■ 26 June 1974 • Neckar, Stuttgart • 43,755 • Ramón Barreto (URU)

▲ **POLAND (1) 1**
Lato 43
SWEDEN (0) 0

● POLAND *Tomaszewski, Szymanowski, Gut, Maszczyk, Gorgon, Zmuda, Lato, Kasperczak, Szarmach [Kazimierz Kmiecik 60], Deyna (c), Gadocha.*
SWEDEN *Hellström, Karlsson, Grip, Nordqvist, Andersson [Jörgen Augustsson 60], Grahn, Tapper [Ahlström 80], Larsson (c), Edström, Torstensson, Sandberg.*

Poland, riding high after their group matches, found the Swedish defence a tougher proposition. Gadocha's corner was headed on by Szarmach for Lato to head in, but Deyna wasn't allowed to take control in midfield and Tomaszewski had to save Tapper's penalty after 63 minutes to preserve the win.

■ 30 June 1974 • Waldstadion, Frankfurt • 53,200 • Rudi Glöckner (EG)

▲ **POLAND (1) 2**
Deyna pen 24, Lato 62
YUGOSLAVIA (1) 1
Karasi 43

● POLAND *Tomaszewski, Szymanowski, Musial, Maszczyk, Gorgon, Zmuda, Lato, Kasperczak, Szarmach [Cmikiewicz 57], Deyna (c) [Domarski 81], Gadocha.*
YUGOSLAVIA *Maric, Buljan, Hadziabdic, Katalinski, Bogicevic, Oblak [Jerkovic 16], Petkovic [Vladimir Petrovic 81], Acimovic (c), Bajevic, Surjak, Karasi.*

Again the Poles were fortunate to get both points, beneficiaries of a penalty awarded when Karasi gave Szarmach a little kick on the calf. He made up for it by taking a through-pass, dummying Tomaszewski, and shooting high into the net – but Lato, as sharp in the area as he was quick on the wing, again headed in a Gadocha corner. Yugoslavia, without Dzajic, were as disappointing as ever.

■ 30 June 1974 • Rheinstadion, Düsseldorf • 67,861 • Pavel Kasakov (USR)

▲ **WEST GERMANY (0) 4**
Overath 51, Bonhof 52, Grabowski 76, Hoeness, pen 89
SWEDEN (1) 2
Edström 24, Sandberg 53

● W. GERMANY *Maier, Vogts, Breitner, Bonhof, Schwarzenbeck, Beckenbauer (c), Hölzenbein [Flohe 83], Hoeness, Müller, Overath, Herzog [Grabowski 64].*
SWEDEN *Hellström, J. Olsson II, Augustsson, Karlsson, Nordqvist, Larsson (c) [Ejderstedt 32], Torstensson, Tapper, Edström, Grahn, Sandberg.*

Probably the match of the tournament. A win would leave West Germany needing only a draw from their last game; anything less would hand the advantage to Poland. And in the first half, less was what they had to make do with. Sweden, keeping their defensive shape, took the lead with another left-footed volley from Edström, this one a wonderful shot that dipped and bent and chewed gum at the same time.

But the loss of Bo Larsson made itself felt when Beckenbauer began streaming out from the back, forcing a good save from the excellent Hellström. As the rain came down, Overath equalized with a shot that hit both posts and Bonhof blasted in a loose ball. Sweden didn't lie down, Sandberg collecting a misplaced header from Schwarzenbeck and driving low across Maier from the left – but the hosts had more ammunition. The ball was worked determinedly across the Swedish penalty area for Grabowski to shoot home, and Ejderstedt brought down Müller for the penalty. A close thing against gutsy opposition, but West Germany had never stopped running and deserved the win.

■ 3 July 1974 • Waldstadion, Frankfurt • 61,249 • Erich Linemayr (AUT)

▲ **WEST GERMANY (0) 1**
Müller 76
POLAND (0) 0

● W. GERMANY *Maier, Vogts, Breitner, Bonhof, Schwarzenbeck, Beckenbauer (c), Grabowski, Hoeness, Müller, Overath, Hölzenbein.*
POLAND *Tomaszewski, Szymanowski, Musial, Maszczyk [Kmiecik 80], Gorgon, Zmuda, Lato, Kasperczak [Cmikiewicz 80], Domarski, Deyna (c), Gadocha.*

The rain kept on falling, like manna for the hosts. Parts of the pitch were waterlogged, the players could barely move the ball ten yards, and the match probably shouldn't have been played. Certainly Poland thought so, conditions underfoot cancelled out their speed on the flanks.

But even in marshland, their wingers were always dangerous. Maier made excellent saves from Lato's free-kick, from Gadocha and Lato after Beckenbauer had completely missed a clearance kick, and from Domarski, whose goal had knocked out England but he wasn't an adequate replacement for the injured Szarmach.

After 53 minutes Hölzenbein, known as a notorious diver in the *Bundesliga*, flew over Zmuda's sliding tackle, but Hoeness had his penalty saved by Tomaszewski. Then, as the rain stopped, a loose ball reached Müller, the last player any defence should have left unmarked near a penalty spot. Poland were hard done by but had stopped looking like a team to contest the Final. West Germany had begun to show some of the form needed to withstand the Dutch, though few expected them to do it.

■ 3 July 1974 • Rheinstadion, Düsseldorf • 37,700 • Luis Pestarino (ARG)

▲ **SWEDEN (1) 2**
Edström 29, Torstensson 85
YUGOSLAVIA (1) 1
Surjak 27

● SWEDEN *Hellström, J. Olsson II, Augustsson, Karlsson, Nordqvist (c), Tapper, Grahn, Persson, Edström, Torstensson, Sandberg.*
YUGOSLAVIA *Maric, Buljan, Hadziabdic, Katalinski, Bogicevic, Miroslav Pavlovic [Luka Peruzovic 77], Petrovic [Karasi 67], Jerkovic, Surjak, Acimovic, Dzajic (c).*

Just reward for the contribution made by Sweden and the towering Edström. As for the Yugoslavs, Scotland were the last opponents not to beat them, which says a few things.

GROUP B	P	W	D	L	F	A	PTS
W. Germany	3	3	0	0	7	2	6
Poland	3	2	0	1	3	2	4
Sweden	3	1	0	2	4	6	2
Yugoslavia	3	0	0	3	2	6	0

West Germany qualified for the Final, Poland for the 3rd-Place Final.

(opposite page) Deyna (white shirt, left) scores from the penalty spot against Yugoslavia.

(left) Tomaszewski makes his second penalty save of the tournament, from Uli Hoeness.

3rd-place Final

■ 6 July 1974 • Olympia, Munich • 74,100 •
Aurelio Angonese (ITA)

▲ **POLAND (0) 1**
Lato 76
BRAZIL (0) 0

● POLAND *Tomaszewski, Szymanowski, Musial, Maszczyk, Gorgon, Zmuda, Lato, Kasperczak [Cmikiewicz 73], Szarmach [Zdzisław Kapka 73], Deyna (c), Gadocha.*
BRAZIL *Leão, Zé Maria, Marinho Chagas, Carpegiani, Alfredo (Mostarda), Marinho Peres (c), Valdomiro, Ademir da Guia [Mirandinha 66], Jairzinho, Rivelino, Dirceu.*

Brazil gave a last cap to the fair-haired Ademir da Guia, whose father Domingos played in the equivalent match of 1938, but he was rarely an influence on yet another dull 3rd-place match. When Lato picked up a pass just inside his own half, Maszczyk pointed the way to goal and Lato outsprinted Alfredo and scuffed the ball past Leão. Soon he was through again, but Leão saved with his foot. Both teams had found their right level, but Brazil had come down from a different plane. In 1994 Zagallo was re-appointed coach on his 63rd birthday. Cmikiewicz came on six times as substitute, a record for a single tournament.

Final

■ 7 July 1974 • Olympia, Munich • 77,833 • Jack Taylor (ENG)

▲ **WEST GERMANY (2) 2**
Breitner pen 25, Müller 43
HOLLAND (1) 1
Neeskens pen 2

● W. GERMANY *Maier, Vogts, Breitner, Bonhof, Schwarzenbeck, Beckenbauer (c), Grabowski, Hoeness, Müller, Overath, Hölzenbein.*
HOLLAND *Jongbloed, Suurbier, Krol, Jansen, Rijsbergen [de Jong 68], Haan, Rep, Neeskens, van Hanegem, Cruyff (c), Rensenbrink [René van de Kerkhof HT].*

No World Cup Final had a more sensational opening, or a quicker goal. Held up for several minutes because Taylor noticed the corner flags were missing, it began with a series of passes among the Dutch, simply keeping possession until Cruyff took the ball in the centre circle and ran at Vogts, beating him on the left and being brought down in the area by Hoeness – penalty, the first in any World Cup

Neeskens scores emphatically from the first penalty awarded in a World Cup Final.

Final. Neeskens thrashed it almost straight as Maier dived to his right.

If you believe van Hanegem, Holland lost the match there and then. Half the team wanted to push on and look for a second goal, the rest to play keep-ball and humiliate the Germans. Memories were apparently going back 30 years, when the Nazis imposed systematic starvation on the Dutch to destroy the Resistance. More to the point perhaps, Vogts' marking of Cruyff began to bite. Virtually all Holland's 15 goals in the tournament started or finished with their captain, who protested about Vogts' treatment at half-time and was booked. By then Taylor had made a bigger dent in Holland's chances.

As against Poland, Hölzenbein ran into the penalty area from the left and went over an outstretched foot, this time Jansen's. There was something oddly inevitable about it, as if Taylor was always likely to give a second penalty the other way.

But this one was far more controversial. Hugh Johns, commentating on ITV, wondered aloud if any contact had been made, and Hölzenbein certainly threw himself forward. Even if Taylor couldn't have been expected to know the winger's reputation, he should surely have given the defender the benefit of the doubt. Instead he said that Jansen 'was certainly not going for the ball'. Which means what? He was deliberately trying to give away a penalty in a World Cup Final? After Hoeness's miss against Poland, Breitner took the kick and beat a stationary Jongbloed.

The turning point, if there was one, came when Cruyff broke away, drew Beckenbauer, and gave the ball to Rep on his left. Maier saved the rather unimaginative shot. Almost on half-time, Bonhof's running made its biggest impact, taking him past Haan to the right-hand goal line. When he pulled the ball back, Müller stopped it with an exaggerated action that looked like a miskick, then shot low across Jongbloed (immobile again) as Krol made a desperate attempt to block. It was Müller's 68th goal in 62 matches for West Germany, an astounding average in such a defensive era. Like Schiavio in 1934, he retired from international football after scoring the winner in the Final for the host country.

And winner it already was. Maier, vastly improved since 1970, made another of his marvellous saves from Neeskens' close-range volley, and Holland pressed throughout the second half – but Beckenbauer and Overath kept the play away from them and Cruyff couldn't escape Vogts, who had his most famous match. General disappointment at Holland's defeat, especially as West Germany had no Netzer to compensate – but the hosts had shown there was more than one way to win a football match, and it was only right that Beckenbauer, Overath, Grabowski and Müller should have World Cup winners' medals, hard though it was on Krol, Neeskens, van Hanegem and the inimitable Cruyff, who was cut down on the one day Holland – and the football world – wanted to see him blossom.

The second penalty in a Final arrives soon after the first. Breitner equalizes for the hosts.

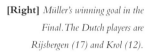

1974

[Right] *Müller's winning goal in the Final. The Dutch players are Rijsbergen (17) and Krol (12).*

[Below] *Another view of Müller's winning goal in the Final.*

[Bottom] *West Germany's two goalscorers after the Final. Breitner (right) escorts the great Gerd into international retirement.*

MOST GOALS IN TOTAL

14	Gerd Müller	WG	1970–74	1 pen.
13	Just Fontaine	FRA	1958	
12	Pelé	BRZ	1958–70	
11	Sándor Kocsis	HUN	1954	
10	Helmut Rahn	WG	1954–58	
10	Teófilo Cubillas	PER	1970–78	2 pen.
10	Grzegorz Lato	POL	1974–82	
10	Gary Lineker	ENG	1986–90	2 pen.

BEST OF OTHER BRITISH

5	Peter McParland	NIR	1958
4	Joe Jordan	SCO	1974–82
2	Ivor Allchurch	WAL	1958

Four players have scored one goal each for the Republic of Ireland: Kevin Sheedy, Niall Quinn (1990), Ray Houghton, John Aldridge (1994).

LEADING GOALSCORERS 1974

7	Grzegorz Lato	POL	
5	Andrzej Szarmach	POL	
5	Johan Neeskens	HOL	3 pen.

The Last Post

Argentina 1978

It was about time Argentina hosted the main event. They'd applied for it in the past and were one of the major footballing powers, so no-one had many qualms when they were awarded the 1978 tournament. Then a military government seized power and changed the picture.

Not that it persuaded FIFA to move the World Cup to an established democracy. Heaven forbid. But it made a great many people uneasy, especially when the likes of Amnesty International sent documentation on torture and other state atrocities to journalists setting out for Buenos Aires. Even those who could ignore this kind of thing had concerns. The first president of the organizing committee, General Actis, was blown up and a policeman died trying to remove another bomb from a press centre. This after the Montoneros, one of the main rebel groups, had promised a ceasefire for the duration of the tournament because it was 'a people's festival'.

Doubts and reservations, however, were swept aside as they invariably are and the junta, deeply in need of a public relations coup, spent the vast sums required to build three new stadia and police the event thoroughly. It passed without much incident off the pitch, but at a cost (more than the 1972 Olympics) in more ways than one.

Of the competing countries, several looked strong in parts. The holders had replaced several of their 1974 team with some talented newcomers but were without Beckenbauer, who'd opted to pick up some easy money in the USA at the end of a wonderful career. Unable to find a replacement, West Germany were using Manni Kaltz, a big attacking right-back, as their sweeper.

If any player was missed even more than the Kaiser, it was Cruyff, who'd simply had enough of life in the goldfish bowl. And van Hanegem dropped out when he couldn't be guaranteed a place in the starting line-up. But Holland retained many of the 1974 side and looked the strongest of the European challengers.

Italy, trying to assimilate the attacking philosophy of a new coach, had beaten an England team with several well-known names (Keegan, Brooking, Channon, Bowles, Emlyn Hughes) who were devoid of plan or leadership. Keegan called it 'the worst team ever picked by Don Revie' and the Italian captain Facchetti agreed: 'The worst England team I have ever seen. Disorganized, confused, of only limited ability.' When Revie accepted a job in the United Arab Emirates before the qualifying games were over, Ron Greenwood stepped in and picked a team which beat Italy 2-0 in the return, but it was too late by then. For the second successive time, England didn't reach the finals.

Brazil, despite a different coach, were just as physical as in 1974. Argentina, like Italy, were trying to go the other way, their coach using two wingers and refusing to pick players from Lorenzo's brutal Boca Juniors. Evolution had been slow (Argentina had a player sent off against both England and Scotland) and results inconclusive (a string of wins over mediocre opposition punctuated by a home defeat by Uruguay), but home advantage would surely count for something.

But it was an open field, and several respected judges, including Rinus Michels and Miljan Miljanic, had a fancy for Scotland, who'd eliminated European champions Czechoslovakia. According to Lou Macari, one of the players in the squad, the 3-1 win at Hampden owed more to grit and fight than sound football method – but it was impressive nonetheless, and there seemed to be no shortage of international class: Buchan and Burns at the back; a midfield of Masson the playmaker and Rioch the destroyer who could pass; Jordan to win the ball up front for Dalglish; dribbling left-wingers in John Robertson and the recalled Willie Johnston. Enough to make people believe the voluble new manager when he intimated that Scotland's third match, against Holland, would be to decide who finished top of the group. Before that, only an ageing Peru followed by Iran, who must have been terrified to hear 'my name is Ally MacLeod and I am a born winner'.

1978

Group 1

Argentina, France, Hungary, Italy

■ 2 June 1978 • Parque Municipal, Mar del Plata • 42,653 • Nicolae Rainea (ROM)

▲ **ITALY (1) 2**
Rossi 29, Zaccarelli 54
FRANCE (1) 1
Lacombe 37

● ITALY *Dino Zoff (c), Claudio Gentile, Antonio Cabrini, Romeo Benetti, Mauro Bellugi, Gaetano Scirea, Franco Causio, Marco Tardelli, Paolo Rossi, Giancarlo Antognoni [Renato Zaccarelli HT], Roberto Bettega. Enzo Bearzot.*
FRANCE *Jean-Paul Bertrand-Demanes, Gérard Janvion, Max Bossis, Jean-Marc Guillou, Patrice Rio, Marius Trésor (c), Christian Dalger, Henri Michel, Bernard Lacombe [Marc Berdoll 75], Michel Platini, Didier Six [Olivier Rouyer 76]. Michel Hidalgo.*

The loss of the veteran Facchetti had forced the Italians to reorganize their defence and you'd think the last thing they needed was to concede such a very early goal. Six hared down the left wing to hit a long cross which Lacombe, no giant, headed past Zoff. In fact it turned out to be just the kick-start Bearzot had been looking for. Forced to come out from the start, Italy outplayed a weakened French team. Their goals were both rather odd, the first going in off the bar and various bits of anatomy including Rossi's leg, the second a first-time ground shot with the keeper possibly unsighted. But there was no doubt about the grip established in midfield by the famous rottweiler Benetti and the young Tardelli who completely subdued Platini, sometimes fairly. Neither of them was a Neeskens, but as a double act they were scary and good.

■ 2 June 1978 • Monumental, Buenos Aires • 76,609 • Antônio Garrido (POR)

▲ **ARGENTINA (1) 2**
Luque 14, Bertoni 83
HUNGARY (1) 1
Csapó 9

● ARGENTINA *Ubaldo Fillol, Jorge Olguin, Alberto Tarantini, Américo Gallego, Luis Galván, Daniel Passarella (c), Daniel Valencia [Norberto Alonso 75], Osvaldo Ardiles, Leopoldo Luque, Mario Kempes, René Houseman [Daniel Bertoni 67]. César Luis Menotti.*
HUNGARY *Sándor Gujdár, Péter Török [Gyözö Martos HT], Zoltán Kereki (c), István Kocsis, József Tóth II, Sándor Pintér, Tibor Nyilasi, Sándor Zombori, Károly Csapó, András Töröcsik, László Nagy. Lajos Baróti.*

▼ SENT OFF: *Töröcsik 87, Nyilasi 89.*

A snowstorm of blue and white tickertape, descending through the floodlights, welcomed the players on to the pitch, one of the great World Cup visuals.

At first the Argentinian team didn't share the festive mood. This was the toughest of the four groups, and although Hungary had just lost a friendly 4-1 at Wembley, they added to Argentina's nervousness with their early goal – Csapó putting in the rebound when Fillol didn't hold Zombori's shot.

The hosts were grateful that Gujdár soon returned the compliment, blocking a Kempes free-kick for Luque to force the ball in as the keeper collided with his leg. After that, Hungary were subjected to a series of bodychecks and small fouls, insignificant on their own but building the frustration. Garrido let most of them go unpunished, though even he had to do something about Passarella's waist-high kick at Pintér. Ironically, it was Hungary's most skilful players who were sent off. Töröcsik, fouled a dozen times without protection, was booked for protesting then sent off for leaving his leg out as Galván ran past. Nyilasi clattered the abrasive Tarantini and walked off with his head held high. Before that, Bertoni had put the ball in the net after Gujdár seemed to have been fouled. Argentina's first appearance had already left a bad taste in the mouth.

■ 6 June 1978 • Parque Municipal, Mar del Plata • 26,533 • Ramón Barreto (URU)

▲ **ITALY (2) 3**
Rossi 34, Bettega 35, Benetti 61
HUNGARY (0) 1
A. Tóth pen 81

● ITALY *Zoff (c), Gentile, Cabrini [Antonello Cuccureddu 79], Benetti, Bellugi, Scirea, Causio, Tardelli, Rossi, Antognoni, Bettega [Francesco Graziani 83].*
HUNGARY *Ferenc Mészáros, Martos, Kocsis, Kereki (c), J. Tóth II, Csapó, Pintér, Zombori, László Pusztai, László Fazekas [István Halász HT], Nagy [András Tóth HT].*

A single match seemed to have made Italy believe in themselves, and they dominated this one, making light of a pitch that had recently been relaid and now cut up in great divots. Facchetti's injury had let in Scirea, who was far better coming forward. The unsung Bellugi was a world-class stopper, Causio smoothness itself on the right, Rossi a nimble replacement for Graziani. Above all, this was Bettega's match. Suave but forceful in the air, he'd scored four goals in one qualifying match and headed a great one against England. Here he scored another as well as hitting the woodwork three times (it was that kind of tournament for him). Rossi scored a poacher's goal and Benetti convulsed the keeper from 20 yards. Bellugi's challenge on Csapó gave away a debatable penalty, but by then the match was won and lost.

■ 6 June 1978 • Monumental, Buenos Aires • 76,609 • Jean Dubach (SWI)

▲ **ARGENTINA (1) 2**
Passarella pen 45, Luque 73
FRANCE (0) 1
Platini 60

● ARGENTINA *Fillol, Olguin, Tarantini, Gallego, Galván, Passarella (c), Valencia [Alonso 61, Oscar Ortíz 70], Ardiles, Luque, Kempes, Houseman.*
FRANCE *Bertrand-Demanes [Dominique Baratelli 55], Patrick Battiston, Bossis, Dominique Bathenay, Christian Lopez, Trésor (c), Dominique Rocheteau, Michel, Lacombe, Platini, Six.*

For drama, tension and atmosphere, this was the match of the tournament. The return of Bathenay, Battiston and the tousle-haired Rocheteau made France much more competitive and many felt they should have won. Platini equalized when Lacombe's lob came back off the bar, Six shot just past the post after running clear, and Argentina's first goal was from a penalty monstrously awarded after the Canadian linesman Werner Winsemann decided the splendid Trésor (his surname means 'treasure') had deliberately handled while falling over. An injury to Bertrand-Demanes, crashing his spine against a goalpost, brought in Baratelli, whose first task was to pick the ball out of the net after Luque had scored with a powerful shot from outside the D.

Again, poor refereeing had done the hosts no harm, but the force was always with them. Menotti's insistence on a more attacking style didn't mean delicate short passes and clever dribbles: this was ball-control at speed, unsettling the opposition with direct running. Even little Ardiles attacked defenders at pace, but the undying memory was of tall men with long black hair (Kempes, Luque, Ortíz) charging like stallions. There was never a more macho combination, and only the coolest of teams were likely to resist them; that or a similar referee.

■ 10 June 1978 • Parque Municipal, Mar del Plata • 23,127 • Arnaldo Coelho (BRZ)

▲ **FRANCE (3) 3**
Lopez 23, Berdoll 38, Rocheteau 42
HUNGARY (1) 1
Zombori 41

● FRANCE *Dominique Dropsy, Janvion, François Bracci, Jean Petit, Lopez, Trésor (c), Rocheteau [Six 75], Claude Papi [Platini HT], Marc Berdoll, Bathenay, Rouyer.*
HUNGARY *Gujdár, Martos, László Bálint, Kereki (c), J. Tóth II, Nyilasi, Pintér, Zombori, Pusztai, Törőcsik, Nagy [Csapó 73].*

Confusion about change strips (black-and-white TV still mattered) led to a delay of 40 minutes and France playing in green and white stripes, the colours of local club Kimberley. Lopez and Zombori scored with spectacular long shots and the French reserves looked skilful, but Platini's Gallic shrug as he came off said it all.

GROUP 1	P	W	D	L	F	A	PTS
Italy	3	3	0	0	6	2	6
Argentina	3	2	0	1	4	3	4
France	3	1	0	2	5	5	2
Hungary	3	0	0	3	3	8	0

Italy and Argentina qualified for the second round.

■ 10 June 1978 • Monumental, Buenos Aires • 76,609 • Avraham Klein (ISR)

▲ **ITALY (0) 1**
Bettega 67
ARGENTINA (0) 0

● ITALY *Zoff (c), Gentile, Cabrini, Benetti, Bellugi [Cuccureddu 6], Scirea, Causio, Tardelli, Rossi, Antognoni [Zaccarelli 73], Bettega.*
ARGENTINA *Fillol, Olguin, Tarantini, Gallego, Galván, Passarella (c), Bertoni, Ardiles, Kempes, Valencia, Ortíz [Houseman 73].*

Benetti, who could pass as well as terrify, drove Italy to a win that made them look the best team in the qualifying stages. The goal was beautifully crafted, Bettega moving in off the left wing by way of one-twos with Antognoni and Rossi before shooting past Fillol as he came out. The two sweepers Scirea and Passarella, born on the same day in 1953, again played superbly in their different styles. Argentina, whose excesses were kept in check by the best referee in the world, disgracefully stopped him taking charge of any of their remaining matches.

Galván and Passarella look on as Tarantini slides in too late to stop Bettega scoring Italy's goal against Argentina.

Group 2

Mexico, Poland, Tunisia, West Germany

■ 1 June 1978 • Monumental, Buenos Aires • 76,609 • Angel Norberto Coerezza (ARG)

▲ **POLAND 0**
WEST GERMANY 0

● POLAND *Jan Tomaszewski, Antoni Szymanowski, Henryk Maculewicz, Bogdan Masztaler [Henryk Kasperczak 83], Jerzy Gorgon, Wladyslaw Zmuda, Grzegorz Lato, Adam Nawalka, Andrzej Szarmach, Kazimierz Deyna (c), Wlodek Lubanski [Zbigniew Boniek 79].* Jacek Gmoch.

   W. GERMANY *Sepp Maier, Berti Vogts (c), Herbert Zimmermann, Rainer Bonhof, Rolf Rüssmann, Manni Kaltz, Rüdi Abramczik, Erich Beer, Klaus Fischer, Heinz Flohe, Hansi Müller.* Helmut Schön.

On another shocking Argentinian pitch, another unappealing opening match. Both sides had declined since 1974. Kaltz was no sweeper, Bonhof no midfield general, Lubanski at last played in the World Cup finals but was past his best. Few chances were made and for the fourth time in a row the tournament began with a goalless draw. Schön, proving that the British don't have a monopoly on classic understatement, called it 'a poor game'.

■ 2 June 1978 • Cordiviola, Rosario • 17,396 • John Gordon (SCO)

▲ **TUNISIA (0) 3**
Kaabi 55, Ghommidh 80, Dhouib 86
MEXICO (1) 1
Vázquez Ayala, pen 45

● TUNISIA *Mokhtar Naili, Mokhtar Dhouib, Ali Kaabi, Amar Jebali, Nejib Ghommidh, 'Jendoubi' (Mohsen Labidi), Temime Lahzami (c) [Khemais Labidi 88], 'Agrebi' (Mohammed Ben Rehaien), Mohammed Ali Akid, Tarak Dhiab, Abderraouf Ben Aziza [Slah Karoui 70].* Abdelmajid Chetali.

   MEXICO *José Pilar Reyes, Jesús Martínez, Eduardo Ramos, Alfredo Tena, Arturo Vázquez Ayala (c), Guillermo Mendizábal [Gerardo Lugo 67], Antonio de la Torre, Leonardo Cuéllar, Victor Rangel, Hugo Sánchez, Raúl Isiordia.* José Antonio Roca.

Tunisia became the first African country to win a finals match, went top of the group, and thoroughly deserved it. Even a dubious penalty, awarded at a critical time, didn't faze them. Tarak looked one of the best players in the tournament and the defenders came up skilfully in attack. Roca agreed that Mexico had been pitiful: 'I think our supporters overestimated our chances.' Temime and Tarak were generally known by their first names.

■ 6 June 1978 • Chateau Carreras, Córdoba • 35,258 • Faruk Bouzo (SYR)

▲ **WEST GERMANY (4) 6**
D. Müller 14, H. Müller 29, Rummenigge 38, 71, Flohe 44, 89
MEXICO (0) 0

● W. GERMANY *Maier, Vogts (c), Bernard Dietz, Bonhof, Rüssmann, Kaltz, Flohe, Dieter Müller, Fischer, H. Müller, Karl-Heinz Rummenigge.*
MEXICO *Pilar Reyes [Pedro Soto 42], Tena, Ramos, Vázquez Ayala (c), Mendizábal, De la Torre, Martínez, Enrique López Zarza [Lugo HT], Sánchez, Cuéllar, Rangel.*

For a side with a modicum of World Cup pedigree, Mexico were an embarrassment. After bungling a free-kick outside the German penalty area, they allowed Rummenigge to run unchallenged into their own before scoring. The Müllers (no relation to Gerd or each other) scored with a ground shot and a cross shot, Rummenigge from a pull-back, Flohe twice from long range as well as hitting both posts with another shot. Some of the running and shooting was irresistible, but Mexico made the midfield a tackle-free zone and were no sort of yardstick. Dietz's first name is spelt correctly (i.e. not Bernhard).

■ 6 June 1978 • Cordiviola, Rosario • 9,624 • Angel Martínez (SPA)

▲ **POLAND (1) 1**
Lato 42
TUNISIA (0) 0

● POLAND *Tomaszewski, Szymanowski, Maculewicz, Kasperczak, Gorgon, Zmuda, Lato, Nawalka, Szarmach [Andrzej Iwan 59], Deyna (c), Lubanski [Boniek 75].*
TUNISIA *Naïli, Jebali, Dhouib, Kaabi, Khaled Gasmi, Jendoubi, Ghommidh, Temime (c), Agrebi, Tarak, Akid.*

Tunisia, showing that their previous result was no fluke, raised their game and were often the better team, Lahzami hitting the bar, Zmuda working overtime on his 24th birthday. But a blunder at the other end decided it, Kaabi missing his kick as the ball dropped over him, the opportunist Lato volleying in.

■ 10 June 1978 • Chateau Carreras, Córdoba • 30,667 • César Orozco (PER)

▲ **TUNISIA 0**
WEST GERMANY 0

● TUNISIA *Naïli, Jebali, Dhouib, Kaabi, Gasmi, Jendoubi, Ghommidh, Temime (c), Agrebi, Tarak, Akid [Ben Aziza 82].*
W. GERMANY *Maier, Vogts (c), Dietz, Bonhof, Rüssmann, Kaltz, Flohe, D. Müller, Fischer, H. Müller, Rummenigge.*

West Germany would have won but for some fine saves by Naïli (playing in place of the veteran Attouga), especially when Fischer was clean through in the second half – but Tunisia deserved the draw. Again they'd lost little in comparison with a major European team. 'The world has laughed at Africa,'

said their manager, 'but now the mockery is over.' The Germans were to agree with that even more wholeheartedly in 1982.

■ 10 June 1978 • Cordiviola, Rosario • 22,651 • Jafar Namdar (IRN)

▲ **POLAND (1) 3**
Boniek 42, 83, Deyna 56
MEXICO (0) 1
Rangel 51

● POLAND *Tomaszewski, Szymanowski, Masztaler, Gorgon, Zmuda, Lato, Kasperczak, Boniek, Deyna (c), Wojciech Rudy [Maculewicz 84], Iwan [Lubanski 75].*
MEXICO *Soto, Vázquez Ayala (c), De la Torre, Cristóbal Ortega, Rigoberto Cisneros, Carlos Gómez, Sánchez, Ignacio Flóres, Cuéllar, Rangel, Javier Cárdenas [Mendizábal HT].*

Even against a demoralized side with little to offer, Poland had to work harder than they would have in 1974, needing two tremendous long shots from Deyna and the new young star Boniek. Cuéllar, with his huge afro and good passing, was again more visible than the two players from whom much had been expected, Rangel and the 19-year-old Sánchez. Mexico were the most persuasive case yet for the abolition of zonal qualification, which they were still using to reach the finals 20 years later. Flores' brother Luis played in the 1986 finals.

GROUP 2	P	W	D	L	F	A	PTS
Poland	3	2	1	0	4	1	5
W. Germany	3	1	2	0	6	0	4
Tunisia	3	1	1	1	3	2	3
Mexico	3	0	0	3	2	12	0

Poland and West Germany qualified for the second round.

Group 3

Austria, Brazil, Spain, Sweden

■ 3 June 1978 • José Amalfitani, Buenos Aires • 40,841 • Károly Palotai (HUN)

▲ **AUSTRIA (1) 2**
Schachner 10, Krankl 79
SPAIN (1) 1
Dani 21

● AUSTRIA *Fritz Koncilia, Robert Sara (c), Gerhard Breitenberger, Josef Hickersberger [Heribert Weber 67], Erich Obermayer, Bruno Pezzey, Walter Schachner [Hans Pirkner 80], Herbert Prohaska, Hans Krankl, Willi Kreuz, Kurt Jara. Helmut Senekowitsch.*
SPAIN *Miguel Angel (González), Marcelino (Pérez), Jesús de la Cruz, Isidoro San José, 'Migueli' (Miguel Bernardo), 'Pirri' (José Martínez) (c), 'Dani' (Daniel Ruíz Bazán), Julio Cardeñosa [Eugenio Leal HT], Rubén Cano, Juan Manuel Asensi, Carlos Rexach ['Quini' (Enrique Castro) 60]. Ladislav Kubala (HUN).*

Austria, slight underdogs, opened with a spectacular goal, Schachner running up the right wing, swerving outside his man and beating Miguel Angel high at his near post. Dani equalized with a low shot that Koncilia should have saved, but the dangerous Krankl (six goals in one of the qualifiers) was quick to sidefoot in a rebound. Austria also hit a post. Weber's first name is correct (i.e. not Herbert).

■ 3 June 1978 • Parque Municipal, Mar del Plata • 38,618 • Clive Thomas (WAL)

▲ **BRAZIL (1) 1**
Reinaldo 45
SWEDEN (1) 1
Sjöberg 37

● BRAZIL *Emerson Leão, 'Toninho' (Antônio Dias), 'Edinho' (Edino Nazareth), José Batista, Oscar (Bernardi), João Amaral, 'Gil' (Gilberto Alves) ['Nelinho' (Manoel Rezende de Matos) 67], 'Zico' (Arthur Antunes Coimbra), Reinaldo (de Lima), Toninho Cerezo [Dirceu (Guimarães) 80], Roberto Rivelino (c). Cláudio Coutinho.*
SWEDEN *Ronnie Hellström, Hasse Borg, Ingemar Erlandsson, Staffan Tapper, Roy Andersson, Björn Nordqvist (c), Lennart Larsson [Ralf Edström 79], Anders Linderoth, Bo Larsson, Thomas Sjöberg, Benny Wendt. Georg 'Åby' Ericsson.*

Brazil had shown their current colours in collecting five yellow cards at Wembley, where someone should have been sent off. Here they were less violent but equally uninspired – Rivelino not the force of old, Zico completely off form. The bearded Sjöberg stabbed the ball home when a flick caught the defence square, but Reinaldo equalized after winning the ball from Cerezo's long high cross. The game ended in farcical controversy. When Zico headed in a corner, the goal was disallowed because time had run out – after only eight seconds of injury-time. The decision, which looked typical of Thomas, was his last in the finals. Nordqvist's 109th cap broke Bobby Moore's world record.

[Right] Clive Thomas points out the exact second his World Cup career ended. Nelinho, Rivelino and Edinho try and take it in.

[Below] Zico (8) heads in a last-minute corner against Sweden, but Brazil's glee is short-lived as the goal is disallowed.

■ 7 June 1978 • José Amalfitani, Buenos Aires •
41,424 • Charles Corver (HOL)

▲ **AUSTRIA (1) 1**
Krankl pen 44
SWEDEN (0) 0

● AUSTRIA *Koncilia, Sara (c), Breitenberger, Hickersberger, Obermayer, Pezzey, Edi Krieger [Weber 71], Prohaska, Krankl, Kreuz, Jara.*
SWEDEN *Hellström, Borg, Erlandsson, Tapper [Conny Torstensson 37], Andersson, Nordqvist (c), L. Larsson, Linderoth [Edström 60], Sjöberg, B. Larsson, Wendt.*

Even when Edström came on, Sweden offered little up front and were again grateful to Hellström, who saved everything Krankl threw at him except the penalty, awarded when he was brought down by Nordqvist. Austria, unexpectedly, were already in the second round.

■ 7 June 1978 • Parque Municipal, Mar del Plata •
34,771 • Sergio Gonella (ITA)

▲ **BRAZIL 0**
SPAIN 0

● BRAZIL *Leão (c), Nelinho [Gil 70], Edinho, Batista, Oscar, Amaral, Zico [Jorge Mendonça 84], Reinaldo, Cerezo, Dirceu, Toninho.*
SPAIN *Miguel Angel, Marcelino, Antonio Olmo, San José, Migueli [Antonio Biosca 51], Cardeñosa, 'Uria' (Francisco Javier Alvarez) [Antonio Guzmán 59], Leal, 'Santillana' (Carlos Alonso), Asensi (c), 'Juanito' (Juan Gómez).*

Again the appalling Mar del Plata pitch didn't help Brazil's passing game and Spain really should have won. Santillana, marvellous in the air for a man of medium height, won the ball in a challenge with

Leão, only for Cardeñosa to shoot straight at Amaral on the line. The latter, a purely defensive sweeper, was Brazil's best player, but that wasn't saying too much. They played a full-back on the wing (Toninho, on his 30th birthday) in place of the disappointing Gil.

■ 11 June 1978 • José Amalfitani, Buenos Aires •
42,132 • Ferdinand Biwersi (WG)

▲ **SPAIN (0) 1**
Asensi 75
SWEDEN (0) 0

● SPAIN *Miguel Angel, Marcelino, Olmo [Pirri HT], San José, Biosca, Cardeñosa, Uria, Leal, Asensi (c), Juanito, Santillana.*
SWEDEN *Hellström, Borg, Erlandsson, Olle Nordin, Andersson, Nordqvist (c), L. Larsson, B. Larsson, Edström [Wendt 60], Sjöberg [Linderoth 66], Torbjörn Nilsson.*

Sweden went out without glory, making little use of Edström's height. Asensi, whose father Vicente played in the 1950 finals, smacked in the only goal from an opening made by Juanito. Too little too late for Spain, who were already looking ahead to 'their' World Cup in four years' time.

■ 11 June 1978 • Parque Municipal, Mar del Plata • 35,221 • Robert Wurtz (FRA)

▲ **BRAZIL (1) 1**
Roberto Dinamite 40
AUSTRIA (0) 0

● BRAZIL *Leão (c), Toninho, José Rodrigues Neto, Batista, Oscar, Amaral, Gil, Cerezo ['Chicão' (Francisco Avanzi) 71], 'Roberto Dinamite' (Roberto de Oliveira), Dirceu, Mendonça [Zico 84].*
AUSTRIA *Koncilia, Sara (c), Breitenberger, Hickersberger [Weber 61], Obermayer, Pezzey, Krieger [Günther Happich 84], Prohaska, Krankl, Kreuz, Jara.*

No Zico, Rivelino or Reinaldo, but a slight improvement from Brazil, albeit against a team that didn't need a result. Dirceu provided some leadership in midfield and Roberto, bigger and stronger than Reinaldo, cracked in Gil's long cross when Pezzey left him badly unmarked. Enough to qualify (a goalless draw would have knocked them out) but not to set any pulses racing, especially in the Argentinian camp.

GROUP 3	P	W	D	L	F	A	PTS
Austria	3	2	0	1	3	2	4
Brazil	3	1	2	0	2	1	4
Spain	3	1	1	1	2	2	3
Sweden	3	0	1	2	1	3	1

Austria and Brazil qualified for the second round.

Group 4

Holland, Iran, Peru, Scotland

■ 3 June 1978 • Chateau Carreras, Córdoba • 37,792 • Ulf Eriksson (SWE)

▲ **PERU (1) 3**
Cueto 43, Cubillas 70, 76
SCOTLAND (1) 1
Jordan 19

● PERU *Ramón Quiroga, Rodolfo Manzo, Jaime Duarte, José Velásquez, Toribio Díaz, Héctor Chumpitáz (c), Juan José Muñante, César Cueto [Percy Rojas 82], Guillermo La Rosa [Hugo Sotil 62], Teófilo Cubillas, Juan Carlos Oblitas. Marcos Calderón.*
SCOTLAND *Allan Rough, Stuart Kennedy, Martin Buchan, Bruce Rioch (c) [Archie Gemmill 70], Kenny Burns, Tom Forsyth, Kenny Dalglish, Asa Hartford, Joe Jordan, Don Masson [Lou Macari 70], Willie Johnston. Ally MacLeod.*

Ally MacLeod, Scotland's manager, perhaps responding to those who considered him short on international experience.

Scotland started as they expected to go on, Jordan putting in the loose ball when Rioch's shot was saved – but then the roof fell in on the house Ally built.

There was talk of the 'ageing' Cubillas being past his best, but he was only 29 – younger than either Rioch or Masson, who were in poor form with Derby County. Cubillas and Cueto ran the midfield and Peru also had weapons up front. Rinus Michels had warned against their wingers Oblitas and Muñante 'who are two of the fastest and most dangerous in the competition'. Muñante, in fact, was considered so valuable that the Peruvian FA paid his Mexican club an insurance premium to secure his services. Against these two, MacLeod picked Buchan, a composed central defender but too slow for a full-back, and the rookie Kennedy. The result was a shambles. It's said that the sum total of MacLeod's half-time team talk was to urge Rough to kick the ball harder to clear the Peruvian midfield!

Quiroga made an important fingertip save from a Dalglish lob, but the Peruvian one-twos had their reward when Cueto scored from close in. In the second half, a lifeline was thrown in the form of a penalty when Cubillas was judged to have brought down Rioch. Masson, whose spot-kick had taken Scotland to the finals, hit this one to the same side but Quiroga made a comfortable save. MacLeod took off Masson and Rioch, but it was too late. Macari, the smallest player on the pitch, was on the end of the wall when Cubillas caressed a free-kick over him with the outside of his foot. That was the clinching goal; a few minutes later he hit the winner from even longer range.

MacLeod used the press conference to blame his players rather than his own preparation ('eight of them didn't play') and the Scottish nightmare was compounded when Johnston was sent home for taking a banned substance. The level to which the team's standing had fallen was expressed by a Dutch journalist when told that Burns was the current Footballer of the Year in England: 'you are pulling my trousers'.

■ 3 June 1978 • San Martín, Mendoza • 33,431 • Alfonso Archundia (MEX)

▲ **HOLLAND (1) 3**
Rensenbrink pen 40,62, pen 78
IRAN (0) 0

● HOLLAND *Jan Jongbloed, Wim Suurbier, Wim Rijsbergen, Wim Jansen, Ruud Krol (c), Willy van de Kerkhof, Johan Neeskens, Arie Haan, René van de Kerkhof [Dick Nanninga 71], Johnny Rep, Rob Rensenbrink.* Ernst Happel (AUT). IRAN *Nasser Hejazi, Hassan Nazari, Nasrullah Abdollahi, Hossein Kazerani, Andranik Eskandarian, Ali Parvin (c), Ebrahim Ghasempour, Muhamad Sadeghi, Hassan Naybagha, Hossein Faraki [Hassan Roshan 52], Ghafoor Djahani.* Heshmat Mohajerani.

After testing positive for a banned substance, Willie Johnston contemplates the end of his Scotland career. Reserve goalkeeper Bobby Clark puts a brave (or something) face on it.

As expected, Holland weren't as good as in 1974, but it didn't matter against a defence that gave away too many free-kicks and penalties. Rensenbrink, doing his best to put on Cruyff's mantle, sent the keeper the wrong way with both spot-kicks and headed in a cross from the right by René van de Kerkhof, who was fouled for the first penalty, Rep for the other. The van de Kerkhofs were twins.

■ 7 June 1978 • San Martín, Mendoza • 28,125 • Adolf Prokop (EG)

▲ **HOLLAND 0**
PERU 0

● HOLLAND *Jongbloed, Suurbier, Rijsbergen, Krol (c), Jan Poortvliet, Neeskens [Nanninga 69], Wim Jansen, Haan, W. van de Kerkhof, R. van de Kerkhof [Rep HT], Rensenbrink.*
PERU *Quiroga, Manzo, Duarte, Velásquez, Díaz, Chumpitáz (c), Muñante, Cueto, La Rosa [Sotil 62], Cubillas, Oblitas.*

As in 1974, the Dutch were happy to play out a goalless draw after winning their first match, using the defensive young Poortvliet in place of Rep. Neither Jongbloed (back again at the age of 37) nor Quiroga had much to do.

■ 7 June 1978 • Chateau Carreras, Córdoba • 7,938 • Youssou Ndiaye (SEN)

▲ **IRAN (0) 1**
Danaifar 60
SCOTLAND (1) 1
Eskandarian o.g. 43

● IRAN *Hejazi, Nazari, Abdollahi, Kazerani, Eskandarian, Parvin (c), Ghasempour, Sadeghi, Iraj Danaifar [Naybagha 89], Faraki [Roshan 83], Djahani.*
SCOTLAND *Rough, William 'Sandy' Jardine, Willie Donachie, Hartford, Burns, Buchan [Forsyth 57], Macari, Gemmill (c), Dalglish [Joe Harper 73], Jordan, John Robertson.*

Scotland's stock crashed even lower, making them the butts of the tournament. Buchan had to go off after having his head cut by Donachie (!) and even their goal was a joke, Eskandarian sticking out a leg after a collision with Jordan. Coming when it did, that should have deflated Iran, but they were well worth their draw, Danaifar holding off Jardine and beating Rough with a low shot at the near post. Dalglish (again) and Robertson were anonymous, but no-one else exactly covered himself in glory. As their bus pulled away after the match, it was serenaded by their own fans singing 'you only want the money'. Back in Britain, the squad was being used to advertise Chrysler cars, a TV ad showing them heading the ball over various vehicles. The prime slot, which must have looked a safe bet, was at half-time in the Iran match. The slogan: 'Both run rings round the opposition'.

Only a small crowd turn up to watch Scotland's untidy performance against Iran.

■ 11 June 1978 • San Martín, Mendoza •
35,130 • Erich Linemayr (AUT)

▲ **SCOTLAND (1) 3**
Dalglish 44, Gemmill pen 46, 68
HOLLAND (1) 2
Rensenbrink pen 34, Rep 71

● SCOTLAND *Rough, Kennedy, Donachie, Rioch (c), Forsyth, Buchan, Gemmill, Hartford, Jordan, Graeme Souness, Dalglish.*
HOLLAND *Jongbloed, Suurbier, Rijsbergen [Piet Wildschut 44], Krol (c), Poortvliet, Neeskens [Jan Boskamp 10], Jansen, Rep, R. van de Kerkhof, W. van de Kerkhof, Rensenbrink.*

A month earlier, Souness had made the goal that won Liverpool the European Cup. MacLeod, who admitted he should have played him against Iran, now sent out the midfield line-up that had been crying out to be picked – and suddenly we were reminded that Jekyll and Hyde was written by a Scot. Amazingly, the Jekylls could still qualify; there was just the little matter of beating Holland by three goals. Even with no luck on their side, they came naggingly close.

Rioch headed against the bar, Dalglish had a goal disallowed, and Jordan might have had a penalty, but Holland got one instead when Kennedy fouled Rep. Rensenbrink converted it (the 1,000th goal scored in the World Cup finals) and there was less than an hour left.

To their enormous credit Scotland didn't give up. Souness hit a high cross to the far post, where Jordan headed down to the unmarked Dalglish who volleyed nervelessly past Jongbloed's arms and legs. Then Souness was bundled over by Willy K. for a penalty. Two goals a minute either side of the interval set up a momentum which Gemmill maintained with one of the best goals in any World Cup. Picking up a loose ball on the right of the Dutch penalty area, he came inside Jansen's lunge, beat Krol on the outside, pushed the ball between Poortvliet's legs, and lifted it over the advancing

Two views of Gemmill's marvellous individual goal against Holland, taking the ball past Poortvliet (2) and clipping it over Jongbloed as René K. arrives too late.

keeper. One more goal and the impossible would be astounding reality.

But Holland, who'd been going through the motions a little after an early injury to Neeskens, roused themselves to score as if on demand. Running through the middle, Rep hit a long-range shot that faded past Rough's right hand, and there was no way back for Scotland. They'd restored some dignity but added to the frustration at what had gone before.

Masson, Rioch, Macari (banned for speaking his mind), Forsyth and Johnston weren't capped again. Remarkably, the Scottish FA allowed MacLeod to keep his job, but he resigned after one more match. It was the last time anything was expected of Scotland in the World Cup.

■ 11 June 1978 • Chateau Carreras, Córdoba • 21,262 • Alojzy Jarguz (POL)

▲ **PERU (3) 4**
Velásquez 2, Cubillas pen 36, pen 39, 79
IRAN (1) 1
Roshan 41

● PERU *Quiroga, Manzo [Germán Leguía 68], Duarte, Velásquez, Díaz, Chumpitáz (c), Muñante, Cueto, La Rosa [Sotil 60], Cubillas, Oblitas.*
IRAN *Hejazi, Nazari, Abdollahi, Kazerani, Javad Allahvardi, Parvin (c), Ghasempour, Sadeghi, Danaifar, Faraki [Djahani 52], Roshan [Behtash Fariba 66].*

Any faint hopes that Iran might do the Scots a favour were extinguished very early, Velásquez heading in Muñante's corner from 12 yards. After that the Iranians fell into their habit of conceding penalties; the first harshly awarded for a shoulder charge on Oblitas, the other when Hejazi brought down Cubillas. Faraki forced a good save from Quiroga and Roshan scored with a low volley, but Cubillas

kicked in a rebound for his tenth goal in World Cup finals. Peru's passing was again good to watch, but no-one had seriously tested their defence.

GROUP 4	P	W	D	L	F	A	PTS
Peru	3	2	1	0	7	2	5
Holland	3	1	1	1	5	3	3
Scotland	3	1	1	1	5	6	3
Iran	3	0	1	2	2	8	1

Peru and Holland qualified for the second round.

2nd Round Group A

Austria, Holland, Italy, West Germany.

■ 14 June 1978 • Monumental, Buenos Aires • 67,547 • Dusan Maksimovic (YUG)

▲ **ITALY 0**
WEST GERMANY 0

● ITALY *Zoff (c), Gentile, Cabrini, Benetti, Bellugi, Scirea, Causio, Tardelli, Rossi, Antognoni [Zaccarelli HT], Bettega*
W. GERMANY *Maier, Vogts (c), Dietz, Bonhof, Rüssmann, Kaltz, Rummenigge, Zimmermann [Harald Konopka 53], Fischer, Flohe [Beer 68], Bernd Hölzenbein.*

A match Italy were disappointed not to win. They might have had a penalty when Kaltz appeared to handle a shot from Bettega, whose finishing was a fraction out all day, especially when he chested down a cross and poked the ball wide from close in. Cabrini hit the bar and Antognoni outplayed Bonhof. Fischer seemed to be fouled in the area by Bellugi, but a German goal would have been a travesty.

Uruguay 1930, the first World Cup winners. (l–r) standing: *trainer Ernesto Figoli, Gestido, Nasazzi, Ballestrero, Mascheroni, Andrade, Fernández, masseur Greco;* kneeling: *Dorado, Scarone, Castro (hiding his missing hand), Cea, Iriarte.*

The official poster for the 1950 tournament.

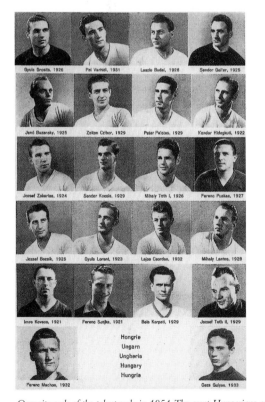

Opposite ends of the talent scale in 1954. The great Hungarians and the not-so-great South Koreans, who lost to them 9-0.

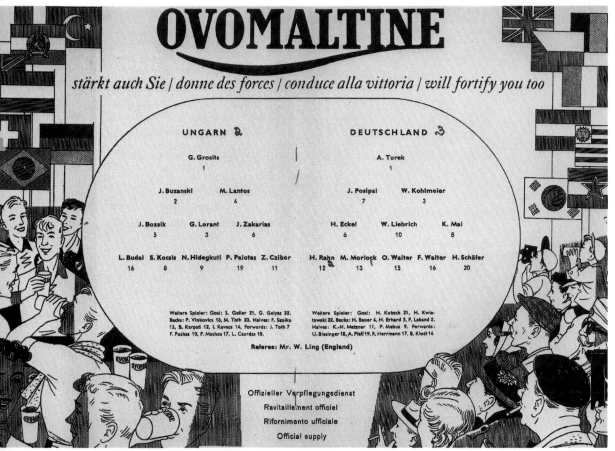

OVOMALTINE

stärkt auch Sie / donne des forces / conduce alla vittoria / will fortify you too

UNGARN					DEUTSCHLAND			

UNGARN

G. Grosits
1

J. Buzanski — M. Lantos
2 — 4

J. Bozsik — G. Lorant — J. Zakarias
5 — 3 — 6

L. Budai — S. Kocsis — N. Hidegkuti — P. Palotas — Z. Czibor
16 — 8 — 9 — 19 — 11

DEUTSCHLAND

A. Turek
1

J. Posipal — W. Kohlmeier
7 — 3

H. Eckel — W. Liebrich — K. Mai
6 — 10 — 8

H. Rahn — M. Morlock — O. Walter — F. Walter — H. Schäfer
12 — 13 — 15 — 16 — 20

Weitere Spieler: Goal: S. Geller 21, G. Gulyas 22.
Backs: P. Vinkovics 13, M. Toth 20. Halves: F. Szolka
15, B. Karpati 12, I. Kovacs 14. Forwards: J. Toth 7
F. Puskas 10, F. Machos 17, L. Csordas 18.

Weitere Spieler: Goal: H. Kubsch 21, H. Kwia-
towski 22. Backs: H. Bauer 4, H. Erhard 5, F. Laband 2.
Halves: K.-H. Metzner 11, P. Mebus 9. Forwards:
U. Biesinger 18, A. Pfaff 19, R. Herrmann 17, B. Klodt 14

Referee: Mr. W. Ling (England)

Offizieller Verpflegungsdienst
Ravitaillement officiel
Rifornimento ufficiale
Official supply

The rather whimsical programme for the 1954 Final, showing the anticipated absence of Puskás in the Hungarian line-up.

Antonio Rattin (third from right) is sent off at Wembley in 1966. The England players are Moore (6) and Peters.

WHITE CITY STADIUM
LONDON

WORLD CHAMPIONSHIP
1966
Jules Rimet Cup

EIGHTH FINAL

SECRETARY.
THE FOOTBALL ASSOCIATION

BLOCK
L
STAND
ENTRANCE
12
2897

FRIDAY JULY 15
KICK-OFF 7.30 p.m.

STANDING ENCLOSURE 7/6

(SEE PLAN & CONDITIONS ON BACK)

ENTRANCE
WESTWAY

A ticket for France v Uruguay in 1966, the only World Cup match played at the White City Stadium, which no longer exists. Every group match was an 'eighth final'.

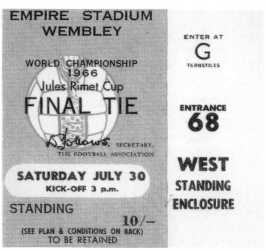

Sir Alf, most certainly the top manager in 1966.

A ticket for the 1966 Final, price 50p.

30 July 1966. Wilson struggles to uphold Moore, who has no such trouble with the gold statuette, flanked by (l–r) Little Nobby and Big Jack, Banksie, Ballie, Peters, the hidden Hunt, Hurst, George Cohen and a tired but happy Bobby Charlton. England – the World Champions.

An advert from 1970. Join a supporters club and meet girls. Yeh, right.

The king and the defender of the faith. Pelé and Bobby Moore after the England-Brazil match in 1970.

A ticket for the England v Brazil match of 1970.

Gérson, who scored Brazil's winning goal, looking older and wearier after the 1970 Final.

Burgnich looks back in anguish as Pelé celebrates his goal in the 1970 Final.

Holland used the same starting line-up in five of their matches in 1974. (l–r): Neeskens, Krol, van Hanegem, Jansen, Suurbier, Rep, Rijsbergen, Rensenbrink, Haan, Jongbloed, Cruyff.

Johan Neeskens blasts home the first penalty in the 1974 Final.

Johan Cruyff had the football world at his feet – until the 1974 Final.

Teófilo Cubillas of Peru (right), a star of the 1970 and 1978 tournaments.

The Kaiser rules, OK. Franz Beckenbauer lifts the new trophy in 1974.

Kenny Dalglish volleys Scotland's first goal in their surprise win over Holland in 1978.

Holland v Italy 1978. Wim Jansen fears for the safety of Ernie Brandts, who receives some typically close attention from Gentile (5) and the fearsome Benetti.

A blizzard of tickertape, one of the abiding memories of Argentina in '78.

Angry Algerian fans wave banknotes as Austria and West Germany go through the motions in 1982.

Polish fans with a Solidarity banner in 1982. The trade union's leader went on to become president of Poland.

The price of fame. Diego Maradona faces a crowd of Belgians in 1982.

The first missed penalty in a World Cup Final. Antonio Cabrini shoots wide in 1982.

Claudio Gentile (left) joins in Marco Tardelli's memorable celebration of his winning goal in the 1982 Final.

Two of Brazil's most skilful players, Júnior and the bearded Sócrates, celebrate the goal against Spain in 1986.

Palm Sunday. Maradona's first goal against England in 1986.

Time to stop shouldering the responsibility. Bryan Robson goes off injured in the match against Morocco in 1986.

Rudi Völler heads West Germany's equalizer in the 1986 Final against Argentina.

Toto Schillaci celebrates his first goal of the 1990 tournament.

The price of fame again. Ruud Gullit held back by Mark Wright in 1990. The idea of paper football shirts may yet catch on.

What's the collective noun for a group of celebrating Cameroonians? Omam Biyick and Roger Milla jump for joy in 1990.

Pat Bonner makes the penalty save that sends the Republic of Ireland into the quarter-finals in 1990.

The spitting image of a great player. Frank Rijkaard (left) and an unsuspecting Rudi Völler are sent off in 1990.

Van der Elst (8) and Gerets (2) are helpless as David Platt volleys England's last-minute winner against Belgium in 1990.

Gazza cried all the way to the bank after Italia '90.

Gary Lineker scored ten goals in the finals, twice as many as any other British player. Here he celebrates the last, against West Germany in 1990.

Comrades in arms. Brehme (left) and Augenthaler after the win over England in the 1990 semi-final.

Ray Houghton's long lob sails in for the Republic of Ireland's goal against Italy in 1994. Gianluca Pagliuca (extreme left) can only wave it on its way.

Houghton turns a somersault after his winning goal against Italy. Terry Phelan, who's never scored for Ireland, wonders how it's done.

Courting the net. Rashidi Yekini savours his goal for Nigeria against Bulgaria in 1994.

Ed de Goey and Ronald Koeman (4) protest Bebeto's controversial goal for Brazil in the 1994 quarter-final.

Saïd Owairan goes past Dirk Medved on the way to scoring a sensational goal for Saudi Arabia against Belgium in 1994.

The moment when Brazil win the World Cup for a record fourth time. Italy's number of wins remains at three as Roberto Baggio puts his penalty over the bar in the shoot-out following the 1994 Final.

■ 14 June 1978 • Chateau Carreras, Córdoba •
25,059 • John Gordon (SCO)

▲ **HOLLAND (3) 5**
Brandts 6, Rensenbrink pen 35, Rep 36, 53,
W. van de Kerkhof 82
AUSTRIA (0) 1
Obermayer 80

● HOLLAND *Piet Schrijvers, Wildschut, Ernie Brandts [Adri van Kraay 66], Haan, Krol (c), Poortvliet, R. van de Kerkhof [Dick Schoenaker 60], Jansen, Rep, W. van de Kerkhof, Rensenbrink.*
AUSTRIA *Koncilia, Sara (c), Breitenberger, Hickersberger, Obermayer, Pezzey, Krieger, Prohaska, Krankl, Kreuz, Jara.*

■ 18 June 1978 • Chateau Carreras, Córdoba •
40,750 • Ramón Barreto (URU)

▲ **HOLLAND (1) 2**
Haan 27, R. van de, Kerkhof 82
WEST GERMANY (1) 2
Abramczik 3, D. Müller 70

● HOLLAND *Schrijvers, Wildschut [Nanninga 79], Brandts, Haan, Krol (c), Poortvliet, Jansen, W. van de Kerkhof, R. van de Kerkhof, Rep, Rensenbrink.*
W. GERMANY *Maier, Vogts (c), Dietz, Bonhof, Rüssmann, Kaltz, Rummenigge, Beer, D. Müller, Hölzenbein, Abramczik.*
▼ SENT OFF: *Nanninga 89.*

An unexpected and slightly exaggerated scoreline, but Holland were certainly on top throughout. The unmarked Brandts, winning his second cap, headed in Haan's free-kick, and Jansen was bodychecked by Prohaska for the penalty. Some poor defence let in Rep to lob the third, Rensenbrink presented him with an open goal for the fourth and set up Willy K. for the fifth. Even Austria's goal was an embarrassment, Obermayer's almost vertical lob somehow dropping in at the far post. The arrival of the Austrian players' wives raised a few smirks, but it hadn't done the Dutch any harm four years earlier.

The champions, shedding their recent poor form, contributed fully to an exciting match. Abramczik scored with a diving header after Schrijvers had saved Bonhof's free-kick, and Müller headed in Beer's cross from the left. Haan's 30-yarder left Maier standing, Rep thrashed the ball against the bar, and René K. rescued the Dutch by cutting inside Kaltz and swerving the ball round Maier. The giant blond Rüssmann handled the ball on the line but couldn't keep it out. Holland still hadn't beaten West Germany since 1956 but remained top of the group.

Nanninga was the first substitute to be sent off in a World Cup tournament (for laughing at a refereeing decision). The van de Kerkhofs weren't identical twins but scored their goals in the same minute of different matches.

■ 18 June 1978 • Monumental, Buenos Aires • 40,000 • Francis Rion (BEL)

▲ **ITALY (1) 1**
Rossi 13
AUSTRIA (0) 0

● ITALY *Zoff (c), Gentile, Cabrini, Benetti, Bellugi [Cuccureddu HT], Scirea, Causio, Tardelli, Rossi, Zaccarelli, Bettega [Graziani 71].*
AUSTRIA *Koncilia, Sara (c), Heinrich Strasser, Krieger, Hickersberger, Obermayer, Pezzey, Prohaska, Krankl, Kreuz, Schachner [Pirkner 63].*

Italy's goal had some skilful beginnings but needed a little help. Rossi backheeled to Causio, Strasser got to the return pass first but let Rossi nick it away from him to score with a low cross-shot. Graziani missed a good late chance. The official attendance figure was 66,695.

■ 21 June 1978 • Chateau Carreras, Córdoba • 38,318 • Avraham Klein (ISR)

▲ **AUSTRIA (0) 3**
Vogts o.g. 59, Krankl 66, 88
WEST GERMANY (1) 2
Rummenigge 19, Hölzenbein 67,

● AUSTRIA *Koncilia, Sara (c), Strasser, Krieger, Hickersberger, Obermayer, Pezzey, Prohaska, Krankl, Kreuz, Schachner [Franz Oberacher 71].*
W. GERMANY *Maier, Vogts (c), Dietz, Bonhof, Rüssmann, Kaltz, Rummenigge, Beer [H. Müller HT], D. Müller [Fischer 60], Hölzenbein, Abramczik.*

Even if the other result went their way, West Germany would have to win by four goals to reach the Final. Instead they lost to Austria for the first time since 1931, thanks to an own goal by their captain, the little white terrier who'd kept Cruyff quiet in 1974 but was now playing his 96th and last international. Krankl regained his goal touch when it didn't matter, scoring with a glorious volley and a cool dribble. Rummenigge converted Dieter Müller's pass and Hölzenbein headed in Bonhof's free-kick. Schön, in the last match of his hugely successful career, had been making bricks without straw.

■ 21 June 1978 • Monumental, Buenos Aires • 67,433 • Angel Martínez (SPA)

▲ **HOLLAND (0) 2**
Brandts 49, Haan 76
ITALY (1) 1
Brandts o.g. 19

● HOLLAND *Schrijvers [Jongbloed 21], Poortvliet, Brandts, Neeskens, Haan, Krol (c), Jansen, W. van de Kerkhof, Rep [van Kraay 65], R. van de Kerkhof, Rensenbrink.*
ITALY *Zoff (c), Cuccureddu, Cabrini, Benetti [Graziani 77], Gentile, Scirea, Causio [Claudio Sala HT], Tardelli, Rossi, Zaccarelli, Bettega.*

Holland needed only a draw but Italy came within two long shots of winning. Benetti sent Bettega through and Brandts came in from behind to knock the ball past Schrijvers, who was injured in the collision. Italy created chances throughout the half, but when Benetti ran his rule down Rensenbrink's leg he was booked for the second time in the tournament, which would keep him out of the Final. Italy's spirit drained away with him.

Even so, it took a ferocious 20-yarder from Brandts, the only player to score for both sides in a finals match, to put Holland in charge; that and some typical tackling. Neeskens should have been sent off, kicking Zaccarelli so hard you could hear the impact on the other side of the ground. But it was difficult to feel sympathy for a team that included Benetti and Tardelli in the same midfield. Haan, from preposterously long range, sealed Holland's place in the Final, but Italy wouldn't have looked out of place there.

GROUP A	P	W	D	L	F	A	PTS
Holland	3	2	1	0	9	4	5
Italy	3	1	1	1	2	2	3
W. Germany	3	0	2	1	4	5	2
Austria	3	1	0	2	4	8	2

Holland qualified for the Final, Italy for the 3rd-place Final.

Group B

Argentina, Brazil, Peru, Poland

■ 14 June 1978 • San Martín, Mendoza • 31,278 • Nicolae Rainea (ROM)

▲ **BRAZIL (2) 3**
Direu 15, 27, Zico pen 72
PERU (0) 0

● BRAZIL *Leão (c), Toninho, Rodrigues Neto, Batista, Oscar, Amaral, Cerezo [Chicão 76], Gil [Zico 70], Roberto Dinamite, Dirceu, Mendonça.*
PERU *Quiroga, Manzo, Duarte, Velásquez, Díaz [José Navarro 11], Chumpitáz (c), Muñante, Cueto, La Rosa, Cubillas, Oblitas [Rojas HT].*

Better from Brazil, but Peru's non-tackling midfield was finally found out, wandering about in their afros like extras in a Shaft film. Dirceu scored the first with a long-range free-kick to the right of the Peruvian goal, the shot bending so much that it curled back inside the right-hand post. His second was a ground shot fumbled by Quiroga and Duarte conceded the penalty by tugging Roberto's shirt. Zico, who'd only just come on, made one of his few contributions to the tournament, but it was a cheap shot.

■ 14 June 1978 • Cordiviola, Rosario • 37,091 • Ulf Eriksson (SWE)

▲ **ARGENTINA (1) 2**
Kempes 16, 72
POLAND (0) 0

● ARGENTINA *Fillol, Olguin, Tarantini, Gallego, Galván, Passarella (c), Houseman [Ortíz 83], Valencia [Ricardo Villa HT], Ardiles, Kempes, Bertoni.*
POLAND *Tomaszewski, Szymanowski, Maculewicz, Masztaler [Wlodek Mazur 60], Zmuda, Nawalka, Lato, Kasperczak, Szarmach, Deyna (c), Boniek.*

With Luque still out injured, Kempes came into his own. The only player Menotti had brought back from Europe, he at last scored in a finals match (his eleventh). His first goal was a classic, a perfectly timed diagonal run to meet Bertoni's left-wing cross with a near-post header, and the second was in the same league, dragging the ball past a defender to shoot low past Tomaszewski. In between, seven minutes before half-time, he made another important contribution, handling on the line to stop Lato's header. Deyna, in his 100th international, hit the penalty too close to Fillol. Ardiles, the dapper playmaker with hair like a black beret, made Kempes' second goal.

■ 18 June 1978 • San Martín, Mendoza •
35,288 • Pat Partridge (ENG)

▲ **POLAND (0) 1**
Szarmach 64
PERU (0) 0

● POLAND *Zygmunt Kukla, Szymanowski, Maculewicz, Masztaler [Kasperczak HT], Gorgon, Zmuda, Nawalka, Lato, Szarmach, Deyna (c), Boniek [Lubanski 86].*
PERU *Quiroga, Manzo, Duarte, Navarro, Chumpitáz (c), Alfredo Quesada, Muñante [Rojas HT], Cueto, La Rosa [Sotil 74], Cubillas, Oblitas.*

The goal brought back memories (Lato's cross met by Szarmach's diving header) and Deyna hit a post – but the two poorest sides in the group played like it, though Quiroga was back on form.

■ 18 June 1978 • Cordiviola, Rosario • 37,326 •
Károly Palotai (HUN)

▲ **ARGENTINA 0**
BRAZIL 0

● ARGENTINA *Fillol, Olguin, Tarantini, Gallego, Galván, Passarella (c), Bertoni, Ardiles [Villa HT], Luque, Kempes, Ortíz [Alonso 61].*
BRAZIL *Leão (c), Toninho, Rodrigues Neto [Edinho 36], Batista, Oscar, Amaral, Gil, Chicão, Roberto Dinamite, Dirceu, Mendonça [Zico 68].*

The South American version of England v Scotland, except this was serious. Seventeen fouls in the first ten minutes, the restored Luque the first to flash his studs, Edinho lucky not to be sent off. Ardiles, whom John Motson called 'the ferret-faced little man', looked the coolest player on the pitch – so the

Brazilians gashed his ankle to let Villa join in. He was later Ardiles' skilful team-mate at Tottenham but behaved like a bearded version of Benetti here. Both sides had reasons to be fairly satisfied, but it wasn't one for the squeamish.

■ 21 June 1978 • San Martín, Mendoza •
39,586 • Juan Silvagno (CHI)

▲ **BRAZIL (1) 3**
Nelinho 13, Roberto Dinamite 58, 63
POLAND (1) 1
Lato 45

● BRAZIL *Leão (c), Toninho, Nelinho, Batista, Oscar, Amaral, Gil, Zico [Mendonça 7], Roberto Dinamite, Cerezo [Rivelino 75], Dirceu.*
POLAND *Kukla, Szymanowski, Maculewicz, Kasperczak [Lubanski 64], Gorgon, Zmuda, Nawalka, Lato, Szarmach, Deyna (c), Boniek.*

Poland hadn't given up hope of reaching the Final, and Lato's goal, exploiting some chaos in the penalty area, gave them a platform for the second half. But Roberto knocked in the rebound after Mendonça hit a post, then repeated the trick, scoring after the Polish woodwork had been hit three times. Before that, Nelinho's wildly over-optimistic shooting at last had its reward, his free-kick searing past Kukla. Dirceu, with his excellent left foot, had another good game. Zico went off injured before he had the chance to disappoint again.

■ 21 June 1978 • Cordiviola, Rosario • 37,326 • Robert Wurtz (FRA)

▲ **ARGENTINA (2) 6**
Kempes 21, 49, Tarantini 43, Luque 50, 72, Houseman 67
PERU (0) 0

● ARGENTINA *Fillol, Olguin, Tarantini, Gallego [Miguel Angel Oviedo 86], Galván, Passarella (c), Bertoni [Houseman 65], Omar Larrosa, Luque, Kempes, Ortíz.*
PERU *Quiroga, Manzo, Duarte, Roberto Rojas, Chumpitáz (c), Velásquez [Raúl Gorriti 52], Muñante, Cueto, Quesada, Cubillas, Oblitas.*

frightening intensity, small comfort for the death of his brother in a car crash during the tournament. The scoreline stopped Brazil reaching the final despite remaining unbeaten in every match, but it was somehow the right one, on an amazing, fervid night.

GROUP B	P	W	D	L	F	A	PTS
Argentina	3	2	1	0	8	0	5
Brazil	3	2	1	0	6	1	5
Poland	3	1	0	2	2	5	2
Peru	3	0	0	3	0	10	0

Argentina qualified for the Final, Brazil for the 3rd-place Final.

The match kicked-off after Brazil v Poland, so the hosts knew what they had to do: win by three goals while scoring at least four. A tall order, but at least the opposition was the least formidable so far. After the match, Brazilians muttered darkly about bribery and corruption, convinced that Quiroga, a naturalized Argentinian, had assisted the country of his birth. Recent allegations mention Argentinian aid worth £50 million finding its way into the Peruvian economy. But perhaps the truth is simply that a weak side were overwhelmed by forces beyond their control. If they really did agree to sell the match, they went about it rather strangely, Muñante hitting a post early on, Quiroga making some desperate saves.

Kempes, now the man of the hour, went past Manzo to score the first, but the important goal was Tarantini's diving header from a corner. After that, Argentina could start believing. Kempes volleyed the third after an exchange of passes in the area, Passarella headed Larrosa's cross back for Luque to fall forward and head in almost on the goal line (not offside), Houseman scored with his first touch, and Luque crashed in the sixth after another interpassing bout of

Mario Kempes, the tournament's leading scorer and decisive player.

1978

3rd-place Final

Final

Liberated from the need for points, Brazil were allowed to play like Brazil, which put their earlier efforts into context. Even Rivelino, in his last international, rolled back the years, and Italy matched them in a pleasing match. Causio inclined his noble brow to convert Rossi's cross then hit a post. Nelinho swerved an incredible shot round Zoff from the right-hand corner of the penalty box, and Dirceu volleyed into the same spot, which meant that the last four goals Zoff conceded in the tournament were all from long range. No blame attached. Two sad sights: Klein refereeing this after being scandalously kept out of the Final and Bettega hitting the woodwork for the umpteenth time in the tournament. For both teams, a case of what might well have been. Patrizio and Claudio Sala were brothers.

For the last time in the tournament, Argentina took full advantage of some lamentable refereeing, this time before the match had even started. After keeping the Dutch waiting for almost ten minutes, they suddenly protested about the protective sheaf on René K.'s right forearm. Since he'd been wearing it for the last five matches without objection, a little crude gamesmanship was clearly involved. Worse, Gonella took the complaint seriously, leading van de Kerkhof off by the arm to have it covered with another, useless layer. Both sides now knew what kind of official they were dealing with (he'd been appointed on the casting vote of another Italian), Holland venting their spleen with savage early tackles on Bertoni and Ardiles.

When the game settled down, the Dutch began to exploit Argentina's vulnerability in the air, Rep twice coming close to scoring. First he rose unopposed to Haan's free-kick only to head wide (first that miss in the 1974 Final, now this), then he cushioned a dreadful defensive header on his thigh before bringing a marvellous save from Fillol. Argentina would have been lost without him – and without Kempes, who opened the scoring after bursting between two defenders and stabbing the ball under Jongbloed on a carpet of tickertape. The movement had begun with Ardiles running past two men.

Holland dominated the second half but were frustrated by endless handballs, needless to say unpunished by bookings. In frustration they replaced Rep with Nanninga, big and direct, who headed the equalizer from René K.'s right-wing cross. Argentina's defence badly missed the height of St Étienne's Osvaldo Piazza.

In injury-time at the end of 90 minutes came the unkindest cut in any World Cup Final. Rensenbrink, running in that hunched way of his, fingers flicking behind him, got to Krol's long free-kick deep inside the penalty area and prodded it past Fillol. The ball hit the left-hand post and Holland's last chance was gone. In extra-time Kempes stormed through again, beating two men. Jongbloed saved at his feet but the ball bounced off Kempes, who prodded it home as two more defenders collided in front of him. Then Bertoni scored gleefully from point-blank range after another cavalry charge and two more lucky rebounds. Holland were the first country to lose consecutive Finals, each time against the hosts. Tarantini was the only player to appear in a Final without being registered with a club.

The most obscene tableau was saved till the end, Passarella receiving the trophy from the hands of General Jorge Rafael Videla, which had the blood of thousands on them. The Mothers of the Plaza de Mayo, protesting day after day about the disappearance of their sons, were glad the World Cup had been staged in Argentina, but only because it brought them to the notice of the world. The tournament had been vivid and unforgettable, but then so is a cattle prod.

Farce and furious. Gonella leads René K. away by the offending arm (note the white plaster on the wrist). Luque (14) and Brandts (22) get ready for the backlash.

LEADING GOALSCORERS 1978

6	Mario Kempes	ARG	
5	Teófilo Cubillas	PER	2 pen
5	Rob Rensenbrink	HOL	4 pen

[Top] *The first goal in the Final. Watched by the moustachioed Luque, Kempes forces the ball under Jongbloed as Haan leaps in too late.*

[Bottom] *Bertoni hammers Argentina's third goal past Jongbloed, watched by Brandts, Kempes and Willy K.*

Rossi fixes It

Spain 1982

Not for the first or last time, FIFA insisted on tampering with the format. Still trying to breed a successful cross between league and cup, they came up with even more of a camel. The top two teams in each group would go into four groups of three, the winners progressing to the semi-finals. There were now 24 countries instead of 16, including an increase in the number of finalists from Africa, Asia and Central America.

Of the teams at the other end of the scale, the champions Argentina came with the same coach and many of the same players from 1978, plus one special newcomer, the stocky bushy-haired Maradona, who'd been left out of the previous finals only because Menotti thought him too young and vulnerable at 17 (he'd first capped him at 16). Now he looked the world's greatest player since Cruyff or even Pelé, a target for Barcelona and every defender in the tournament.

West Germany, who'd thrown out the old wood, were the European Champions and had won all eight qualifiers with a goal tally of 33-3. Rummenigge was now a front player of the highest class and there were formidable new defenders in Briegel, Stielike and Karlheinz Förster, but their blond young playmaker Bernd Schuster was out injured.

Italy hadn't looked altogether convincing in qualifying, but at least Rossi was back after serving a suspension of less than two years for his involvement in a major match-fixing scandal. He had yet to embed himself back in the team; Antognoni had only just recovered from a life-threatening skull fracture, and Bettega and Benetti were gone – but the defence was better than ever and the whole team had been together for four more years. Spain, whose national team rarely matched the success of their club sides, were cursed with unexceptional players just when their time came to host the tournament.

Three of the British Isles countries had qualified and the other two came close. The Republic of Ireland were unfortunate to finish a very close third in a strong group which saw Holland eliminated. Wales beat Czechoslovakia but were undone by a 2-2 draw with Iceland in Swansea, where the floodlights failed. England had made their fans ride a remarkable rollercoaster. Defeats in Romania and Switzerland were followed by a convincing win in Hungary and another defeat, strangest of all, in Norway ('Your boys took a helluva beating!'). But Switzerland won in Romania to let them through, after which they put together an unbeaten run, though injuries to Brooking and the talismanic Keegan were a worry.

Northern Ireland, under their benign but pragmatic manager Billy Bingham, who'd played in the 1958 finals, came second in a group won by Scotland, who'd replaced MacLeod with the unimpeachable figure of Jock Stein. Although they scored only nine goals in eight qualifying games, their attack looked better than that and at last there was some organization at the back.

But they were unlucky with the draw. Originally scheduled to meet Argentina in the opening match (with the Falklands War still unresolved), they were moved to another group when FIFA realized there was no guarantee that the South American countries would be kept apart. So Scotland found themselves drawn alongside a strong Soviet side and the hot favourites.

Brazil, under a new coach, were looking their old selves again, a very passable impersonation of the 1970 team: thin in defence, explosively brilliant everywhere else. They'd beaten England at Wembley and in their last match before the finals had thrashed the Republic of Ireland 7-0. The 'beautiful game' was back and the rest of the field would be hoping to admire it at a distance for as long as possible.

Group 1

Cameroon, Italy, Peru, Poland

■ 14 June 1982 • Balaidos, Vigo • 22,000 •
Michel Vautrot (FRA)

▲ **ITALY 0**
POLAND 0

● ITALY *Dino Zoff (c), Claudio Gentile, Antonio Cabrini, Giampiero Marini, Fulvio Collovati, Gaetano Scirea, Bruno Conti, Marco Tardelli, Paolo Rossi, Giancarlo Antognoni, Francesco Graziani.* Enzo Bearzot.
POLAND *Józef Mlynarczyk, Stefan Majewski, Pawel Janas, Wladyslaw Zmuda (c), Jan Jalocha, Waldemar Matysik, Zbigniew Boniek, Andrzej Buncol, Grzegorz Lato, Andrzej Iwan [Marek Kusto 72], Wlodek Smolarek.* Antoni Piechniczek.

Now regarded as one of Italy's three sub-standard performances in the group, it was rather better than that. Some good moves from both sides, though Rossi wasn't quite there yet and Boniek (signed by Juventus and up against six of his future team-mates) was playing too deep. Zoff, now 40, had a relatively quiet time in his 100th international.

■ 15 June 1982 • Riazor, La Coruña • 15,000 •
Franz Wöhrer (AUT)

▲ **CAMEROON 0**
PERU 0

● CAMEROON *Thomas Nkono (c), Michel Kaham, Ephrem Mbom, Elie Onana, René Ndjeya, Ibrahim Aoudou, Emmanuel Kunde, Théophile Abega, Grégoire Mbida, Jacques Nguea [Paul Bahoken 72], Roger Milla [Jean-Pierre Tokoto 89].* Jean Vincent (FRA).
PERU *Ramón Quiroga, Jaime Duarte, Toribio Díaz (c), Salvador Salguero, Jorge Olaechea, José Velásquez, César Cueto, Teófilo Cubillas [Gerónimo Barbadillo 56], Julio César Uribe, Germán Leguía [Guillermo La Rosa 56], Juan Carlos Oblitas.* 'Tim' (Elba de Pádua Lima) (BRZ).

Uribe had looked one of the best players in the world during the win in Paris six weeks earlier, subtle and intricate, but here he simply didn't show. Cameroon, meanwhile, were a minor revelation. Milla, with his gap-toothed grin and excellent control, was the most charismatic player on the pitch. His original surname was Miller (some say Müller). Both coaches had played in previous finals: Vincent in 1954 and 1958; the 67-year-old Tim (oldest in any World Cup tournament) back in 1938.

Dino Zoff began the tournament by winning his 100th cap and ended it as the oldest World Cup winner.

■ 18 June 1982 • Balaidos, Vigo • 25,000 •
Walter Eschweiler (WG)

▲ **ITALY (1) 1**   Conti 19
PERU (0) 1   Díaz 85

● ITALY *Zoff (c), Gentile, Cabrini, Marini, Collovati, Scirea, Conti, Tardelli, Rossi [Franco Causio HT], Antognoni, Graziani.*
PERU *Quiroga, Duarte, Díaz (c), Salguero, Olaechea, Velásquez, Cueto, Cubillas, Uribe [La Rosa 65], Barbadillo [Leguía 65], Oblitas.*

Italy played less well this time but should still have won, against a team now clearly in decline. Conti, a new class act, turned his man and shot in off the bar from long range, but a deflected free-kick (Italians call it a Collovati own goal) ended Peru's run of 493 minutes without a goal, a record until Bolivia in 1994.

■ 19 June 1982 • Riazor, La Coruña • 12,000 •
Alexis Ponnet (BEL)

▲ **CAMEROON 0**
POLAND 0

● CAMEROON *Nkono (c), Kaham, M'bom, Onana, Ndjeya, Aoudou, Kunde, Abega, Mbida, Nguea [Tokoto HT], Milla.*
POLAND *Mlynarczyk, Majewski, Janas, Zmuda (c), Jalocha, Andrzej Palasz [Kusto 66], Boniek, Buncol, Lato, Iwan [Andrzej Szarmach 25], Smolarek.*

Same again from both teams.

■ 22 June 1982 • Riazor, La Coruña • 16,000 •
Mario Rubio Vázquez (MEX)

▲ **POLAND (0) 5**
Smolarek 56, Lato 59, Boniek 61, Buncol 68, Ciolek 77
PERU (0) 1
La Rosa 83

● POLAND *Mlynarczyk, Majewski, Janas, Zmuda (c), Jalocha [Marek Dziuba 27], Matysik, Janusz Kupcewicz, Buncol, Lato, Boniek, Smolarek [Wlodek Ciolek 74].*
PERU *Quiroga, Duarte, Díaz (c), Salguero, Olaechea, Velásquez, Cueto, Cubillas [Uribe 50], La Rosa, Leguía, Oblitas [Barbadillo 50].*

After a first half in keeping with the group so far, Peru left their floodgates open; Kupcewicz capitalizing on a mistake by Velásquez to set up Smolarek. Lato, balder but not much slower, scored his 45th goal for Poland, his tenth in World Cup finals. La Rosa scored the goal his 1978 performances deserved, but it was a dismal end for Cubillas & Co.

23 June 1982 • Balaidos, Vigo • 17,000 •
Bogdan Dochev (BUL)

CAMEROON (0) 1
Mbida 62
ITALY (0) 1
Graziani 61

CAMEROON *Nkono (c), Kaham, Mbom, Onana, Ndjeya, Aoudou, Kunde, Abega, Mbida, Tokoto, Milla.*
ITALY *Zoff (c), Gentile, Cabrini, Tardelli, Collovati, Scirea, Gabriele Oriali, Conti, Rossi, Antognoni, Graziani.*

THE COMPLETE BOOK OF THE WORLD CUP

In that modern rarity, a match without substitutes, Italy qualified without glory, scoring one more goal than Cameroon, who were eliminated without losing a match. The agile Nkono slipped as Graziani's header drifted over him, and Mbida lifted in a close-range volley.

GROUP 1	P	W	D	L	F	A	PTS
Poland	3	1	2	0	5	1	4
Italy	3	0	3	0	2	2	3
Cameroon	3	0	3	0	1	1	3
Peru	3	0	2	1	2	6	2

Poland and Italy qualified for the second round.

Group 2

Algeria, Austria, Chile, West Germany

■ 16 June 1982 • El Molinón, Gijón • 25,000 •
Enrique Labo Revoredo (PER)

▲ **ALGERIA (0) 2**
Madjer 53, Belloumi 69
WEST GERMANY (0) 1
Rummenigge 67

● ALGERIA *Mehdi Cerbah, Chaabane Merzekane, Mahmoud Guendouz, Nourredine Kourichi, Faouzi Mansouri, Ali Fergani (c), Mustafa Dahleb, Lakhdar Belloumi, Rabah Madjer [Salah Larbes 88], Djamel Zidane [Tedj Bensaoula 64], Salah Assad.* Rachid Mekhloufi, with Mahiedine Khalef.
W. GERMANY *Harald Schumacher, Manni Kaltz, Hans-Peter Briegel, Wolfgang Dremmler, Karlheinz Förster, Uli Stielike, Pierre Littbarski, Felix Magath [Klaus Fischer 83], Horst Hrubesch, Paul Breitner, Karl-Heinz Rummenigge (c).* Jupp Derwall.

So what's so surprising? The win merely maintained Algeria's 100 per cent record against West Germany, whom they'd beaten 2-0 in 1964. Seriously, the European champions were unrecognizable, especially in midfield, where Breitner, for all his abilities, didn't provide enough creative backup for Magath. Rummenigge wasn't fully fit and Littbarski had a late goal disallowed.

But enough of them. Algeria's big names, two of the best players produced in North Africa, scored their goals. Madjer flipped the ball in after a run by Belloumi, who then pushed a left-wing cross into an empty net. Embarrassment for Derwall ('We're so strong we'll win without problems'), and West Germany were already in danger of failing to reach the next stage for the first time ever. Note the different ways of writing Förster and Rummenigge's first names.

■ 17 June 1982 • Carlos Tartiere, Oviedo •
22,000 • Juan Cardellino (URU)

▲ **AUSTRIA (1) 1**
Schachner 22
CHILE (0) 0

● AUSTRIA *Fritz Koncilia, Bernd Krauss, Erich Obermayer (c), Josef Degeorgi [Ernst Baumeister 78] Bruno Pezzey, Roland Hattenberger, Reinhold Hintermaier, Herbert Prohaska, Heribert Weber [Gernot Jurtin 80], Hans Krankl, Walter Schachner.* Georg Schmidt.
CHILE *Mario Osbén, Antonio Lizardo Garrido, René Valenzuela, Elias Figueroa (c), Vladimir Bigorra, Eduardo Bonvallet, Rodolfo Dubó, Miguel Angel Neira [Manuel Rojas 73], Gustavo Moscoso [Miguel Angel Gamboa 66], Patricio Yáñez, Carlos Caszely.* Luis Santibañez.

For the first time, two countries had qualified from most of the European groups, so Austria were here despite losing twice to West Germany. Meanwhile Chile had two wins over the reigning South American champions. But the arithmetic didn't hold up here; Austria were slightly the better side in a drab match. The great Figueroa, a veteran of 1966, was still a force at centre-half, so there was only one goal, Schachner's slow-motion header. Three minutes later, Caszely, who'd been sent off in Chile's first match in 1974, missed a penalty, the only player to achieve this unenviable double in World Cup finals.

■ 20 June 1982 • El Molinón, Gijón • 40,000 • Bruno Galler (SWI)

▲ **WEST GERMANY (1) 4**
Rummenigge 9, 57, 67, Reinders 82
CHILE (0) 1
Moscoso 89

● W. GERMANY *Schumacher, Kaltz, Briegel, Dremmler, Kh. Förster, Stielike, Littbarski [Uwe Reinders 80], Magath, Hrubesch, Breitner [Lothar Matthäus 61], Rummenigge (c).*
CHILE *Osbén, Garrido, Valenzuela, Figueroa (c), Bigorra, Bonvallet, Dubó, Mario Soto [Juan Carlos Letelier HT], Moscoso, Gamboa [Neira 67], Yáñez.*

More like the Germans we know. Breitner, back from international retirement after more than five years, had a better game and Rummenigge looked every inch the European Footballer of the Year, scoring three good goals, one with a powerful header.

■ 21 June 1982 • Carlos Tartiere, Oviedo • 22,000 • Tony Boskovic (AUS)

▲ **AUSTRIA (0) 2**
Schachner 56, Krankl 67
ALGERIA (0) 0

● AUSTRIA *Koncilia, Krauss, Obermayer (c), Degeorgi, Pezzey, Hattenberger, Hintermaier, Prohaska [Weber 81], Krankl, Baumeister [Kurt Welzl HT], Schachner.*
ALGERIA *Cerbah, Merzekane, Guendouz, Kourichi, Mansouri, Fergani (c), Dahleb [Djamel Tlemcani 75], Belloumi [Bensaoula 66], Madjer, Zidane, Assad.*

Without appearing a dominant force, Austria made Algeria's earlier win look a one-off, shackling the influential Fergani, glad that Belloumi was off form. So was Krankl, but like the rest of the team he did just enough.

■ 24 June 1982 • Carlos Tartiere, Oviedo • 18,000 • Rómulo Méndez Molina (GUA)

▲ **ALGERIA (3) 3**
Assad 8, 31, Bensaoula 34
CHILE (0) 2
Neira pen 60, Letelier 74

● ALGERIA *Cerbah, Merzekane, Guendouz, Kourichi, Mansouri [Dahleb 73], Fergani (c), Larbes, Bensaoula, Abdelmajid Bourrebou [Hocine Yahi 31], Madjer, Assad.*
CHILE *Osbén, Mario Galindo, Valenzuela, Figueroa (c), Bigorra, Bonvallet [Soto 38], Dubó, Neira, Moscoso, Yáñez, Caszely [Letelier 54].*

Algeria became the first African country to win two matches in the finals, but ultimately had only themselves to blame. Skilfully dominant in the first half, they conceded two important goals, the second a fine individual run by Letelier. If the score had stayed 3-0, only a 4-3 win or better would have saved West Germany. The 35-year-old Figueroa was winning his last cap.

■ 25 June 1982 • El Molinón, Gijón • 41,000 • Bob Valentine (SCO)

▲ **WEST GERMANY (1) 1**
Hrubesch 11
AUSTRIA (0) 0

● W. GERMANY *Schumacher, Kaltz, Briegel, Dremmler, Kh. Förster, Stielike, Littbarski, Magath, Hrubesch [Fischer 69], Breitner, Rummenigge (c) [Matthäus 67].*
AUSTRIA *Koncilia, Krauss, Obermayer (c), Degeorgi, Pezzey, Hattenberger, Hintermaier, Prohaska, Weber, Krankl, Schachner.*

Scandalous, they said – but there's no evidence that the two teams agreed the result beforehand. Morality aside (as always), why would Austria want to see a strong team like West Germany go through? The truth seems to be that the Germans needed the result, got an early goal (a clumsy header), then neither side had any interest in forcing the pace. Still, it was very hard on Algeria, whose fans waved banknotes through the wire fencing in tearful fury. Penny for their thoughts before the Final.

GROUP 2	P	W	D	L	F	A	PTS
W. Germany	3	2	0	1	6	3	4
Austria	3	2	0	1	3	1	4
Algeria	3	2	0	1	5	5	4
Chile	3	0	0	3	3	8	0

West Germany and Austria qualified for the second round.

Group 3

Argentina, Belgium, El Salvador, Hungary

■ 13 June 1982 • Nou Camp, Barcelona • 95,000 • Vojtech Christov (CZE)

▲ **BELGIUM (0) 1**
Vandenbergh 63
ARGENTINA (0) 0

● BELGIUM *Jean-Marie Pfaff, Eric Gerets (c), Marc Baecke, Luc Millecamps, Maurits De Schrijver, Guy Vandersmissen, Ludo Coeck, Frankie Vercauteren, Jan Ceulemans, Alex Czerniatynski, Erwin Vandenbergh. Guy Thys.*
ARGENTINA *Ubaldo Fillol, Jorge Olguin, Alberto Tarantini, Américo Gallego, Luis Galván, Daniel Passarella (c), Daniel Bertoni, Osvaldo Ardiles, Mario Kempes, Diego Maradona, Ramón Díaz [Jorge Valdano 63]. César Luis Menotti.*

Nine of the Argentinian starting line-up had played in 1978, but the blend didn't work against the gritty Belgians, European runners-up two years previously. They held Maradona in check and Vandenbergh converted their best chance – eventually. When Vercauteren's long ball put him clear, he and Fillol went into a strange little dance of hesitation before the shot finally came; the first goal in an opening match for 20 years. Ten minutes later Maradona hit the bar with a free-kick.

MOST GOALS BY ONE TEAM			
10-1	Hungary	1982	v El Salvador
9-0	Hungary	1954	v S. Korea
9-0	Yugoslavia	1974	v Zaire

■ 15 June 1982 • Nuevo Estadio, Elche • 6,000 •
Ibrahim Youssef Al Doy (BHR)

▲ **HUNGARY (3) 10**
Nyilasi 4, 83, Pölöskei 11, Fazekas 24, 55,
Tóth 51, Kiss 69, 73, 77, Szentes 71
EL SALVADOR (0) 1
Ramírez Zapata 65

● HUNGARY *Ferenc Mészáros, László Bálint, Gyözö Martos, József Tóth II, Imre Garaba, Sándor Müller [Lázár Szentes 69], Tibor Nyilasi (c), Sándor Sallai, András Törőcsik [László Kiss 57], László Fazekas, Gábor Pölöskei. Kálmán Mészöly.*
EL SALVADOR *Luis Mora Guevara, Mario Castillo, José Francisco Jovel, Jaime Rodríguez, Carlos Recinos, José Luis Rugamas [Luis Ramírez Zapata 28], Joaquin Alonso Ventura [Ramón Fagoaga 75], Norberto Huezo (c), Francisco Hernández, Jorge González, José María Rivas. Mauricio 'Pipo' Rodríguez.*

El Salvador scored their only finals goal – but the exchange rate was extortionate. Hungary racked up a record total, including seven goals in one half, another first. After Törőcsik had somehow failed to dip his bread in, Kiss scored the fastest finals hat-trick and the only one by a substitute. Most of the goals were hammered in from close range with the defence in tatters, while Ramírez Zapata scored in a goalmouth scramble. Mészöly said the scoreline gave Hungary half a goal advantage over Argentina; a draw would be enough.

■ 18 June 1982 • José Rico Pérez, Alicante •
32,093 • Belaid Lacarne (ALG)

▲ **ARGENTINA (2) 4**
Bertoni 27, Maradona 28, 57, Ardiles 61
HUNGARY (0) 1
Pölöskei 76

● ARGENTINA *Fillol, Olguin, Tarantini [Juan Barbas 51], Gallego, Galván, Passarella (c), Bertoni, Ardiles, Kempes, Maradona, Valdano [Gabriel Calderón 25].*
HUNGARY *Mészáros, Bálint, J. Tóth II, Martos [Fazekas HT], Garaba, József Varga, Nyilasi (c), Sallai, Kiss [Szentes 63], Tibor Rab, Pölöskei.*

A one-man *tour de force*. Displaying the right stuff after his anonymity against Belgium, Maradona won it on his own, all muscular brilliance and strut, like Pelé but angrier. He thrashed in two goals but might have had four more; and the Hungarian defence was so disorientated they even allowed Ardiles to score from close in. Some consolation for a country who'd just lost Port Stanley back to the British.

■ 19 June 1982 • Nuevo Estadio, Elche • 6,000 •
Malcolm Moffatt (NIR)

▲ **BELGIUM (1) 1**
Coeck 18
EL SALVADOR (0) 0

● BELGIUM *Pfaff, Gerets (c), Baecke, L. Millecamps, Walter Meeuws, Vandersmissen [François Van der Elst HT], Coeck, Vercauteren, Vandenbergh, Czerniatynski, Ceulemans [Wilfried Van Moer 80].*
EL SALVADOR *Mora Guevara, Francisco Osorto [Miguel Angel Díaz HT], Jovel, Rodríguez, Recinos, Fagoaga, Ventura, Huezo (c), Ramírez Zapata, González, Rivas.*

It looks a very unlikely scoreline, but even El Salvador didn't concede ten goals every game, and Belgium lacked the width in attack to break down a packed defence. The 20-year-old Mora Guevara made some good saves and the only goal was unsatisfactory, Coeck's very long shot dropping just inside a post. François Van der Elst was the brother of Leo (1986) and a different player from Franky (1986–94).

■ 22 June 1982 • Nuevo Estadio, Elche • 22,000 • Clive White (ENG)

▲ **BELGIUM (0) 1**
Czerniatynski 76
HUNGARY (1) 1
Varga 27

● BELGIUM *Pfaff, Gerets (c) [Gérard Plessers 62], L. Millecamps, Baecke, Meeuws, Vandersmissen [Van Moer HT], Coeck, Vercauteren, Vandenbergh, Czerniatynski, Ceulemans.*
HUNGARY *Mészáros, Martos, Attila Kerekes, Garaba, Varga, Müller [Sallai 68], Nyilasi (c), Fazekas, Törőcsik, Kiss [Ferenc Csongrádi 71], Pölöskei.*

Belgium scraped the draw they needed when the rugged Ceulemans made a goal for Czerniatynski. Hungary, who'd won their qualifying group despite losing twice to England, fell very flat, especially Törőcsik and the style guru Nyilasi.

■ 23 June 1982 • Rico Pérez, Alicante • 18,000 • Luis Barrancos (BOL)

▲ **ARGENTINA (1) 2**
Passarella pen 23, Bertoni 54
EL SALVADOR (0) 0

● ARGENTINA *Fillol, Olguin, Tarantini, Gallego, Galván, Passarella (c), Bertoni [Díaz 68], Ardiles, Kempes, Maradona, Calderón [Santiago Santamaría 81].*
EL SALVADOR *Mora Guevara, Osorto [Díaz 32], Jovel, Rodríguez, Recinos, Fagoaga, Ventura [Mauricio Alfaro 80], Huezo (c), Ramírez Zapata, González, Rivas.*

More credit to the minnows, who went behind to a penalty awarded for what looked like a dive by Calderón, who was no great improvement on Díaz. Argentina had hardly looked like World Champions and were now in the most difficult second-round group.

GROUP 3	P	W	D	L	F	A	PTS
Belgium	3	2	1	0	3	1	5
Argentina	3	2	0	1	6	2	4
Hungary	3	1	1	1	12	6	3
El Salvador	3	0	0	3	1	13	0

Belgium and Argentina qualified for the second round.

Group 4

Czechoslovakia, England, France, Kuwait

■ 16 June 1982 • San Mamés, Bilbao • 44,172 •
Antônio Garrido (POR)

▲ **ENGLAND (1) 3**
Robson 27 sec, 67, Mariner 83
FRANCE (1) 1
Soler 25

● **ENGLAND** *Peter Shilton, Mick Mills (c), Kenny Sansom
[Phil Neal 90], Bryan Robson, Terry Butcher, Phil
Thompson, Steve Coppell, Ray Wilkins, Paul Mariner, Trevor
Francis, Graham Rix. Ron Greenwood.*

FRANCE *Jean-Luc Ettori, Patrick Battiston, Max Bossis, René
Girard, Christian Lopez, Marius Trésor, Dominique Rocheteau
[Didier Six 71], Alain Giresse, Jean-François Larios [Jean
Tigana 74], Michel Platini (c), Gérard Soler. Michel Hidalgo.*

Coppell took a throw-in on the right, Butcher's back-
header found Robson utterly alone in front of goal, and a
gymnastic left-footed volley forced the ball past Ettori.
England were back in the World Cup finals for the first
time in 12 years – and how! Less than half a minute gone.

But the goal didn't give them the expected
momentum. The defence, with Coppell and Rix playing
deep on the flanks, was solid enough, but Brooking's injury
and Hoddle's absence left them short of a playmaker
(Wilkins was already crabbing the ball sideways). Soler, sent
clear on the left by Giresse, scored with a smart cross-shot,
and France had the better of things for half the match.

What saved England was the drive and energy of
Robson (at last an English version of Neeskens and
Tardelli) and errors in the French defence. When
Francis crossed from the right, Robson leapt up to
score with an athletic header, but little Ettori had come
too far off his line. Then Trésor, of all people, miskicked
a shot by Francis to let in Mariner behind him. The jury
was still out on both teams.

*Bryan Robson scores his acrobatic and very early goal against France.
Supporting cast (l–r): Trésor, Ettori, Mariner and Larios.*

Robson heads his second goal as Ettori comes out too far and Lopez can't get across in time.

more idle than ever. The penalty was awarded for a foul, if that's what it was, on Vízek. Kuwait, convincing winners of the Asia-Oceania group, were busy and confident, their equalizer a beauty – Al-Dakhil's flying long shot clipping the bar on its way in. The stadium was also known as El Prado.

■ 17 June 1982 • José Zorrilla, Valladolid • 12,000 • Benjamin Dwomoh (GHA)

▲ **CZECHOSLOVAKIA (1) 1**
Panenka pen 21
KUWAIT (0) 1
Al-Dakhil 58

● CZECHOSLOVAKIA *Zdenek Hruska, Jozef Barmos, Ladislav Jurkemik, Jan Fiala, Jozef Kukucka, Jan Berger, Antonín Panenka, Tomás Kriz [Premysl Bicovsky 63], Petr Janecka [Vlastimil Petrzela 69], Zdenek Nehoda (c), Ladislav Vízek. Jozef Venglos.*
KUWAIT *Ahmad Al-Tarabulsi, Naeem Sa'ad Mubarak, Mahboub Jum'ah Mubarak, Abdullah Mayouf, Walid Al-Jasem Mubarak, Abdullah Al-Buloushi, Sa'ad Al-Houti (c), Mohammed Ahmad Karam [Fathi Kamil Marzouq 57], Faisal Al-Dakhil, Jasem Yacoub, Abdul Aziz Al-Anbari. Carlos Alberto Parreira (BRZ).*

■ 20 June 1982 • San Mamés, Bilbao • 44,182 • Charles Corver (HOL)

▲ **ENGLAND (0) 2**
Francis 63, Barmos o.g. 66
CZECHOSLOVAKIA (0) 0

● ENGLAND *Shilton, Mills (c), Sansom, Robson [Glenn Hoddle HT], Butcher, Thompson, Coppell, Wilkins, Mariner, Francis, Rix.*
CZECHOSLOVAKIA *Stanislav Seman [Karel Stromsík 75], Barmos, Jurkemik, Fiala, Rostislav Vojácek, Libor Radimec, Pavel Chaloupka, Berger, Vízek, Nehoda (c), Janecka [Marián Masny 78].*

Czechoslovakia, who'd qualified despite winning only half their eight matches, were as drippy as expected: Nehoda losing his sharpness; Panenka

Again England were solid but uninventive; again they were gifted two goals. Seman dropped a corner straight in front of Francis and wasn't capped again, and Barmos turned Mariner's low cross just inside a post. Mariner, who'd scored in each of the previous five games, tried to claim it, but there are limits. England were already through, but they'd need more from their midfield against the stronger teams.

■ 21 June 1982 • José Zorrilla, Valladolid • 30,043 • Miroslav Stupar (USSR)

▲ **FRANCE (2) 4**
Genghini 31, Platini 43, Six 48, Bossis 89
KUWAIT (0) 1
Al-Buloushi 75

● FRANCE *Ettori, Manuel Amoros, Bossis, Gérard Janvion [Christian Lopez 59], Trésor, Giresse, Bernard Genghini, Platini (c) [Girard 81], Soler, Bernard Lacombe, Six.*
KUWAIT *Al-Tarabulsi, Naeem Sa'ad, Mahboub, Mayouf, Al-Jasem [Humoud Al-Shemmari 76], Al-Buloushi, Al-Houti (c), Karam [Fathi Kamil HT], Al-Dakhil, Yacoub, Al-Anbari.*

■ 24 June 1982 • José Zorrilla, Valladolid • 28,000 • Paolo Casarin (ITA)

▲ **CZECHOSLOVAKIA (0) 1**
Panenka pen 84
FRANCE (0) 1
Six 66

● FRANCE *Ettori, Amoros, Bossis, Janvion, Trésor, Giresse, Genghini, Platini (c), Soler [Girard 88], Lacombe [Alain Couriol 70], Six.*
CZECHOSLOVAKIA *Stromsík, Barmos, Fiala, Vojácek, Radimec, Nehoda (c), Bicovsky, Frantisek Stambachr, Janecka [Panenka 70], Vízek, Kriz [Masny 31].*
▼ SENT OFF: *Vízek 87.*

Kuwait may well have fancied their chances, but the French midfield was too talented for them. Genghini curled in a free-kick, Platini was sent clear to push the ball past the keeper then made the third for Six. In one of the tournament's memorable moments, Giresse had a goal disallowed. The Kuwaiti defence, hearing a whistle in the crowd, hesitated then protested. Their general manager Sheikh Al-Sabah, resplendent in his robes, called the players off the pitch. Stupar wrongly disallowed the goal and didn't referee another World Cup match. Bossis made up for it by scoring from a tight angle at close range.

France had little trouble achieving the draw they needed against a side who contributed nothing to the competition and went out gracelessly, Vízek getting himself sent off for fouling Soler. Six put in the rebound when Lacombe's shot was blocked and Vízek won another penalty. Panenka and Masny, important players when Czechoslovakia won the European Championship in 1976, weren't capped again.

GROUP 4	P	W	D	L	F	A	PTS
England	3	3	0	0	6	1	6
France	3	1	1	1	6	5	3
Czechoslovakia	3	0	2	1	2	4	2
Kuwait	3	0	1	2	2	6	1

England and France qualified for the second round.

■ 25 June 1982 • San Mamés, Bilbao • 31,000 • Gilberto Aristizábal (COL)

▲ **ENGLAND (1) 1**
Francis 27
KUWAIT (0) 0

● ENGLAND *Shilton, Neal, Mills (c), Hoddle, Steve Foster, Thompson, Coppell, Wilkins, Mariner, Francis, Rix.*
KUWAIT *Al-Tarabulsi, Naeem Sa'ad, Mahboub, Mayouf, Al-Jasem [Al-Shemmari 75], Al-Buloushi, Al-Houti (c), Fathi Kamil, Yousef Al-Suwayed, Al-Dakhil, Al-Anbari.*

Yes, no problem, though it was just as well that Kuwait weren't an attacking force. Hoddle's many admirers had to admit he didn't really take his chance; but Francis looked sharp in the group matches and scored with a low cross-shot after exchanging passes with Mariner following Shilton's long punt. Al-Houti and the 35-year-old Al-Tarabulsi, both impressive, weren't capped again.

Group 5

Honduras, Northern Ireland, Spain, Yugoslavia

■ 16 June 1982 • Luis Casanova, Valencia • 49,562 • Arturo Ithurralde (ARG)

▲ **HONDURAS (1) 1**
Zelaya 8
SPAIN (0) 1
López Ufarte pen 65

● HONDURAS *Julio César Arzu, César Gutiérrez, Jaime Villegas, Anthony Costly, José Fernando Bulnes, Ramón Maradiaga (c), Gilberto (Yearwood), Héctor Zelaya, Prudencio Norales [Carlos Caballero 68], Porfirio Betancourt, José Roberto Figueroa.* 'Chelato Ucles' (José de la Paz Herrera).
SPAIN *Luis Arkonada (c), José Camacho, Rafael Gordillo, Joaquin (Alonso) [José Sánchez HT], Miguel Tendillo, José Alexanko, Miguel Alonso, Jesús Zamora, Jesús Satrústegui, Roberto López Ufarte, 'Juanito' (Juan Gómez) [Enrique Saura HT].* José Santamaría (URU).

The hosts against the least fancied team in the group: we're allowed to make comparisons with bullrings. But Spain were whistled off at the end.

It's not that they were downright bad (the goalkeeper and defence were among the best in Europe), just lacking any great players up front.

Juanito, tricky and hot-tempered, did little, and Satrústegui was no great finisher. Honduras were well organized, took the lead when Zelaya kept his nerve in the penalty area, and had chances to double it. Arzu in goal, Costly at centre-half and Gilberto in midfield were their stars. One English paper had its headline already prepared: Manuel Labour. Norales is the correct spelling (not Morales).

■ 17 June 1982 • La Romareda, Saragossa • 18,000 • Erik Fredriksson (SWE)

▲ **NORTHERN IRELAND 0**
YUGOSLAVIA 0

● N. IRELAND *Pat Jennings, Jimmy Nicholl, Mal Donaghy, David McCreery, Chris Nicholl, John McClelland, Gerry Armstrong, Martin O'Neill (c), Billy Hamilton, Sammy McIlroy, Norman Whiteside.* Billy Bingham.
YUGOSLAVIA *Dragan Pantelic, Nikola Jovanovic, Milos Hrstic, Velimir Zajec, Nenad Stojkovic, Ivan Gudelj, Vladimir Petrovic, Edhem Sljivo, Ivo Surjak (c), Safet Susic, Zlatko Vujovic.* Miljan Miljanic.

Northern Ireland, in the finals for the first time since 1958, set out their stall for a draw, achieved it without too much strain, and should have had a penalty when the teenaged Whiteside, winning his first cap, was clearly fouled in the area. O'Neill and McIlroy were talented and careful in midfield, Armstrong and Hamilton hard-working up front, and the pace of McClelland was invaluable alongside Chris Nicholl. Yugoslavia had so many players with clubs abroad that Miljanic hadn't bothered to arrange any friendlies since December, an approach which smacked of exasperation (and didn't work).

■ 20 June 1982 • Luis Casanova, Valencia •
50,000 • Henning Lund-Sørensen (DEN)

▲ **SPAIN (1) 2**
Juanito pen 14, Saura 66
YUGOSLAVIA (1) 1
Gudelj 10

● SPAIN *Arkonada (c), Camacho, Gordillo, M. Alonso, Tendillo, Alexanko, Sánchez [Saura 63], Zamora, Satrústegui ['Quini' (Enrique Castro) 63], López Ufarte, Juanito.*
YUGOSLAVIA *Pantelic, Jovanovic (Vahid Halilhodzic 74], Zlatko Krmpotic, Stojkovic, Zajec, Gudelj, Vujovic [Milos Sestic 83], Petrovic, Susic, Sljivo, Surjak (c).*

Whatever else Spain were going to lack in this tournament, it wasn't refereeing generosity. Their latest penalty was awarded for a foul on Alonso by Zajec, who was careful to trip his man outside the area – as seen on TV. Even then Spain needed a refereeing top-up, Juanito scoring with the retake after López Ufarte put the original kick wide. Gudelj headed in a Petrovic free-kick, but Saura scored the winner from a pass by the other substitute Quini. Relief around the stadium, but it was Spain's only win in the tournament.

YOUNGEST PLAYERS
yrs/days
17/41	Norman Whiteside	NIR	1982
17/235	Pelé	BRZ	1958
17/353	Rigobert Song	CAM	1994

Edu, aged 16, was in Brazil's 1966 squad.

■ 21 June 1982 • La Romareda, Saragossa •
15,000 • Chan Tam Sun (HKG)

▲ **HONDURAS (0) 1**
Laing 60
NORTHERN IRELAND (1) 1
Armstrong 10

● HONDURAS *Arzu, Gutiérrez, Villegas, Costly, José Luis Cruz, Maradiaga (c), Gilberto, Zelaya, Norales [Tony Laing 58], Betancourt, Figueroa.*
N. IRELAND *Jennings, J. Nicholl, Donaghy, McCreery, C. Nicholl, McClelland, Armstrong, M. O'Neill (c) [Patrick Joseph 'Felix' Healy 77], Hamilton, McIlroy, Whiteside [Noel Brotherston 65].*

Bingham, budgeting for four points, expected two of them here, but Honduras again did well. The 37-year-old Jennings made a good save but couldn't keep out Laing's header from the subsequent corner. Healy was the only player to appear in a finals match while with an Irish club (Coleraine).

■ 24 June 1982 • La Romareda, Saragossa •
12,000 • Gastón Castro (CHI)

▲ **YUGOSLAVIA (0) 1**
Petrovic pen 87
HONDURAS (0) 0

● YUGOSLAVIA *Pantelic, Jovanovic [Halilhodzic HT], Krmpotic, Stojkovic, Zajec, Gudelj, Vujovic [Sestic 60], Petrovic, Surjak (c), Susic, Sljivo.*
HONDURAS *Arzu, Domingo Drummond, Villegas, Costly, Bulnes, Maradiaga (c), Gilberto, Zelaya, Cruz [Laing 65], Betancourt, Figueroa.*
▼ SENT OFF: *Gilberto 88.*

Really tough on Honduras, who again looked the equal of the Europeans. After missing at least two good chances, they were beaten by another harsh penalty, for a challenge by Villegas on Sestic, and had their best player sent off for an off-the-ball incident. The result left Northern Ireland needing a win over the hosts to survive.

■ 25 June 1982 • Luis Casanova, Valencia • 49,562 • Héctor Ortíz (PAR)

▲ **NORTHERN IRELAND (0) 1**
Armstrong 47
SPAIN (0) 0

● N. IRELAND *Jennings, J. Nicholl, Donaghy, McCreery, C. Nicholl, McClelland, Armstrong, M. O'Neill (c), Hamilton, McIlroy [Tommy Cassidy 50], Whiteside [Sammy Nelson 73].*
SPAIN *Arkonada (c), Camacho, Gordillo, M. Alonso, Tendillo, Alexanko, Sánchez, López Ufarte [Ricardo Gallego 78], Satrústegui [Quini HT], Saura, Juanito.*
▼ SENT OFF: *Donaghy 61.*

This was *Boy's Own* stuff. Arguably the best performance by a British team in any World Cup –

admittedly against a sub-standard team without its playmaker (Zamora) – but one reinforced by a referee who hadn't taken charge of an international for two years. The crowd should also have been Spain's ally, but Bingham had gauged its mood: 'Intimidating – but they also put pressure on their own team.' Northern Ireland defended coolly but needed a goal, which they got when Hamilton brushed his marker aside on the way to the right-hand goal line and pulled the ball back low. Arkonada, once the best keeper in Europe, could only palm it straight to Armstrong, who fired it low into the net.

After that, Rorke's Drift – but the Irish had been well briefed: stay on your feet when the ball's in the penalty area; don't give the referee any excuse outside it. They gave him only one, the merest push on Camacho making Donaghy the first British player to be sent off in a finals match – this while the Spaniards were hardly observing the niceties. Jennings, idiosyncratic and brilliant, cleverly avoided the possibility of a penalty by flipping the ball over Juanito's head, and in the end Spain were happy to settle for a 1-0 defeat; another goal would have eliminated them. Northern Ireland couldn't have picked a better time, a more vibrant night, to record their only win over Spain.

GROUP 5	P	W	D	L	F	A	PTS
N. Ireland	3	1	2	0	2	1	4
Spain	3	1	1	1	3	3	3
Yugoslavia	3	1	1	1	2	2	3
Honduras	3	0	2	1	2	3	2
Northern Ireland and Spain qualified for the second round.							

Northern Ireland's most famous World Cup goal.
Armstrong gives Arkonada no chance to redeem his error.

Group 6

Brazil, New Zealand, Scotland, USSR

■ 14 June 1982 • Sánchez Pizjuán, Seville •
50,000 • Augusto Lamo Castillo (SPA)

▲ **BRAZIL (0) 2**
Sócrates 75, Éder 87
USSR (1) 1
Bal 34

● BRAZIL *Waldir Peres, Leandro (Souza Ferreira),
Leovegildo Júnior, Paulo Roberto Falcão, Oscar (Bernardi),
'Luizinho' (Luiz Ferreira), Dirceu (Guimarães) [Paulo
Isidoro (de Jesus) HT], Sócrates (de Souza) (c), 'Serginho'
(Sérgio Bernardino), 'Zico' (Arthur Antunes Coimbra), Éder
(de Assis).* Telê Santana.
USSR *Renat Dasayev, Tengiz Sulakvelidze, Anatoly
Demianenko, Sergei Baltacha, Aleksandr Chivadze (c),
Vladimir Bessonov, Andrei Bal, Yuri Gavrilov [Yuri
Susloparov 74], Vitaly Daraselia, Ramaz Shengalia [Sergei
Andreyev 88], Oleg Blokhin.* Konstantin Beskov.

This USSR side was less than the sum of its parts, all of
them international class or better – but it matched the
favourites for most of the match and took the lead
with a goal which showed that this Brazilian team
contained another obligatory ingredient from 1970: a
dreadful goalkeeper. The ball was moved left to right
across the Brazilian penalty area for Bal to shoot from
30 yards. The balding Waldir had been voted Brazil's
Player of the Year in 1975 but now stood stiff-legged
and let the ball in off his shin. A beauty.

It took Brazil a long time to get back on terms,
but it was worth the anxious wait. The Soviets had
three attempts at clearing their lines but sent the ball
straight to the lanky, bearded Sócrates, who

sidestepped twice to the right before unleashing a
heatseeker into the top left-hand corner. The winner
was even better, Paulo Isidoro laying the ball back
from the right and Falcão stepping over it for Éder to
flip it up and volley in at the near post. Dasayev,
perhaps the best keeper in the tournament, didn't
move. Flair and shooting power of the highest order.
A beautiful game, alright.

■ 15 June 1982 • La Rosaleda, Malaga •
22,000 • David Socha (USA)

▲ **SCOTLAND (3) 5**
Dalglish 18, Wark 30, 33, Robertson 73,
Archibald 79
NEW ZEALAND (0) 2
Sumner 54, Wooddin 65

● SCOTLAND *Allan Rough, Danny McGrain (c), Frank
Gray, John Wark, Allan Evans, Alan Hansen, Gordon
Strachan, Graeme Souness, Alan Brazil [Steve Archibald
53], Kenny Dalglish [David Narey 83], John Robertson.*
Jock Stein.
N. ZEALAND *Frank Van Hattum, John Hill, Sam
Malcolmson [Duncan Cole 77], Bobby Almond [Ricki
Herbert 66], Adrian Elrick, Keith Mackay, Allan Boath,
Steve Sumner (c), Ken Cresswell, Wynton Rufer, Steve
Wooddin.* John Adshead (ENG).

As in 1974, Scotland met the whipping-boys first and
made a meal of it, or at least a messy snack. No
problems in the first half, with Strachan brisk and
clever on the right. Wark, well-known as a midfield
opportunist, headed two goals after Dalglish had
forced the ball in as he was tackled. But after the
break the 19-year-old Rufer sent over a cross,
McGrain and the woeful Rough hesitated, and
Sumner poked the ball in. Then Wooddin drove in
Hill's long ball. Crisis.

Pulse rates were lowered by Robertson's curling free-kick and Archibald's header, but the margin wasn't what it might have been, and Brazil were next.

■ 18 June 1982 • Benito Villamarín, Seville • 47,379 • Luis Siles (COS)

▲ **BRAZIL (1) 4**
Zico 33, Oscar 49, Éder 65, Falcão 87
SCOTLAND (1) 1
Narey 18

● BRAZIL *Waldir Peres, Leandro, Júnior, Cerezo, Oscar, Luizinho, Falcão, Sócrates (c), Serginho [Paulo Isidoro 82], Zico, Éder.*
SCOTLAND *Rough, Narey, Gray, Wark, Willie Miller, Hansen, Strachan [Dalglish 65], Souness (c), Archibald, Asa Hartford [Alex McLeish 69], Robertson.*

The dropping of Dalglish wasn't a factor. Brazil destroyed Scotland with a style of play that had supposedly vanished for ever. The ball-control, movement and angles of passing, all done without apparent effort, were the stuff of mythical beaches, with apparently no need for defence. If Sócrates was the natural leader, Falcão organized everything, Cerezo fetched and carried (better looking than it sounds) and Zico played well because he was surrounded by similarly gifted players. Three of their goals were out of the top drawer.

Before that, Scotland scored a good one of their own. Souness pitched a long diagonal ball to the right-hand corner of the area and Wark headed into the path of the charging Narey, whose first touch wasn't great but whose second sent the ball screaming into the top near corner for his only international goal.

Zico equalized with a free-kick curled in at pace off the top of a post, then Scotland really should have

prevented the second, Souness being left to mark the towering Oscar at Júnior's near-post corner. The third goal was almost embarrassing, Brazil walking the ball out of defence to set Éder free on the left. His reputation for ferocious shooting went before him, and he put it to good use, hitting a delicate chip as Rough tensed for the thunderbolt.

The last goal, if anything, was even better, a string of passes ending with Sócrates laying the ball back for Falcão to shoot past four defenders and in off a post. No contest, but at least Scotland wouldn't be the last to suffer, and it was in a good cause.

■ 19 June 1982 • La Rosaleda, Malaga • 17,000 • Yousef El Ghoul (LBY)

▲ **USSR (1) 3**
Gavrilov 25, Blokhin 48, Baltacha 69
NEW ZEALAND (0) 0

● USSR *Dasayev, Sulakvelidze, Demianenko, Baltacha, Chivadze (c), Bessonov, Bal, Gavrilov [Sergei Rodionov 79], Daraselia [Khoren Oganesian HT], Shengalia, Blokhin.*
N. ZEALAND *Van Hattum, Glenn Dods, Herbert, Boath, Elrick, Mackay, Cole, Sumner (c), Cresswell, Rufer, Wooddin.*

New Zealand were well in the game for the first 20 minutes, forcing an important save from Dasayev, but an unlucky goal did for them. Van Hattum, preferred to Richard Wilson who'd kept ten consecutive clean sheets in the qualifiers, had a shot covered until it hit one of the Soviet players and gave Gavrilov a simple tap-in.

■ 22 June 1982 • La Rosaleda, Malaga •
30,000 • Nicolae Rainea (ROM)

▲ **SCOTLAND (1) 2**
Jordan 15, Souness 87
USSR (0) 2
Chivadze 60, Shengalia 84

● SCOTLAND *Rough, Narey, Gray, Wark, Miller, Hansen, Strachan [McGrain 71], Souness (c), Archibald, Joe Jordan [Brazil 71], Robertson.*
USSR *Dasayev, Sulakvelidze, Demianenko, Baltacha, Chivadze (c), Bessonov, Bal, Gavrilov, Sergei Borovsky, Shengalia [Andreyev 89], Blokhin.*

■ 23 June 1982 • Benito Villamarín, Seville •
32,000 • Damir Matovinovic (YUG)

▲ **BRAZIL (2) 4**
Zico 28, 31, Falcão 55, Serginho 69
NEW ZEALAND (0) 0

● BRAZIL *Waldir Peres, Leandro, Júnior, Cerezo, Oscar ['Edinho' (Edino Nazareth) 73], Luizinho, Falcão, Sócrates (c), Serginho [Paulo Isidoro 67], Zico, Éder.*
N. ZEALAND *Van Hattum, Dods, Herbert, Almond, Elrick, Mackay, Boath, Sumner (c), Cresswell [Cole 77], Rufer [Brian Turner 77], Wooddin.*

Needing a win to qualify, Scotland recalled the veteran Jordan, who showed his fangs by running on to Narey's long ball to give them a deserved lead. But there was always the feeling that the USSR had too many shots in their locker. Chivadze scored unconvincingly after Gavrilov's drive was stopped, but the goal that knocked Scotland out was entirely self-inflicted. Miller and the smooth Hansen collided under a long ball by the left touchline and Shengalia ran on to swerve past a stationary Rough. Souness' late slapshot only emphasized his overall contribution. With his team needing real generalship at the highest level, he didn't deliver. But if Jock Stein deserved a better crop of players, at least this time the exit was dignified.

Brazil were at half-throttle, so the scoreline remained respectable. Zico's goals were wasted on a brave but limited team; his first a sweet volley, the second a ground shot, both from right-wing crosses. Falcão ran on and bided his time before scoring at the near post, and even the lumbering Serginho stabbed one in, though it was hard to believe there wasn't a better reserve centre-forward in the whole of Brazil. The injuries to Reinaldo and Careca would probably be felt sooner or later. Meanwhile the All Whites hadn't disgraced themselves in a terribly hard group.

GROUP 6	P	W	D	L	F	A	PTS
Brazil	3	3	0	0	10	2	6
USSR	3	1	1	1	6	4	3
Scotland	3	1	1	1	8	8	3
N. Zealand	3	0	0	3	2	12	0
Brazil and USSR qualified for the second round.							

2nd Round
Group A

Belgium, Poland, USSR

■ 28 June 1982 • Nou Camp, Barcelona •
30,000 • Luis Siles (COS)

▲ **POLAND (2) 3**
Boniek 4, 27, 53
BELGIUM (0) 0

● POLAND *Mlynarczyk, Dziuba, Majewski, Janas, Zmuda
(c), Matysik, Lato, Kupcewicz [Ciolek 82], Buncol, Boniek,
Smolarek.*
BELGIUM *Théo Custers, Michel Renquin, L. Millecamps,
Meeuws (c), Plessers [Baecke 87], Van Moer [Van der Elst HT],
Coeck, Vercauteren, Vandenbergh, Czerniatynski, Ceulemans.*

After two poor performances, Boniek had been
pushed up front against Peru – and now the move
paid off in full. Suddenly here was one of the best
strikers in Europe, scoring a marvellously varied hat-
trick. First he lashed in a square pass from Lato (who
was winning his 100th cap), then knocked a header
over Custers as he came out, and finally broke
through to take the ball round the keeper. Juventus
had spent their money well. Vandenbergh hit the bar
but Belgium were disorganized, and the dropping of
Pfaff for misbehaviour didn't help. His replacement
wasn't capped again (yes, Custers' last stand).

■ 1 July 1982 • Nou Camp, Barcelona • 25,000 •
Michel Vautrot (FRA)

▲ **USSR (0) 1**
Oganesian 49
BELGIUM (0) 0

● USSR *Dasayev, Borovsky, Demianenko, Baltacha,
Chivadze (c), Bessonov, Bal [Daraselia 88], Gavrilov,
Oganesian, Shengalia [Rodionov 89], Blokhin.*
BELGIUM *Jacky Munaron, Renquin, L. Millecamps,
Meeuws (c), De Schrijver [Marc Millecamps 65],
Vandersmissen [Czerniatynski 67], René Verheyen, Coeck,
Vandenbergh, Vercauteren, Ceulemans.*

Vandenbergh, normally so lethal, missed two good
chances, and Belgium were unlucky that
Oganesian's mishit volley bounced in. Shengalia, for
once, and Blokhin, as usual, had a poor match. Luc
and Marc Millecamps were brothers.

■ 4 July 1982 • Nou Camp, Barcelona • 45,000 •
Bob Valentine (SCO)

▲ **POLAND 0**
USSR 0

● POLAND *Mlynarczyk, Dziuba, Majewski, Janas, Zmuda
(c), Matysik, Kupcewicz [Ciolek 52], Buncol, Lato, Boniek,
Smolarek.*
USSR *Dasayev, Sulakvelidze, Demianenko, Bessonov,
Baltacha, Chivadze (c), Borovsky, Gavrilov [Daraselia 79],
Oganesian, Shengalia [Andreyev 58], Blokhin.*

Poland needed only a draw and packed the midfield
to get it. The main talking-point was the way the
Spanish police, brutal throughout the tournament,
waded in to remove banners supporting the Polish

trade union Solidarity, apparently at the request of Soviet television.

GROUP A	P	W	D	L	F	A	PTS
Poland	2	1	1	0	3	0	3
USSR	2	1	1	0	1	0	3
Belgium	2	0	0	2	0	4	0

Poland qualified for the semi-finals.

Group B

England, Spain, West Germany

■ 29 June 1982 • Bernabéu, Madrid • 75,000 •
Arnaldo Coelho (BRZ)

▲ **ENGLAND 0**
WEST GERMANY 0

● ENGLAND *Shilton, Mills (c), Sansom, Robson, Butcher, Thompson, Coppell, Wilkins, Mariner, Francis [Tony Woodcock 76], Rix.*
W. GERMANY *Schumacher, Kaltz, Briegel, Stielike, Kh. Förster, Bernd Förster, Rummenigge (c), Hansi Müller [Fischer 74], Reinders [Littbarski 63], Breitner, Dremmler.*

Drab and grim, two well-organized sides cancelling each other out. England did little up front and were lucky that Rummenigge's long shot hit the bar in the last few minutes. The only hopes raised were Spanish. The Försters were brothers.

■ 2 July 1982 • Bernabéu, Madrid • 90,089 •
Paolo Casarin (ITA)

▲ **WEST GERMANY (0) 2**
Littbarski 50, Fischer 76
SPAIN (0) 1
Zamora 83

● W. GERMANY *Schumacher, Kaltz, Briegel, B. Förster, Kh. Förster, Stielike, Rummenigge (c) [Reinders HT], Breitner, Fischer, Dremmler, Littbarski.*
SPAIN *Arkonada (c), Camacho, Gordillo, M. Alonso, Tendillo, Alexanko, Santiago Urkiaga, Juanito [López Ufarte HT], 'Santillana' (Carlos Alonso), Zamora, Quini [Sánchez 65].*

The defeat by Northern Ireland had sent Spain into a tougher group than expected, and they now paid for it against a side that at last raised its game, even (especially?) when the injured Rummenigge had to go off. Littbarski's recall made a big difference. Small and tricky, he put in the rebound after Arkonada couldn't hold Dremmler's shot, then turned cleverly on the ball to set up Fischer, who pushed it almost cruelly past a covering defender. Despite Zamora's header, the hosts were eliminated without making a mark.

LEADING GOALSCORERS 1982

6	Paolo Rossi	ITA
5	Karl-Heinz Rummenigge	WG
4	Zbigniew Boniek	POL
4	Zico	BRZ

OLDEST PLAYERS IN A FINAL

yrs/days			
40/133	Dino Zoff	ITA	1982
37/241	Gunnar Gren	SWE	1958
37/212	Jan Jongbloed	HOL	1978
37/32	Nílton Santos	BRZ	1962

■ 5 July 1982 • Bernabéu, Madrid • 65,000 • Alexis Ponnet (BEL)

▲ **ENGLAND 0**
SPAIN 0

● SPAIN *Arkonada (c), Camacho, Urkiaga, Gordillo, Tendillo [Antonio Maceda 73], Alexanko, M. Alonso, Zamora, Satrústegui, Santillana, Saura [Pedro Uralde 67].*
ENGLAND *Shilton, Mills (c), Sansom, Robson, Butcher, Thompson, Francis, Wilkins, Mariner, Woodcock [Kevin Keegan 63], Rix [Trevor Brooking 63].*

England needed to win while scoring at least two goals, but they'd managed a diminishing number in each match so far, and even the use of three strikers didn't change things. Greenwood had his reservations about Hoddle (and the 1986 finals suggested he may have been right), but surely anything was better than the Wilkins–Rix axis, the latter allegedly kept in by Don Howe, his coach at Arsenal and assistant manager here. Spain allowed Shilton to make a save with two forwards descending on him, but the clearest chances were missed by the England substitutes, their best players for so long. Brooking turned elegantly inside a man and shot straight at Arkonada, then Keegan put a far post header wide from Robson's cross ('No excuses, I should have buried it'). After a World Cup finals career of 27 minutes, neither was capped again; nor were Mills and five of the Spaniards. England were out without losing a match but without taking many risks to stay in, as if Greenwood had settled for the quiet life to prepare for his retirement.

GROUP B	P	W	D	L	F	A	PTS
W. Germany	2	1	1	0	2	1	3
England	2	0	2	0	0	0	2
Spain	2	0	1	1	1	2	1

West Germany qualified for the semi-finals.

Group C

Argentina, Brazil, Italy

■ 29 June 1982 • Sarriá, Barcelona • 39,000 • Nicolae Rainea (ROM)

▲ **ITALY (0) 2**
Tardelli 57, Cabrini 67
ARGENTINA (0) 1
Passarella 83

● ITALY *Zoff (c), Gentile, Cabrini, Tardelli, Collovati, Scirea, Oriali [Marini 75], Conti, Rossi [Alessandro Altobelli 80], Antognoni, Graziani.*
ARGENTINA *Fillol, Olguin, Tarantini, Gallego, Galván, Passarella (c), Bertoni, Ardiles, Díaz [Calderón 58], Maradona, Kempes [Daniel Valencia 58].*
▼ SENT OFF: *Gallego 85.*

Few gave Italy a chance against the resurgent World Champions, but they'd closed ranks after the group matches, refusing to give interviews to their own press, and this seemed to add to team spirit. In the first half Rainea booked five players, including some who complained that he wasn't booking others for violent conduct! The only sending-off was for a late foul on Tardelli, one of the chief perpetrators. Someone kept a TV camera on Gentile, which was a real revelation, showing how he kept Maradona quiet by bumping, pushing and shirt-tugging all afternoon, invariably on the blind side of the referee. There's no protection against this kind of thing, and although Maradona (to his great credit) stuck it out without exploding, his contribution was inevitably diminished. Ardiles too, was left with a shirt torn down the front as Italy tightened their grip.

In the second half, they moved on to phase two, bringing their talented defenders upfield to score twice. Tardelli left Fillol doing the splits from Antognoni's pass, then Conti set up an open goal for Cabrini, who was confirming his promise of 1978. Maradona and Passarella hit the bar and the latter smacked in a free-kick with Zoff complaining that the whistle hadn't gone – but Italy were just about worth their win.

■ 2 July 1982 • Sarriá, Barcelona • 44,000 • Mario Rubio Vázquez (MEX)

▲ **BRAZIL (1) 3**
Zico 12, Serginho 68, Júnior 74
ARGENTINA (0) 1
Díaz 89

● BRAZIL *Waldir Peres, Leandro [Edevaldo (de Freitas) 82], Júnior, Falcão, Oscar, Luizinho, Cerezo, Sócrates (c), Serginho, Zico [João Batista 84], Éder.*
ARGENTINA *Fillol, Olguin, Tarantini, Barbas, Galván, Passarella (c), Bertoni [Santamaría 64], Ardiles, Kempes [Díaz HT], Maradona, Calderón.*

▼ SENT OFF: *Maradona 87.*

Argentina saw their reign come to an undignified end, comprehensively beaten and with their best player sent off – but really there was little they could have done against a side that moved up a level from merely brilliant. All the Brazilian goals were state-of-the-art.

When Éder lined up a 35-yard free-kick, nobody scoffed. Sure enough, the shot crashed against the bar, Zico beating Serginho to the rebound with no defender in sight to protect a stunned Fillol. Then Éder curled the ball inside to Zico, whose perfect pass through the defence sent Falcão clear on the right, and even Serginho couldn't miss the far-post header. The third was the best, Zico again threading the ball through for the skilful Júnior to continue his run and push the ball past Fillol. At the death, Tarantini's vengeful challenge on Batista forced the ball through to Díaz, whose tremendous shot into the top corner didn't compensate for his wretched tournament. Earlier, almost as soon as he came on, Batista had flattened Barbas, Maradona getting himself sent off for exacting revenge. Frustrated by Italian fouling and Brazilian brilliance, there was nevertheless no doubt about his great talent, and his time would surely come.

■ 5 July 1982 • Sarriá, Barcelona • 44,000 • Avraham Klein (ISR)

▲ **ITALY (2) 3**
Rossi 5, 25, 74
BRAZIL (1) 2
Sócrates 12, Falcão 68

● ITALY *Zoff (c), Gentile, Cabrini, Tardelli [Marini 75], Collovati [Giuseppe Bergomi 34], Scirea, Oriali, Conti, Rossi, Antognoni, Graziani.*
BRAZIL *Waldir Peres, Leandro, Júnior, Cerezo, Oscar, Luizinho, Falcão, Sócrates (c), Serginho [Paulo Isidoro 69], Zico, Éder.*

A graphic illustration of Maradona's treatment by Gentile, who was born in Libya and inevitably nicknamed Gaddafi. Cabrini and Scirea are on hand should the little man escape.

If Hungary-Uruguay 1954 really was the greatest World Cup match, it now had a rival. Even Italy's improved showing against Argentina hadn't melted the bookmakers' stony hearts, especially as Brazil needed only a draw – but Bearzot's men now played the game of their lives, and it was *just* enough.

A good start helped. Conti, full of confidence after his performances so far, kept possession on the right, avoiding two half-hearted tackles, before swinging the ball across to the left. Cabrini dinked in an excellent outswinger and Rossi scored his first goal of the tournament with a neat downward header across the keeper.

Even Italian supporters doubted it could last, and it didn't for long. Zico escaped the murderous Gentile with a marvellous backheeled turn, then his clever angled ball set Sócrates free on the right. The shot beat Zoff at the near post, puffing the chalk on the goal line. But Cerezo knocked a carefree square pass towards three of his team-mates deep in their own half. None

of them expected it; Rossi stole it away to the edge of the area, and shot right through Waldir Peres.

The longer the lead lasted, the more possible an Italian victory became, and Rossi should have made it certain in the second half, after the selfless Graziani had beaten his man on the left and knocked the ball across goal. With only poor old Waldir to beat, Rossi scooped the ball wide. Within minutes, it looked as disastrous a miss as expected; Brazil equalized again.

Júnior swerved inside from the left wing and gave the ball to the unmarked Falcão on the right-hand side of the Italian area. Cerezo made another of his brave and powerful runs (Zoff had already saved superbly at his feet), taking out three defenders to leave a gap for Falcão, who visibly took aim before scoring with a strong left-foot shot which left Zoff screaming at his defence. Falcão's face, demented with delight, was one of the images of the tournament.

But this was a day of great Italian resilience. From a corner on the right, the ball fell to Tardelli, whose weak

Rossi puts the seal on one of the great matches by completing his hat-trick. The Brazilians are Leandro, Falcão and Waldir Peres.

shot turned into a perfect short through-pass for Rossi, who swivelled and shot past Waldir from the six-yard line. Brazil kept pressing, but Italy went on making chances, Antognoni having a goal understandably but wrongly disallowed for offside. With two minutes left, Éder's free-kick from the left was met by Oscar's header at the far post, only for Zoff to dive and hold the ball just in front of the line; amazing reflexes for a middle-aged man. Oscar couldn't believe his eyes. You will, Oscar, you will.

Italy had put an end to Brazil's run of 24 unbeaten matches, mainly because their defence – which kept its concentration under extreme pressure – was altogether more talented. Júnior looked good coming forward but it's hard to remember him making a tackle, and the thought of Waldir, Luizinho and Leandro with winners medals was as unappealing as Félix and Everaldo in 1970. Scirea, Bergomi (impressively cold-blooded for an 18-year-old) and the mop-haired Collovati had been immense, and Antognoni matched the Brazilians for poise, but of course it was Rossi's match.

Maradona's difficult first World Cup ends in a sending-off against Brazil. Tarantini offers consolation.

GROUP C	P	W	D	L	F	A	PTS
Italy	2	2	0	0	5	3	4
Brazil	2	1	0	1	5	4	2
Argentina	2	0	0	2	2	5	0

Italy qualified for the semi-finals.

Group D

Austria, France, Northern Ireland

■ 28 June 1982 • Vicente Calderón, Madrid • 30,000 • Károly Palotai (HUN)

▲ **FRANCE (1) 1**
Genghini 39
AUSTRIA (0) 0

● FRANCE *Ettori, Battiston, Bossis, Janvion, Trésor (c), Giresse, Genghini [Girard 85], Soler, Lacombe [Rocheteau 15], Tigana, Six.*
AUSTRIA *Koncilia, Krauss, Obermayer (c), Degeorgi [Baumeister HT], Pezzey, Hattenberger, Hintermaier, Prohaska, Kurt Jara [Welzl HT], Krankl, Schachner.*

By finishing second to England and winning just one of their first three matches, France found themselves in the easiest second-round group and made the most of it. Their win here was more clear-cut than the score suggests, Tigana a very acceptable deputy for Platini. Genghini hit a post before scoring with a swinging free-kick, and Koncilia had to make a string of saves. Prohaska, supposedly the playmaker, played far too deep, and Degeorgi crashed into an advertising hoarding. Austria were making an untidy exit.

■ 1 July 1982 • Vicente Calderón, Madrid • 24,000 • Adolf Prokop (EG)

▲ **AUSTRIA (0) 2**
Pezzey 53, Hintermaier 67
NORTHERN IRELAND (1) 2
Hamilton 28, 74

● AUSTRIA *Koncilia, Krauss, Obermayer (c), Pezzey, Johann Pregesbauer [Hintermaier HT], Anton Pichler, Baumeister, Prohaska, Max Hagmayr [Welzl HT], Jurtin, Schachner.*
N. IRELAND *Jim Platt, J. Nicholl, Nelson, McCreery, C. Nicholl, McClelland, Armstrong, M. O'Neill (c), Hamilton, McIlroy, Whiteside [Brotherston 67].*

The Irish were still riding their cloud, doing great things with a front three that consisted of a Watford reserve (Armstrong), a Third Division player (Hamilton) and a 17-year-old with a single League match behind him. Armstrong, a revelation in Spain (losing weight in the heat apparently helped) made another of his strong runs down the right, and Hamilton headed in the cross. Then the Austrians woke up, Prohaska hitting a post, Pezzey scoring from the resulting corner. Schachner had a goal dubiously disallowed before Hintermaier's rising shot put them ahead. But Jimmy Nicholl beat Koncilia to a loose ball on the right, and Hamilton

headed in again. Admirable stuff, but Northern Ireland now had to beat France, who were coming into form.

■ 4 July 1982 • Vicente Calderón, Madrid • 30,000 • Alojzy Jarguz (POL)

▲ **FRANCE (1) 4**
Giresse 33, 80, Rocheteau 46, 68
NORTHERN IRELAND (0) 1
Armstrong 75

● FRANCE *Ettori, Amoros, Bossis, Tigana, Janvion, Trésor, Giresse, Genghini, Soler [Six 63], Platini (c), Rocheteau [Couriol 83].*
N. IRELAND *Jennings, J. Nicholl, Donaghy, McCreery [John O'Neill 85], C. Nicholl, McClelland, Armstrong, M. O'Neill (c), Hamilton, McIlroy, Whiteside.*

After 26 minutes, with honours roughly even, Martin O'Neill broke through to score, only for the goal to be wrongly disallowed. With their limited resources, that was the last thing Northern Ireland needed, and the last real chance they had. Giresse, the hardworking star of the French midfield, cracked in Platini's pull-back and headed the fourth, small though he was. The revitalized Rocheteau ran from halfway to score the second and beat two defenders for the third. Armstrong, the best British player in the tournament, put in the rebound when Ettori couldn't hold Whiteside's shot. Death with glory for the Irish, who deserved a better scoreline. Had O'Neill's goal been allowed, who knows how this brittle French side would have responded?

[Right] Schumacher (left) starts his assault on French hopes in the semi-final. Battiston collapses at his feet as Breitner distances himself from the deed.

GROUP D	P	W	D	L	F	A	PTS
France	2	2	0	0	5	1	4
Austria	2	0	1	1	2	3	1
N. Ireland	2	0	1	1	3	6	1

France qualified for the semi-finals.

Semi-finals

■ 8 July 1982 • Nou Camp, Barcelona • 55,000 •
Juan Cardellino (URU)

▲ **ITALY (1) 2**
Rossi 22, 73
POLAND (0) 0

● ITALY *Zoff (c), Bergomi, Cabrini, Tardelli, Collovati, Scirea, Oriali, Conti, Rossi, Antognoni [Marini 28], Graziani [Altobelli 70].*
POLAND *Mlynarczyk, Dziuba, Majewski, Janas, Zmuda (c), Matysik, Kupcewicz, Buncol, Lato, Ciolek [Palasz HT], Smolarek [Kusto 77].*

The rest of the tournament was largely processional for Italy, especially against a Polish team which had lost Boniek to a pointless booking in the previous match. Although Kupcewicz grazed a post, at the other end Rossi was on a roll. He stabbed in from close range when Tardelli's dive distracted the defence at a free-kick, then fell gently forward to head the second after Conti had beaten two men on the left. Italy's only worry, and it was nothing minor, was the injury that would keep Antognoni out of the Final.

■ 8 July 1982 • Sánchez Pizjuán, Seville •
71,000 • Charles Corver (HOL)

▲ **WEST GERMANY (1) (1) 3**
Littbarski 18, Rummenigge 103, Fischer 108
FRANCE (1) (1) 3
Platini pen 27, Trésor 93, Giresse 99
West Germany 5-4 pens.

● W. GERMANY *Schumacher, Kaltz (c), Briegel [Rummenigge 97], B. Förster, Kh. Förster, Stielike, Magath [Hrubesch 73], Breitner, Fischer, Dremmler, Littbarski.*
FRANCE *Ettori, Amoros, Bossis, Janvion, Trésor, Giresse, Genghini [Battiston 50, Lopez 60], Six, Tigana, Platini (c), Rocheteau*
☐ PENALTY SHOOT-OUT: *Giresse 1-0, Kaltz 1-1, Amoros 2-1, Breitner 2-2, Rocheteau 3-2, Stielike saved, Six saved, Littbarski 3-3, Platini 4-3, Rummenigge 4-4, Bossis saved, Hrubesch 4-5.*

If it didn't equal Italy-Brazil for sustained skill, this more than matched it for drama. France, unrecognizable as the team that had lost to England, played some wonderful stuff through midfield, but West Germany had been dining out on this kind of comeback since 1954. The scoreline was about right, though few were pleased by the result or the way of deciding it. It was the first World Cup match to end in a penalty shoot-out.

[Top] *The aftermath of Schumacher's challenge. While Six tends to the stricken Battiston, Platini makes an impassioned plea for justice.*

[Middle] *Fischer, half-hidden and falling, equalizes with a classy overhead kick.*

[Bottom] *Schumacher adds insult to injury by saving Bossis' penalty in the semi-final shoot-out.*

Another penalty had started the French scoring, after Bernd Förster pulled back Rocheteau. Before that, Littbarski had scored easily when Ettori saved from Fischer. In the second half, Battiston ran clear on to Platini's pass and was violently bodychecked by Schumacher's follow-through, probably the worst-looking foul in any World Cup. No free-kick, no red card, just concussion and broken teeth for Battiston (Schumacher rather crassly offered to pay to have them capped) who was stretchered off and given oxygen. When people wonder if Michael Schumacher is a relative, this is what they mean. A dreadful piece of refereeing by the man who'd allowed Brazil to kick lumps out of England in 1978.

France almost gained revenge in the last minute (Amoros hit the bar) and appeared to have done so in extra-time, Trésor hooking in a splendid volley from a cross by Giresse, who drove the third in off a post. But Battiston's injury had forced them to use their second substitute, and there was no-one to chase Rummenigge's fresh legs when they came on, so Schumacher's thuggery helped win the match. Rummenigge knocked in a cross at the near post and the veteran Fischer equalized with one of his trademark overhead kicks, two goals in keeping with a marvellous match.

When Stielike missed his penalty in the shoot-out, the hard man fell to his knees in despair, but Schumacher saved from Six and the outstanding Bossis, and the hulking Hrubesch showed a delicate touch with the last kick. Sad for France and everyone who admired them, but the Germans had contributed fully to a splendid occasion. Mind you, if they were satisfied, so too were the Italians, who now had less to fear.

3rd-place Final

Final

■ 10 July 1982 • José Rico Pérez, Alicante •
28,000 • Antônio Garrido (POR)

▲ **POLAND (2) 3**
Szarmach 42, Majewski 45, Kupcewicz 47
FRANCE (1) 2
Girard 14, Couriol 75

● POLAND *Mlynarczyk, Dziuba, Majewski, Janas, Zmuda (c), Matysik [Roman Wójcicki HT], Lato, Kupcewicz, Szarmach, Boniek, Buncol.*
FRANCE *Jean Castaneda, Amoros, Janvion [Lopez 66], Girard, Philippe Mahut, Trésor (c), Couriol, Tigana [Six 83], Soler, Larios, Bruno Bellone.*

11 July 1982 • Bernabéu, Madrid • 90,089 •
Arnaldo Coelho (BRZ)

ITALY (0) 3
Rossi 56, Tardelli 68, Altobelli 80
WEST GERMANY (0) 1
Breitner 83

ITALY *Zoff (c), Bergomi, Cabrini, Gentile, Oriali, Collovati, Scirea, Tardelli, Conti, Rossi, Graziani [Altobelli 7, Causio 89].*

W. GERMANY *Schumacher, Kaltz, Briegel, B. Förster, Kh. Förster, Stielike, Littbarski, Dremmler [Hrubesch 62], Breitner, Fischer, Rummenigge (c) [H. Müller 70].*

Entertaining enough, for what it was worth. The French gave their reserves a run-out, and two of them scored their goals, both from passes by Tigana. But these only sandwiched Poland's three quick strikes either side of the interval. Szarmach bundled the ball in off a post; the bearded Majewski headed in when Castaneda missed a corner; and Kupcewicz scored with a low free-kick. It was the last international match for Lato and Szarmach, remnants of Poland's best-ever team.

Did we say processional? Already without their midfield general, Italy lost their centre-forward almost immediately, missed a penalty, and still won with plenty to spare. Conti and Tardelli took over the playmaking, and again the quality of their defensive players made a vital difference, contributing to all

All fall down as Rossi scores his sixth consecutive goal, the first of the Final. (l–r): Kh. Förster, Stielike, Cabrini, Rossi, Schumacher, Briegel and Altobelli.

three goals. The strapping Briegel, a former decathlete, had been seen as the future of the game – but every Italian goal came down his flank and he gave away a penalty after 24 minutes by crudely hauling down Conti. Cabrini, who'd once had a spot-kick saved at Highbury, became the first player to miss one in a World Cup Final, scuffing the ball low and wide. But West Germany's name wasn't written on the Cup this time.

Rummenigge still wasn't fully fit (Stielike was furious about it afterwards), so Bearzot let Gentile loose on Littbarski, who disappeared without trace. At the other end, a quickly taken free-kick found Gentile in yards of space on the right, and his low cross would have been put in by Cabrini if Rossi's head hadn't got there first; he'd now scored Italy's last six goals. The next began with Conti carrying the ball and Scirea backheeling it deep in the German penalty area then pushing the return pass across to Tardelli; he turned away from a defender before lashing in the cross-shot. His celebration, all fists and larynx, was the most vivid in any Final. Altobelli scored the third by calmly going round Schumacher. Breitner's low shot made him only the third player to score in two Finals, but it was the merest coat of gloss. West Germany lost to a European country for the first time since the 1978 finals.

Like Menotti in 1978, Bearzot had been vindicated, though he owed even more to his defenders (there were an awful lot of them) than to Rossi, whose rehabilitation was remarkable. At the start of the tournament, an even greater striker, Denis Law, had been adamant that 'you can't be out of the game for two years and come back in a tournament like the World Cup'. Now the Germans were left wishing there were longer bans for fixing the results of Italian football matches.

Altobelli (half hidden) is about to complete the scoring for Italy. Kh. Förster and Kaltz (20) had close views of all three Italian goals.

West Germany's starting line-up in the Final (l–r): Littbarski, Kh. Förster, Fischer, Dremmler, B. Förster, Breitner, Stielike, Briegel, Kaltz, Schumacher, Rummenigge.

The Hand of the Baskervilles
Mexico 1986

At first glance, it looked as if FIFA weren't entirely to blame for revisiting Mexico's heat and altitude (Colombia, the original choice, and Brazil both pulled out) but the truth was murkier than that. Canada and the USA were both allowed to present their cases, but there was evidence that the decision had already been taken; one of FIFA's vice-presidents, Guillermo Cañedo, was a leading executive with the private Mexican television company Televisa. Asked about the prohibitively high ticket prices, Cañedo replied that 'people always have TV'. Havelange said his conscience was clear and 'other people may write or say what they like'. What many wrote and said (even those from Thatcher's Britain) was how shocked they were by the ongoing gulf between Mexico's rich and poor. Havelange had no convincing answers when asked why FIFA simply didn't fill the empty seats with needy children or ban Camel cigarettes as a major sponsor.

As for the altitude, teams were fitter by now and appeared to suffer less distress – but most of the fancied teams had other problems. The holders Italy came with the same coach and several of the same players but a patchy recent record. France had won all 12 of their matches in 1984, including the European Championship in which Platini scored nine goals in five games. But that was at home, the team had begun to creak a little in the two years since, and there was still no reliable striker.

Maradona was at his peak for Argentina but seemed to lack a quality supporting cast. West Germany had Beckenbauer as manager but no midfield general (the brilliant Schuster was now refusing to play for the national team). Brazil were strong at the back and had Careca up front but were still relying on their 1982 creative players, who were all over 30: Zico, Sócrates, Falcão, Júnior. Mexico, who'd been doing well under their Yugoslav coach, seemed to have been strengthened by the inclusion of Hugo Sánchez, now with Real Madrid – but had lost 3-0 to England a month earlier

and would again have to lean heavily on home support.

England had qualified far more comfortably this time, without losing a match. The messianic Bryan Robson had a troublesome shoulder but there was a quick new striker in Gary Lineker, the First Division's leading scorer. High hopes but fingers crossed. Northern Ireland came through from the same group after holding out for a goalless draw at Wembley and showing their usual grit by winning 1-0 in Romania.

Scotland were there yet again, after a long haul tinged with tragedy. Jock Stein, still their manager, had died of a heart attack while watching the 1-1 draw in Cardiff which sent them through to a play-off with Australia. Then the 0-0 draw in Melbourne owed much to Jim Leighton's form in goal. But again, the Scots were unfortunate with the draw for the finals, finding themselves in the 'Group of Death' with West Germany, the exciting Danes (in the finals for the first time) and Uruguay, many people's favourites with their array of world-class defenders and Francescoli in midfield.

FIFA had carried out their threat to increase the number of qualifiers to 24, partly to uphold their president João Havelange's old election promises to Africa and Asia, who provided his power base. The second stage mini-leagues were scrapped in favour of a knockout format, a return to the 1970 system but with an extra match. To fit 24 into the 16 needed for the second round, the four third-placed teams with the best records would join the top two in each of six groups. The phrase 'keep it simple' only applied on the pitch.

Not everything had changed from the last time the tournament came to Mexico; more than ever, the organizers were kowtowing to the wishes of TV companies. Not only were some kick-offs scheduled for the hottest part of the day, but matches were to end on the dot of full time, to fit in with broadcasting deadlines. Very snug. As in someone's pocket.

1986

Group A

Argentina, Bulgaria, Italy, South Korea

■ 31 May 1986 • Azteca, Mexico City • 95,000 • Erik Fredriksson (SWE)

▲ **BULGARIA (0) 1**
Sirakov 85
ITALY (1) 1
Altobelli 43

● BULGARIA *Borislav Mikhailov, Radoslav Zdravkov, Georgi Dimitrov (c), Nikolai Arabov, Aleksandar Markov, Nasko Sirakov, Anjo Sadkov, Stoicho Mladenov, Zivko Gospodinov [Andrej Zheliaskov 73], Plamen Getov, Bojidar Iskrenov [Kostadin Kostadinov 64]. Ivan Vutzov.*
ITALY *Giovanni Galli, Giuseppe Bergomi, Antonio Cabrini, Fernando De Napoli, Pietro Vierchowod, Gaetano Scirea (c), Bruno Conti [Gianluca Vialli 65], Salvatore Bagni, Giuseppe Galderisi, Antonio Di Gennaro, Alessandro Altobelli. Enzo Bearzot.*

Calling this the best opening match since 1962 sounds like damning with faint praise; in fact it was a perfectly adequate contest, which Italy should have won against an unambitious team. Altobelli met a long cross with a sidefooted volley at the far post, but the holders missed chances and Sirakov equalized with a low header from Zdravkov's cross.

■ 2 June 1986 • Olímpico, Mexico City • 40,000 • Victoriano Sánchez Arminio (SPA)

▲ **ARGENTINA (2) 3**
Valdano 6, 46, Ruggeri 18
SOUTH KOREA (0) 1
Park Chang-sun 73

● ARGENTINA *Nery Pumpido, Néstor Clausen, José Luis Brown, Oscar Ruggeri, Oscar Garré, Ricardo Giusti, Sergio Batista [Julio Olarticoechea 76], Jorge Burruchaga, Diego Maradona (c), Pedro Pasculli [Carlos Tápia 75], Jorge Valdano. Carlos Bilardo.*
S. KOREA *Oh Yun-kyo, Park Kyung-joon, Huh Jung-moo, Cho Min-kook, Jung Yong-hwan, Kim Yong-se [Joo Byung-ok HT], Kim Pyung-suk [Cho Kwang-rae 22], Kim Joo-sung, Park Chang-sun (c), Choi Soon-ho, Cha Bum-kun. Kim Jung-nam.*

South Korea, back in the finals for the first time since 1954, impressed people with their determination and long-range goal, but were less comfortable at the back. Valdano shot the first and scored the last at the far post, and Ruggeri thumped in a header. All three goals stemmed from Maradona, who was the best player on the pitch despite nursing a long-standing injury which the Koreans tried to aggravate. The first two goals came from free-kicks after he was tripped.

■ 5 June 1986 • Cuauhtemoc, Puebla • 32,000 •
Jan Keizer (HOL)

▲ **ARGENTINA (1) 1**
Maradona 33
ITALY (1) 1
Altobelli pen 6

● ARGENTINA *Pumpido, Brown, José Luis Cuciuffo,
Ruggeri, Garré, Giusti, Batista [Olarticoechea 59],
Burruchaga, Maradona (c), Cláudio Borghi [Héctor Enrique
76], Valdano.*
ITALY *Galli, Bergomi, Cabrini, De Napoli [Giuseppe Baresi
87], Vierchowod, Scirea (c), Conti [Vialli 64], Bagni, Galderisi,
Di Gennaro, Altobelli.*

Italy took the lead when Garré was judged to have
handled intentionally, but Bilardo had correctly
identified Altobelli as Italy's only attacking threat and
put Ruggeri on him, with the result that Italy were
barely worth the draw, although Conti hit a post in
the second half. Maradona was man-marked too, by
Bagni, but escaped to push in a volley with that
famous left foot. The second half, like so many others
in the tournament, degenerated in a rash of bookings.

GROUP A	P	W	D	L	F	A	PTS
Argentina	3	2	1	0	6	2	5
Italy	3	1	2	0	5	4	4
Bulgaria	3	0	2	1	2	4	2
S. Korea	3	0	1	2	4	7	1

Argentina, Italy and Bulgaria qualified for the second round.

■ 5 June 1986 • Olímpico, Mexico City •
45,000 • Fallaj Al-Shanar (SAU)

▲ **BULGARIA (1) 1**
Getov 11
SOUTH KOREA (0) 1
Kim Jong-boo 69

● BULGARIA *Mikhailov, Zdravkov, Dimitrov (c), Arabov,
Petar Petrov, Sirakov, Sadkov, Mladenov, Gospodinov, Getov
[Zheliaskov 58], Iskrenov [Kostadinov HT].*
S. KOREA *Oh Yun-kyo, Park Kyung-joon, Huh Jung-
moo, Cho Yung-jeung, Jung Yong-hwan, Cho Kwang-rae [Cho
Min-kook 71], Park Chang-sun (c), No Soon-jin [Kim Jong-
boo HT], Kim Joo-sung, Byun Byung-joo, Cha Bum-kun.*

Bulgaria presumably saw this as their latest great
opportunity to win a game in the finals, but the
Koreans refused to lie down after Getov had pushed in
Mladenov's cross. Kim Joo-sung and Park Chang-sun
came close before Kim Jong-boo eventually got to a
cross before Dimitrov and pushed it past the keeper.

■ 10 June 1986 • Cuauhtemoc, Puebla • 20,000 •
David Socha (USA)

▲ **ITALY (1) 3**
Altobelli 18, 73, Cho Kwang-rae o.g. 82
SOUTH KOREA (0) 2
Choi Soon-ho 62, Huh Jung-moo 89

● ITALY *Galli, Vierchowod, Cabrini, De Napoli, Fulvio
Collovati, Scirea (c), Conti, Bagni [Baresi 68], Galderisi
[Vialli 88], Di Gennaro, Altobelli.*
S. KOREA *Oh Yun-kyo, Cho Kwang-rae, Park Kyung-
joon, Huh Jung-moo, Jung Yong-hwan, Cho Yung-jeung, Kim
Joo-sung [Chung Jong-soo HT], Park Chang-sun (c), Cha
Bum-kun, Byun Byung-joo [Kim Jong-boo 70], Choi Soon-ho.*

A repeat of the 1966 disaster against North Korea would have knocked Italy out, but they were in no great danger of that, even after the gangling Choi Soon-ho had stepped outside a tackle before thumping an equalizer from the edge of the box. Again the Italian attack relied too much on Altobelli, but it didn't matter this time. He scored twice (the first with incredible arrogance in the box), provoked Cho Kwang-rae into an own goal, and would have had a hat-trick if he hadn't hit the post with a penalty awarded for a foul by Park Kyung-joon on Galderisi. Huh Jung-moo scored from a flick by Cha Bum-kun, Korea's best-known player, who played in the *Bundesliga*. Baresi's more famous brother Franco played in the 1990 and 1994 finals.

■ 10 June 1986 • Olímpico, Mexico City • 45,000 • Berny Ulloa (COS)

▲ **ARGENTINA (1) 2**
Valdano 3, Burruchaga 79
BULGARIA (0) 0

● ARGENTINA *Pumpido, Brown, Cuciuffo, Ruggeri, Garré, Giusti, Batista [Enrique HT], Burruchaga, Maradona (c), Borghi [Olarticoechea HT], Valdano.*
BULGARIA *Mikhailov, Petrov, Dimitrov (c), Zheliaskov, A. Markov, Sirakov [Zdravkov 72], Sadkov, Georgi Yordanov, Plamen Markov, Getov, Mladenov [Boycho Velichkov 54].*

Bulgaria had seen the results from other groups and knew that a narrow defeat would send them through. They packed their team with midfielders and no forwards, conceded goals from crosses by Cuciuffo and Maradona – yet still qualified for the first time despite taking only two points from three games.

Group B

Belgium, Iraq, Mexico, Paraguay

■ 3 June 1986 • Azteca, Mexico City • 110,000 • Carlos Esposito (ARG)

▲ **MEXICO (2) 2**
Quirarte 23, Sánchez 39
BELGIUM (1) 1
Vandenbergh 45

● MEXICO *Pablo Larios, Mario Trejo, Fernando Quirarte, Félix Cruz Barbosa, Raúl Servín, Javier Aguirre, Tomás Boy (c) [Miguel España 69], Carlos Muñoz, Manuel Negrete, Luis Flóres [Francisco Javier Cruz 79], Hugo Sánchez.* Bora Milutinovic (YUG).
BELGIUM *Jean-Marie Pfaff, Eric Gerets, Franky Van der Elst, Hugo Broos, Michel De Wolf, Enzo Scifo, Frankie Vercauteren, René Vandereycken, Jan Ceulemans (c), Erwin Vandenbergh [Stefan Demol 66], Filip Desmet [Nico Claesen 64].* Guy Thys.

The hosts had a better team than in 1970, guided by the tall veteran Boy, whose dead-ball kicks led to the two goals. Quirarte headed in his indirect free-kick and Aguirre glanced on his corner for Sánchez to head in from very close range at the far post. Vandenbergh headed in Gerets' long throw, but Belgium were too defensive for their own good. Rather like Rossi before him, Gerets had been amnestied after being found guilty in a famous bribery case. Spelling variations: Stéphane De Mol, Philippe De Smet.

■ 4 June 1986 • Luis Gutiérrez Dosal, Toluca •
24,000 • Edwin Picon-Ackong (MAU)

▲ **PARAGUAY (1) 1**
Romero 35
IRAQ (0) 0

● PARAGUAY *Roberto Fernández, Juan Torales, César Zabala,*
Wladimiro Schettina, Rogelio Delgado (c), Adolfino Cañete, Julio
César Romero, Jorge Núñez, Buenaventura Ferreira, Alfredo
Mendoza [Jorge Guasch 88], Roberto Cabañas. Cayetano Ré.
IRAQ *Raad Hammoudi (c), Khalil Allawi, Salim Nadhum,*
Samir Mahmoud, Ali Shihab, Haris Hassan [Abdulrahim
Aufi 67], Ahmed Rhadi Amaiesh, Saïd Hussein, Basil Kourkis
Hanna [Qasim Basim 84], Natiq Abidoun, Ghanim Al-
Roubai. Evaristo (de Macedo) (BRZ).

Iraq were unlucky when Rhadi put the ball in the
net just after the half-time whistle had gone, but
Paraguay were too clever for them. Their star player
(nicknamed Romerito in Brazil, where he played for
Fluminense) ran on to Cañete's pass to lob the
keeper. Kourkis is sometimes seen spelt Gorgis.

■ 7 June 1986 • Azteca, Mexico City • 114,600 •
George Courtney (ENG)

▲ **MEXICO (1) 1**
Flóres 3
PARAGUAY (0) 1
Romero 85

● MEXICO *Larios, Cruz Barbosa, Trejo, Quirarte, Servín,*
Aguirre, Boy (c) [España 57], Muñoz, Negrete, Flóres [F. J.
Cruz 77], Sánchez.
PARAGUAY *Fernández, Torales [Ramón Angel Hicks*
75], Zabala, Schettina, Delgado (c), Cañete, Romero,
Núñez, Cabañas, Ferreira, Mendoza [Guasch 62].

A dramatic top-and-tail. Boy sent Servín down the
left for a cross which Flóres chested down before
shooting home, then the next 80 minutes were
punctuated by bookings. Romero headed in
Cañete's cross and Sánchez was brought down in the
area with two minutes left, only for his image of a
returning messiah to be dented when Fernández
touched his penalty on to a post. The crowd's first
disappointment, but both sides were surely through
to the next round.

■ 8 June 1986 • Luis Gutiérrez Dosal, Toluca •
10,000 • Jesús Díaz Palacio (COL)

▲ **BELGIUM (2) 2**
Scifo 16, Claesen pen 19
IRAQ (0) 1
Rhadi 59

● BELGIUM *Pfaff, Gerets, F. Van der Elst, Demol [Georges*
Grün 68], De Wolf, Scifo [Leo Clijsters 66], Vercauteren,
Vandereycken, Ceulemans (c), Desmet, Claesen.
IRAQ *Raad (c), Allawi, Nadhum, Samir Mahmoud,*
Shihab, Haris Hassan, Al-Roubai, Rhadi, Kourkis,
Abidoun, Karim Minshid [Aufi 81].
SENT OFF: *Kourkis 52.*

Belgium badly needed the win and got it without too
much trouble, though Iraq's physical style was again
hard to deal with. The 20-year-old playmaker Scifo,
who'd turned down Italy to play for Belgium, scored
with a cross-shot from a Ceulemans pass, and
Vercauteren was brought down by Khalil Allawi for
the penalty. Kourkis was sent off for fouling De Wolf.

■ 11 June 1986 • Azteca, Mexico City •
103,763 • Zoran Petrovic (YUG)

▲ **MEXICO** (0) 1
Quirarte 54
IRAQ (0) 0

● MEXICO *Larios, Rafael Amador [Alejandro Domínguez 61], Quirarte, Cruz Barbosa, Servín, Aguirre, Boy (c), España, Negrete, Flóres, Carlos de los Cobos [F. J. Cruz 78].*
IRAQ *Abdulfattah Jassim, Maad Ibrahim Majid, Khalil Allawi (c), Nadhum, Shihab, Rhadi, Minshid, Abidoun [Aufi 60], Ainid Tiveresh [Shakir Hamza 68], Basim, Al-Roubai.*

Again the Iraqis offered little more than snapping aggression, but Mexico made hard work of it, scoring from another set piece, a defender heading in Negrete's indirect free-kick. Sánchez was suspended after bookings in each of the previous two games.

■ 11 June 1986 • Luis Gutiérrez Dosal, Toluca •
10,000 • Bogdan Dochev (BUL)

▲ **BELGIUM** (1) 2
Vercauteren 31, Veyt 59
PARAGUAY (0) 2
Cabañas 50, 76

● BELGIUM *Pfaff, Michel Renquin, Grün [Leo Van der Elst 89], Vercauteren, Broos, Patrick Vervoort, Demol, Scifo, Ceulemans (c), Claesen, Veyt.*
PARAGUAY *Fernández, Torales, Zabala, Guasch, Delgado (c), Núñez, Romero, Cañete, Ferreira, Mendoza [Hicks 67], Cabañas.*

Paraguay were already in the second round, the Belgians virtually there with them, so this was mainly for entertainment and experiment. Belgium's

new back line was a considerable improvement. Ceulemans, big and rawboned but always influential, ran from the halfway line to set up Vercauteren, who chipped the keeper, as did Veyt from Vervoort's pass, but Cabañas capitalized on a bad back-pass by Broos and put in Delgado's cross. Scifo scored gloriously from a free-kick but hadn't noticed that it was indirect. Five minutes from time Ré became the first coach to be shown a red card in a finals match.

GROUP B	P	W	D	L	F	A	PTS
Mexico	3	2	1	0	4	2	5
Paraguay	3	1	2	0	4	3	4
Belgium	3	1	1	1	5	5	3
Iraq	3	0	0	3	1	4	0

Mexico, Paraguay and Belgium qualified for the second round.

Group C

Canada, France, Hungary, USSR

■ 1 June 1986 • Campo Nuevo, León • 35,748 •
Hernán Silva Arce (CHI)

▲ **FRANCE** (0) 1
Papin 79
CANADA (0) 0

● FRANCE *Joël Bats, Manuel Amoros, Patrick Battiston, Luis Fernandez, Thierry Tusseau, Max Bossis, Alain Giresse, Jean Tigana, Jean-Pierre Papin, Michel Platini (c), Dominique Rocheteau [Yannick Stopyra 70]. Henri Michel.*
CANADA *Paul Dolan, Bobby Lenarduzzi, Ian Bridge, Paul James [Branko Segota 82], Randy Samuel, Bruce Wilson (c), Randy Ragan, Dave Norman, Mike Sweeney [Jamie Lowery 55], Carl Valentine, Igor Vrablic. Tony Waiters (ENG).*

1986

France naturally dominated the part-timers – several of whom didn't even have a club – but suffered from their chronic lack of a goalscorer up front. Papin, who eventually shot in after Stopyra had headed on a long cross by Fernandez, wasn't yet the razor-sharp striker who became European Footballer of the Year. Canada, coached by a former England international goalkeeper, had their moments but the lively Vrablic was given little support.

■ 2 June 1986 • Revolución, Irapuato • 16,500 • Luigi Agnolin (ITA)

▲ **USSR (3) 6**
Yakovenko 2, Aleinikov 3, Belanov pen 24, Yaremchuk 66, Dajka o.g. 75, Rodionov 83
HUNGARY (0) 0

● USSR *Renat Dasayev, Vladimir Bessonov, Oleg Kuznetsov, Nikolai Larionov, Anatoly Demianenko (c), Vasily Rats, Pavel Yakovenko [Vadim Yevtushenko 72], Aleksandr Zavarov, Igor Belanov [Sergei Rodionov 69], Sergei Aleinikov, Ivan Yaremchuk.* Valery Lobanovsky.
HUNGARY *Péter Disztl, Sándor Sallai, Antal Róth [Győző Burcsa 13], József Kardos, Zoltán Péter [László Dajka 63], Imre Garaba, Antal Nagy (c), Lajos Détári, József Kiprich, Marton Esterházy, György Bognár.* György Mezey.

Hungary were without the injured Nyilasi, but his World Cup record was spotty and anyway the USSR were simply too strong, though six goals was an unusual haul for them. They were helped by Mezey taking off a defender after the two early goals, but there was no doubting their stamina in the thin air. Lobanovsky, recently appointed coach, was also the manager at Dynamo Kiev, who'd just run away with the Cup-Winners Cup; nine of that team played here. Aleinikov's thumping long shot was the pick of the goals and they would have equalled the record of

seven different goalscorers if Yevtushenko hadn't missed a penalty three minutes after coming on. Dajka's own goal is sometimes credited to Yaremchuk. Larionov, Demianenko and Yakovenko shared the same birthday.

■ 5 June 1986 • Campo Nuevo, León • 36,540 • Romualdo Arppi (BRZ)

▲ **FRANCE (0) 1** Fernandez 62
USSR (0) 1 Rats 54

● FRANCE *Bats, William Ayache, Amoros, Fernandez, Bossis, Battiston, Giresse [Philippe Vercruysse 83], Tigana, Papin [Bruno Bellone 76], Platini (c), Stopyra.*
USSR *Dasayev, Bessonov, Kuznetsov, Larionov, Demianenko (c), Rats, Yakovenko [Rodionov 69], Zavarov [Oleg Blokhin 59], Belanov, Aleinikov, Yaremchuk.*

A fine match, in which both teams looked real contenders. The USSR's goal was another tremendous long shot (Rats beating Bats launched a few headlines) but Giresse put the sturdy Fernandez through and a draw was the right result. Platini, who hit the post with a free-kick, was plagued with tendonitis and had yet another quiet World Cup match.

GROUP C	P	W	D	L	F	A	PTS
USSR	3	2	1	0	9	1	5
France	3	2	1	0	5	1	5
Hungary	3	1	0	2	2	9	2
Canada	3	0	0	3	0	5	0
USSR and France qualified for the second round.							

■ 6 June 1986 • Revolución, Irapuato • 13,800 •
Jamal Al Sharif (SYR)

▲ **HUNGARY (1) 2**
Esterházy 2, Détári 75
CANADA (0) 0

● HUNGARY *József Szendrei, Sallai, Kardos, Garaba, József Varga, Nagy (c) [Dajka 61], Détári, Burcsa [Róth 28], Kiprich, Esterházy, Bognár.*
CANADA *Tino Lettieri, Lenarduzzi, Bridge, James [Segota 54], Samuel, Wilson (c) [Sweeney 41], Ragan, Norman, Gerry Gray, Valentine, Vrablic.*
▼ SENT OFF: *Sweeney 86.*

Hungary kept their hopes alive, but without impressing anyone. Their first goal was the result of a mistake by Wilson, who had a rough time and was substituted. The highly-rated Détári put in a rebound for the second. Canada didn't build on their stubborn performance against France. Vrablic and Segota missed chances and Sweeney was sent off for a second bookable offence, a foul on Bognár.

■ 9 June 1986 • Campo Nuevo, León • 31,420 •
Carlos Alberto da Silva Valente (POR)

▲ **FRANCE (1) 3**
Stopyra 30, Tigana 63, Rocheteau 84
HUNGARY (0) 0

● FRANCE *Bats, Ayache, Amoros, Fernandez, Bossis, Battiston, Giresse, Tigana, Papin [Rocheteau 61], Platini (c), Stopyra [Jean-Marc Ferreri 71].*
HUNGARY *Disztl, Sallai, Kardos, Garaba (c), Varga, Róth, Péter Hannich [Nagy HT], Dajka, Détári, Kálmán Kovács [Bognár 66], Esterházy.*

In emphasizing the gulf between the teams, France could have had more goals, Battiston, Fernandez and Stopyra missing clear chances. Although Détári hit the bar, Hungary looked desperately short on morale. Stopyra headed in Ayache's long cross at the far post and Rocheteau converted Platini's cross from the left, but Tigana's goal was the best of the three. Exchanging passes with Platini and Rocheteau, he shot in sweetly at the near post. Surprisingly it was his only goal for France in an eventual 52 matches, but he'd had a hand in a few others.

■ 9 June 1986 • Revolución, Irapuato • 14,200 •
Idrissa Traoré (MLI)

▲ **USSR (0) 2**
Blokhin 58, Zavarov 75
CANADA (0) 0

● USSR *Viktor Chanov, Andrei Bal, Kuznetsov, Gennady Morozov, Aleksandr Bubnov, Gennady Litovchenko, Aleinikov, Yevtushenko, Rodionov, Oleg Protasov [Belanov 56], Blokhin (c) [Zavarov 61].*
CANADA *Lettieri, Lenarduzzi, Bridge, James [Segota 64], Samuel, Wilson (c), Ragan, Norman, Gray [George Pakos 69], Valentine, Dale Mitchell.*

Blokhin, once fearsomely fast (European Footballer of the Year 11 years earlier), was allowed a romp against the bottom team, scored from Belanov's pass and made the second for Zavarov. Canada tried hard for a goal and Mitchell came close with a free-kick.

Group D

Algeria, Brazil, Northern Ireland, Spain

■ 1 June 1986 • Jalisco, Guadalajara • 35,748 • Chris Bambridge (AUS)

▲ **BRAZIL (0) 1**
Sócrates 61
SPAIN (0) 0

● BRAZIL *Carlos (Gallo), Édson Boaro, 'Branco' (Cláudio Vaz), Elzo (Coelho), Júlio César (da Silva), 'Edinho' (Edino Nazareth) (c), Leovegildo Júnior [Paulo Roberto Falcão 78], 'Alemão' (Ricardo de Brito), Walter Casagrande ['Müller' (Luís Corrêa) 65], Sócrates (de Souza), 'Careca' (Antônio de Oliveira). Telê Santana.*
SPAIN *Andoni Zubizarreta, Tomás (Reñones), Andoni Goikoetxea, Antonio Maceda, José Camacho (c), 'Michel' (Miguel González), Víctor (Muñoz), Francisco (López) [Juan Antonio Señor 81], Julio Salinas, Julio Alberto (Moreno), Emilio Butragueño. Miguel Muñoz.*

■ 3 June 1986 • Tres de Marzo, Guadalajara • 22,000 • Valery Butenko (USR)

▲ **ALGERIA (0) 1**
Zidane 59
NORTHERN IRELAND (1) 1
Whiteside 6

● ALGERIA *Larbi El-Hadi, Abdullah Medjadi, Faouzi Mansouri, Nourredine Kourichi, Mahmoud Guendouz (c), Mohammed Kaci Saïd, Salah Assad, Halim Ben Mabrouk, Djamel Zidane [Lakhdar Belloumi 72], Karim Maroc, Rabah Madjer [Rachid Harkouk 27]. Rabah Saadane.*
N. IRELAND *Pat Jennings, Jimmy Nicholl, Mal Donaghy, Nigel Worthington, Alan McDonald, John O'Neill, David McCreery, Steve Penney [Ian Stewart 67], Billy Hamilton, Sammy McIlroy (c), Norman Whiteside [Colin Clarke 81]. Billy Bingham.*

Two of the surprise teams of 1982 were in obvious decline, both scoring from free-kicks, neither showing much except commitment. Harkouk was a unique phenomenon in World Cup tournaments, an African player with an English club (Notts Co). Medjadi was known as Abdullah Liégeon in France.

Spain had no luck. Two first-choice players were ill, and TV replays showed the ball crossing the line after their best player Michel hit the bar. When Careca struck the bar nine minutes later, Sócrates headed in from an offside position. Careca was a lithe threat up front and the back line was excellent; Branco a progressive left back; Júlio César and Edinho the best central defensive partnership in the world. Goikoetxea was a different player from Jon Andoni Goikoetxea who played in the 1994 finals.

■ 6 June 1986 • Jalisco, Guadalajara • 47,000 • Rómulo Méndez Molina (GUA)

▲ **BRAZIL (0) 1**
Careca 66
ALGERIA (0) 0

● BRAZIL *Carlos, Édson Boaro [Falcão 10], Branco, Elzo, Júlio César, Edinho (c), Júnior, Alemão, Sócrates, Careca, Casagrande [Müller 58].*
ALGERIA *Nasreddine Drid, Medjadi, Mansouri, Fodil Megharia, Guendouz (c), Kaci Saïd, Assad [Tedj Bensaoula 67], Ben Mabrouk, Djamel Menad, Belloumi [Zidane 75], Madjer.*

Edinho had to kick clear when Belloumi's shot beat Carlos, but Drid was the busier keeper. Careca scored the only goal when Megharia missed Müller's low cross. Of some concern was the performance of Sócrates, loping around to no great effect, and the need to use Júnior in midfield.

■ 7 June 1986 • Tres de Marzo, Guadalajara • 28,000 • Horst Brummeier (AUT)

▲ **SPAIN (2) 2**
Butragueño 1, Salinas 18
NORTHERN IRELAND (0) 1
Clarke 46

● SPAIN *Zubizarreta, Tomás, Goikoetxea, Víctor, Ricardo Gallego, Camacho (c), Michel, Francisco, Rafael Gordillo [Ramón Calderé 53], Salinas [Señor 78], Butragueño.*
N. IRELAND *Jennings, Nicholl, Donaghy, Worthington [Hamilton 70], McDonald, O'Neill, McCreery, Penney [Stewart 54], Clarke, McIlroy (c), Whiteside.*

The early goals were too much for Northern Ireland to make up. Butragueño scored from Michel's pass and the hefty Salinas smacked the ball in after some clever passing by Butragueño and Francisco. The Irish replied with a bizarre goal; Zubizarreta slicing a clearance kick up in the air; Gallego heading the ball back; Clarke heading over the keeper as he came out. Gordillo's return gave Spain extra quality on the left but only for this one match; a broken leg kept him out of the rest of the tournament. The Official FIFA Report says Hippolito Rincón came on as substitute for Salinas, an error confirmed by the Spanish FA.

■ 12 June 1986 • Tecnológico, Monterrey • 23,980 • Shizuo Takada (JPN)

▲ **SPAIN (1) 3**
Calderé 15, 68, Eloy 71
ALGERIA (0) 0

● SPAIN *Zubizarreta, Tomás, Goikoetxea, Gallego, Camacho (c), Michel [Señor 61], Víctor, Francisco, Calderé, Salinas, Butragueño [Eloy (Olaya) HT].*
ALGERIA *Drid [Larbi 18], Mansouri, Megharia, Kourichi, Guendouz (c), Kaci Saïd, Madjer, Maroc, Harkouk, Belloumi, Zidane [Menad 60].*

Drid's early injury made little difference: Algeria were a shadow of the 1982 side, and rough with it. Calderé, a sharp runner on both flanks, drove in a pass from Salinas and finished off a move between Eloy and Francisco, but was then found to have taken the stimulant ephedrine, administered by the local hospital for a gastric complaint. The Spanish Federation was fined and the team doctor cautioned, but Calderé escaped a ban.

■ 12 June 1986 • Jalisco, Guadalajara • 46,500 • Siegfried Kirschen (EG)

▲ **BRAZIL (2) 3**
Careca 15, 87, Josimar 41
NORTHERN IRELAND (0) 0

● BRAZIL *Carlos, Josimar (Pereira), Branco, Elzo, Júlio César, Edinho (c), Júnior, Alemão, Sócrates ['Zico' (Arthur Antunes Coimbra) 67], Careca, Müller [Casagrande 27].*
N IRELAND *Jennings, Nicholl, Donaghy, David Campbell [Gerry Armstrong 70], McDonald, O'Neill, McCreery, Stewart, Clarke, McIlroy (c), Whiteside [Hamilton 67].*

All three goals were too good for a side who were never a threat. Müller, marked by two players near the right corner flag, drove in a low cross which Careca hammered through Jennings' dive. Josimar, the new cap who'd given Müller the ball, came up again and steadied himself before cracking a 25-yarder into the top corner, reducing Jennings to a desperate hop. The third has been shown less often but was even better, Careca coming inside to collect Zico's backheel and fire in low at the near post. Jennings, one of the all-time greats and not disgraced now, ended his international career on a neat note, a world record 119th cap on his 41st birthday.

GROUP D	P	W	D	L	F	A	PTS
Brazil	3	3	0	0	5	0	6
Spain	3	2	0	1	5	2	4
N. Ireland	3	0	1	2	2	6	1
Algeria	3	0	1	2	1	5	1

Brazil and Spain qualified for the second round.

Group E

Denmark, Scotland, Uruguay, West Germany

■ 4 June 1986 • La Corregidora, Queretaro • 30,500 • Vojtech Christov (CZE)

▲ **URUGUAY (1) 1**
Alzamendi 4
WEST GERMANY (0) 1
Allofs 84

● URUGUAY *Fernando Alvez, Eduardo Acevedo, Victor Diogo, Miguel Angel Bossio, José Batista, Nelson Gutiérrez, Jorge Barrios (c) [Mario Saralegui 55], Antonio Alzamendi [Venancio Ramos 81], Sergio Santín, Jorge da Silva, Enzo Francescoli.* Omar Borras.
W. GERMANY *Harald Schumacher (c), Klaus Augenthaler, Thomas Berthold, Karlheinz Förster, Hans-Peter Briegel, Andreas Brehme [Pierre Littbarski HT], Lothar Matthäus [Karl-Heinz Rummenigge 73], Felix Magath, Norbert Eder, Rudi Völler, Klaus Allofs.* Franz Beckenbauer.

Uruguay took an early lead against a team missing Rummenigge and Littbarski, both recovering from injury. Alzamendi escaped Matthäus and went round the keeper before hitting the bar with a shot that didn't reach the net but clearly crossed the line. But German teams don't bow the knee, and the two substitutions gave them more oomph up front. Allofs shot in after good work by the tubby Magath, whom Beckenbauer was reluctantly using as his playmaker.

The first Danish team to play in the World Cup finals. (l–r) standing: Arnesen, Busk, Laudrup, Nielsen, J. Olsen, Bertelsen; kneeling: Berggreen, M. Olsen, Lerby, Rasmussen, Elkjaer.

■ 4 June 1986 • Neza 86, Nezahualcoyotl • 18,000 • Lajos Nemeth (HUN)

▲ **DENMARK (0) 1**
Elkjaer 57
SCOTLAND (0) 0

● DENMARK *Troels Rasmussen, Morten Olsen (c), Søren Busk, Ivan Nielsen, Klaus Berggreen, Søren Lerby, Jesper Olsen [Jan Mølby 79], Jens-Jørn Bertelsen, Frank Arnesen [John Sivebæk 75], Preben Elkjaer, Michael Laudrup. Sepp Piontek (WG).*
SCOTLAND *Jim Leighton, Richard Gough, Maurice Malpas, Steve Nicol, Robert 'Roy' Aitken, Alex McLeish, Willie Miller, Graeme Souness (c), Gordon Strachan [Eamonn Bannon 75], Charlie Nicholas, Paul Sturrock [Frank McAvennie 61]. Alex Ferguson.*

Scotland were made to look ordinary by the best team Denmark have ever put out; so strong that the likes of Mølby and Jesper Olsen weren't guaranteed a place. Once the veteran Morten Olsen had taken a grip at the back, the front two began to stretch the Scottish defence, Elkjaer with his strong running, Laudrup one of the most gifted young players in the world. The goal, though, was untidy, Elkjaer taking a rebound off Miller's legs before shooting in off a post. Strachan ran his heart out and used the ball well, but Souness was disappointing again, and the much vaunted Nicholas was badly fouled by Berggreen.

■ 8 June 1986 • La Corregidora, Queretaro • 25,000 • Ioan Igna (ROM)

▲ **WEST GERMANY (1) 2**
Völler 22, Allofs 49
SCOTLAND (1) 1
Strachan 17

● W. GERMANY *Schumacher (c), Berthold, Briegel [Ditmar Jakobs 62], Matthäus, Förster, Augenthaler, Littbarski [Rummenigge 75], Magath, Éder, Völler, Allofs.*
SCOTLAND *Leighton, Gough, Nicol [McAvennie 60], Aitken, Malpas, Miller, David Narey, Souness (c), Strachan, Bannon [Davie Cooper 74], Steve Archibald.*

Again little Strachan was Scotland's only star, thoroughly deserving his goal, a marvellous strike from the right-hand side of the penalty area. Cooper's trickery caused a few problems at the end and Archibald did some intelligent running but had no support. Meanwhile the opportunism of the West German strikers turned the match, each making a goal for the other. Allofs' left-wing cross set up an open goal for Völler, who later held back a defender as the ball ran to Allofs. Ditmar is the correct spelling in this case (not Dietmar).

■ 8 June 1986 • Neza 86, Nezahualcoyotl • 26,500 • Antonio Márquez (MEX)

▲ **DENMARK (2) 6**
Elkjaer 11, 68, 79, Lerby 41, Laudrup 51, J. Olsen 88
URUGUAY (1) 1
Francescoli pen 45

● DENMARK *Rasmussen, M. Olsen (c), Busk, Nielsen, Berggreen, Lerby, Henrik Andersen, Bertelsen [Mølby 56], Arnesen, Elkjaer, Laudrup [J. Olsen 81].*
URUGUAY *Alvez, Acevedo (c), Diogo, Bossio, Batista, Gutiérrez, Saralegui, Santín [José Salazar 56], Da Silva, Francescoli, Alzamendi [Ramos 57].*
▼ SENT OFF: *Bossio 19.*

Hard to know what to think of this. Denmark were direct and skilful and had everything a modern power team needs, but Uruguay were a man short for the last 70 minutes and lost their appetite for a struggle. Laudrup scored the best goal of the six, almost tip-toeing past two defenders and the goalkeeper. Elkjaer, jutting-jawed and relentless, ran on to Laudrup's pass for the first goal, put in a rebound, went round Alvez for the third, and crossed for Lerby and Jesper Olsen to score. Francescoli was fouled by Busk for the penalty, but Uruguay's credentials had taken an enormous blow.

■ 13 June 1986 • Neza 86, Nezahualcoyotl • 20,000 • Joël Quiniou (FRA)

▲ **SCOTLAND 0**
URUGUAY 0

● SCOTLAND *Leighton, Gough, Arthur Albiston, Nicol [Cooper 70], Miller (c), Narey, Strachan, Paul McStay, Graeme Sharp, Aitken, Sturrock [Nicholas 70].*
URUGUAY *Alvez, Acevedo, Gutiérrez, Batista, Diogo, Dario Pereyra, Ramos [Saralegui 70], Santín, Wilmar Cabrera, Barrios (c), Francescoli [Alzamendi 83].*
▼ SENT OFF: *Batista 55 sec.*

Batista (on the ground, left) is shown the red card after less than a minute. Gutiérrez (2) and Barrios (armband) argue his case with referee Quiniou.

The tournament's oddball format meant that the Scots would still qualify if they beat Uruguay, despite having lost their first two matches. But Ferguson picked the weakest Scotland team in recent memory and even a ludicrous early sending-off didn't help them.

Immediately after the kick-off, Batista took Strachan's legs and was sent off by a referee who, some say, took out the red card by mistake. It was the fastest dismissal in a finals match. But Francescoli, on his own upfield, held the ball up superbly, and Scotland made few chances against that strong defence. The best was missed by Nicol, from Strachan's low cross. Only six yards out from an empty net, he somehow prodded it back towards Alvez. Without winning a match, and after losing one 6-1, Uruguay were through, but yet again Scotland hadn't done enough to be mourned. Someone counted that they'd had seven shots on target in three matches.

GROUP E	P	W	D	L	F	A	PTS
Denmark	3	3	0	0	9	1	6
W. Germany	3	1	1	1	3	4	3
Uruguay	3	0	2	1	2	7	2
Scotland	3	0	1	2	1	3	1

Denmark, West Germany and Uruguay qualified for the second round.

Group F

England, Morocco, Poland, Portugal

■ 13 June 1986 • La Corregidora, Queretaro • 28,500 • Alexis Ponnet (BEL)

▲ **DENMARK (1) 2**
J. Olsen pen 43, Eriksen 62
WEST GERMANY (0) 0

● DENMARK *Lars Høgh, M. Olsen (c), Busk, Sivebæk, Andersen, Lerby, Mølby, J. Olsen [Allan Simonsen 70], Arnesen, Elkjaer, Laudrup [John Eriksen HT].*
   W. GERMANY *Schumacher (c), Berthold, Förster [Rummenigge 70], Brehme, Matthias Herget, Jakobs, Eder, Matthäus, Völler, Wolfgang Rolff [Littbarski HT], Allofs.*
▼ SENT OFF: *Arnesen 88.*

■ 2 June 1986 • Universitário, Monterrey • 19,694 • José Luis Martínez Bazán (URU)

▲ **MOROCCO 0**
POLAND 0

● MOROCCO *'Zaki' (Ezaki Badou) (c), Khalifa (Labid), Abdelmajid Lamriss, Mustafa El Biyaz, Nourredine Bouyahiaoui, Abdelmajid Dolmy, Mustafa El Haddaoui [Abdelaziz Soulaimani 87], Aziz Bouderbala, 'Krimau' (Abdelkarim Merry), Mohammed Timoumi [Abderrazak Khairi 89], Mustafa Merry. José Faria (BRZ).*
   POLAND *Józef Mlynarczyk, Marek Ostrowski, Roman Wójcicki, Stefan Majewski, Waldemar Matysik, Dariusz Kubicki [Kazimierz Przybys HT], Ryszard Komornicki, Andrzej Buncol, Wlodek Smolarek, Zbigniew Boniek (c), Dariusz Dziekanowski [Jan Urban 55]. Antoni Piechniczek.*

West Germany made several chances – Høgh making a superb save from Völler, Brehme hitting a post – but Morten Olsen, still a fine attacking sweeper at 36, was tripped by Rolff for the penalty, and Arnesen's low cross gave Eriksen an open goal. Arnesen's sending-off, for a kick at Matthäus, would cost Denmark their midfield organizer, but they seemed to have all the talent in the world to replace him. Simonsen, the forerunner of this talented team and European Footballer of the Year back in 1977, made a token appearance in the finals.

The more sophisticated team had the three best players on the pitch and more of the play, but seemed happy with the draw. Yes, Morocco should have done better.

Timoumi, Bouderbala and Krimau were more gifted than anyone in the Polish team. Boniek, now 30, was playing deep again, and the highly-regarded Dziekanowski had to be replaced, his substitute hitting a post near the end. Perhaps the Poles were one of the teams still feeling the effects of the heat and altitude. Khairi was on the field for only 27 seconds, a finals record. Krimau and Mustafa Merry were brothers.

■ 3 June 1986 • Tecnológico, Monterrey • 19,998 • Volker Roth (WG)

▲ **PORTUGAL (0) 1**
Carlos Manuel 75
ENGLAND (0) 0

● PORTUGAL *Manuel Bento (c), Alvaro (Magalhães), Frederico (Rosa), Antônio J. Oliveira, Augusto Inácio, Diamantino (Miranda) [José Antônio (Bargiela) 83], Antônio André, Carlos Manuel (Correia), Fernando Gomes [Paulo Futre 71], Jaime Pacheco, Antônio de Sousa. José Torres.*
ENGLAND *Peter Shilton, M. Gary Stevens, Kenny Sansom, Bryan Robson (c) [Steve Hodge 80], Terry Butcher, Terry Fenwick, Glenn Hoddle, Ray Wilkins, Mark Hateley, Gary Lineker, Chris Waddle [Peter Beardsley 80]. Bobby Robson.*

England's recent unbeaten run included a meritorious win in the USSR, but they now ran up against a brick wall and lost faith in themselves. Portugal had lost their last warm-up match 3-1 at home, but earlier in the season they'd become the only country to beat West Germany in a World Cup qualifier: 1-0 away with a goal by Carlos Manuel.

England created chances, one in particular when Lineker stretched for a cross from the left and put it just wide – but suddenly the use of a big man (Hateley) served by a winger (Waddle) looked woefully predictable. Portugal attacked so infrequently that their goal probably had something to do with England's loss of concentration. Diamantino beat Sansom on the inside and Stevens went AWOL when Carlos Manuel appeared unmarked at the far post to lift the low cross over Shilton, the first goal he'd conceded in the last five finals matches.

The 20-year-old Futre came on to run at England's defence and Shilton had to make a good save at his feet when he was clean through. A sobering match. One source lists André as a first name, but the leading Portuguese statisticians and almanac call him Antônio Ferreira André.

Carlos Manuel celebrates his goal against England, Portugal's first in the finals for 20 years.

1986

■ 6 June 1986 • Tecnológico, Monterrey •
20,200 • Gabriel González (PAR)

▲ **ENGLAND 0**
MOROCCO 0

● MOROCCO *Zaki (c), Khalifa, Lamriss ['Hcina' (Lahcen Ouadani) 73], El Biyaz, Bouyahiaoui, Khairi, Dolmy, Bouderbala, Krimau, Timouni, M. Merry [Soulaimani 87].*
ENGLAND *Shilton, M. G. Stevens, Sansom, Robson (c) [Hodge `41], Butcher, Fenwick, Hoddle, Wilkins, Hateley [Gary A. Stevens 75], Lineker, Waddle.*
▼ SENT OFF: *Wilkins 42.*

Nightmare heaped on nightmare for England, who were fortunate that Morocco were almost pathologically cautious. Against a team that lost its inspirational captain and played with ten men for the last 50 minutes, they kept possession and played for another draw. Put it down to modesty in the face of history, but they risked not going through.

Robson's protective harness didn't help his shoulder when he fell in the Moroccan penalty area. Led off with his arm in a sling, he seemed to be taking his team's hopes with him. Almost immediately Wilkins was penalized, threw the ball towards the referee, and became the only England player sent off in a finals match, for a second bookable offence two minutes after his first. England's reputation and position in the group were lower than anyone could have expected.

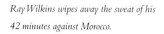

Ray Wilkins wipes away the sweat of his 42 minutes against Morocco.

■ 7 June 1986 • Universitário, Monterrey •
19,915 • Ali Ben Nasser (TUN)

▲ **POLAND (0) 1**
Smolarek 68
PORTUGAL (0) 0

● POLAND *Mlynarczyk, Ostrowski, Wójcicki, Majewski, Matysik, Urban, Komornicki [Jan Karas 56], Krzysztof Pawlak, Smolarek [Andrzej Zgutczynski 75], Boniek (c), Dziekanowski.*
PORTUGAL *Vítor Damas, Alvaro, Frederico, Oliveira, Inácio, Diamantino, André [Jaime Magalhães 73], Carlos Manuel, Gomes (c) [Futre HT], Pacheco, Sousa.*

A dose of vice-versa for the Portuguese, dominating possession before conceding a breakaway goal to a far-post cross. Futre again caused problems with his ball-control at speed and should probably have started the game in place of the tall Gomes, who was prolific but overrated. The 38-year-old Damas had to replace the 37-year-old Bento, who'd broken a leg in training and didn't play for Portugal again.

■ 11 June 1986 • Tres de Marzo, Guadalajara •
18,000 • Alan Snoddy (NIR)

▲ **MOROCCO (2) 3**
Khairi 18, 27, Krimau 61
PORTUGAL (0) 1
Diamantino 79

● MOROCCO *Zaki (c), Khalifa, Lamriss [Azzeddine Amanallah 69], El Biyaz, Bouayhiaoui, Khairi, Dolmy, El Haddaoui [Soulaimani 71], Bouderbala, Krimau, Timouni.*
PORTUGAL *Damas, Alvaro [Rui Aguas 55], Frederico, Oliveira, Inácio, J. Magalhães, Carlos Manuel, Gomes (c), Futre, Pacheco, Sousa [Diamantino 65].*

When Morocco decided to come out of their shell, they did it in style, becoming the first African country not only to qualify from a finals group but to win it. Khairi smashed in a loose ball from outside the area and met Khalifa's lob with an instant ground shot; Krimau drove in Timoumi's cross; and Morocco could afford to leave Diamantino unmarked near the end. Portugal's win over England seemed a long time ago.

■ 11 June 1986 • Universitário, Monterrey • 22,600 • André Daina (SWI)

▲ **ENGLAND (3) 3**
Lineker 9, 14, 34
POLAND (0) 0

● ENGLAND *Shilton (c), M. G. Stevens, Sansom, Peter Reid, Butcher, Fenwick, Trevor Steven, Hoddle, Lineker [Kerry Dixon 84], Beardsley [Waddle 75], Hodge.*
POLAND *Mlynarczyk, Ostrowski, Majewski, Matysik [Buncol HT], Wójcicki, Pawlak, Urban, Komornicki [Karas 23], Smolarek, Boniek (c), Dziekanowski.*

Amazingly a draw would still be enough for England to qualify, but in the event they suddenly woke up and played a swaggering first half. It's said that Bobby Robson gave in to player power, but if so he was only doing what Schön had done in the 1970s, and anyway the players got it right. They dropped the winger and target man, used Steven and Hodge wide in midfield, and played Beardsley just behind Lineker, who used the extra space to score a hat-trick that saved everybody's bacon and uplifted a whole country.

All three goals came down the Polish right. Lineker took a square pass and moved the ball to the other wing then forced himself in front of Majewski to scoop in Steven's low cross. Beardsley, lying deep with his back to goal, hit a perfect first-time ball out to the left, where Hodge put in a long cross which Lineker met at full tilt. In the previous two matches, his half-volley would probably have gone into the stands; here it flew just under the bar. There was a similar rub of the green for the third goal, but again Lineker took it well, turning to half-volley into the roof of the net after Mlynarczyk, normally so reliable, had dropped an easy corner. Hodge had a goal disallowed for offside and Lineker might have scored again in the second half, but let's not be greedy. It was the end of England's four consecutive finals matches without a goal. At the 32nd attempt, they'd won one by more than two goals.

[Above] *Lineker gets there before Majewski and Mlynarczyk to score England's first goal of the tournament. Relief for Reid and everyone back home.*
[Top Right] *Lineker (10) prepares to take advantage of Mlynarczyk's error and complete his hat-trick.*

GROUP F	P	W	D	L	F	A	PTS
Morocco	3	1	2	0	3	1	4
England	3	1	1	1	3	1	3
Poland	3	1	1	1	1	3	3
Portugal	3	1	0	2	2	4	2

Morocco, England and Poland qualified for the second round.

2nd Round

■ 15 June 1986 • Azteca, Mexico City • 114,580 • Romualdo Arppi (BRZ)

▲ **MEXICO (1) 2**
Negrete 34, Servín 61
BULGARIA (0) 0

● MEXICO *Larios, Amador, Quirarte, Cruz Barbosa, Servín, Muñoz, España, Negrete, Aguirre, Boy (c) [de los Cobos 79], Sánchez.*
BULGARIA *Mikhailov, Zdravkov, Arabov, Petrov, Dimitrov (c), Sadkov, Yordanov, Gospodinov, Getov [Sirakov 59], Kostadinov, Atanas Pashev [Iskrenov 70].*

Bulgaria were heavily criticized for adding nothing to the tournament – but perhaps, as in 1970, they simply couldn't cope with Mexican conditions. Both the goals were spectacular – Negrete's volley in mid-air and Servín's diving header – but Mexico couldn't have asked for more compliant opposition.

■ 15 June 1986 • Campo Nuevo, León • 32,277 • Erik Fredriksson (SWE)

▲ **BELGIUM (0) (2) 4**
Scifo 54, Ceulemans 77, Demol 102, Claesen 108
USSR (1) (2) 3
Belanov 27, 69, pen 111

● BELGIUM *Pfaff, Gerets [L. Van der Elst 112], Grün [Clijsters 99], Renquin, Vervoort, Demol, Scifo, Vercauteren, Ceulemans (c), Claesen, Veyt.*
USSR *Dasayev, Bessonov, Kuznetsov, Bal, Demianenko (c), Rats, Yakovenko [Yevtushenko 78], Zavarov [Rodionov 71], Belanov, Aleinikov, Yaremchuk.*

The USSR, their fitness again making light of the conditions, dominated entire periods of play and took the lead when Belanov swerved to his right and hit a long-range cross-shot that careered through the thin air into the top corner. He had a tremendous match and a very good tournament, but that single shot was probably what made him European Footballer of the Year. He later restored the lead by drilling Zavarov's cross under Pfaff.

But the Belgians, unimpressive until now, gave the Soviet defence endless trouble with high crosses. Vercauteren made goals for Scifo and Demol, Vervoort for Ceulemans (who looked offside) and Claesen volleyed in a Clijsters header. Belanov put away a penalty after he'd been fouled and Rodionov's marvellous shot hit the angle of post and bar. The USSR's elimination was the tournament's loss, but it was hard to begrudge Belgium their win.

■ 16 June 1986 • Jalisco, Guadalajara • 45,000 •
Volker Roth (WG)

▲ **BRAZIL (1) 4**
Sócrates pen 29, Josimar 56, Edinho 78,
Careca pen 83
POLAND (0) 0

● BRAZIL *Carlos, Josimar, Branco, Elzo, Júlio César,
Edinho (c), Júnior, Alemão, Careca, Sócrates [Zico 69],
Müller [Silas (do Prado) 73].*
POLAND *Mlynarczyk, Przybys [Jan Furtok 59],
Wójcicki, Majewski, Ostrowski, Ryszard Tarasiewicz
[Wladyslaw Zmuda 83], Boniek (c), Karas, Urban,
Smolarek, Dziekanowski.*

■ 16 June 1986 • Cuauhtemoc, Puebla • 26,000 •
Luigi Agnolin (ITA)

▲ **ARGENTINA (1) 1**
Pasculli 41
URUGUAY (0) 0

● ARGENTINA *Pumpido, Brown, Cuciuffo, Ruggeri,
Garré, Giusti, Batista [Olarticoechea 85], Burruchaga,
Maradona (c), Pasculli, Valdano.*
URUGUAY *Alvez, Bossio, Gutiérrez, Acevedo [Rubén
Paz 60], Eliséo Rivero, Barrios (c), Pereyra, Santín, Cabrera
[Da Silva HT], Ramos, Francescoli.*

Poland were inferior but desperately unlucky. Don't
look at the scoreline, think of Dziekanowski's chip
hitting the post and a huge long shot from Karas
coming back off the bar, both with the score still 0-0.
After that, it was a triumph for skill. Careca was barged
in the penalty area, Sócrates taking the penalty
without a run-up. Josimar improved on his goal
against the Irish by stepping through three tackles on
the right before blasting the ball over the keeper from
a tight angle, like a table tennis shot with top spin. He
scored in each of his first two internationals, rare for a
full-back.

Edinho, so hot-headed in 1978 but now the ideal
central defender, scored the third by running the length of
the field to pick up Careca's backheel and beat a defender
and the keeper with a single turn. The fourth goal also
came from a long-range break-out, Mlynarczyk bringing
down Zico, sent clear by Careca, whose spot-kick hit a
post and crept in near the other one. Awesome in the end
by Brazil. Zmuda was brought on for the last seven
minutes to equal Seeler's total of 21 finals matches, still
the record.

Uruguay, having received a fine and a warning from
FIFA, couldn't subject Maradona to the kind of
tackling they wanted, leaving him free to dominate
the match. All the sharper for losing seven pounds in
training, he was still a meaty 11 stone spread over 5′6″,
three inches shorter than Pelé. Hard to believe this
was the same player who'd had two such unhappy
years with Barcelona, plagued by hepatitis in the first,
victim of a crippling foul in the next. He skipped past
tackles and made chances for Pasculli and Valdano, hit
the bar with a free-kick and had a goal disallowed.
Ironically he wasn't directly involved in the goal,
Acevedo's error letting Pasculli in at the end of
Valdano's low cross. Uruguay's famous past was
looking increasingly distant.

1986

■ 17 June 1986 • Olímpico, Mexico City •
71,449 • Carlos Esposito (ARG)

▲ **FRANCE (1) 2**
Platini 15, Stopyra 57
ITALY (0) 0

● FRANCE *Bats, Ayache, Amoros, Fernandez [Tusseau 73], Bossis, Battiston, Giresse, Tigana, Stopyra, Platini (c) [Ferreri 84], Rocheteau.*
ITALY *Galli, Bergomi, Cabrini, De Napoli, Vierchowod, Scirea (c), Conti, Bagni, Altobelli, Baresi [Di Gennaro HT], Galderisi [Vialli 57].*

Italy, who'd been living off Altobelli and recent glories, were found out and well beaten. Rocheteau sent Platini through the middle to chip over Galli, who was no replacement for Zoff, and Stopyra drove in Tigana's left-wing cross at the far post. A crewcut Vialli replaced the anonymous Galderisi, who didn't score a goal in his ten internationals and was one of six Italians (including heroes like Conti and Scirea) not to be capped again.

■ 17 June 1986 • Universitário, Monterrey •
19,800 • Zoran Petrovic (YUG)

▲ **WEST GERMANY (0) 1**
Matthäus 88
MOROCCO (0) 0

● W. GERMANY *Schumacher, Berthold, Briegel, Éder, Jakobs, Förster, Rummenigge (c), Matthäus, Völler [Littbarski HT], Magath, Allofs.*
MOROCCO *Zaki (c), Khalifa, Lamriss, Hcina, Bouyahiaoui, Khairi, Dolmy, El Haddaoui, Bouderbala, Krimau, Timoumi.*

Morocco's Brazilian coach claimed he was waiting to bring on two fresh attackers in extra-time, but Matthäus didn't give him the chance, hitting a free-kick along the ground past a badly placed wall and just inside the post. Morocco had only themselves to blame. Yet again (it becomes repetitive) they'd looked the better side but were too defensive, especially as they were surely more accustomed to 36°C heat than the Germans.

■ 18 June 1986 • Azteca, Mexico City • 98,728 •
Jamal Al-Sharif (SYR)

▲ **ENGLAND (1) 3**
Lineker 31, 72, Beardsley 56
PARAGUAY (0) 0

● ENGLAND *Shilton (c), M. G. Stevens, Sansom, Reid [G. A. Stevens 57], Butcher, Alvin Martin, Steven, Hoddle, Lineker, Beardsley [Hateley 80], Hodge.*
PARAGUAY *Fernández, Torales [Guasch 64], Zabala, Schettina, Delgado (c), Núñez, Romero, Cañete, Ferreira, Mendoza, Cabañas.*

Paraguay were no pushovers but England now expected to win matches. Hoddle did well and the front two kept their enthusiasm in the face of some brutal tackling. Beardsley scored his goal, a rebound when Fernández couldn't hold a shot, while Lineker was off the field after being elbowed in the throat. He took his revenge with a low cross-shot from the right. Earlier, Hoddle had pulled a cross back from the left-hand goal line for Lineker to touch it into an empty net. England kept a close watch on Romero and were well worth their win. Not for the first time in Mexico, the official crowd figure looks like something invented to placate the critics.

Quarter-finals

■ 18 June 1986 • La Corregidora, Queretaro • 38,500 • Jan Keizer (HOL)

▲ **SPAIN (1) 5**
Butragueño 43, 57, 79, pen 88,
Goikoetxea pen 68
DENMARK (1) 1
J. Olsen pen 32

● SPAIN *Zubizarreta, Tomás, Camacho (c), Víctor, Goikoetxea, Gallego, Julio Alberto, Calderé, Salinas [Eloy HT], Michel [Francisco 83], Butragueño.*
DENMARK *Høgh, M. Olsen (c), Nielsen, Busk, Andersen [Eriksen 60], Lerby, Bertelsen, Berggreen, J. Olsen [Mølby 70], Elkjaer, Laudrup.*

■ 21 June 1986 • Jalisco, Guadalajara • 65,677 • Ioan Igna (ROM)

▲ **FRANCE (1) (1) 1**
Platini 41
BRAZIL (1) (1) 1
Careca 17
France 4-3 pens.

● FRANCE *Bats, Amoros, Tusseau, Fernandez, Bossis, Battiston, Giresse [Ferreri 84], Tigana, Stopyra, Platini (c), Rocheteau [Bellone 99].*
BRAZIL *Carlos, Josimar, Branco, Elzo, Júlio César, Edinho (c), Júnior [Silas FT], Alemão, Sócrates, Careca, Müller [Zico 71].*
□ PENALTY SHOOT-OUT: *Sócrates saved, Stopyra 0-1, Alemão 1-1, Amoros 1-2, Zico 2-2, Bellone 2-3, Branco 3-3, Platini missed, Júlio César hit post, Fernandez 3-4.*

An incredible turn-around. Denmark took the lead when Berggreen was brought down by Gallego and would have been ahead at half-time but for the most traumatizing error in their football history. Jesper Olsen dropped back and out to the right to collect a short free-kick from Høgh, rolled it around to kill a little time, then knocked it square without looking, straight into the path of Butragueño, who slipped it past Høgh without breaking stride.

The goal cut into Denmark's confidence, and Arnesen wasn't here to lift it. The fair-haired Butragueño, known as 'El Buitre' (the vulture) headed in a corner, converted Eloy's cross, and was brought down for both penalties. Easy to blame Olsen, or some imagined lack of Danish bottle, but it was really just a freak result, and a sad one for the tournament. No disrespect to Spain and Butragueño, but they were unlikely to play like this again.

This was the match of the round. Müller hit a post and the bar and Bats had to make some important saves, but France were always in the match, Rocheteau missing an open goal, Stopyra twice coming close. They went behind to a fine goal, Müller and Júnior drawing the defence by exchanging tight little passes on the right before moving the ball inside to the unmarked Careca, who swept it first time over Bats. The equalizer was less tidy but thoroughly deserved. Giresse sent Rocheteau clear on the right, the low cross deflected

off Edinho into the path of Stopyra, who missed his stumbling header under pressure from Carlos. The ball ran on for Platini to prod home at the far post. It was his 31st birthday, his 41st goal for France (still the record) and the only one Carlos conceded in five finals matches.

The crucial moment arrived in the 73rd minute. Zico's perfect sliced pass sent Branco into the area, where Bats dived at his feet and the referee awarded a penalty. Sócrates and Careca had taken the spot-kicks against Poland, but Zico stepped up for this one. In 1978 he'd scored from a penalty within two minutes of coming on as substitute against Peru. Now, in an eerily similar repeat, he took another one, but Bats made the save. Three minutes from the end of extra-time, Platini's through-ball sent Bellone clear to go round Carlos, who brought him down without punishment. The ball went straight down the other end and Sócrates missed an open goal from Careca's low cross. Penalty shoot-out.

Sócrates, taking the first kick, got his come-uppance for his cocky approach against Poland, Bats saving easily to his right. But Platini, the world's great dead-ball expert, shot over the bar. Then Júlio

César hit the left-hand post and Brazil were the latest quality side to be eliminated. Sócrates, Zico and Rocheteau weren't capped again. The end of an era.

■ 21 June 1986 • Universitário, Monterrey • 44,386 • Jesús Díaz Palacio (COL)

▲ **WEST GERMANY 0**
MEXICO 0
West Germany 4-1 pens.

● W. GERMANY *Schumacher, Berthold, Briegel, Eder [Littbarski 115], Brehme, Jakobs, Förster, Rummenigge (c) [Dieter Hoeness 58], Matthäus, Magath, Allofs.*
MEXICO *Larios, Amador [F. J. Cruz 70], Quirarte, Cruz Barbosa, Servín, Muñoz, España, Negrete, Aguirre, Boy (c) [de los Cobos 32], Sánchez.*

▼ SENT OFF: *Berthold 64, Aguirre 99.*

□ PENALTY SHOOT-OUT: *Allofs 1-0, Negrete 1-1, Brehme 2-1, Quirarte saved, Matthäus 3-1, Servín saved, Littbarski 4-1.*

West Germany were still uninspired but the hosts couldn't take advantage. Boy was caught by Brehme's crunching tackle; Sánchez had another poor match; and Schumacher made a number of late saves as well as two in the shoot-out. The referee, who didn't look in full control, showed seven yellow cards as well as the two red. Hoeness' more famous brother Uli played in the 1974 Final.

Bats saves Zico's penalty in the quarter-final.

22 June 1986 • Azteca, Mexico City •
114,580 • Ali Ben Nasser (TUN)

▲ **ARGENTINA (0) 2**
Maradona 51, 55
ENGLAND (0) 1
Lineker 81

● ARGENTINA *Pumpido, Cuciuffo, Olarticoechea, Batista, Ruggeri, Brown, Giusti, Enrique, Burruchaga [Tápia 75], Maradona (c), Valdano.*
ENGLAND *Shilton (c), M.G. Stevens, Sansom, Reid [Waddle 69], Butcher, Fenwick, Steven [John Barnes 74], Hoddle, Lineker, Beardsley, Hodge.*

The most controversial World Cup moment since the over-the-line goal in 1966 – but England were struggling before it happened. Bilardo, always flexible, again varied his tactics to match the opposition's strengths, man-marking Lineker and Beardsley and stationing Giusti wide on the right to block Hodge. This effectively left Argentina without conventional full-backs, but Robson, not thinking on his feet, didn't bring on a winger till Maradona had done the damage.

When Hodge sliced a clearance kick back towards his own penalty spot, the two captains went for it, Shilton slightly too slow off his line but Maradona still unlikely to get there first. At the last second, he made up for his lack of inches by getting his hand to the ball before Shilton's punch, sending it bouncing into the empty net.

Ben Nasser took his share of the flak, but it happened fast enough to deceive most people in the stadium, and anyway it wasn't the referee who

[Left] Maradona uses his hand in more conventional fashion before the kick-off against England. Referee Ben Nasser (second left) has no trouble seeing it so far, though Shilton's expression suggests he knows what's coming.

handled the ball. A grubby little moment, with major implications, especially when Maradona scored one of the almighty goals, picking the ball up near halfway and going past three tackles before dummying Shilton. Barry Davies got it exactly right: 'You have to say that's magnificent.'

When Barnes went past two defenders on the left and crossed for Lineker to score with a header, people were suddenly wise after the event: why wasn't he on from the start? Because he hadn't been playing well for England, who'd just won their last two matches 3-0. In the dying minutes Barnes put in another cross, but a defender somehow touched the ball away when Lineker seemed certain to head in again. Excruciating.

The 'Hand of God' was crucial, of course – but England hadn't had a shot on goal before it, and they had a right to expect more from Glenn Hoddle. Tall

Maradona's devilish handball. Shilton's fist is inches away from where all Englishmen would like to see it.

and enviably gifted, his ball-control and passing among the very best (ask Ardiles), he was a controversial figure since his successful first international in 1979. Fans wanted him in, managers generally preferred Wilkins and McDermott. Now, with Wilkins out and a midfield geared to win him the ball, with Lineker up front, he didn't perform in the heat of the kitchen; the bottom line when discussing his England career. He'll be hoping for much better as manager in France '98.

■ 22 June 1986 • Cuauhtemoc, Puebla • 45,000 • Siegfried Kirschen (EG)

▲ **BELGIUM (1) (1) 1**
Ceulemans 34
SPAIN (0) (1) 1
Señor 84
Belgium 5-4 pens.

● BELGIUM *Pfaff, Gerets, Renquin, Grün, Vervoort, Demol, Scifo, Vercauteren [L. Van der Elst 106], Ceulemans (c), Claesen, Veyt [Broos 83].*
SPAIN *Zubizarreta, Tomás [Señor HT], 'Chendo' (Miguel Portlan), Gallego, Víctor, Camacho (c), Julio Alberto, Calderé, Salinas [Eloy 63], Michel, Butragueño.*
□ PENALTY SHOOT-OUT: *Señor 1-0, Claesen 1-1, Eloy saved, Scifo 1-2, Chendo 2-2, Broos 2-3, Butragueño 3-3, Vervoort 3-4, Víctor 4-4, L. Van der Elst 4-5.*

More intestinal fortitude from Belgium, who survived the loss of Vandenbergh and Vandereycken, both flown home for surgery. The defence was again superb, conceding only Señor's desperate long-range volley from Víctor's corner. Salinas missed a good chance but so did Veyt. Ceulemans had put Belgium ahead with a splendid diving header from Vercauteren's cross. Pfaff, back to his best after the nonsense of 1982, made the only save in the shoot-out.

[Top Left] *Barnes' cross beats Ruggeri (19) for Lineker to head the goal that gives England hope against Argentina.*

[Left] *Agonisingly close to a repeat performance. Lineker, face contorted with the effort, just fails to connect with another Barnes centre.*

Semi-finals

■ 25 June 1986 • Jalisco, Guadalajara • 47,500 • Luigi Agnolin (ITA)

▲ **WEST GERMANY (1) 2**
Brehme 9, Völler 89
FRANCE (0) 0

● W. GERMANY *Schumacher, Brehme, Briegel, Eder, Förster, Jakobs, Rummenigge (c) [Völler 57], Matthäus, Allofs, Magath, Rolff.*
FRANCE *Bats, Ayache, Amoros, Fernandez, Bossis, Battiston, Giresse [Vercruysse 71], Tigana, Stopyra, Platini (c), Bellone [Daniel Xuereb 66].*

The one thing France didn't want, against such rugged opponents, was to concede an early goal, especially one like this. Magath tapped a free-kick to Brehme, whose low shot was horribly fumbled by Bats, a hero against Brazil and for the past two seasons. The French naturally came forward, but were handicapped by Platini's tendons, Giresse's age (he wasn't capped again) and the absence of the injury-prone Rocheteau. Bossis shot over an empty goal from six yards and Schumacher, the villain of 1982, turned the knife with his usual quota of saves. In the last minute Völler ran on to lift the ball over Bats before scoring. For the second successive time France had lost in the semi-final to West Germany, who were praised for making the most of what they had. But perhaps if Rocheteau and Platini had been fully fit, France would have done the same. Xuereb was the only finals player whose surname began with X!

■ 25 June 1986 • Azteca, Mexico City • 110,420 • Antonio Márquez (MEX)

▲ **ARGENTINA (0) 2**
Maradona 51, 63
BELGIUM (0) 0

● ARGENTINA *Pumpido, Cuciuffo, Olarticoechea, Batista, Ruggeri, Brown, Giusti, Enrique, Burruchaga [Ricardo Bochini 85], Maradona (c), Valdano.*
BELGIUM *Pfaff, Gerets, Renquin [Desmet 53], Vervoort, Demol, Grün, Scifo, Vercauteren, Ceulemans (c), Claesen, Veyt.*

Another one-man show, another double whammy. Both teams saturated the midfield but Belgium, toothless in attack, could only hold out for so long. Running into the penalty area from the right, Maradona's mind was made up for him when Pfaff came off his line slightly too soon, to be beaten by a flick of that left foot. The second goal was on a par with his second against England, running at the heart of a very good defence, taking out three opponents and jagging to his left before hooking the ball past the keeper. Belgium were dogged but had no answer. Credit also to Argentina's midfield, where Burruchaga had emerged as a knowing second-in-command.

3rd-place Final

■ 28 June 1986 • Cuauhtemoc, Puebla •
21,500 • George Courtney (ENG)

▲ **FRANCE (2) (2) 4**
Ferreri 27, Papin 43, Genghini 104,
Amoros pen 111
BELGIUM (1) (2) 2
Ceulemans 11, Claesen 73

● FRANCE *Albert Rust, Michel Bibard, Amoros, Tigana [Tusseau 84], Yvon Le Roux [Bossis 56], Battiston (c), Vercruysse, Bernard Genghini, Papin, Ferreri, Bellone.*
BELGIUM *Pfaff, Gerets, Renquin [F. Van der Elst HT], Vervoort, Grün, Demol, Raymond Mommens, Scifo [L. Van der Elst 65], Ceulemans (c), Claesen, Veyt.*

The only 3rd-place Final to go to extra-time. Bellone helped make the first two goals and Genghini scored from Ferreri's lobbed pass. Amoros, winning his 39th cap out of 82, still the French record, picked up his only international goal after Gerets brought him down. Ceulemans scored at one end after Bellone had missed at the other and Claesen put in Veyt's cross. The 32-year-old Rust won his only cap.

Final

■ 29 June 1986 • Azteca, Mexico City •
114,580 • Romualdo Arppi (BRZ)

▲ **ARGENTINA (1) 3**
Brown 23, Valdano 56, Burruchaga 85
WEST GERMANY (0) 2
Rummenigge 74, Völler 82

● ARGENTINA *Pumpido, Cuciuffo, Olarticoechea, Enrique, Ruggeri, Brown, Giusti, Batista, Burruchaga [Marcelo Trobbiani 89], Maradona (c), Valdano.*
W. GERMANY *Schumacher, Berthold, Briegel, Jakobs, Förster, Eder, Matthäus, Brehme, Allofs [Völler HT], Magath [Hoeness 61], Rummenigge (c).*

Beckenbauer, who admitted he didn't have the players to win the title, put Matthäus on Maradona, hoped for the best, and might have got it if he hadn't been undermined by the sudden fallibility of Schumacher, until then the best goalkeeper in the competition. After three consecutive clean sheets, he suddenly charged out for Burruchaga's free-kick and was stranded in mid air when Brown headed in. Urged by his team-mates to stay back (according to his autobiography) he allowed Valdano to run in from the right and push the ball past his outstretched foot. Then Burruchaga was clean through, only to be called back for a non-existent offside.

Still, 2-0 seemed to be enough – but ye of little faith should have remembered that this was West Germany, and they do things differently there. Dull side though they were, with Rummenigge still unfit and Magath invisible in midfield, they hauled themselves back into it, releasing Matthäus from his marking duties and scoring twice from Brehme's left-wing corners. The first was helped on by Völler for Rummenigge to slide in and force it home; the second was headed back by Berthold for Völler to get his head bravely in front of Pumpido's fists. Hard for Argentina to defend against these with Brown having cracked a bone in his shoulder.

The Germans felt they lost it there and then. Intoxicated by the comeback, they pressed forward instead of playing for extra-time, giving Maradona enough room to thread a pass through to Burruchaga in the inside-right channel. He ran on and shot across Schumacher, who again stayed on his line. Seven of the Germans weren't capped again, including Briegel, Förster (still only 27) and Rummenigge, the only player to captain the losing team in two Finals. West Germany might have won at least one if he'd been fully fit either time, or if Schuster had played.

Meanwhile his opposite number had a relatively quiet match but still made the winning goal, just reward after the frustrations of 1982. No other World Cup tournament has been so dominated by a single player, with a left foot in the Puskás class and that cheating left hand.

LEADING GOALSCORERS 1986

6	Gary Lineker	ENG	
5	Emilio Butragueño	SPA	1 pen
5	Careca	BRZ	1 pen
5	Diego Maradona	ARG	

SHORTEST FINALS CAREERS

mins

1	Marcelo Trobbiani	ARG	1986	v WG
2	Khemais Labidi	TUN	1978	v MEX
2	Miguel Pardeza	SPA	1990	v BEL
2	Magnus Erlingmark	SWE	1994	v RUS
2	Petar Mikhtarski	BUL	1994	v MEX
3	Ion Vladoiu	ROM	1994	v SWI
3	Corneliu Papura	ROM	1994	v COL & ARG
4	Miguel Angel Oviedo	ARG	1978	v PER
4	Marco Etcheverry	BOL	1994	v GER

BRITISH

| 6 | Kerry Dixon | ENG | 1986 | v POL |

Schumacher jumps highest but misses, and Brown (half hidden) heads the first goal of the Final. Impish glee from Maradona down below.

Rummenigge sparks one of West Germany's famous comebacks by scoring from close range in the Final.

The greatest player of his generation, still doing important things with his hand.

Penalties of Fame

Italy 1990

No-one was unduly surprised when Italy became the first European country to host the World Cup more than once. They'd been the first to host the European Championship twice (before most countries had held it once) and generally knew their way through the corridors of power. That and a strong national team gave them a serious head start. Azeglio Vicini, Bearzot's successor as coach, who'd been in charge of the Under-21 team which won the European title in 1986, had brought several of those players into the senior squad. The defence, in which Bergomi was now the captain, had been reinforced by the young Paolo Maldini and another great sweeper in Franco Baresi, conceding only one goal in the last nine games. But there were problems and controversies up front (only two goals in the last seven), where Vicini seemed reluctant to use the talents of Roberto Baggio. Much would depend on Vialli, who'd just scored the goals that won Sampdoria the Cup-Winners' Cup.

Argentina had several of the same players as in 1986, again led by Maradona, but had won only one of their last ten games, 2-1 in Israel. They had to take what comfort they could from their second match being staged on Maradona's home club ground.

West Germany had failed to win the European Championship at home two years earlier but had many more talented players than in 1986. Brehme, Matthäus and Völler were reinforced by world-class newcomers like Buchwald, Kohler and the dashing blond Klinsmann, and three of the squad played with Inter in Milan. But Beckenbauer, still the manager, was having to use the veteran Augenthaler as sweeper.

Brazil had a new coach and another strong defence, but no replacements for their old midfield stars. Careca was still there but his obvious partner, the immensely gifted Romário, hadn't played since breaking a leg in March. Winners of the Copa América the previous year

and the only team to have beaten Italy this season, they were established as joint second favourites or thereabouts.

Ahead of them in the ratings were the Dutch, back in the finals with a team that lost little in comparison with Cruyff & Co, European Champions arriving with a battery of all-time greats including Rijkaard and Ronald Koeman, the dreadlocked Gullit and van Basten, the complete centre-forward. Although Gullit had been out for almost a year with injury, they were the big stumbling block in England's group.

Nevertheless England had reason to be cheerful. After their disastrous European finals (three defeats out of three, including a hat-trick by van Basten), Bobby Robson was allowed to stay on and quickly brought in a great new defensive talent in the lightning-quick Des Walker. England qualified without conceding a goal and Lineker had recovered from jaundice, but they were grateful that Poland hit the bar in injury-time at the end of their last match.

The Republic of Ireland, who'd beaten England in Euro '88 and were drawn in the same group again, were coached by Jack Charlton, of 1966 fame, who'd overlooked their midfield skills in favour of an approach that involved banging the ball towards the corner flags to turn opposition defences. Rarely a pretty sight, it was effective enough to take them to the finals for the first time at the expense of their neighbours from the North. The organizers, fearful of English, Irish and Dutch fans all thrown together, packed them all off to Sardinia and policed them brutally, scenes that were to be repeated – on a reduced scale – at England's qualifying match in Rome seven years later.

Scotland, present for the fifth time in a row, again found themselves in the same group as Brazil but fancied their chances against Sweden, who'd twice drawn 0-0 with England in the qualifiers; and manager Andy Roxburgh wasn't alone in thinking 'we have nothing to fear from Costa Rica'.

Group A

Austria, Czechoslovakia, Italy, USA

■ 9 June 1990 • Olimpico, Rome • 72,303 • José Ramiz Wright (BRZ)

▲ **ITALY (0) 1**
Schillaci 79
AUSTRIA (0) 0

● ITALY *Walter Zenga, Giuseppe Bergomi (c), Paolo Maldini, Carlo Ancelotti [Luigi De Agostini HT], Riccardo Ferri, Franco Baresi, Roberto Donadoni, Fernando De Napoli, Andrea Carnevale [Salvatore Schillaci 75], Giuseppe Giannini, Gianluca Vialli. Azeglio Vicini.*
AUSTRIA *Klaus Lindenberger, Kurt Russ, Michael Streiter, Ernst Aigner, Robert Pecl, Peter Schöttel, Peter Artner [Manfred Zsak 62], Manfred Linzmaier [Alfred Hörtnagl 77], Toni Polster (c), Andreas Ogris, Andreas Herzog. Josef Hickersberger.*

■ 10 June 1990 • Comunale, Florence • 33,266 • Kurt Röthlisberger (SWI)

▲ **CZECHOSLOVAKIA (2) 5**
Skuhravy 26, 79, Bílek pen 39, Hasek 51, Luhovy 89
USA (0) 1
Caligiuri 60

● CZECHOSLOVAKIA *Jan Stejskal, Miroslav Kadlec, Ján Kocian, Frantisek Straka, Michal Bílek, Ivan Hasek (c), Jozef Chovanec, Lubos Kubík, Lubomír Moravcík [Vladimír Weiss 83], Tomás Skuhravy, Ivo Knoflícek [Milan Luhovy 76]. Jozef Venglos.*
USA *Tony Meola, Steve Trittschuh, Mike Windischmann (c), Desmond Armstrong, Paul Caligiuri, John Stollmeyer [Marcelo Balboa 64], Tab Ramos, John Harkes, Eric Wynalda, Peter Vermes, Bruce Murray [Chris Sullivan 78]. Bob Gansler.*
SENT OFF: *Wynalda 52.*

▼

Italy's goalscoring problems graphically illustrated. Attacking rather than counter-attacking, they had most of the match, but Carnevale missed at least four chances (two saved by Lindenberger) and was substituted. The staring eyes of his replacement, who scored his first goal for Italy with an emphatic header, were to become a feature of the tournament. Vialli, always more of an all-round forward than an out-and-out striker, may have had mixed feelings about providing the cross for the goal.

After watching the opening match of the tournament, Windischmann allegedly described his team as 'the Cameroon of our group', which raised a few chuckles after this overwhelming defeat. Rodney Marsh was nearer the mark when he said most unfancied teams had a puncher's chance but the USA didn't have a puncher. They conceded two penalties, two goals from corners, another to Luhovy from close range, and had Wynalda sent off for pushing Kadlec. Only Caligiuri's fine solo goal and Meola's late penalty save from Bílek relieved the embarrassment. Note the slight difference in the spelling of Stejskal and Kocian's first names.

■ 14 June 1990 • Olimpico, Rome • 73,423 •
Edgardo Codesal (MEX)

▲ **ITALY (1) 1**
Giannini 11
USA (0) 0

● ITALY *Zenga, Bergomi (c), Maldini, Nicola Berti, Ferri, Baresi, Donadoni, De Napoli, Carnevale [Schillaci 52], Giannini, Vialli.*
USA *Meola, Jimmy Banks [Stollmeyer 80], Windischmann (c), John Doyle, Armstrong, Balboa, Caligiuri, Harkes, Ramos, Vermes, Murray [Sullivan 82].*

Vicini gave the same starting line-up a second chance against the whipping-boys, but they struggled again, even after Giannini's low drive gave them an early lead. Vialli hit the post with a penalty after 33 minutes (it really wasn't his tournament) and even the introduction of Schillaci didn't help much. Italy were through to the next round, but minus any dancing in the streets.

■ 15 June 1990 • Comunale, Florence • 38,962 •
George Smith (SCO)

▲ **CZECHOSLOVAKIA (1) 1**
Bílek pen 29
AUSTRIA (0) 0

● CZECHOSLOVAKIA *Stejskal, Kadlec, Kocian, Václav Nemecek, Hasek (c), Moravcík, Chovanec [Július Bielik 30], Bílek, Kubík, Skuhravy, Knoflícek [Weiss 81].*
AUSTRIA *Lindenberger, Aigner, Pecl, Anton Pfeffer, Russ [Streiter HT], Hörtnagl, Zsak, Schöttel [Ogris HT], Herzog, Polster (c), Gerhard Rodax.*

Like the hosts, Czechoslovakia qualified at the earliest opportunity, against a dismal and dirty Austrian team who got little from the vaunted pairing of Polster (who later had the gall to criticize his coach) and Rodax. Pfeffer's back pass let in Chovanec, who had to go off after the foul by Lindenberger that conceded the penalty.

■ 19 June 1990 • Olimpico, Rome • 73,303 • Joël Quiniou (FRA)

▲ **ITALY (1) 2**
Schillaci 9, Baggio 78
CZECHOSLOVAKIA (0) 0

● ITALY *Zenga, Bergomi (c), Maldini, Berti, Ferri, Baresi, Donadoni [De Agostini 51], De Napoli [Pietro Vierchowod 66], Schillaci, Giannini, Roberto Baggio.*
CZECHOSLOVAKIA *Stejskal, Kadlec, Vladimír Kinier, Nemecek [Bielik HT], Hasek (c), Moravcík, Chovanec, Bílek, Weiss [Stanislav Griga 59], Skuhravy, Knoflícek.*

Vicini changed his front two and was rewarded with a much better performance and a special goal, Baggio taking a return pass from Giannini and almost sauntering past two defenders in a long run on goal. First, Schillaci scored with another header but Italy were rather lucky to be staying in Rome for the second round; Griga had a headed goal wrongly disallowed for offside after 64 minutes.

■ 19 June 1990 • Comunale, Florence • 34,857 • Jamal Al-Sharif (SYR)

▲ **AUSTRIA (0) 2**
Ogris 49, Rodax 63
USA (0) 1
Murray 84

● AUSTRIA *Lindenberger, Artner, Streiter, Aigner, Pecl, Pfeffer, Ogris, Zsak, Polster (c) [Andreas Reisinger HT], Herzog, Rodax [Gerald Glatzmayer 84].*
USA *Meola, Banks [Wynalda 55], Windischmann (c), Doyle, Armstrong, Balboa, Caligiuri [Brian Bliss 71], Harkes, Ramos, Vermes, Murray.*
▼ SENT OFF: *Artner 34.*

Bad-tempered and bad. Nine bookings and Artner sent off for a dangerous tackle on Vermes. Ogris' goal was all his own work and Streiter's run set up Rodax. Murray's goal from a cross by Ramos was some consolation for a side whose own World Cup was due in four years' time.

BOOKINGS IN A MATCH

9	1990	Austria (5)	v	USA (4)
9	1994	Italy (5)	v	Nigeria (4)
8	1986	Mexico (5)	v	W. Germany (3)
8	1994	Bulgaria (4)	v	Greece (4)
8	1994	Spain (4)	v	Switzerland (4)
8	1994	Germany (5)	v	Bulgaria (3)

A tenth player (another Austrian) was sent off in the 1990 match. Two players were sent off in the Mexico-WG match, one of whom had previously been booked. Italy also had another player sent off.

GROUP A	P	W	D	L	F	A	PTS
Italy	3	3	0	0	4	0	6
Czechoslovakia	3	2	0	1	6	3	4
Austria	3	1	0	2	2	3	2
USA	3	0	0	3	2	8	0

Italy and Czechoslovakia qualified for the second round.

Group B

Argentina, Cameroon, Romania, USSR

■ 8 June 1990 • Giuseppe Meazza, Milan • 73,780 • Michel Vautrot (FRA)

▲ **CAMEROON (0) 1**
Omam Biyick 67
ARGENTINA (0) 0

● CAMEROON *Thomas Nkono, Stephen Tataw (c), Bertin Ebwelle, Victor Ndip, Benjamin Massing, Emmanuel Kunde, Cyrille Makanaky [Roger Milla 82], Émile Mbouh, François Omam Biyick, André Kana Biyick, Louis Paul Mfede [Thomas Libiih 65]. Valery Nepomniachi (USR).*
ARGENTINA *Nery Pumpido, Néstor Fabbri, Roberto Sensini [Gabriel Calderón 69], Juan Simón, Oscar Ruggeri [Claudio Caniggia HT], Néstor Lorenzo, Jorge Burruchaga, Sergio Batista, Abel Balbo, Diego Maradona (c), José Basualdo. Carlos Bilardo.*
▼ SENT OFF: *Kana-Biyick 61, Massing 88.*

Not quite the sensation it appears, given the teams' recent records, but still a surprise. Cameroon massed in defence and paid Maradona strict attention, though both sendings-off were for fouls on the lively Caniggia; the second an assault that seemed to start halfway across the pitch. The only goal was scrappy, Omam Biyick climbing way above the defence to head down straight at Pumpido, who let the ball in off his leg. The Biyicks were brothers. The stadium, renamed after the star of 1934 and 1938, is still generally known as the San Siro.

■ 9 June 1990 • San Nicola, Bari • 42,907 • Juan Cardellino (URU)

▲ **ROMANIA (1) 2**
Lacatus 41, pen 55
USSR (0) 0

● ROMANIA *Silviu Lung (c), Mircea Rednic, Michael Klein, Gheorghe Popescu, Ioan Andone, Ionut Lupescu, Ioan Ovidiu Sabau, Florin Raducioiu [Gavril Balint 80], Marius Lacatus [Ilie Dumitrescu 87], Iosif Rotariu, Daniel Timofte.* Emerich Jenei.
USSR *Renat Dasayev (c), Sergei Gorlukovich, Vladimir Bessonov, Vasily Rats, Vagiz Khidiatulin, Oleg Kuznetsov, Sergei Aleinikov, Gennady Litovchenko [Ivan Yaremchuk 66], Oleg Protasov, Aleksandr Zavarov, Igor Dobrovolsky [Aleksandr Borodyuk 71].* Valery Lobanovsky.

Even without their playmaker Hagi, Romania had things stacked in their favour. Yakovenko and Alexei Mikhailichenko were out for the duration, Protasov and Zavarov missed early chances, and the penalty was given for a handball which Khidiatulin committed outside the area. Lacatus, who opened the scoring with a powerful shot, also missed an open goal.

■ 13 June 1990 • San Paolo, Naples • 55,759 • Erik Fredriksson (SWE)

▲ **ARGENTINA (1) 2**
Troglio 27, Burruchaga 78
USSR (0) 0

● ARGENTINA *Pumpido [Sergio Goycochea 9], José Serrizuela, Julio Olarticoechea, Simón, Pedro Monzón [Lorenzo 79], Basualdo, Burruchaga, Batista, Pedro Troglio, Maradona (c), Caniggia.*
USSR *Aleksandr Uvarov, Bessonov, Gorlukovich, Khidiatulin, Kuznetsov (c), Andrei Zygmantovich, Aleinikov, Igor Shalimov, Protasov [Litovchenko 75], Zavarov [Vladimir Liuti 85], Dobrovolsky.*
▼ SENT OFF: *Bessonov 47.*

Pumpido broke his right leg in a collision with Olarticoechea – but, with respect, it was the USSR who had all the bad luck in this group. The previous year, Maradona had perpetrated another divine handball, earning a penalty (!) in the UEFA Cup Final, which Napoli won. Now, in the same stadium, he palmed away Kuznetsov's flick-on but the referee didn't see it. After that, Troglio headed in Olarticoechea's cross from the left and Burruchaga took advantage of Kuznetsov's back pass. The USSR, full of very good players who kept missing chances, were the first side to be eliminated from the tournament.

Omam Biyick climbs way up there to head the goal that shocked Argentina. The sight leaves Sensini (17) open-mouthed.

■ 14 June 1990 • San Nicola, Bari • 38,687 •
Hernán Silva Arce (CHI)

▲ **CAMEROON (0) 2**
Milla 76, 86
ROMANIA (0) 1
Balint 88

● CAMEROON *Nkono, Tataw (c), Ebwelle, Ndip, Jules Denis Onana, Kunde [Jean-Claude Pagal 70], Makanaky, Mbouh, Omam Biyick, Mfede, Emmanuel Maboang Kessack [Milla 57].*
ROMANIA *Lung (c), Rednic, Klein, Popescu, Andone, Rotariu, Lacatus, Sabau, Raducioiu [Balint 63], Gheorghe Hagi [Dumitrescu 56], Timofte.*

Cameroon, again uncomplicated and aggressive, gave the 38-year-old Milla a run-out worthy of the name and he scored two flamboyant goals, barging Andone off the ball for the first, showing great acceleration before thrashing in the second, each time celebrating with a little dance round the corner post. Brought out of virtual retirement (from a club on Réunion, an island in the Indian Ocean), he was the oldest player to score in a finals match, a record he hadn't finished with yet. Lacatus hit a post but Cameroon could afford Balint's late strike, from a position that looked offside.

■ 18 June 1990 • San Paolo, Naples • 52,733 •
Carlos Alberto da Silva Valente (POR)

▲ **ARGENTINA (0) 1**
Monzón 61
ROMANIA (0) 1
Balint 68

● ARGENTINA *Goycochea, Serrizuela, Olarticoechea, Simón, Monzón, Basualdo, Burruchaga [Gustavo Dezotti 62], Batista, Troglio [Ricardo Giusti 53], Maradona (c), Caniggia.*
ROMANIA *Lung (c), Rednic, Klein, Popescu, Andone, Rotariu, Lacatus, Sabau [Dorin Mateut 81], Balint [Danut Lupu 73], Hagi, Lupescu.*

Romania needed a draw to be sure of qualifying and Balint made sure they got it after Sabau headed back a cross by Lacatus. Monzón had headed Argentina in front from a corner by Maradona, who was overshadowed by Hagi, 'the Maradona of the Carpathians'.

Roger Milla, 38-year-old goalscorer and great World Cup personality.

Group C

Brazil, Costa Rica, Scotland, Sweden

■ 18 June 1990 • San Nicola, Bari • 37,307 •
José Ramiz Wright (BRZ)

▲ **USSR (2) 4**
Protasov 20, Zygmantovich 29, Zavarov 52,
Dobrovolsky 63
CAMEROON (0) 0

● USSR *Uvarov, Gorlukovich, Anatoly Demianenko (c),
Khidiatulin, Kuznetsov, Zygmantovich, Aleinikov,
Litovchenko [Yaremchuk 74], Protasov, Shalimov
[Zavarov HT], Dobrovolsky.*
CAMEROON *Nkono, Tataw (c), Ebwelle, Ndip, Onana,
Kunde [Milla 35], Makanaky [Pagal 58], Mbouh, Omam
Biyick, Kana Biyick, Mfede.*

Too late the USSR showed what they were made of,
at last taking their goalscoring opportunities.
Protasov put in a cross by Zygmantovich, who
knocked in the second after Aleinikov went round
the keeper. Dobrovolsky slid in the fourth.
Cameroon, in their sixth finals match, suffered their
first defeat.

GROUP B	P	W	D	L	F	A	PTS
Cameroon	3	2	0	1	3	5	4
Romania	3	1	1	1	4	3	3
Argentina	3	1	1	1	3	2	3
USSR	3	1	0	2	4	4	2

Cameroon, Romania and Argentina qualified for
the second round.

■ 10 June 1990 • Delle Alpi, Turin • 62,628 •
Tullio Lanese (ITA)

▲ **BRAZIL (1) 2**
Careca 40, 62
SWEDEN (0) 1
Brolin 78

●

BRAZIL *Cláudio Taffarel, 'Jorginho' (Jorge Amorim),
'Branco (Cláudio Vaz), Mauro Galvão, Ricardo Gomes (c),
José Carlos Mozer, 'Müller' (Luís Corrêa), 'Dunga' (Carlos
Bledorn Verri), 'Careca' (Antônio de Oliveira), 'Alemão'
(Ricardo de Brito), Valdo (Cândido) [Silas (do Prado) 85].
Sebastião Lazaroni.*
SWEDEN *Thomas Ravelli, Roland Nilsson, Roger Ljung
[Glenn Strömberg 70], Stefan Schwarz, Peter Larsson, Jonas
Thern (c), Anders Limpar, Klas Ingesson, Tomas Brolin,
Joakim Nilsson, Mats Magnusson [Stefan Pettersson HT].
Olle Nordin.*

Without hitting any heights, Brazil made efficiency
good-looking, if that's possible. Their five-man
defence and functional attack were too much for a
Swedish team enlivened only by the babyfaced
Brolin, who scored with a clever turn and shot. Both
the Brazilian goals were well made and crisply taken.
Careca, still slim and sharp, ran on to Branco's
through-ball and dummied the keeper, then put
Müller's low cross into an empty net.

■ 11 June 1990 • Luigi Ferraris, Genoa •
30,867 • Juan Carlos Loustau (ARG)

▲ **COSTA RICA (0) 1**
Cayasso 49
SCOTLAND (0) 0

● COSTA RICA *Luis Conejo, Germán Chavarría, José Carlos Chávez, Roger Flóres (c), Héctor Marchena, Mauricio Montero, Ronald González, Oscar Ramírez, Juan Cayasso, Roger Gómez, Claudio Jara [Hernán Medford 86].* Bora Milutinovic (YUG).
SCOTLAND *Jim Leighton, Richard Gough [Stewart McKimmie HT], Maurice Malpas, Robert 'Roy' Aitken (c), Alex McLeish, Dave McPherson, Jim Bett [Ally McCoist 74], Paul McStay, Mo Johnston, Stuart McCall, Alan McInally.* Andy Roxburgh.

If Roxburgh's pre-match quote was memorable, so was a post-match headline: 'Scotland Plunged Into Cayasso'. Milutinovic, who'd coached Mexico in the previous finals, made controversial changes to the squad as soon as he took charge, and they paid off. The goal was cleverly started and finished, Cayasso clipping Jara's backheel over Leighton. Costa Rica were the first Central American team to win a World Cup match in Europe, but yet again this looked an ordinary Scotland team.

GROUP C	P	W	D	L	F	A	PTS
Brazil	3	3	0	0	4	1	6
Costa Rica	3	2	0	1	3	2	4
Scotland	3	1	0	2	2	3	2
Sweden	3	0	0	3	3	6	0

Brazil and Costa Rica qualified for the second round.

■ 16 June 1990 • Delle Alpi, Turin • 40,000 • Neji
Jouini (TUN)

▲ **BRAZIL (1) 1**
Müller 33
COSTA RICA (0) 0

● BRAZIL *Taffarel, Jorginho, Branco, Mauro Galvão, Ricardo Gomes (c), Mozer, Müller, Dunga, Careca ['Bebeto' (Roberto Gama) 84], Alemão, Valdo [Silas 86].*
COSTA RICA *Conejo, Chavarría, Chávez, Flóres (c), Montero, González, Ramírez, Marchena, Cayasso [Alexandre Guimarães 78], Gómez, Jara [Roy Myers 71].*

Further determined defence by the underdogs, but Brazil should have won by a greater margin. Müller and defender Marchena hit the Costa Rican crossbar, and Conejo made a number of saves. The goal was streaky, Müller's shot going in off Montero, but Brazil were rightly and swiftly through to the next round. The official attendance figure was 58,007.

■ 16 June 1990 • Luigi Ferraris, Genoa •
31,823 • Carlos Maciel (PAR)

▲ **SCOTLAND (1) 2**
McCall 10, Johnston pen 82
SWEDEN (0) 1
Strömberg 87

● SCOTLAND *Leighton, Craig Levein, Malpas, Aitken (c), McLeish, McPherson, Robert Fleck [McCoist 85], Murdo MacLeod, Johnston, McCall, Gordon Durie [McStay 75].*
SWEDEN *Ravelli, R. Nilsson, Schwarz, Thern, Larsson [Strömberg 75], Glenn Hysén (c), Limpar, Ingesson, Brolin, J. Nilsson, Pettersson [Johnny Ekström 63].*

Ordinary team or not, Scotland's morale was in better shape than Sweden's, and the team changes helped. McCall slid the ball in from close range after McPherson helped on a corner from the right, and Aitken would have scored if Roland Nilsson hadn't fouled him for the penalty. A long lob was coolly touched in by Strömberg, a distinctive figure with his long fair hair; but the Scots were worthy winners.

■ 20 June 1990 • Luigi Ferraris, Genoa • 30,223 • Zoran Petrovic (YUG)

▲ **COSTA RICA (0) 2**
Flóres 74, Medford 87
SWEDEN (1) 1
Ekström 31

● COSTA RICA *Conejo, Chavarría [Guimarães 75], Montero, Chávez, Flóres (c), González, Ramírez, Marchena, Cayasso, Gómez [Medford 60], Jara.*
SWEDEN *Ravelli, R. Nilsson, Schwarz, Ingesson, Larsson, Hysén (c), Brolin [Mats Gren 34], Strömberg [Leif Engqvist 82], Ekström, J. Nilsson, Pettersson.*

Sweden, a disappointment to their fans, achieved the unique feat of losing all three group matches by the same score, this time after taking the lead through Ekström, once one of their golden boys, who put in the rebound when Conejo saved a free-kick from Schwarz. Another free-kick, by González, was headed in by the veteran captain Flóres, then the lively Medford ran through to shoot across Ravelli, putting Costa Rica in the next round and Scotland's first match in perspective.

■ 20 June 1990 • Delle Alpi, Turin • 62,502 • Helmut Kohl (AUT)

▲ **BRAZIL (0) 1**
Müller 81
SCOTLAND (0) 0

● BRAZIL *Taffarel, Jorginho, Branco, Mauro Galvão, Ricardo Gomes (c), Ricardo Rocha, Romário (de Souza) [Müller 65], Dunga, Careca, Alemão, Valdo*
SCOTLAND *Leighton, McKimmie, Malpas, Aitken (c), McLeish, McPherson, McStay, MacLeod [Gary Gillespie 38], Johnston, McCall, McCoist [Fleck 78].*

Eighty minutes of clock-watching – exactly what Scotland wanted – suddenly meant nothing when Alemão, Brazil's driving midfielder, shot firmly but not overpoweringly from the edge of the box. Leighton, an international-class keeper for most of the decade, had recently been in poor form with Manchester United, and was dropped for the FA Cup Final replay. Here he couldn't hold Alemão's shot, did well to save Careca's follow-up, but could only watch as the ball trundled behind him almost to the goal line before Müller squeezed it in from a narrow angle. On another day, in better times, his error would have gone unpunished. As it was, Scotland were out and still hadn't qualified for the second stage after seven attempts. Leighton was left out for more than three years but recovered to become an important member of the squad that reached the 1998 finals.

Group D

Colombia, United Arab Emirates, West Germany, Yugoslavia

■ 9 June 1990 • Renato Dall'Ara, Bologna • 30,791 • George Courtney (ENG)

▲ **COLOMBIA (0) 2**
Redín 50, Valderrama 85
UNITED ARAB EMIRATES (0) 0

● COLOMBIA *René Higuita, Luis Herrera, Gilardo Gómez, Andrés Escobar, Luis Perea, Gabriel Gómez, Bernardo Redín, Leonel Alvarez, Freddy Rincón, Carlos Valderrama (c), Arnoldo Iguarán [Carlos Enrique Estrada 75].* Francisco Maturana.

EMIRATES *Muhsin Musabah Faraj, Eissa Meer Abdulrahman, Ibrahim Meer Abdulrahman [Abdullah Ali Sultan 74], Khalil Ghanem Mubarak, Mohammed Yousuf Hussain, Abdulrahman Mohammed Abdullah, Nasser Khamis Mubarak, Ali Thani Juma'a, Adnan Khamis Al-Taliyani, Hussain Ghuloum Abbas [Zuhair Bakhit Bilal 53], Fahad Khamis Mubarak (c).* Carlos Alberto Parreira (BRZ).

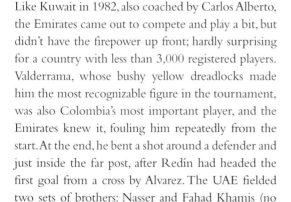

■ 10 June 1990 • Giuseppe Meazza, Milan • 74,765 • Peter Mikkelsen (DEN)

▲ **WEST GERMANY (2) 4**
Matthäus 28, 63, Klinsmann 39, Völler 69
YUGOSLAVIA (0) 1
Jozic 54

● W. GERMANY *Bodo Illgner, Stefan Reuter, Andreas Brehme, Thomas Berthold, Guido Buchwald, Klaus Augenthaler, Thomas Hässler [Pierre Littbarski 74], Uwe Bein [Andreas Möller 74], Rudi Völler, Lothar Matthäus (c), Jürgen Klinsmann.* Franz Beckenbauer.

YUGOSLAVIA *Tomislav Ivkovic, Faruk Hadzibegic, Mirsad Baljic, Predrag Spasic, Zoran Vulic, Davor Jozic, Dragan Stojkovic, Safet Susic [Robert Prosinecki 55], Srecko Katanec, Dejan Savicevic [Dragoljub Brnovic 55], Zlatko Vujovic (c).* Ivica Osim.

Like Kuwait in 1982, also coached by Carlos Alberto, the Emirates came out to compete and play a bit, but didn't have the firepower up front; hardly surprising for a country with less than 3,000 registered players. Valderrama, whose bushy yellow dreadlocks made him the most recognizable figure in the tournament, was also Colombia's most important player, and the Emirates knew it, fouling him repeatedly from the start. At the end, he bent a shot around a defender and just inside the far post, after Redín had headed the first goal from a cross by Alvarez. The UAE fielded two sets of brothers: Nasser and Fahad Khamis (no relation to Adnan Khamis) and the Meers.

For the first time since 1966, West Germany opened their account with a compelling display of power football. Stojkovic, Savicevic and the 35-year-old Susic, some of the most extravagantly gifted players of their generation, were simply swept aside. Buchwald, tall and surprisingly skilful but an adhesive marker, blotted out Savicevic. Matthäus did the same to Stojkovic as well as scoring with two ferocious long shots, one with each foot; the first after sidestepping a tackle, the second after hurdling a defender on his way through the middle. The ultimate all-round midfielder.

His team-mates were almost as good. Brehme whipped in a low cross for Klinsmann to score with a spectacular diving header, then fired in a shot which Ivkovic fumbled for Völler to be credited with the fourth. Jozic headed a Stojkovic free-kick in off a post, but the Yugoslavs, and the rest of the competition, were left breathless.

■ 14 June 1990 • Renato Dall'Ara, Bologna •
32,257 • Luigi Agnolin (ITA)

▲ **YUGOSLAVIA (0) 1**
Jozic 75
COLOMBIA (0) 0

● YUGOSLAVIA *Ivkovic, Vujadin Stanojkovic, Brnovic, Hadzibegic, Jozic, Spasic, Stojkovic, Susic, Katanec [Robert Jarni HT], Vujovic (c) [Darko Pancev 55], Refik Sabanadzovic.*
COLOMBIA *Higuita, Herrera, Gilardo Gómez, Escobar, Perea, Gabriel Gómez, Redín [Estrada 80], Rincón [Rubén Dario Hernández 69], Iguarán, Valderrama (c), Alvarez.*

Against far less formidable opposition, Yugoslavia hauled themselves back into the competition. Stojkovic crossed for Jozic, a skilful sweeper, to chest down and shoot into the roof of the net. The long-haired Higuita, whose rushes from goal recalled Quiroga of 1978 fame, saved Hadzibegic's penalty with 11 minutes left.

■ 15 June 1990 • Giuseppe Meazza, Milan •
71,167 • Alexei Spirin (USR)

▲ **WEST GERMANY (2) 5**
Völler 35, 74, Klinsmann 37, Matthäus 48, Bein 58
UNITED ARAB EMIRATES (0) 1
Khalid Ismail 47

● W. GERMANY *Illgner, Berthold [Littbarski HT], Brehme, Reuter, Buchwald, Augenthaler, Hässler, Bein, Völler, Matthäus (c), Klinsmann [Karlheinz Riedle 71].*
EMIRATES *Faraj, Eissa Meer, Ibrahim Meer [Abdulrahman Mohammed Al-Haddad 87], Khalil Ghanem, Mohammed Yousuf, Abdulrahman Mohammed (c), Nasser Khamis, Juma'a, Al-Taliyani, Ghuloum Abbas, Khalid Ismail [Hassan Mohammed Hussain 82].*

The Germans, continuing in the same vein, should have had ten. With the score still 0-0, their two strikers missed three good chances, hit a post and forced a close-range save from Faraj. Eventually Klinsmann crossed for Völler to head in then scored himself from Reuter's centre. Khalid Ismail calmly trapped a deflected pass before shooting across Illgner, but there was no comeback against a team like this. Another Matthäus piledriver immediately made it 3-1, and Bein thumped a shot high into the net. The German victory was firmly sealed a quarter of an hour later by Völler's second goal of the match.

■ 19 June 1990 • Giuseppe Meazza, Milan •
72,510 • Alan Snoddy (NIR)

▲ **COLOMBIA (0) 1**
Rincón 90
WEST GERMANY (0) 1
Littbarski 88

● COLOMBIA *Higuita, Herrera, Gilardo Gómez, Escobar, Perea, Gabriel Gómez, Luis Alfonso Fajardo, Alvarez, Rincón, Valderrama (c), Estrada.*
W. GERMANY *Illgner, Reuter, Hans Pflügler, Berthold, Buchwald, Augenthaler, Hässler [Olaf Thon 87], Bein [Littbarski HT], Völler, Matthäus (c), Klinsmann.*

Colombia needed a draw to qualify, fell behind to Littbarski's near-post shot with only two minutes left, then staged an improbable recovery when Rincón ran through to slip the ball between Illgner's legs as he came out. The Colombians won few friends with their play-acting, Valderrama at one point lying face-down for three minutes while the referee left him to it.

■ 19 June 1990 • Renato Dall'Ara, Bologna •
27,833 • Shizuo Takada (JPN)

▲ **YUGOSLAVIA (2) 4**
Susic 4, Pancev 7, 46, Prosinecki 90
UNITED ARAB EMIRATES (1) 1
Juma'a 20

● YUGOSLAVIA *Ivkovic, Stanojkovic, Brnovic, Hadzibegic,
Jozic, Spasic, Stojkovic, Susic, Pancev, Sabanadzovic
[Prosinecki 80], Vujovic (c) [Vulic 65].*
EMIRATES *Faraj, Eissa Meer, Ibrahim Meer, Khalil
Ghanem, Al-Haddad, Abdulrahman Mohammed (c), Nasser
Khamis [Sultan 35], Juma'a [Fahad Khamis HT], Al-
Taliyani, Ghuloum Abbas, Khalid Ismail.*
▼ SENT OFF: *Khalil Ghanem 76.*

Easy as expected for the revitalized Yugoslavs.
Pancev, soon to become the most feared striker in
Europe, scored twice from close range. The Emirates
again pulled it back to 2-1, but their involvement
ended on the wrong note when Khalil Ghanem was
sent off for a second bookable offence.

GROUP D	P	W	D	L	F	A	PTS
W. Germany	3	2	1	0	10	3	5
Yugoslavia	3	2	0	1	6	5	4
Colombia	3	1	1	1	3	2	3
Emirates	3	0	0	3	2	11	0

West Germany, Yugoslavia and Colombia
qualified for the second round.

Group E

Belgium, South Korea, Spain, Uruguay

■ 12 June 1990 • Marc'Antonio Bentegodi,
Verona • 32,790 • Vincent Mauro (USA)

▲ **BELGIUM (0) 2**
Degryse 53, De Wolf 64
SOUTH KOREA (0) 0

● BELGIUM *Michel Preud'homme, Eric Gerets (c), Michel
De Wolf, Leo Clijsters, Stefan Demol, Bruno Versavel, Marc
Emmers, Franky Van der Elst, Marc Degryse, Enzo Scifo,
Marc Van der Linden [Jan Ceulemans HT].* Guy Thys.
S. KOREA *Choi In-yung, Park Kyung-joon, Gu Sang-
bum, Hong Myung-bo, Chung Yong-hwan (c), Choi Kang-
hee, Kim Joo-sung, Noh Soo-jin [Lee Tae-ho 62], Hwang
Seon-hong, Lee Yung-jin [Cho Min-kook HT], Choi Soon-
ho.* Lee Hoe-taik.

Versavel hit a post after only six minutes, but it took
the introduction of Ceulemans, now 33 but still a
force, to kindle the Belgians. Degryse, chasing Scifo's
long ball, hit a stratospheric lob over the keeper, and
De Wolf smashed in a shot from the left. Choi In-
yung had to make several good saves and South
Korea rarely troubled Belgium's ageing defence.
Degryse is also written as two words: De Gryse.

LEADING GOALSCORERS 1990

6	Salvatore Schillaci	ITA	1 pen
5	Tomás Skuhravy	CZE	
4	Michel	SPA	1 pen
4	Roger Milla	CAM	
4	Lothar Matthäus	WG	1 pen
4	Gary Lineker	ENG	2 pen

■ 13 June 1990 • Friuli, Udine • 35,713 • Helmut Kohl (AUT)

▲ **SPAIN 0**
URUGUAY 0

● SPAIN *Andoni Zubizarreta, 'Chendo' (Miguel Portlan), Manuel Jiménez, Genaro Andrinua, Manuel Sanchís jnr, Rafael Martín Vázquez, 'Michel' (Miguel González), Roberto (Fernández), Emilio Butragueño (c), Francisco Villaroya [Alberto Gorriz 80], Manolo (Sánchez) [Rafael (Rafa) Paz 80]. Luis Suárez.*
URUGUAY *Fernando Alvez, José Herrera, Alfonso Domínguez, Nelson Gutiérrez, Hugo De León, José Perdomo, Antonio Alzamendi [Carlos Aguilera 65], Rubén Pereira [Carlos Gabriel Correa 65], Enzo Francescoli (c), Rubén Paz, Rubén Sosa. Oscar Washington Tabarez.*

■ 17 June 1990 • Marc'Antonio Bentegodi, Verona • 33,759 • Siegfried Kirschen (EG)

▲ **BELGIUM (2) 3**
Clijsters 15, Scifo 22, Ceulemans 46
URUGUAY (0) 1
Bengoechea 72

● BELGIUM *Preud'homme, Gerets, De Wolf, Clijsters [Emmers HT], Georges Grün, Demol, Versavel [Patrick Vervoort 73], Van der Elst, Degryse, Scifo, Ceulemans (c).*
URUGUAY *Alvez, Herrera, Domínguez, Gutiérrez, De León, Perdomo, Alzamendi [Aguilera HT], Santiago Ostolaza [Pablo Bengoechea 57], Francescoli (c), Paz, Sosa.*
▼ SENT OFF: *Gerets 36.*

Uruguay's win at Wembley had just ended England's run of 17 matches without defeat, and their coach stressed they were determined to shake off the reputation for dirty play they'd reinforced in 1986. But in its place there was nothing but tedium, from both teams. Zubizarreta pushed Alzamendi's shot on to the bar and Sosa drove a penalty over the top after Villaroya had handled with 20 minutes left. Martín (Vázquez) is part of the surname, not a first name.

Belgium caught the Uruguayans cold (the veteran Clijsters heading in De Wolf's cross, Scifo scoring with a ground shot from nearly 30 yards) and Ceulemans' powerful shot helped them survive the sending-off of Gerets for two bookable offences. Bengoechea's volley was good but not enough, and Herrera had to work hard on his 25th birthday.

GROUP E	P	W	D	L	F	A	PTS
Spain	3	2	1	0	5	2	5
Belgium	3	2	0	1	6	3	4
Uruguay	3	1	1	1	2	3	3
S. Korea	3	0	0	3	1	6	0

Spain, Belgium and Uruguay qualified for the second round.

OLDEST CAPTAINS
yrs/days
40/292	Peter Shilton	ENG	1990
40/133	Dino Zoff	ITA	1982
37/343	Manuel Bento	POR	1986

OLDEST OUTFIELD CAPTAIN
| 36/308 | Morten Olsen | DEN | 1986 |

■ 17 June 1990 • Friuli, Udine • 32,733 • Elias Jácome (ECU)

▲ **SPAIN (1) 3**
Michel 23, 63, 82
SOUTH KOREA (1) 1
Hwang Bo-kwan 43

● SPAIN *Zubizarreta, Chendo, Gorriz, Andrinua, Sanchís, Martín Vázquez, Michel, Roberto [José María Bakero 82], Butragueño (c) [Fernando (Gómez) 78], Villaroya, Julio Salinas.*
S. KOREA *Choi In-yung, Park Kyung-joon [Chung Jong-soo 69], Gu Sang-bum, Hong Myung-bo, Yoon Deuk-yeo, Choi Kang-hee, Kim Joo-sung, Hwang Bo-kwan, Byun Byung-joo, Chung Hae-won [Noh Soo-jin 52], Choi Soon-ho (c).*

South Korea tried to kick Spain out of their stride, equalized with a thunderous drive from outside the area, but were generally outplayed. Butragueño might have had a penalty, Salinas had a goal controversially disallowed, and Michel, a midfield star with Real Madrid throughout the 1980s, scored three classy goals: a volley, a free-kick, and a dribble on the left.

■ 21 June 1990 • Marc'Antonio Bentegodi, Verona • 35,950 • Juan Carlos Loustau (ARG)

▲ **SPAIN (2) 2**
Michel pen 26, Gorriz 38
BELGIUM (1) 1
Vervoort 29

● SPAIN *Zubizarreta, Chendo, Gorriz, Andrinua, Sanchís, Martín Vázquez, Michel, Roberto, Butragueño (c) [Rafael Alkorta 83], Villaroya, Salinas [Miguel Pardeza 88].*
BELGIUM *Preud'homme, Lorenzo Staelens [Van der Linden 79], De Wolf, Demol, Philippe Albert, Emmers [Pascal Plovie 31], Vervoort, Van der Elst, Degryse, Scifo, Ceulemans (c).*

Michel had another good match, putting away the penalty after Preud'homme fouled Salinas, and hitting a free-kick to the far post for Gorriz to head home. For the second match in a row, one of Spain's opponents missed a penalty, Scifo hitting the bar after Staelens was brought down by Gorriz on the hour. Vervoort cracked home a free-kick, but a draw would have been a fairer result.

■ 21 June 1990 • Friuli, Udine • 29,039 • Tullio Lanese (ITA)

▲ **URUGUAY (0) 1**
Fonseca 90
SOUTH KOREA (0) 0

● URUGUAY *Alvez, Herrera, Domínguez, Gutiérrez, De León, Perdomo, Sergio Martínez, Ostolaza [Aguilera HT], Francescoli (c), Paz, Sosa [Daniel Fonseca 63].*
S. KOREA *Choi In-yung, Park Kyung-joon, Choi Kang-hee, Chung Jong-soo, Hong Myung-bo, Yoon Deuk-yeo, Kim Joo-sung, Hwang Bo-kwan [Chung Hae-won 78], Byun Byung-joo [Hwang Seon-hong 42], Lee Heung-sil, Choi Soon-ho (c).*
▼ SENT OFF: *Yoon Deuk-yeo 70.*

Uruguay, who needed a win to be sure of qualifying, achieved one in a finals match for the first time since 1970 but left it late, the toothy Fonseca scoring with a header deep into injury-time. South Korea committed their usual quota of fouls and had a player sent off for time-wasting. The Official FIFA Report lists Alzamendi in place of Ostolaza, an error.

Group F

Egypt, England, Holland, Republic of Ireland

■ 11 June 1990 • Renato Sant'Elia, Cagliari •
35,238 • Aron Schmidhuber (WG)

▲ **ENGLAND (1) 1**
Lineker 9
REP. IRELAND (0) 1
Sheedy 73

● ENGLAND *Peter Shilton, M. Gary Stevens, Stuart Pearce, Bryan Robson (c), Terry Butcher, Des Walker, Chris Waddle, Paul Gascoigne, Gary Lineker [Steve Bull 84], Peter Beardsley [Steve McMahon 69], John Barnes.* Bobby Robson.
IRELAND *Pat Bonner, Chris Morris, Steve Staunton, Paul McGrath, Mick McCarthy (c), Kevin Moran, Ray Houghton, Andy Townsend, Tony Cascarino, John Aldridge [Alan McLoughlin 64], Kevin Sheedy.* Jack Charlton (ENG).

'No Football, We're English.' – the headline in *La Gazzetta dello Sport* got it about right, but they surely meant to include the Republic. Charlton's long-ball tactics were no prettier for being predictable, and England fell into the trap of copying them, playing into the hands of Ireland's straightforward stoppers. For an hour, England consoled themselves with the prospect of ending this grim business with a win. Lineker reached Waddle's through-ball, dummied Bonner and chested it past him in the same motion, then chased it into an empty net ahead of McCarthy and Morris. But a mistake by McMahon gave away the equalizer, the ball bobbling away from him on the edge of his own area for Sheedy to shoot low past Shilton. Bryan Robson, carrying yet another injury (a toe this time), wasn't the force of old.

Moran was winning his 50th cap. Italian statisticians apparently calculated that the ball was in play for only 49 minutes!

England's preparations had been dogged by the kind of press attention their manager had been living with for years. Isabella Ciaravolo, a Sardinian liaison officer, was transferred elsewhere after unsubstantiated reports of extra-curricular activities with some of the England players. After the Ireland match, one of the tabloids, which had been conducting a savage campaign against Bobby Robson since 1988, ran the line 'The *Sun* speaks its mind. Bring them home'. Watch this space for developments.

■ 12 June 1990 • Della Favorita, Palermo •
33,288 • Emilio Soriano Aladrén (SPA)

▲ **EGYPT (0) 1**
Abdelghani pen 82
HOLLAND (0) 1
Kieft 58

● EGYPT *Ahmed Shoubeir, Ibrahim Hassan, Rabbi Yassin, Ahmed Ramzy [Magdi Tolba 70], Hisham Yakan, Hani Ramzy, 'El-Kass' (Ahmed Abdou), Magdi Abdelghani, Gamal Abdelhamid (c) [Adel Abdelrahman 70], Ismail Youssef, Hossam Hassan.* Mahmoud El-Gohary.
HOLLAND *Hans van Breukelen, Berry van Aerle, Adri van Tiggelen, Jan Wouters, Graeme Rutjes, Ronald Koeman, Gerald Vanenburg [Wim Kieft HT], Frank Rijkaard, Marco van Basten, Ruud Gullit (c), Erwin Koeman [Richard Witschge 69].* Leo Beenhakker.

Although the unfancied countries had generally given a good account of themselves so far, this was the one match expected to restore the status quo: predictions of 5-0 were about the average. But Gullit wasn't fully fit, van Basten had a shocker, and Egypt were no mugs (they'd recently won 3-1 in Scotland).

It took a typical piece of poaching by Kieft, after Rijkaard dummied van Basten's cross, to put the Dutch ahead. But Egypt deservedly equalized when the persistent Hossam Hassan was fouled in the area. Beenhakker, brought in very late in preference to the players' choice Johan Cruyff, suddenly had a huge task on his hands. The Koemans were brothers, the Hassans twins.

■ 16 June 1990 • Renato Sant'Elia, Cagliari • 35,267 • Zoran Petrovic (YUG)

▲ **ENGLAND 0**
HOLLAND 0

● ENGLAND *Shilton, Paul Parker, Pearce, Robson (c) [David Platt 64], Butcher, Walker, Mark Wright, Waddle [Bull 58], Gascoigne, Lineker, Barnes.*
HOLLAND *van Breukelen, van Aerle, van Tiggelen, Wouters, Rijkaard, R. Koeman, Witschge, Gullit (c), van Basten, Hans Gillhaus, John van't Schip [Kieft 74].*

Once again in a finals tournament, Bobby Robson allegedly submitted to a version of player power; this time installing a so-called sweeper system, i.e. five at the back, more than enough to stifle this incredibly lifeless Dutch team. Parker, small and quick, was a particular success in place of Stevens. England also had the better of things up front, Gascoigne running at defenders with skill and muscle, Lineker having a goal disallowed for handball, Pearce shooting straight in from an indirect free-kick. Encouraging, although the earth hadn't quite moved yet. Shilton, first capped in 1970, kept a clean sheet in his 120th international, which broke Pat Jennings' European record. Van Tiggelen was celebrating his 33rd birthday.

Mark Wright celebrates his only goal for England in the match against Egypt.

■ 17 June 1990 • Della Favorita, Palermo • 33,288 • Marcel Van Langenhove (BEL)

▲ **EGYPT 0**
REP. IRELAND 0

● EGYPT *Shoubeir, I. Hassan, Yassin (c), H. Ramzy, Yakan, Tolba [Taher Abou Zeid 59], Osman Oraby, El-Kass [Abdelhamid 76], Abdelghani, Youssef, H. Hassan.*
IRELAND *Bonner, Morris, Staunton, McGrath, McCarthy (c), Moran, Houghton, Townsend, Cascarino [Niall Quinn 84], Aldridge [McLoughlin 64], Sheedy.*

The funniest moment in the World Cup: listening to Jack Charlton, high priest of non-football, accusing the Egyptians of killing the game. The result left all four teams absolutely equal, increasing the possibility that the drawing of lots would decide who qualified.

1990

■ 21 June 1990 • Renato Sant'Elia, Cagliari •
34,959 • Kurt Röthlisberger (SWI)

▲ **ENGLAND (0) 1**
Wright 58
EGYPT (0) 0

● ENGLAND *Shilton (c), Parker, Pearce, McMahon, Walker,
Wright, Waddle [Platt 87], Gascoigne, Bull [Beardsley 84],
Lineker, Barnes.*
EGYPT *Shoubeir, I. Hassan, H. Ramzy, Yakan, Yassin,
Youssef, Abdelghani, Abdelhamid (c) [Abdelrahman 78], A.
Ramzy, El-Kass [Tareq Soliman 78], H. Hassan.*

■ 21 June 1990 • Della Favorita, Palermo •
33,288 • Michel Vautrot (FRA)

▲ **HOLLAND (1) 1**
Gullit 10
REP. IRELAND (0) 1
Quinn 71

● IRELAND *Bonner, Morris, Staunton, McGrath,
McCarthy (c), Moran, Houghton, Townsend, Quinn,
Aldridge [Cascarino 62], Sheedy [Ronnie Whelan 62].*
HOLLAND *van Breukelen, van Aerle, van Tiggelen,
Wouters, Rijkaard, R. Koeman, Witschge [Henk Fräser 59],
Gullit (c), van Basten, Kieft [John van Loen 79], Gillhaus.*

The only win in the group. Even with Robson injured again and Butcher dropped to make way for an extra attacker, England's defence was rarely threatened, allowing Shilton to keep his ninth clean sheet in World Cup finals, a new record. Wright, kept out of the 1986 tournament by a broken leg but now the best of the back four, scored his only goal for England by beating the keeper to Gascoigne's free-kick and heading it in off Yakan. Fine as far as it went, but that seemed to be no further than the next round, especially if Bull stayed in instead of Beardsley.

When Gullit accelerated beautifully past his man on the right and finished with a ground shot across Bonner, it seemed that class was about to come out on top at last. But whatever Ireland lacked it wasn't heart. Houghton had a goal disallowed and Sheedy shot over the bar with Aldridge better placed. Eventually the Republic scored the kind of goal Big Jack probably fantasized about. Bonner banged a huge kick downfield, van Aerle's back pass surprised his goalkeeper, and the 6'4" Quinn slid in on his stilts to reach the loose ball. Both teams qualified along with England, but it was a group nobody wanted to dwell on.

GROUP F	P	W	D	L	F	A	PTS
England	3	1	2	0	2	1	4
Rep. Ireland	3	0	3	0	2	2	3
Holland	3	0	3	0	2	2	3
Egypt	3	0	2	1	1	2	2

England, Republic of Ireland and Holland qualified for
the second round. Second and third places decided by
drawing of lots.

MINUTES WITHOUT CONCEDING A GOAL

517	Walter Zenga	ITA	1990
500	Peter Shilton	ENG	1982–86
475	Sepp Maier	WG	1974–78
458	Emerson Leão	BRZ	1978
442	Gordon Banks	ENG	1966
401	Carlos	BRZ	1986

2nd Round

■ 23 June 1990 • San Paolo, Naples • 50,026 •
Tullio Lanese (ITA)

▲ **CAMEROON (0) (0) 2**
Milla 106, 109
COLOMBIA (0) (0) 1
Redín 116

● CAMEROON *Nkono, Tataw (c), Ebwelle, Ndip, Onana, Kana Biyick, Maboang, Mbouh, Omam Biyick, Mfede [Milla 54], Makanaky [Bonaventure Djonkep 70].*
COLOMBIA *Higuita, Herrera, Gilardo Gómez, Escobar, Perea, Gabriel Gómez [Redín 80], Fajardo [Iguarán 63], Alvarez, Rincón, Valderrama (c), Estrada.*

■ 23 June 1990 • San Nicola, Bari • 15,000 •
Siegfried Kirschen (EG)

▲ **CZECHOSLOVAKIA (1) 4**
Skuhravy 11, 62, 82, Kubík 77
COSTA RICA (0) 1
González 56

● CZECHOSLOVAKIA *Stejskal, Kadlec, Bílek, Kocian, Straka, Hasek (c), Moravcík, Chovanec, Skuhravy, Kubík, Knoflícek.*
COSTA RICA *Hermidio Barrantes, Chavarría [Guimarães 65], Chávez, Flóres (c), Montero, Marchena, Marvin Obando [Medford HT], González, Ramírez, Cayasso, Jara.*

Billed as a colourful clash of styles, the match wended its dreary way through the first 90 minutes, alleviated only by Rincón's shot against the bar. Then, in extra-time the two biggest characters in the tournament came face to face, and one of them lost out both times. First Higuita left a glaring gap at his near post when Milla broke through, then he indulged in his well-known habit of dribbling the ball upfield. Trying to drag it back with the sole of his foot, he lost it to Milla, who ran on, an evil grin on his face, to put it in the empty net.

Redín's goal came too late to stop Cameroon going through to the next stage. It was the only time an African country has reached the quarter-finals, and Higuita's last match in the finals: he missed the 1994 tournament after being imprisoned on charges relating to kidnapping. Having scored from three penalties in internationals, he spent the time inside practising free-kicks.

Barrantes, not as spectacular as Conejo, did nothing very wrong, and the 19-year-old González headed a fine equalizer from Marchena's free-kick – but at last someone was taking advantage of Costa Rica's weakness under the high ball. Skuhravy, heavily built and good in the air, scored a hat-trick of headers and had a goal disallowed, Kubík curled in a free-kick, and Moravcík hit the bar. Costa Rica were well beaten but not at all disgraced. The official attendance figure (probably tickets sold) was 47,673.

■ 24 June 1990 • Delle Alpi Turin • 61,381 • Joël Quiniou (FRA)

▲ **ARGENTINA (0) 1**
Caniggia 81
BRAZIL (0) 0

● ARGENTINA *Goycochea, Basualdo, Ruggeri, Simón, Monzón, Olarticoechea, Burruchaga, Giusti, Caniggia, Maradona (c), Troglio [Calderón 62].*
BRAZIL *Taffarel, Jorginho, Branco, Mauro Galvão [Silas 84], Ricardo Gomes (c), Ricardo Rocha, Müller, Dunga, Careca, Alemão [Renato (Portaluppi) 84], Valdo.*

▼ SENT OFF: *Ricardo Gomes 83.*

■ 24 June 1990 • Giuseppe Meazza, Milan • 74,559 • Juan Carlos Loustau (ARG)

▲ **WEST GERMANY (0) 2**
Klinsmann 50, Brehme 84
HOLLAND (0) 1
● R. Koeman pen 88

W. GERMANY *Illgner, Berthold, Brehme, Buchwald, Jürgen Kohler, Augenthaler, Littbarski, Reuter, Völler, Matthäus (c), Klinsmann [Riedle 78].*
HOLLAND *van Breukelen, van Aerle [Kieft 67], van Tiggelen, Wouters, Rijkaard, R. Koeman, van't Schip, Aron Winter, van Basten, Gullit (c), Witschge [Gillhaus 78].*

▼ SENT OFF: *Rijkaard 21, Völler 21.*

There was the usual post-match guff about a misguided attempt to make the Brazilian team more 'European'. In fact they played some of the best football in the tournament, losing because they missed chances and had no luck. Dunga hit the post with a header, Goycochea pushed Careca's shot against a post and saved from Alemão, Müller shot over the bar. In the way of these things, Argentina made only one real chance and took it. If Maradona wasn't at his best in this tournament, it was mainly because his inflamed toenail left him with a badly swollen foot. Playing in pain, he attracted defenders like flies and managed to get a pass away with Ricardo Gomes pushing his shoulder down. Caniggia was completely free on his left to take the ball around Taffarel. One moment of inspiration had been enough, but it was very hard on Brazil, whose frustration culminated in the sending-off of their captain. Someone at FIFA calculated that they'd made 56 chances in their four matches, scoring from four of them. Renato is now known as Renato Gaúcho in Brazil.

The early sendings-off led to one of the great individual performances in the World Cup. Rijkaard was booked for a vicious foul on Völler, who was cautioned for complaining to the referee. When van Breukelen collected the ensuing free-kick, Völler dived in with his feet, Rijkaard got involved, and both were sent off, Rijkaard spitting twice on his way past. The look on Völler's face was a picture.

Deprived of his partner, Klinsmann simply rose to the occasion. Explosive and tireless, he scored from Buchwald's cross, crashed a shot against the post, ran the whole Dutch defence to distraction, and went off to a standing ovation. Brehme curled in the second goal with his right foot from the left wing. Koeman's penalty, dubiously awarded for Kohler's tackle on van Basten, was no kind of balm for the most disappointing team in any finals tournament.

[Left] *Milla (centre) scores his second goal despite Higuita's desperate attempt to atone for the error of his ways.*

■ 25 June 1990 • Luigi Ferraris, Genoa •
31,818 • José Ramiz Wright (BRZ)

▲ **REP. IRELAND 0**
ROMANIA 0
Ireland 5-4 pens.

● IRELAND *Bonner, Morris, Staunton [David O'Leary 94],*
McGrath, McCarthy (c), Moran, Houghton, Townsend,
Quinn, Aldridge [Cascarino 23], Sheedy.
ROMANIA *Lung (c), Rednic, Klein, Popescu, Andone,*
Rotariu, Sabau [Timofte 98], Balint, Raducioiu [Lupu 75],
Hagi, Lupescu.

□ PENALTY SHOOT-OUT: *Hagi 1-0, Sheedy 1-1, Lupu*
2-1, Houghton 2-2, Rotariu 3-2, Townsend 3-3, Lupescu
4-3, Cascarino 4-4, Timofte saved, O'Leary 4-5.

Romania didn't quite have the quality to break
through the predictable blockade, and Bonner easily
saved Timofte's nervous little kick in the shoot-out.
McGrath was excellent as usual, but there was little
else to admire about the Irish except their fans.

Bonner saves Timofte's weak penalty in the shoot-out.

■ 25 June 1990 • Olimpico, Rome • 73,303 •
George Courtney (ENG)

▲ **ITALY (0) 2**
Schillaci 65, Serena 83
URUGUAY (0) 0

● ITALY *Zenga, Bergomi (c), Maldini, Berti [Aldo Serena 52],*
Ferri, Baresi, De Agostini, De Napoli, Schillaci, Giannini,
Baggio [Vierchowod 79].
URUGUAY *Alvez, José Pintos Saldanha, Domínguez,*
Gutiérrez, De León, Perdomo, Aguilera [Sosa 55], Ostolaza
[Alzamendi 79], Fonseca, Francescoli (c), Pereira.

After a defensive first half, Schillaci twice came close,
but Uruguay missed the best chance of the match,
Zenga making a save after De Napoli's misplaced
header let Aguilera through. Soon afterwards Serena
nutmegged Gutiérrez to set up Schillaci, who by
now was expecting to score every time he touched
the ball, sweeping an instant long shot high into the
net. Serena, on his 30th birthday, sealed the match
with a header from Giannini's free-kick.

■ 26 June 1990 • Marc'Antonio Bentegodi,
Verona • 34,822 • Aron Schmidhuber (WG)

▲ **YUGOSLAVIA (0) (1) 2**
Stojkovic 77, 93
SPAIN (0) (1) 1
Salinas 83

● YUGOSLAVIA *Ivkovic, Spasic, Brnovic, Hadzibegic,*
Sabanadzovic, Jozic, Stojkovic, Katanec [Vulic 79], Pancev
[Savicevic 56], Susic, Vujovic (c).
SPAIN *Zubizarreta, Chendo, Gorriz, Andrinua [Jiménez*
48], Sanchís, Villaroya, Martín Vázquez, Michel, Roberto,
Butragueño (c) [Rafa Paz 79], Salinas.

Spain hit the post twice and scored a deserved equalizer when the hardworking Martín Vázquez shot from the right and Salinas scored at the far post. But they were undone by two marvellous pieces of finishing from Stojkovic, who'd been brilliant but frustrating since his debut at the age of 18 in 1983. Vujovic crossed from the left, Katanec got a touch, Stojkovic shaped to blast the ball first time then trapped it to let a defender slide past, a wonderfully cool piece of skill, before shooting low into the far corner. When Roberto gave away a free-kick, Stojkovic whipped it around the wall and just inside the post. Savicevic, later a star at Milan, helped to keep possession until the end.

■ 26 June 1990 • Renato Dall' Ara, Bologna •
34,520 • Peter Mikkelsen (DEN)

▲ **ENGLAND (0) (0) 1**
Platt 119
BELGIUM (0) (0) 0

● ENGLAND *Shilton, Parker, Pearce, McMahon [Platt 71], Butcher (c), Walker, Wright, Waddle, Gascoigne, Lineker, Barnes [Bull 74].*
BELGIUM *Preud'homme, Gerets, De Wolf, Demol, Clijsters, Grün, Van der Elst, Scifo, Versavel [Vervoort 107], Degryse [Nico Claesen 65], Ceulemans (c).*

This dramatic match might have been settled a lot sooner. England's five-man defence couldn't stop Ceulemans and Scifo hitting the post, and Barnes had a goal wrongly disallowed for offside. Regularly criticized for his England performances, he played his full part here despite being double marked. Belgium's veterans lasted the pace well, but Claesen did little as substitute and wasn't capped again.

Extra-time, which England were playing for the first time since the 1970 World Cup, was almost at an end and they seemed to have settled for the penalty shoot-out. But Shilton shouted at them to keep attacking, and the bearded Gerets, still a quality right-back at 36, made his last World Cup gesture by bringing down Gascoigne, who took the inswinging free-kick himself. As it dropped over Platt's right shoulder in a packed penalty area, he swivelled and hooked it across Preud'homme for the first and most important of his 27 goals for England, who were in the quarter-finals again, and this time with no Maradona to have a hand in things. The *Sun's* view by now: 'We never seriously doubted England's chances of clawing their way through the World Cup field.' Read on, it gets better.

CLEAN SHEETS			
10	Peter Shilton	ENG	1982–90
8	Sepp Maier	WG	1974–78
8	Emerson Leão	BRZ	1974–78
7	Gylmar	BRZ	1958–66
6	Gordon Banks	ENG	1966–70

England's last-minute winner against Belgium. (l–r): Vervoort, Clijsters, Gerets, Pearce, Preud'homme, Parker, Wright, the goalscorer Platt. The ball is just visible behind Clijsters' hand.

*Q*uarter-finals

■ 30 June 1990 • Comunale, Florence • 38,971 •
Kurt Röthlisberger (SWI)

▲ **ARGENTINA 0**
YUGOSLAVIA 0
Argentina 3-2 pens.

● ARGENTINA *Goycochea, Serrizuela, Olarticoechea [Troglio 55], Simón, Ruggeri, Basualdo, Burruchaga, Giusti, Caniggia, Maradona (c), Calderón [Dezotti 86].*
YUGOSLAVIA *Ivkovic, Vulic, Spasic, Brnovic, Hadzibegic, Sabanadzovic, Jozic, Stojkovic, Susic [Savicevic 63], Prosinecki, Vujovic (c).*

▼ SENT OFF: *Sabanadzovic 31.*

□ PENALTY SHOOT-OUT: *Serrizuela 1-0, Stojkovic hit bar, Burruchaga 2-0, Prosinecki 2-1, Maradona saved, Savicevic 2-2, Troglio hit post, Brnovic saved, Dezotti 3-2, Hadzibegic saved.*

Hot-blooded from start to finish (five Argentinians booked), the skilful Yugoslavs had the better of it until Sabanadzovic was sent off for a second bookable offence, the usual one of fouling Maradona. After that, Ruggeri's header dropped on to the bar and Burruchaga had a very late goal controversially disallowed for handball. Most of the real drama, however, was packed into a fluctuating penalty shoot-out. When Maradona missed Argentina's third, the Yugoslavs weren't the only ones to rejoice, but Goycochea again proved an important shot-stopper. The fair-haired Prosinecki showed a promise he hasn't quite fulfilled.

■ 30 June 1990 • Olimpico, Rome • 73,303 •
Carlos Alberto da Silva Valente (POR)

▲ **ITALY (1) 1**
Schillaci 38
REP. IRELAND (0) 0

● ITALY *Zenga, Bergomi (c), Maldini, De Agostini, Ferri, Baresi, Donadoni, De Napoli, Schillaci, Giannini [Ancelotti 63], Baggio [Serena 71].*
IRELAND *Bonner, Morris, Staunton, McGrath, McCarthy (c), Moran, Houghton, Townsend, Quinn [Cascarino 53], Aldridge [John Sheridan 78], Sheedy.*

Italy expected a tough match and got it, but the result was never really in doubt. Quinn caused occasional problems with his height, but the Irish defence couldn't hold Toto Schillaci, who hit the underside of the bar and had a goal dubiously disallowed for offside, as well as scoring the only goal, an instant strike after Baggio beat three men and Donadoni's high shot knocked Bonner off his feet. There was much talk afterwards of the Republic's great World Cup adventure, ended by a single goal from the host country – but they scored only two goals in five games, none of which were won, and contributed little to the tournament except defensive organization. For various reasons, there were sighs of relief when they left it.

CONSECUTIVE CLEAN SHEETS			
5	Walter Zenga	ITA	1990
4	Gylmar	BRZ	1958
4	Gordon Banks	ENG	1966
4	Emerson Leão	BRZ	1974
4	Sepp Maier	WG	1978
4	Emerson Leão	BRZ	1978
4	Peter Shilton	ENG	1982
4	Carlos	BRZ	1986

■ 1 July 1990 • Giuseppe Meazza, Milan • 73,347 • Helmut Kohl (AUT)

▲ **WEST GERMANY (1) 1**
Matthäus pen 24
CZECHOSLOVAKIA (0) 0

● W. GERMANY *Illgner, Berthold, Brehme, Buchwald, Kohler, Augenthaler, Littbarski, Bein [Möller 82], Riedle, Matthäus (c), Klinsmann.*
CZECHOSLOVAKIA *Stejskal, Kadlec, Bílek [Nemecek 68], Kocian, Straka, Hasek (c), Moravčík, Chovanec, Skuhravy, Kubík [Griga 80], Knoflícek.*
▼ SENT OFF: *Moravčík 70.*

Moravčík's ludicrous dismissal, for kicking his boot away in annoyance, did Czechoslovakia's cause no good, but they'd looked intimidated from the start. Hasek (twice) and Bílek cleared off the line, Buchwald missed an open goal, and Riedle might have had a penalty when Stejskal brought him down. Klinsmann did get one, for a foul by Straka, and if West Germany were less exciting than in the group matches, Czechoslovakia hardly had a shot on goal.

Two views of Platt's headed goal in the quarter-final, watched by Lineker (10). The Cameroon players are Massing (4), Nkono and Ebwelle (5).

■ 1 July 1990 • San Paolo, Naples • 55,205 • Edgardo Codesal (MEX)

▲ **ENGLAND (1) (2) 3**
Platt 25, Lineker pen 83, pen 104
CAMEROON (0) (2) 2
Kunde pen 61, Ekeke 65

● ENGLAND *Shilton, Parker, Pearce, Platt, Butcher (c) [Trevor Steven 74], Walker, Wright, Waddle, Lineker, Gascoigne, Barnes [Beardsley HT].*
CAMEROON *Nkono, Massing, Ebwelle, Mfede [Eugène Ekeke 62], Tataw (c), Kunde, Libiih, Pagal, Omam Biyick, Makanaky, Maboang [Milla HT].*

Lineker's two penalties against Cameroon.

Something wondrous strange happened here. Emerging from their earlier shell, Cameroon shredded England's massed defence time after time, only to be let down by indiscipline (they were without four first choices through suspension) and poor finishing. In the first half, Libiih missed two opportunities and Shilton rushed out to block a volley when Omam Biyick was clean through. So England were able to hold on to the lead provided by Platt's downward header from Pearce's left-wing cross.

Then Milla came on and again changed the flow. Unnecessarily fouled by Gascoigne for the penalty, he then delayed his short pass to send Ekeke through

the ruins of the defence to chip the ball beyond Shilton. With Steven at right back and Wright forced out to the wing with a bandaged head (another Milla contribution), England were in obvious disarray.

But their most important players kept their nerve when it mattered. Gascoigne's square pass found Lineker, who turned a defender and was brought down in the area. It was the first penalty England had been awarded in 53 matches, and there were only seven minutes left. In all the pressure, Lineker sent Nkono the wrong way. In extra-time he did the same, finding the other side of the net, when Gascoigne's through-ball sent him clear. Nkono, booked for protesting, was backed up by the TV replays: if he touched Lineker at all, it was with his head! Not the way he'd have chosen to end an impressive international career. African teams had been progressing through successive World Cups one step at a time, and Cameroon had been the most convincing so far, but England would have been disappointed if they'd lost to any of their opponents so far. The next, though, were a different matter.

*S*emi-finals

■ 3 July 1990 • San Paolo, Naples • 59,978 •
Michel Vautrot (FRA)

▲ **ARGENTINA (0) (1) 1**
Caniggia 67
ITALY (1) (1) 1
Schillaci 17
Argentina 4-3 pens.

● ARGENTINA *Goycochea, Serrizuela, Olarticoechea, Simón, Ruggeri, Basualdo [Batista 98], Burruchaga, Giusti, Caniggia, Maradona (c), Calderón [Troglio HT].*
ITALY *Zenga, Bergomi (c), Maldini, De Agostini, Ferri, Baresi, Donadoni, De Napoli, Schillaci, Giannini [Baggio 75], Vialli [Serena 70].*

▼ SENT OFF: *Giusti 109.*

□ PENALTY SHOOT-OUT: *Baresi 1-0, Serrizuela 1-1, Baggio 2-1, Burruchaga 2-2, De Agostini 3-2, Olarticoechea 3-3, Donadoni saved, Maradona 3-4, Serena saved.*

Goycochea saves Donadoni's penalty in the shoot-out.

Argentina showed their intentions from the start, bringing down Vialli, Maldini and De Napoli in the first four minutes. Giusti was sent off for flattening Baggio, and Vautrot had to issue a warning to both captains. Somewhere in all that, Italy took the lead when Giannini headed down for Vialli to shoot, Goycochea to save, and the inevitable Schillaci to put in the rebound from what looked like an offside position. The Sicilian bricklayer's son, who'd recently spent seven seasons in the second and third divisions, seemed to be rising to his destiny like Rossi in 1982.

But Italy appeared nervous after half-time, relying on their defence to keep yet another clean sheet. Argentina began to make chances. Olarticoechea crossed from the left, Zenga came out when he should have stayed put, and Caniggia got to the ball before him, glancing a back-header inside the far post. It was the first goal Italy had conceded in 11 matches.

Baggio and Serena were brought on but couldn't change the flow. Schillaci was caught offside eight times and Giusti's sending-off came too late to matter. When Donadoni, gaunt and skilful, had his penalty saved in the shoot-out, Italy had to hope that Maradona would miss his kick as he did in the previous round, but this time there was no mistake and Argentina had sneaked into a second successive Final. Caniggia, their one real striker, wouldn't be with them. After several attempts to handle the ball as it went over his head, he eventually succeeded and picked up his second booking of the tournament, the daftest reason yet for missing a World Cup Final.

For the hosts, nothing but terrible anticlimax – but perhaps it had been in the stars. This was their first match of the tournament outside Rome, they played it on Maradona's home ground, it was the 17th international staged in Naples, Schillaci scored after 17 minutes, and Donadoni was wearing No. 17. Some things just aren't meant to be.

■ 4 July 1990 • Delle Alpi, Turin • 62,628 • José
Ramiz Wright (BRZ)

▲ **WEST GERMANY (0) (1) 1**
Brehme 59
ENGLAND (0) (1) 1
Lineker 80
West Germany 4-3 pens.

● W. GERMANY *Illgner, Berthold, Brehme, Matthäus (c),
Kohler, Augenthaler, Buchwald, Hässler [Reuter 68], Völler
[Riedle 38], Thon, Klinsmann.*
ENGLAND *Shilton, Parker, Pearce, Platt, Butcher (c)
[Steven 70], Walker, Wright, Beardsley, Lineker, Gascoigne,
Waddle.*
□ PENALTY SHOOT-OUT: *Lineker 1-0, Brehme 1-1,
Beardsley 2-1, Matthäus 2-2, Platt 3-2, Riedle 3-3, Pearce
saved, Thon 3-4, Waddle shot over.*

An epic. England looked secure at the back, Wright
playing with a padded bandage over his left eye, but
West Germany's performance was their least
convincing of the tournament, especially after
Völler, back after suspension, suffered a shin injury.
Hässler and Thon were brought in to take some of
the load off Matthäus, who was on a yellow card –
but England had the better of the first half, though
neither side created any real chances.

[From the top] *Brehme's free-kick hits Parker's foot on its way
over Shilton for the opening goal of the semi-final.*

Kohler arrives too late to stop Lineker equalizing with ten minutes left.

Illgner's legs keep out Pearce's penalty in the shoot-out.

Yet again Shilton dives the right way, but Thon scores with West Germany's last kick.

A pile of celebrating Germans is no sight for a grieving Englishman.
Waddle, who missed England's last penalty, is comforted (but not really) by Matthäus.

The first goal was unexpected and flukey, the ball hitting Parker's leg and ballooning over Shilton. Brehme had now scored from free-kicks in successive semi-finals, but with considerable help each time. England looked on their way out, but suddenly three German defenders were confused by Parker's long cross from the right, Lineker flicked it away with his thigh and shot low across the keeper with his left foot. For the first time in any World Cup, a country would play extra-time in three consecutive matches.

It was this additional half hour that raised the match to its present status. Waddle's low drive hit a post, Buchwald did the same, Shilton made excellent saves from Matthäus and Klinsmann, Platt had a headed goal rightly disallowed for offside, and Gascoigne's tackle on Berthold earned him a booking that would keep him out of the Final if England reached it. Gazza's challenges had already given away two goals and this one was astoundingly pointless; Berthold was out on the touchline and no threat to anybody. As Bobby Robson said, 'daft azza brush'.

The penalty shoot-out, the first England had been involved in, was as feverish as they come. West Germany's experience in this lottery was probably decisive: the only country to take part in three World Cup shoot-outs, they've won them all (and we all know about the rematch in Euro '96). Here the normally reliable Pearce hit Illgner's leg and Waddle blazed high into the night sky, images we've had to relive time

Time finally tolls for the 40-year-old Shilts, whose long international career ends with the 3rd-place Final. He was still playing in League matches seven years later.

and again, along with that of Gascoigne wiping his tears with his shirt, the sight that allegedly started the current football craze, so it was doubly irritating.

Just a thought here. Dave Beasant was in the squad. Much taller than Shilton, nine years younger, and a well-known shot-stopper. Two years earlier, his penalty save in the Final had won Wimbledon the FA Cup. Imagine the criticism if Robson had sent him on in the last minute of extra-time and England had still lost the shoot-out. Yes, but maybe it was the kind of imaginative thinking England needed. Instead Shilton went the right way for each kick but couldn't reach them.

West Germany set records by playing their 67th finals match and reaching the Final for the sixth time and the third in a row. They were (whisper it) a better team than England, but not necessarily on this fraught night, which ended in tears, and not just those of a clown.

3rd-place Final

■ 7 July 1990 • San Nicola, Bari • 51,426 • Joël Quiniou (FRA)

▲ **ITALY (0) 2**
Baggio 71, Schillaci pen 85
ENGLAND (0) 1
Platt 81

● ITALY *Zenga, Bergomi (c), Maldini, Ancelotti, Vierchowod, Baresi, Ciro Ferrara, Giannini [Ferri 90], Schillaci, Baggio, De Agostini [Berti 67].*
ENGLAND *Shilton (c), M. G. Stevens, Tony Dorigo, McMahon [Waddle 72], Walker, Parker, Wright [Neil Webb 72], Steven, Lineker, Platt, Beardsley.*

A harmless match came to some sort of life when Baggio caught Shilton rolling the ball on the ground, stole it away, exchanged passes with Schillaci, and looked offside when he scored – a red nose for England's veteran keeper in his last international. Platt, one of the finds of the tournament, headed a crisp equalizer from a left-wing cross by the nimble Dorigo, but Parker was judged to have brought down Schillaci, whose penalty made him the tournament's leading scorer. Like England's Fair Play award, it was little consolation. Italy were third after winning six matches and drawing the other, Argentina finished higher after winning two and losing two. If that's fair, FIFA are bananas.

Berti had a headed goal wrongly disallowed in the last minute, and our tabloid friends turned full circle in one of their leaders: 'Around Gazza and his young gang we can build a team to rule the world. Four years on, remember you read it first in *The Sun*.' How could we forget? England didn't qualify for the 1994 finals.

Maradona (10) and Augenthaler watch Monzón become the first player to be sent off in a World Cup Final, for a foul on the prostrate Klinsmann.

Final

■ 8 July 1990 • Olimpico, Rome • 73,603 •
Edgardo Codesal (MEX)

▲ **WEST GERMANY (0) 1**
Brehme pen 84
ARGENTINA (0) 0

● W. GERMANY *Illgner, Berthold [Reuter 73], Brehme, Buchwald, Kohler, Augenthaler, Hässler, Matthäus (c), Littbarski, Völler, Klinsmann.*
ARGENTINA *Goycochea, Simón, Sensini, Basualdo, Serrizuela, Ruggeri [Monzón HT], Burruchaga [Calderón 53], Troglio, Lorenzo, Maradona (c), Dezotti.*
▼ SENT OFF: *Monzón 64, Dezotti 86.*

Because it's a World Cup Final, we're expected to give it due respect with a full report, blow by blow, but the heart's not in it.

Argentina, with four players suspended, would have forced extra-time again if the unimpressive Codesal hadn't given a penalty when Völler went down in a tackle by Sensini. Matthäus, suffering a painful ankle, left the kick to Brehme, whose low shot edged past Goycochea. The two sendings-off, the first in a Final, were almost expected: Monzón for a spectacular foul on Klinsmann, Dezotti the first in the queue to grab Völler by the throat. Maradona, man-marked out of it by Buchwald, who towered over him, shed tears in Gazza-esque quantities; a sight for sore English eyes.

Argentina were the first team to fail to score in a Final. West Germany, in their last World Cup as a separate nation, were worthy enough winners but scored only a single goal in each of their last three matches: two from the penalty spot, the other (in a match decided on penalties) with a deflected free-kick. There were more red cards (16) and a lower goals-per-game average (2.21) than in any other finals tournament. With the possible exceptions of 1962 and the only other time Italy were the hosts, it was the worst ever.

An emotional Gascoigne after the semi-final.

1994

The Long Drought

USA 1994

If FIFA hoped that awarding the World Cup to the land of the dollar would at last crack the supposedly lucrative United States market, it was a triumph of hope over experience. But at least the infrastructure wasn't bad. What visitors were likely to see were matches played in well-appointed stadia, with excellent transport facilities, catering services and communications, an experienced and minimal police presence, and the highest average crowds in World Cup history. If the price was allowing a mediocre USA team free entry, it was worth every cent.

Of the stronger countries, a reunified Germany had a new coach but rather too many old players, though Klinsmann was in his pomp and Sammer a powerful recruit from East Germany. Brazil were without four regular central defenders but others simply stepped off the conveyor belt, and Romário had just scored 30 goals in 33 league games for Barcelona as well as the two goals that sent Brazil through at Uruguay's expense. Italy, who'd rather staggered over the finishing line, were still strong at the back but again in search of a reliable goalscorer.

A talented French team (Papin, Cantona, Ginola) stayed at home after losing their last two home games to very late goals, the first against Israel, the second in the very last minute, thanks to a misjudgement by Ginola. Nothing much was expected of their conquerors Bulgaria.

Argentina had gone 31 matches without losing, which included winning the Copa América twice in a row; but a 5-0 home defeat by Colombia made them recall the 33-year-old Maradona to help them squeeze through in a play-off, beating Australia with a deflected goal. Colombia, still led by Valderrama, with Asprilla a new threat in attack, were naturally included among the favourites.

So too, for the first time, were a team from Africa. Nigeria had just won the African Nations Cup with a blend of skill and power that people had been expecting from the continent for years. Yekini, Okacha, Amunike and Amokachi were expected to become big names in the forthcoming month.

Certainly more so than Saunders, McAllister or Carlton Palmer. For the first time since they entered the World Cup, none of the four British countries reached the finals. Scotland, Wales and Northern Ireland all finished fourth in their groups, while England's five wins included four against Turkey and San Marino. New manager Graham Taylor picked some shocking players and 'a pig's arse of a team' (his words, everyone's opinion) against Norway, who won 2-0. So did Holland, in the decisive match, thanks to a referee who should have sent Ronald Koeman off for a professional foul but let him stay on to score from a free-kick. In Taylor's last match in charge, England conceded a goal in the first nine seconds against San Marino, which said it all.

The Republic of Ireland were there again, still playing the same way under Jack Charlton but qualifying on goal difference and unlikely to figure at the sharp end of the tournament, especially as it was being played in fearful heat and humidity (FIFA again scheduled some noontime kick-offs). Nigeria, we were allowed to suppose, would be rather less apprehensive.

After 20 years as president, Havelange was still showing who was boss, banning Pelé from the opening ceremony for daring to criticize the head of the Brazilian FA, Ricardo Teixeira, who happened to be Havelange's son-in-law. Havelange later announced his intention to step down at the end of the 1998 finals. Promises, promises.

Group A

Colombia, Romania, Switzerland, USA

■ 18 June 1994 • Pontiac Silverdome, Detroit • 73,425 • Francisco Lamolina (ARG)

▲ **SWITZERLAND (1) 1**
Bregy 39
USA (1) 1
Wynalda 44

● SWITZERLAND *Marco Pascolo, Marc Hottiger, Dominique Herr, Alain Geiger (c), Yvan Quentin, Christophe Ohrel, Ciriaco Sforza [Thomas Wyss 77], Georges Bregy, Stéphane Chapuisat, Alain Sutter, Thomas Bickel [Néstor Subiat 72].* Roy Hodgson (ENG).
USA *Tony Meola (c), Cle Kooiman, Paul Caligiuri, Tab Ramos, Alexi Lalas, Marcelo Balboa, Thomas Dooley, John Harkes, Mike Sorber, Ernie Stewart [Cobi Jones 80], Eric Wynalda [Roy Wegerle 57].* Bora Milutinovic (YUG).

■ 18 June 1994 • Rose Bowl, Pasadena • 91,865 • Jamal Al-Sharif (SYR)

▲ **ROMANIA (2) 3**
Raducioiu 16, 89, Hagi 34
COLOMBIA (1) 1
Valencia 43

● ROMANIA *Bogdan Stelea, Dan Petrescu, Miodrag Belodedici, Gheorghe Popescu, Daniel Prodan, Gheorghe Mihali, Ionut Lupescu, Dorinel Munteanu, Florin Raducioiu [Corneliu Papura 89], Gheorghe Hagi (c), Ilie Dumitrescu [Tibor Selymes 67].* Anghel Iordanescu.
COLOMBIA *Oscar Córdoba, Andrés Escobar, Luis Herrera, Wilson Pérez, Luis Perea, Leonel Alvarez, Carlos Valderrama (c), Gabriel Gómez, Freddy Rincón, Adolfo Valencia, Faustino Asprilla.* Francisco Maturana.

Switzerland's first finals match since 1966 was also the first played indoors, which had the players sweating like cheeses. Both goals came from well-taken free-kicks, Bregy curling his shot round the wall, Wynalda in off the bar from 30 yards. Dooley and Sutter should have scored, but players were soon beginning to slip and slide on the damp grass, and everyone looked drained by the end. Harkes (Derby County) and Wegerle (Coventry City) played their club football in England.

Romania had only qualified because Paul Bodin hit the crossbar with a penalty in Cardiff, and Colombia were many people's favourites, Pelé included – but the form guide was no help here. Playing six men in midfield to smother Colombia's close-passing game, Romania channelled everything through Hagi, who at last convinced everyone that ten years of hype hadn't been misplaced.

Above all, Romania put away their chances. Raducioiu cut inside two defenders and whipped his shot across Córdoba, then broke clear and resisted the keeper's challenge before lashing the ball into an empty net, each time running on to passes from Hagi, who also scored one of the monster World Cup goals. From out near the left-hand touchline, he fired the ball in at the far post with his left foot. It may have been a fluke (he glanced towards a team-mate at the far post) but we'll believe he meant it, because his second glance was at the goal itself, and because we want to. Valencia headed in a corner at the near post, but neither Valderrama nor Asprilla

was an influence. Death threats against Gómez reminded people where some of football's money came from in that country.

■ 22 June 1994 • Pontiac Silverdome, Detroit • 61,428 • Neji Jouini (TUN)

▲ **SWITZERLAND (1) 4**
Sutter 16, Chapuisat 53, Knup 66, Bregy 72
ROMANIA (1) 1
Hagi 36

● SWITZERLAND *Pascolo, Hottiger, Herr, Geiger (c), Quentin, Ohrel [Patrick Sylvestre 83], Sforza, Bregy, Adrian Knup, Sutter [Bickel 70], Chapuisat.*
ROMANIA *Stelea, Petrescu, Belodedici, Popescu, Prodan, Mihali, Lupescu [Basarab Pandaru 84], Munteanu, Hagi (c), Dumitrescu [Ion Vladoiu 70], Raducioiu.*
▼ SENT OFF: *Vladoiu [73].*

Something of a shock, given the results of the first matches and the half-time score in this one – but perhaps the Swiss were simply acclimatized to the greenhouse effect. The return of Knup, and therefore a more attacking formation, was also a factor. Sutter, his fair hair tied back, cracked the ball in low from the D, but Hagi equalized with an equally good shot from 25 yards. Chapuisat scored in a scramble, Sforza's strong clever run made an open goal for Knup, and Bregy's free-kick skimmed a defender's head on its way in (some sources mistakenly credited it to Knup). To complete Romania's disarray, Vladoiu was sent off for showing his studs to Ohrel. It was Switzerland's first win in the finals since 1954.

■ 22 June 1994 • Rose Bowl, Pasadena • 93,194 • Fabio Baldas (ITA)

▲ **USA (1) 2**
Escobar o.g. 34, Stewart 52
COLOMBIA (0) 1
Valencia 89

● USA *Meola (c), Fernando Clavijo, Caligiuri, Ramos, Lalas, Balboa, Dooley, Harkes, Sorber, Stewart [Jones 66], Wynalda [Wegerle 61].*
COLOMBIA *Córdoba, Herrera, Perea, Escobar, Pérez, Valderrama (c), Rincón, Hernán Gaviria, Alvarez, Anthony de Avila [Valencia HT], Asprilla [Iván Valenciano HT].*

When the draw was made, there was every prospect of the host nation being eliminated at the group stage for the first time – but the USA had few problems with this ghost of a Colombian team. After both sides had hit a post, Escobar turned Harkes' optimistic cross-shot into his own net. Then Ramos hit a through-ball, Córdoba rushed out too soon, and Stewart touched it past him and in off the near post. The tall Lalas, whose long red hair and goatee made him as recognizable as Valderrama, had a thumping goal wrongly disallowed for offside. Asprilla was at his irritating worst and had to be substituted, and Valencia's goal, a rebound after a fine save by Meola, couldn't stop the USA winning a finals match for the first time since beating England in 1950. The game had an horrific postscript ten days later when Escobar, a slim and talented central defender, was shot dead in Medellín, capital of his country's drug trade, because his own goal had apparently cost someone some money in bets. It cast a dirty shadow over the tournament.

■ 26 June 1994 • Stanford, Palo Alto • 83,769 •
Peter Mikkelsen (DEN)

▲ **COLOMBIA (1) 2**
Gaviria 44, Lozano 89
SWITZERLAND (0) 0

● COLOMBIA *Córdoba, Herrera, Escobar, Alexis Mendoza, Pérez, Valderrama (c), Gaviria [Harold Lozano 78], Rincón, Alvarez, Valencia [de Avila 63], Asprilla.*
SWITZERLAND *Pascolo, Hottiger, Herr, Geiger (c), Quentin, Ohrel, Sforza, Bregy, Sutter [Marco Grassi 81], Knup [Subiat 81], Chapuisat.*

GROUP A	P	W	D	L	F	A	PTS
Romania	3	2	0	1	5	5	6
Switzerland	3	1	1	1	5	4	4
USA	3	1	1	1	3	3	4
Colombia	3	1	0	2	4	5	3

Romania, Switzerland and USA qualified for the second round.

After Pascolo fumbled Gaviria's leaping header, de Avila slipped a short ball inside to Lozano who beat Herr and scored with a low cross shot. But Switzerland were already through and Colombia already out.

■ 26 June 1994 • Rose Bowl, Pasadena •
93,869 • Mario van der Ende (HOL)

▲ **ROMANIA (1) 1**
Petrescu 17
USA (0) 0

● ROMANIA *Florian Prunea, Petrescu, Belodedici [Mihali 87], Popescu, Prodan, Selymes, Lupescu, Munteanu, Hagi (c), Dumitrescu, Raducioiu [Constantin Gâlca 84].*
USA *Meola (c), Clavijo, Caligiuri, Ramos [Jones 63], Lalas, Balboa, Dooley, Harkes, Sorber [Wegerle 74], Stewart, Wynalda.*

If the American balloon didn't exactly burst, there was a definite sense of deflation. Romania, needing at least a draw, were relieved when Harkes hit a post early on. Raducioiu twisted away from a defender before pushing a short pass inside Caligiuri for Petrescu to shoot in low at the near post. Florian (Prunea) and Florin (Raducioiu) are both correct.

Group B

Brazil, Cameroon, Russia, Sweden

■ 19 June 1994 • Rose Bowl, Pasadena • 83,959
• Alberto Tejada (PER)

▲ **CAMEROON (1) 2**
Embe 31, Omam Biyick 47
SWEDEN (1) 2
Ljung 8, Dahlin 75

● CAMEROON *Joseph-Antoine Bell, Stephen Tataw (c), Raymond Kalla, Rigobert Song, Hans Agbo, Thomas Libiih, Émile Mbouh, Louis-Paul Mfede [Emmanuel Maboang Kessack 86], Marc Vivien Foe, François Omam Biyick, David Embe [Georges Mouyeme 79]. Henri Michel (FRA).*
SWEDEN *Thomas Ravelli, Roland Nilsson, Roger Ljung, Stefan Schwarz, Patrik Andersson, Joachim Björklund, Klas Ingesson [Kennet Andersson 75], Jonas Thern (c), Jesper Blomqvist [Henrik Larsson 60], Martin Dahlin, Tomas Brolin. Tommy Svensson.*

Interesting and fun, though neither side looked like title contenders. Ljung, unmarked despite ten Cameroon players in the penalty area, headed in Thern's free-kick at the far post. Omam Biyick blocked a clearance on the left before squaring the ball to Embe (fractionally onside) to equalize and Omam Biyick scored after Patrik Andersson misjudged Song's long free-kick.

Sweden were saved when the dreadlocked Larsson hit the bar from 30 yards and Dahlin let the ball bounce, chested it down, and half-volleyed past Bell, who was at last getting a game in the finals at the age of 39. Michel had coached France in 1986.

■ 20 June 1994 • Stanford, Palo Alto • 81,061 • Lim Kee Chong (MAU)

▲ **BRAZIL (1) 2**
Romário 26, Raí pen 53
RUSSIA (0) 0

● BRAZIL *Cláudio Taffarel, 'Jorginho' (Jorge Amorim), Leonardo (Nascimento), Mauro Silva, Ricardo Rocha [Aldair (Nascimento) 74], Márcio Santos, 'Zinho' (Crizam de Oliveira), 'Dunga' (Carlos Bledorn Verri) ['Mazinho' (Iomar do Nascimento) 85], 'Bebeto' (Roberto Gama), Raí (de Souza) (c), Romário (de Souza). Carlos Alberto Parreira.*
RUSSIA *Dmitry Kharin (c), Vladislav Ternavsky, Yuri Nikiforov, Sergei Gorlukovich, Valery Karpin, Andrei Piatnitsky, Dmitry Radchenko [Aleksandr Borodyuk 77], Dmitry Kuznetsov, Ilya Tsymbalar, Dmitry Khlestov, Sergei Yuran [Oleg Salenko 55]. Pavel Sadyrin.*

Russia didn't really stand a chance. Earlier in the season, 14 players had written to the Minister for Sport demanding the sacking of the coach. Instead Sadyrin stayed and seven of the rebels were left out, including some vital attacking players: Shalimov, Kanchelskis, Kolyvanov, Kiriakov and Dobrovolsky. Without them, Russia couldn't break drown Brazil's strong defence in which Jorginho had been world-class for years and Leonardo looked a bright new wing-back. Romário won a push and shove with his marker to stab in Bebeto's corner and was fouled by Ternavsky for the penalty, converted by Raí, younger brother of Sócrates.

■ 24 June 1994 • Stanford, Palo Alto • 83,401 • Arturo Brizio Carter (MEX)

▲ **BRAZIL (1) 3**
Romário 39, Márcio Santos 66, Bebeto 73
CAMEROON (0) 0

● BRAZIL *Taffarel, Jorginho, Leonardo, Mauro Silva, Aldair, Márcio Santos, Zinho [Paulo Sérgio [Silvestre] 75], Dunga, Bebeto, Raí (c) [Müller (Luíz Corrêa) 80], Romário.*
CAMEROON *Bell, Tataw (c), Kalla, Song, Agbo, Libiih, Mbouh, Mfede [Maboang 70], Omam Biyick, Foe, Embe [Roger Milla 65].*
▼ SENT OFF: *Song 63.*

Cameroon, who'd threatened to boycott the game unless they were paid bonuses from the qualifying competition, were no match for Brazil's solidity and Romário's neat genius. He outran three defenders before toe-poking the ball past a hesitant keeper, and made the third goal with a shot that Bell did well to save, Bebeto turning in the loose ball from a narrow angle. In between, Márcio Santos came in unmarked to score with a plunging header. Cameroon set two World Cup age records: Milla the oldest player (42), Song the youngest to be sent off (17 years 358 days).

1994

■ 24 June 1994 • Pontiac Silverdome, Detroit •
71,528 • Joël Quiniou (FRA)

▲ **SWEDEN (1) 3**
Brolin pen 38, Dahlin 59, 81
RUSSIA (1) 1
Salenko pen 4

● SWEDEN *Ravelli, R. Nilsson, Ljung, Schwarz,
P.Andersson, Björklund [Magnus Erlingmark 88], Ingesson,
Thern (c), K.Andersson [Larsson 84], Dahlin, Brolin.*
RUSSIA *Kharin (c), Gorlukovich, Nikiforov, Khlestov,
Kuznetsov, Dmitry Popov [Karpin 40], Borodyuk [Dmitry
Galiamin 51], Aleksandr Mostovoi, Viktor Onopko, Salenko,
Radchenko.*
▼ SENT OFF: *Gorlukovich 49.*

After the exchange of penalties, for fouls by Ljung
and Gorlukovich, Dahlin took over. The first black
player capped by Sweden, sharp and athletic, he was
lucky to stay on after a violent challenge on Khlestov
but won the penalty and scored with two marvellous,
very different headers. The second came from a cross
by Kennet Andersson, who brought back memories

of José Torres with his height and mobility. Russia
were on their way out, Gorlukovich going early after
a foul on Dahlin, Sadyrin soon to follow.

■ 28 June 1994 • Stanford, Palo Alto • 74,914 •
Jamal Al-Sharif (SYR)

▲ **RUSSIA (3) 6**
Salenko 16, 41, pen 44, 73, 75, Radchenko 82
CAMEROON (0) 1
Milla 47

● RUSSIA *Stanislav Cherchesov, Omari Tetradze, Nikiforov,
Ternavsky, Karpin, Tsymbalar, Igor Ledyakov [Vladimir
Beschastnykh 77], Khlestov, Onopko (c), Salenko, Igor
Korneyev [Radchenko 64].*
CAMEROON *Jacques Songo'o, Tataw (c), Kalla, Victor
Ndip, Agbo, Libiih, André Kana Biyick, Mfede [Milla HT],
Foe, Omam Biyick, Embe [Alphonse Tchami 47].*

As in 1990, the doomed Russians thrashed
Cameroon, who were ageing imitations of that side.
Salenko, with the help of a dubious penalty, became
the first to score five goals in a finals match. Two
players collided to let him in for the first,
his second was an open goal, Tetradze set
him up for another, and he went through
unchallenged for the fifth as his marker
stood and appealed for offside.
Radchenko also ran clear to score with a
shot that went in off Songo'o. Cameroon's
only consolation was a close-range goal
by the eternal Milla, the fastest by any
substitute, marking the end of an
extraordinary career.

*Salenko clips the ball over
Songo'o for the last of his
record five goals against
Cameroon.*

GOALS IN A GAME

5	Oleg Salenko	RUS	1994 v CAM	1 pen
4	Ernest Wilimowski	POL	1938 v BRZ	
4	Ademir	BRZ	1950 v SWE	
4	Sándor Kocsis	HUN	1954 v WG	
4	Just Fontaine	FRA	1958 v WG	
4	Eusébio	POR	1966 v NKO	2 pen
4	Emilio Butragueño	SPA	1986 v DEN	1 pen

Leônidas (BRZ) and Gustav Wetterström (SWE), who scored three against Poland and Cuba respectively in 1938, were once credited with four, as was Juan Schiaffino (URU), who scored twice against Bolivia in 1950.

OLDEST PLAYERS

yrs/days

42/39	Roger Milla	CAM	1994
41/00	Pat Jennings	NIR	1986
40/292	Peter Shilton	ENG	1990
40/133	Dino Zoff	ITA	1982
39/260	Angel Labruna	ARG	1958
39/259	Joseph-Antoine Bell	CAM	1994
39/145	Stanley Matthews	ENG	1954
38/246	Vítor Damas	POR	1986

A member of the Cameroon delegation claimed Milla was 46!

OLDEST GOALSCORERS

yrs/days

42/39	Roger Milla	CAM	1994
37/236	Gunnar Gren	SWE	1958
36/279	Obdulio Varela	URU	1954
36/64	Tom Finney	ENG	1958
35/279	John Aldridge	EIR	1994
35/264	Nils Liedholm	SWE	1958
35/67	Safet Susic	YUG	1990

Milla also scored in two matches in 1990 aged 38.

■ 28 June 1994 • Pontiac Silverdome, Detroit • 77,217 • Sándor Puhl (HUN)

▲ **BRAZIL (0) 1**
Romário 47
SWEDEN (1) 1
K. Andersson 23

● BRAZIL *Taffarel, Jorginho, Leonardo, Mauro Silva [Mazinho HT], Aldair, Márcio Santos, Zinho, Dunga, Bebeto, Raí (c) [Paulo Sérgio 83], Romário.*
SWEDEN *Ravelli, R. Nilsson, Ljung, Schwarz [Håkan Mild 75], P. Andersson, Pontus Kâmark, Larsson [Blomqvist 62], Thern (c), K. Andersson, Ingesson, Brolin.*

Kennet Andersson's goal was a superb piece of finishing, a volleyed lob of great touch and control beyond Taffarel. Meanwhile all of Romário's goals in the tournament were scored with a kind of economic brilliance. Here he darted at the centre of the Swedish defence, beating two men through speed and angle of running, before nudging the ball wide of Ravelli. Sweden, improving with every match, deserved the draw but Brazil still looked the strongest team in the competition.

GROUP B	P	W	D	L	F	A	PTS
Brazil	3	2	1	0	6	1	7
Sweden	3	1	2	0	6	4	5
Russia	3	1	0	2	7	6	3
Cameroon	3	0	1	2	3	11	1

Brazil and Sweden qualified for the second round.

Group C

Bolivia, South Korea, Spain, West Germany

■ 17 June 1994 • Soldier Field, Chicago • 63,117 • Arturo Brizio Carter (MEX)

▲ **GERMANY (0) 1**
Klinsmann 61
BOLIVIA (0) 0

● GERMANY *Bodo Illgner, Thomas Berthold, Andreas Brehme, Stefan Effenberg, Jürgen Kohler, Matthias Sammer, Thomas Hässler [Thomas Strunz 82], Lothar Matthäus (c), Karlheinz Riedle [Mario Basler 60], Andreas Möller, Jürgen Klinsmann.* Berti Vogts.
BOLIVIA *Carlos Trucco, Marco Sandy, Miguel Angel Rimba, Gustavo Quinteros, Luis Cristaldo, Carlos Borja (c), José Melgar, Vladimir Soria, Julio César Baldivieso [Jaime Moreno 65], Erwin Sánchez, William Ramallo [Marco Etcheverry 78].* Xabier Azkargorta (SPA).
▼ SENT OFF: *Etcheverry 82.*

A tournament that ended with a missed penalty also began with one. As part of the opening ceremony, singer Diana Ross showed that her links with the game were as tenuous as we thought by hooking the ball wide from only a few yards out. The following year, she opened another World Cup, this time the rugby league version at Wembley. She wasn't asked to take a kick at goal.

In Chicago, Germany became the first team to pick up three points for a win, but there was no smooth transition from 1990. Riedle missed chances in the first half and was substituted in the second, the whole team seemed reluctant to mix it physically and the goal was a mess. A long pass bounced off Hässler, Trucco came out too far, and Klinsmann rolled the ball into an empty net from the edge of the area. Bolivia, who'd qualified for the first time since 1950, might have done better if the long-haired Etcheverry, their great hope, hadn't become involved in some nonsense on the touchline. Playing his first competitive match in six months because of injury, his finals career lasted four minutes.

■ 17 June 1994 • Cotton Bowl, Dallas • 56,247 • Peter Mikkelsen (DEN)

▲ **SOUTH KOREA (0) 2**
Hong Myung-bo 85, Seo Jung-won 89
SPAIN (0) 2
Salinas 51, Goikoetxea 56

● S. KOREA *Choi In-yung (c), Kim Pan-keun, Park Jung-bae, Lee Yung-jin, Shin Hong-gi, Hong Myung-bo, Noh Jung-yoon [Ha Seok-ju 72], Kim Joo-sung [Seo Jung-won 58], Ko Jeong-woon, Choi Yung-il, Hwang Sun-hong.* Kim Ho.
SPAIN *Santiago Cañizares, Albert Ferrer, 'Sergi' (Sergio Barjuán), Rafael Alkorta, Miguel Angel Nadal (c), Abelardo (Fernández), Julen Guerrero [José Luis Caminero HT], Jon Andoni Goikoetxea, Julio Salinas [Felipe (Miñambres) 62], Fernando Hierro, Luis Enrique (Martínez).* Javier Clemente.
▼ SENT OFF: *Nadal 25.*

Despite losing Nadal for a foul on Ko Jeong-woon, Spain established a two-goal lead with a close-range shot and Goikoetxea's header, but the ten men couldn't hold out in extreme heat (43°C) and humidity. The Koreans, fast and incredibly fit, pulled one back with a free-kick (the deflection left Cañizares turning his back in disgust) then Seo Jung-won coolly drilled a shot in low at the near post.

■ 21 June 1994 • Soldier Field, Chicago •
63,113 • Ernesto Filippi Cavani (URU)

▲ **GERMANY (0) 1**
Klinsmann 48
SPAIN (1) 1
Goikoetxea 14

● GERMANY *Illgner, Berthold, Brehme, Matthäus (c), Kohler,*
Strunz, Effenberg, Hässler, Sammer, Möller [Rudi Völler 61],
Klinsmann.
SPAIN *Andoni Zubizarreta (c), Ferrer, Sergi, Alkorta, Abelardo,*
Goikoetxea [José María Bakero 63], Hierro, Salinas, Josep
Guardiola [Francisco Camarasa 76], Caminero, Luis Enrique.

Spain had the better of the first half, when Germany
left Klinsmann alone up front. The arrival of Völler, still
sharp at 34, improved the balance, and Hässler's
outswinging free-kick was headed down and in by
Klinsmann. But Spain's defence did well, the powerful
Hierro moving back to sweeper in the manner born.
Their goal, though, was laughable. Goikoetxea's cross
from the right, no more than eight yards from the goal
line, drifted over Illgner and in off the far post.

■ 23 June 1994 • Foxboro, nr Boston • 53,456 •
Leslie Mottram (SCO)

▲ **BOLIVIA 0**
SOUTH KOREA 0

● BOLIVIA *Trucco, Sandy, Rimba, Quinteros, Cristaldo,*
Borja (c), Melgar, Soria, Baldivieso, Sánchez, Ramallo
[Alvaro Peña 66].
S. KOREA *Choi In-yung (c), Kim Pan-keun, Park Jung-*
bae, Shin Hong-gi, Hong Myung-bo, Lee Yung-jin, Kim Joo-
sung, Seo Jung-won [Ha Seok-ju 65], Ko Jeong-woon, Noh
Jung-yoon [Choi Yung-il 71], Hwang Sun-hong.
▼ SENT OFF: *Cristaldo 83.*

South Korea had high hopes of winning a match in
the finals for the first time, Bolivia of scoring their
first goal. Neither came to pass in a scrappy match.
Again the Koreans never stopped running (even
though the referee played eight minutes of injury-
time) but this time their shooting was also hurried.
Cristaldo was controversially sent off for a challenge
on Kim Pan-keun.

■ 27 June 1994 • Cotton Bowl, Dallas • 63,998 •
Joël Quiniou (FRA)

▲ **GERMANY (3) 3**
Klinsmann 12, 37, Riedle 20
SOUTH KOREA (0) 2
Hwang Sun-hong 52, Hong Myung-bo 63

● GERMANY *Illgner, Berthold, Brehme, Matthäus (c)*
[Möller 63], Kohler, Guido Buchwald, Effenberg [Thomas
Helmer 74], Hässler, Sammer, Riedle, Klinsmann.
S. KOREA *Choi In-yung (c) [Lee Woon-jae HT], Choi Yung-*
il, Hong Myung-bo, Park Jung-bae, Shin Hong-gi, Kim Pan-
keun, Lee Yung-jin [Chung Jong-son 39], Ko Jeong-woon, Kim
Joo-sung, Cho Jin-ho [Seo Jung-won HT], Hwang Sun-hong.

Once again the heat came to South Korea's aid, but this
time not to their rescue. Klinsmann, maintaining his
excellent form, flipped up Hässler's low cross, spun
round and volleyed in. Then he hit a post for Riedle to
thrash in the rebound, and finally chested down another
cross before scoring with a shot that Choi In-yung
fumbled in. The change of goalkeepers at half-time
came too late, but South Korea bowed out with two fine
goals. Park Jung-bae's pass sent Hwang Sun-hong
streaking clear to touch the ball cleverly past Illgner,
then Hong Myung-bo smashed in a clearance from 25
yards. The match was played on Ko Jeong-woon's 28th
birthday. Effenberg, sent home by Vogts after making a
gesture to the crowd, hasn't been capped since.

■ 27 June 1994 • Soldier Field, Chicago •
63,089 • Rodrigo Badilla (COS)

▲ **SPAIN (1) 3**
Guardiola pen 19, Caminero 66, 71
BOLIVIA (0) 1
Sánchez 67

● SPAIN *Zubizarreta (c), Ferrer, 'Voro' (Salvador González), Abelardo, Goikoetxea, Caminero, Guardiola [Bakero 67], Felipe [Hierro HT], Sergi, Salinas, Guerrero.*
BOLIVIA *Trucco, Sandy, Rimba, Juan Manuel Peña, Mauricio Ramos [Moreno HT], Borja (c), Modesto Soruco, Melgar, Soria [Ramiro Castillo 61], Sánchez, Ramallo.*

In their sixth finals match, 64 years after the first, Bolivia at last scored their first goal, with the aid of a big deflection. Spain had their luck early on – Ramallo hitting the bar, the penalty controversially awarded – but were much the better side. Caminero scored from a narrow angle after good work by Sergi on the left, then chested down a cross before coolly stubbing it across the keeper. In between, a Spanish defender lunged at Sánchez' fierce 25-yarder and lifted it past Zubizarreta. Castillo was only 29 when he hanged himself in 1997.

GROUP C	P	W	D	L	F	A	PTS
Germany	3	2	1	0	5	3	7
Spain	3	1	2	0	6	4	5
S. Korea	3	0	2	1	4	5	2
Bolivia	3	0	1	2	1	4	1

Germany and Spain qualified for the second round.

Group D

Argentina, Bulgaria, Greece, Nigeria.

■ 21 June 1994 • Foxboro, Boston • 53,486 •
Arturo Angeles (USA)

▲ **ARGENTINA (2) 4**
Batistuta 2, 44, pen 89, Maradona 60
GREECE (0) 0

● ARGENTINA *Luis Islas, Roberto Sensini, Fernando Cáceres, Oscar Ruggeri, José Chamot, Diego Simeone, Fernando Redondo, Gabriel Batistuta, Abel Balbo [Alejandro Mancuso 79], Diego Maradona (c) [Ariel Ortega 82], Claudio Caniggia. Alfio Basile.*
GREECE *Antonis Minou, Stratos Apostolakis, Thanasis Kolitsidakis, Stelios Manolas, Yiannis Kalitzakis, Dimitris Saravakos (c), Nikos Nioplias, Panayotis Tsaluhidis, Nikos Tsiantakis [Spiros Maragos HT], Savas Kofidis, Nikos Mahlas [Tasos Mitropoulos 59]. Alkis Panagoulias.*

Argentina, uncertain about their form, couldn't have asked for an easier start. Greece might not have qualified if the horrors in Bosnia hadn't prompted FIFA to suspend Yugoslavia. They'd recently lost 5-0 at Wembley and the last thing they needed was to concede an early goal. But Batistuta was allowed a long run from deep, his eventual shot slipping past the keeper. Then he dummied a return pass to Chamot before smashing the ball in from the edge of the area. The penalty was given for accidental handball by Apostolakis. Argentina's best goal involved two one-twos on the edge of the box followed by a flashing left-footer from Maradona, who celebrated by glaring into a camera lens on the touchline, in-your-face as always. Suddenly rejuvenated and slimline, he was once again the glue in the team. How did he do it?

■ 21 June 1994 • Cotton Bowl, Dallas • 44,932 • Rodrigo Badilla (COS)

▲ **NIGERIA (2) 3**
Yekini 21, Amokachi 43, Amunike 55
BULGARIA (0) 0

● NIGERIA *Peter Rufai (c), Chidi Nwanu, Augustine Eguavoen, Uche Okechukwu, Ben Iroha, Finidi George [Emeka Ezeugo 76], Samson Siasia [Mutiu Adepoju 68], Sunday Oliseh, Rashidi Yekini, Emmanuel Amunike, Daniel Amokachi. Clemens Westerhof (HOL).*
BULGARIA *Borislav Mikhailov (c), Emil Kremenliev, Petar Hubchev, Trifon Ivanov, Tsanko Tsvetanov, Zlatko Yankov, Daniel Borimirov [Ivailo Yordanov 72], Yordan Letchkov [Nasko Sirakov 58], Krasimir Balakov, Emil Kostadinov, Christo Stoitchkov. Dimitar Penev.*

Stoitchkov was unlucky to have a goal mysteriously disallowed from a free-kick – but Nigeria were 2-0 up by then and fulfilling all expectations. George drove a low cross into the six-yard box, where three team-mates were sprinting in on it. Yekini, apparently described as 'a humble and religious stud', got there first and followed the ball into the net, which he grasped in his hands while making joyful faces. George also provided the crosses for the other two goals, Amokachi pushing a defender off the ball then sweeping extravagantly around the keeper, Amunike scoring with a diving header. Like so many in the team, Yekini and Amokachi were great slabs of men but with intricate control. If you'd been told that one of these teams was going to reach the semi-finals, you'd have had no trouble believing it.

■ 25 June 1994 • Foxboro, Boston • 54,453 • Bo Karlsson (SWE)

▲ **ARGENTINA (2) 2**
Caniggia 22, 29
NIGERIA (1) 1
Siasia 8

● ARGENTINA *Islas, Sensini [Hernán Díaz 87], Cáceres, Ruggeri, Chamot, Simeone, Maradona (c), Redondo, Balbo [Mancuso 71], Batistuta, Caniggia.*
NIGERIA *Rufai (c), Nwanu, Eguavoen, Okechukwu, Mike Emenalo, George, Siasia [Adepoju 57], Oliseh [Augustine 'JJ' Okocha 87], Amunike, Yekini, Amokachi.*

The first cracks in the Nigerian massif. They scored another splendid goal, Siasia stepping inside a defender before chipping the ball over Islas as he rushed out to the edge of the penalty area. But they fell asleep at a free-kick, which Maradona took quickly and Caniggia curled beyond Rufai. The second goal also followed a free-kick, Maradona backheeling the ball for Batistuta to shoot low around the wall, Rufai fumbling the ball for Caniggia to kick it into the roof of the net.

Quite a comeback for Caniggia, whose ban for cocaine use had ended just a month before the finals – but it wasn't the big drugs story of the tournament. In his eagerness to lose weight quickly, Maradona had taken a cocktail that included 'five inhibited substances in each urine sample ... ephedrine and allied substances ... increasing concentration and physical capacity'. That wasn't the beginning or the end of it, of course. He'd tested positive for cocaine in 1991, was appointed to lead an anti-drugs drive in 1996, then was discovered taking cocaine again in 1997. If he hadn't been caught in Boston, he'd have played more matches in World Cup finals than anyone else. As it was, his 21 gives him a share in the record. Hero or villain, he was very much the headline player of his age, impossible to ignore or forget.

MATCHES AS CAPTAIN

16	Diego Maradona	ARG	1986–94
14	Dino Zoff	ITA	1978–82
13	Kaziu Deyna	POL	1974–78

■ 26 June 1994 • Soldier Field, Chicago • 63,160 • Ali Mohammed Bujsaim (UAE)

▲ **BULGARIA (1) 4**
Stoitchkov pen 5, pen 55, Letchkov 66, Borimirov 89
GREECE (0) 0

● BULGARIA *Mikhailov (c), Kremenliev, Hubchev, Ivanov, Tsvetanov [Ilian Kiriakov 76], Letchkov, Yankov, Balakov, Sirakov, Stoitchkov, Kostadinov [Borimirov 81].*
GREECE *Ilias Atmatzidis, Apostolakis (c), Kalitzakis, Vaios Karayannis, Kyriakos Karataidis, Nioplias, Maragos, Minas Hantzidis [Mitropoulos HT], Mahlas, Kofidis, Alexis Alexoudis [Vasilis Dimitriadis 57].*

No surprise that Bulgaria won a finals match for the first time; Greece were their softest opposition yet. Stoitchkov put away two penalties and brought a good save from Atmatzidis with his free-kick, Borimirov stabbing in the rebound. Letchkov, the balding general, played a delayed one-two with

Kostadinov and ran on to shoot in off a post. As usual, coach Panagoulias had his own succinct account of the proceedings: 'Beaten by that flat-footed poof Ivanov or whatever his name is.' His success in taking Greece to the finals for the first time was already almost forgotten.

■ 30 June 1994 • Cotton Bowl, Dallas • 63,998 • Neji Jouini (TUN)

▲ **BULGARIA (0) 2**
Stoitchkov 61, Sirakov 89
ARGENTINA (0) 0

● BULGARIA *Mikhailov (c), Kremenliev, Hubchev, Ivanov, Tsvetanov, Letchkov [Borimirov 77], Yankov, Balakov, Sirakov, Stoitchkov, Kostadinov [Kiriakov 74].*
ARGENTINA *Islas, Díaz, Cáceres, Ruggeri (c), Chamot, Simeone, Redondo, Leo Rodríguez [Ramón Medina Bello 66], Balbo, Batistuta, Caniggia [Ortega 26].*
▼ SENT OFF: *Tsvetanov 67.*

Like waiting for a bus. It takes 32 years for the first to arrive, then two come along together, this one carrying greater kudos. Maradona's absence had its effect, as did the fact that Argentina were already through. Even after Stoitchkov sprinted clear to prod the ball wide of Islas, they were top of the group – until Sirakov's header from a corner and an even later goal in the other match relegated them to third. Mikhailov, sporting a new hair transplant, did well in goal. Tsvetanov was sent off for bringing down Ortega, his second bookable offence.

■ 30 June 1994 • Foxboro, Boston • 53,001 • Leslie Mottram (SCO)

▲ **NIGERIA (1) 2**
George 45, Amokachi 90
GREECE (0) 0

● NIGERIA *Rufai, Stephen Keshi (c), Okechukwu, Nwanu, Emenalo, George [Adepoju 83], Siasia, Oliseh, Amunike, Yekini [Okocha 68], Amokachi.*
GREECE *Christos Karkamanis, Kalitzakis, Karayannis, Alexis Alexiou, Tsaluhidis, Nioplias, Mitropoulos (c) [Tsiantakis 79], Hantzidis, Kofidis, Alekos Alexandris, Mahlas [Dimitriadis 79].*

George celebrated his goal (a smart chip) by going down on all fours and cocking a leg. Deep into injury-time Amokachi wasted a wonderful strike on such a weak team, taking out four defenders before blasting a tremendous right-footer into the top corner. The goal vaulted Nigeria to the top of the group. The full first name of Alexoudis, Alexandris and Alexiou is Alexandros.

GROUP D	P	W	D	L	F	A	PTS
Nigeria	3	2	0	1	6	2	6
Bulgaria	3	2	0	1	6	3	6
Argentina	3	2	0	1	6	3	6
Greece	3	0	0	3	0	10	0

Nigeria, Bulgaria and Argentina qualified for the second round.

Group E

Republic of Ireland, Italy, Mexico, Norway

■ 18 June 1994 • Giants Stadium, New Jersey • 74,826 • Mario van der Ende (HOL)

▲ **REP. IRELAND (1) 1**
Houghton 12
ITALY (0) 0

● IRELAND *Pat Bonner, Denis Irwin, Terry Phelan, Roy Keane, Phil Babb, Paul McGrath, Ray Houghton [Jason McAteer 67], John Sheridan, Tommy Coyne [John Aldridge 89], Andy Townsend (c), Steve Staunton.* Jack Charlton (ENG).
ITALY *Gianluca Pagliuca, Mauro Tassotti, Paolo Maldini, Dino Baggio, Alessandro Costacurta, Franco Baresi (c), Roberto Donadoni, Demetrio Albertini, Beppe Signori, [Nicola Berti 83], Roberto Baggio, Alberigo Evani [Daniele Massaro HT].* Arrigo Sacchi.

Two years earlier Houghton had scored the only goal of another opening group match, crippling England's chances in the European Championship. Here he chested down Baresi's weak header and hooked a long-range volley over Pagliuca. The move had started with a typical Irish mortar bomb, forcing Costacurta into an aerial duel with Coyne.

Sacchi had packed the team with midfielders and stationed little Signori (Serie A's leading scorer for the past two seasons) out on the left. As a result, Italy couldn't find their way through a defence in which Babb was an ideal partner for the 34-year-old McGrath, still a great player despite dodgy knees. At the other end, Sheridan hit the bar. It was the Republic's first win in the finals and Big Jack seemed vindicated again.

■ 19 June 1994 • Robert F. Kennedy, Washington DC • 52,359 • Sándor Puhl (HUN)

▲ **NORWAY (0) 1**
Rekdal 85
MEXICO (0) 0

● NORWAY *Erik Thorstvedt, Alf-Inge Håland, Rune Bratseth (c), Stig Inge Bjørnebye, Erik Mykland [Kjetil Rekdal 77], Øyvind Leonhardsen, Henning Berg, Jahn Ivar Jakobsen [Gunnar Halle HT], Jostein Flo, Lars Bohinen, Jan Åge Fjørtoft.* Egil Olsen.
MEXICO *Jorge Campos, Claudio Suárez, Raúl Gutiérrez [Marcelino Bernal 70], Ignacio Ambriz (c), Ramón Ramírez, Luis García, Joaquin del Olmo, Juan Ramírez, Luis Valdez [Benjamin Galindo HT], Hugo Sánchez, Luis Alves Zague.* Miguel Mejía Barón.

Norway had surprisingly finished ahead of Holland and England in qualifying, and their support play and discipline were enough even in these conditions. When Fjørtoft was fouled, the ball ran on to Rekdal, who outpaced Suárez before scoring with a cross-shot. Alves Zague, who had a Brazilian father, was sometimes known as 'Zaguinho'. In the last minute his diving header came back off a post, hit his head as he lay on the ground, and was kicked clear by Berg. Jakobsen had his nickname 'Mini' printed on the back of his shirt.

The start and finish of Ireland's goal against Italy. The ball leaves Houghton's foot ... and is retrieved by Pagliuca.

■ 23 June 1994 • Giants Stadium, New Jersey •
74,624 • Heinz Hellmut Krug (GER)

▲ **ITALY (0) 1**
D. Baggio 69
NORWAY (0) 0

● ITALY *Pagliuca, Antonio Benarrivo, Maldini, D. Baggio,
Costacurta, Baresi (c) [Luigi Apolloni 48], Berti, Albertini,
Signori, R. Baggio [Luca Marchegiani 22], Pierluigi
Casiraghi [Massaro 69].*
NORWAY *Thorstvedt, Håland, Bratseth (c), Bjørnebye,
Berg, Mykland [Rekdal 80], Leonhardsen, Sigurd Rushfeldt
[Jakobsen HT], Bohinen, Flo, Fjørtoft.*

▼ SENT OFF: *Pagliuca 21.*

■ 24 June 1994 • Citrus Bowl, Orlando •
61,219 • Kurt Röthlisberger (SWI)

▲ **MEXICO (1) 2**
L. García 43, 66
REP. IRELAND (0) 1
Aldridge 84

● MEXICO *Campos, Jorge Rodríguez [Gutiérrez 80],
Suárez, J. Ramírez, Del Olmo, Bernal, L. García,
Ambriz (c), Alberto García Aspe, Carlos Hermosillo [Luis
Salvador 80], Alves Zague.*
IRELAND *Bonner, Irwin, Phelan, Keane, Babb, McGrath,
Houghton, Sheridan, Coyne [Aldridge 66], Townsend (c),
Staunton [McAteer 65].*

A match to enter Italian folklore. When Pagliuca
brought down Leonhardsen to become the first
goalkeeper ever sent off in the finals, Italy were not
only left with ten men for most of the match but
took off Roberto Baggio (gasp) to make way for a
substitute keeper. Then Baresi was injured and
Maldini finished the match limping on the wing,
Massaro moving to left-back. Impossible odds.

Norway were subsequently criticized for playing
for a point instead of crushing the invalids – but
perhaps they were pacing themselves to conserve
energy. Italy, too, would probably have settled for a
draw, but Dino Baggio scored with a powerful
header after leading the charge to attack Signori's
free-kick. Bratseth had a goal disallowed with eight
minutes left, but the thin blue line deserved to hold
out. The referee's second name is no misprint (i.e.
not the more common spelling Helmut).

In a frying midday sun, Mexico again finished less
strongly than the Europeans – but they'd done the
damage by then, Luis García scoring with sharp
ground shots from the edge of the penalty area.
Ireland's two subs (and best players) combined for
their goal, McAteer cutting back a good cross from
the right for the veteran Aldridge to score. Campos,
also capped as an outfield player, wearing a multi-
coloured jersey of his own design, was more of a
personality than a great goalkeeper. He should have
stopped Aldridge's downward header.

*Big Jack engages in a little touchline debate during
Ireland's group match with Mexico.*

Earlier there'd been some fun and games when an official delayed Aldridge's entrance as substitute, provoking strong words from the striker and his manager. Charlton had earlier criticized a decision not to allow players to drink water during matches (it wasn't true: they were simply told to do it on the touchline) and FIFA now lost patience, issuing a one-match ban from the bench and a £10,000 fine. The Official Report (a distinct minority) says Gutiérrez substituted Del Olmo.

■ 28 June 1994 • Giants Stadium, New Jersey • 76,322 • José Torres Cadena (COL)

▲ **NORWAY 0**
REP. IRELAND 0

● **NORWAY** *Thorstvedt, Halle [Jakobsen 33], Erland Johnsen, Bratseth (c), Bjørnebye, Flo, Berg, Leonhardsen [Bohinen 67], Gøran Sørloth, Mykland, Rekdal.*
IRELAND *Bonner, Gary Kelly, Staunton, Keane, Babb, McGrath, McAteer, Houghton, Townsend (c) [Ronnie Whelan 74], Sheridan, Aldridge [David Kelly 64].*

Norway's passivity (or problems with the heat) cost them a place in the next round, the only team eliminated with four points. Gary Kelly and Staunton were excellent replacements at full-back and Charlton used a two-way radio to communicate with his bench. The Republic were in the second round for the second time, but the fires of Orlando were waiting again.

■ 28 June 1994 • Robert F. Kennedy, Washington DC • 53,186 • Francisco Lamolina (ARG)

▲ **ITALY (0) 1**
Massaro 48
MEXICO (0) 1
Bernal 58

● **ITALY** *Marchegiani, Benarrivo, Apolloni, D. Baggio [Donadoni 64], Costacurta, Maldini (c), Berti, Albertini, Casiraghi [Massaro HT], R. Baggio, Signori.*
MEXICO *Campos, Rodríguez, Suárez, J. Ramírez, Del Olmo, Bernal, L. García [Juan Carlos Chávez 80], Ambriz (c), García Aspe, Hermosillo, Alves Zague.*

Baresi's absence forced Maldini into the middle, but he played as if he'd been there all his life, enjoying his 26th birthday until the ankle flared up again. Massaro, first capped in 1982, scored his first senior international goal after chesting down Albertini's through-ball, but Bernal drove in a ground shot after avoiding Signori's tackle; a goal that moved Mexico from bottom to top and eliminated Norway. Italy had to wait for the result of Russia v Cameroon to be sure they'd qualified.

GROUP E	P	W	D	L	F	A	PTS
Mexico	3	1	1	1	3	3	4
Rep. Ireland	3	1	1	1	2	2	4
Italy	3	1	1	1	2	2	4
Norway	3	1	1	1	1	1	4

Mexico, Republic of Ireland and Italy qualified for the second round. Ireland placed second as a result of beating Italy. The only time all four teams finished with the same number of points.

Group F

Belgium, Holland, Morocco, Saudi Arabia

■ 19 June 1994 • Citrus Bowl, Orlando • 60,790 • José Torres Cadena (COL)

▲ **BELGIUM (1) 1**
Degryse 11
MOROCCO (0) 0

● BELGIUM *Michel Preud'homme, Georges Grün (c), Michel De Wolf, Rudi Smidts, Lorenzo Staelens, Franky Van der Elst, Marc Degryse, Enzo Scifo, Danny Boffin [Vital Borkelmans 84], Josip Weber, Luc Nilis [Marc Emmers 53].* Paul Van Himst.
MOROCCO *Khalil Azmi [Zakaria Alaoui 88], Nasser Abdullah, Smahi Triki, Larbi Hababi, Abdelkarim El-Hadrioui, Nourredine Naybet, Mustafa El-Haddaoui (c) [Ahmed Bahja 68], Rachid Azzouzi, Rachid Daoudi, Mustafa Hadji, Mohammed Chaouch [Aziz Samadi 81].* Abdullah Blinda.

There was still no getting away from the heat (Van Himst said he was soaking wet 'and I was only sitting on the bench') but Morocco couldn't quite make it count. Chaouch twice hit the bar, the second time via a save by Preud'homme. At the other end Azmi came out for a cross by Nilis but Degryse got his head to it before him. Under a new rule allowing goalkeepers to be replaced, Morocco became the first team to use three substitutes in a finals match.

■ 20 June 1994 • Robert F. Kennedy, Washington DC • 52,535 • Manuel Díaz Vega (SPA)

▲ **HOLLAND (0) 2**
Jonk 50 , Taument 86
SAUDI ARABIA (1) 1
Amin 19

● HOLLAND *Ed de Goey, Ulrich van Gobbel, Ronald Koeman (c), Frank de Boer, Wim Jonk, Frank Rijkaard, Marc Overmars [Gaston Taument 57], Jan Wouters, Dennis Bergkamp, Brian Roy [Peter van Vossen 80], Ronald de Boer.* Dick Advocaat.
SAUDI *Mohammed Al-Deayah, Abdullah Al-Dossari, Mohammed Al-Khlawi, Mohammed Al-Jawad, Ahmed Madani, Fuad Amin, Fahad Al-Bishi, Khalid Al-Muwalid, Talal Jebreen, Majed Abdullah Mohammed (c) [Hamzah Falatah 45], Saïd Owairan [Hamza Saleh 68].* Jorge Solari (ARG).

Holland, not a patch on their 1988 side but skilful as always, were given a fright by a talented and committed side. Saudi Arabia, appearing in the finals for the first time, had ironically sacked their Dutch coach in February (Leo Beenhakker, who'd coached Holland in the 1990 finals) for training them too hard. Here they took the lead through Amin's header from a free-kick but obviously hadn't been briefed about Jonk's reputation for long-range shooting. His 30-yarder swerved past the keeper's left hand. Worse was to follow for Al-Deayah, who came a long way off his line but missed his punch, the cross bouncing behind him for Taument to head in. Solari had played for Argentina in the 1966 finals. The de Boers were twins.

■ 25 June 1994 • Citrus Bowl, Orlando •
62,387 • Renato Marsiglia (BRZ)

▲ **BELGIUM (0) 1**
Albert 65
HOLLAND (0) 0

● BELGIUM *Preud'homme, Emmers [Dirk Medved 77], Grün (c), De Wolf, Philippe Albert, Borkelmans [Smidts 60], Scifo, Van der Elst, Staelens, Degryse, Weber.*
HOLLAND *De Goey, Stan Valckx, Koeman (c), F. de Boer, Rijkaard, Jonk, Wouters, Taument [Overmars 63], Bergkamp, Roy, R. de Boer [Rob Witschge HT].*

Albert, a classy attacking defender later signed by Newcastle, shot in off the near post from a corner, and Scifo had a goal disallowed – but Belgium were indebted to the 35-year-old Preud'homme, who gave the goalkeeping performance of the tournament, saving from Koeman, Bergkamp, Rijkaard, you name it, finally touching a shot from Overmars on to the bar in the last minute.

■ 25 June 1994 • Giants Stadium, New Jersey •
72,404 • Philip Don (ENG)

▲ **SAUDI ARABIA (2) 2**
Al-Jaber pen 8, Amin 45
MOROCCO (1) 1
Chaouch 27

● SAUDI *Al-Deayah, Al-Khlawi, Al-Jawad (c), Awad Al-Anazi [Abdullah Zebermawi 29], Madani, Amin, Al-Bishi, Al-Muwalid, Al-Jebreen, Owairan, Sami Al-Jaber [Fahad Al-Ghesheyan 79].*
MOROCCO *Azmi (c), Abdullah [Abdelsalam Laghrissi 56], Taher El-Khalej, Triki, Naybet, Azzouzi, El-Hadrioui, Daoudi, Hababi [Hadji 72], Chaouch, Bahja.*

In the first finals meeting between two Arab countries, Saudi Arabia became only the second Asian team to win a match, the first since North Korea in 1966. Naybet fouled Al-Jaber for the penalty, Chaouch was left with a tap-in after some brilliant work by Bahja on the goal line, foxing four men – but another error by Azmi gave away the winning goal, Amin's long shot bouncing in off his hands.

■ 29 June 1994 • Citrus Bowl, Orlando •
60,578 • Alberto Tejada (PER)

▲ **HOLLAND (1) 2**
Bergkamp 43, Roy 78
MOROCCO (0) 1
Nader 47

● HOLLAND *De Goey, Valckx, Koeman (c), F. de Boer, Aron Winter, Jonk, Wouters, Witschge, Overmars [Taument 57], Bergkamp, van Vossen [Roy 68].*
MOROCCO *Alaoui, Samadi, Rachid Neqrouz, Triki, El-Hadrioui, Abdelmajid Bouyboub [Hadji HT], El-Khalej (c), Azzouzi [Daoudi 62], Hababi, Hassan Nader, Bahja.*

Holland got the win they needed to be sure of qualifying, but were again made to work for it, Nader driving in a square pass for the equalizer. Bergkamp, who'd calmly lifted the ball over the keeper for the first goal, swerved past a defender to set up Roy for the winner. In a tight group, Morocco lost all three matches despite playing well, while Holland needed Bergkamp's good form to make up for Koeman's increasing fallibility in defence.

2nd Round

■ 29 June 1994 • Robert F. Kennedy, Washington DC • 52,959 • Heinz Hellmut Krug (GER)

▲ **SAUDI ARABIA (1) 1**
Owairan 5
BELGIUM (0) 0

● SAUDI *Al-Deayah, Al-Khlawi, Zebermawi, Al-Jawad, Madani, Al-Bishi, Jebreen, Saleh, Majed Abdullah (c) [Al-Muwalid HT], Owairan [Al-Dossari 61], Falatah.*
BELGIUM *Preud'homme, Medved, Albert, De Wolf, Smidts, Staelens, Van der Elst, Boffin, Scifo (c), Degryse [Nilis 23], Marc Wilmots [Weber 53].*

Belgium, expected to stroll through as group winners, had more of the play, but Owairan's goal was worthy of winning any match. Playing with a bandaged wrist, he took a pass well inside his own half, burst between two Belgians, beat another on the outside, a fourth on the inside, then hooked the ball high past Preud'homme. Saudi Arabia were the first Asian country to win two matches and qualify for the next round. Majed Abdullah, 'Pelé of the Desert', won his 147th and last cap, recognized by FIFA as the current world record.

GROUP F	P	W	D	L	F	A	PTS
Holland	3	2	0	1	4	3	6
Saudi Arabia	3	2	0	1	4	3	6
Belgium	3	2	0	1	2	1	6
Morocco	3	0	0	3	2	5	0

Holland, Saudi Arabia and Belgium qualified for the second round.

■ 2 July 1994 • Soldier Field, Chicago • 60,246 • Kurt Röthlisberger (SWI)

▲ **GERMANY (3) 3**
Völler 6, 40, Klinsmann 11,
BELGIUM (1) 2
Grün 8, Albert 89

● GERMANY *Illgner, Helmer, Matthäus (c) [Brehme HT], Kohler, Berthold, Buchwald, Hässler, Sammer, Martin Wagner, Völler, Klinsmann [Stefan Kuntz 85].*
BELGIUM *Preud'homme, Grün (c), Albert, De Wolf, Smidts [Boffin 65], Staelens, Van der Elst, Emmers, Scifo, Nilis [Alex Czerniatynski 77], Weber.*

This was Belgium's penance for losing to Saudi Arabia, a match with the champions and their famous strikers. Völler scored the first goal by heading the ball on and running through to nick the ball deftly over Preud'homme, who should have stopped the header that made it 3–1. Völler's slick one-two with Klinsmann led to the second goal. Grün stabbed in the equalizer from a free-kick and Albert played a one-two before going past Kohler in the penalty area, a definite touch of the Beckenbauers. Germany hadn't lost to Belgium since 1954 and were the better side here – but they had a little help; Röthlisberger was sent home after admitting he should have awarded a penalty for a foul by Helmer on Weber.

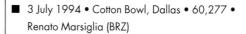

1994

■ 2 July 1994 • Robert F. Kennedy, Washington DC • 53,121 • Mario van der Ende (HOL)

▲ **SPAIN (1) 3**
Hierro 15, Luis Enrique 74, Beguiristain pen 87
SWITZERLAND (0) 0

● SPAIN *Zubizarreta (c), Alkorta, Ferrer, Camarasa, Nadal, Abelardo, Hierro [Jorge Otero 75], Bakero, Sergi, Goikoetxea [Aitor Beguiristain 60], Luis Enrique.*
SWITZERLAND *Pascolo, Hottiger, Herr, Geiger (c), Quentin [Jürg Studer 57], Ohrel [Subiat 72], Sforza, Bregy, Bickel, Knup, Chapuisat.*

A miserable 26th birthday for Knup. After 18 matches going back to 1925, Spain remained unbeaten against Switzerland. Hierro ran through to score as the Swiss stopped playing, expecting a whistle when Sergi ran back from an offside position. Luis Enrique celebrated his goal with a shirt–over–the–face routine for which Ravanelli took out the British patent, and Pascolo brought down Ferrer for the penalty. The Swiss badly missed the skills of Sutter, who'd aggravated a serious toe injury when Hodgson picked him for the meaningless last group match. Switzerland have played 22 matches in the finals without keeping a single clean sheet.

Remember the old joke about the goalkeeper who put his head in his hands and dropped it? Pat Bonner after his blunder against Holland (see opposite).

■ 3 July 1994 • Cotton Bowl, Dallas • 60,277 • Renato Marsiglia (BRZ)

▲ **SWEDEN (1) 3**
Dahlin 6, K.Andersson 51, 88
SAUDI ARABIA (0) 1
Al-Ghesheyan 85

● SWEDEN *Ravelli, R. Nilsson, Ljung, Schwarz, P. Andersson, Björklund [Kåmark 54], Brolin, Thern (c) [Mild 70], K.Andersson, Ingesson, Dahlin.*
SAUDI *Al-Deayah, Zebermawi, Madani, Al-Jawad (c) [Al-Ghesheyan 54], Al-Khlawi, Al-Jaber, Amin, Saleh, Owairan, Al-Bishi [Al-Muwalid 62], Falatah.*

Again the Saudis decorated the match with an excellent goal, Al-Ghesheyan cutting inside and thrashing a high shot inside Ravelli. But although Sweden visibly wilted in the heat, they were always in control. Once again Dahlin headed in a cross by Kennet Andersson, the star of the front line, who scored with two low shots, the first after holding off a defender, the second in off a post.

■ 3 July 1994 • Rose Bowl, Pasadena • 90,469 • Pierluigi Pairetto (ITA)

▲ **ROMANIA (2) 3**
Dumitrescu 11, 18, Hagi 56
ARGENTINA (1) 2
Batistuta pen 16, Balbo 75

● ROMANIA *Prunea, Petrescu, Prodan, Belodedici, Lupescu, Popescu, Selymes, Munteanu, Hagi (c) [Gâlca 86], Dumitrescu [Papura 88], Mihali.*
ARGENTINA *Islas, Sensini [Medina Bello 63], Cáceres, Ruggeri (c), Chamot, José Basualdo, Simeone, Redondo, Ortega, Balbo, Batistuta.*

A feast of a match. While Argentina missed Maradona, Romania made up for Raducioiu's suspension by pushing Dumitrescu up front, and he responded with two superb goals. His first was merely a beautifully struck free-kick from out on the left, dipping over Islas into the side netting. The second was a gem, Hagi pushing an angled pass between three defenders, Dumitrescu twisting his body coolly to side-foot it in at the near post. Batistuta was awarded an equalizing penalty for a challenge by Prodan but Romania were full of flair on the break and scored another fine goal, Dumitrescu setting up Hagi to shoot high past Islas. Balbo pulled one back when Prunea badly fumbled Cáceres' low shot – but it wasn't enough. Iordanescu took a strange gamble by substituting both his goalscorers, but Argentina couldn't force extra-time.

■ 4 July 1994 • Citrus Bowl, Orlando • 61,355 • Peter Mikkelsen (DEN)

▲ **HOLLAND (2) 2**
Bergkamp 11, Jonk 41
REP. IRELAND (0) 0

● HOLLAND *De Goey, Winter, Valckx, Koeman (c), F. de Boer, Rijkaard, Jonk, Witschge [Arthur Numan 78], Overmars, Bergkamp, van Vossen [Roy 69].*
IRELAND *Bonner, G. Kelly, Phelan, Keane, Babb, McGrath, Houghton, Townsend (c), Coyne [Tony Cascarino 73], Sheridan, Staunton [McAteer 62].*

A match remembered for Bonner's appalling blunder, but the first goal was almost as bad, Overmars pouncing on Phelan's weak header and sprinting away to set up Bergkamp. Jonk's long-range shot wasn't one of his best, but Bonner let it slip horribly through his hands, which he then used to hold his head. Roy missed two easy chances late on.

Charlton's tactics in the second half are still hard to understand. Two goals down, he continued to use only a single striker, and when he eventually replaced the hardworking Coyne, it was with a blunt instrument like Cascarino instead of Aldridge. And why was the impressive McAteer left on the bench? The Republic have played nine matches in the World Cup finals, winning one and scoring four goals. When the team were given a reception on their return home, the half-empty field suggested that even for their fans it was all wearing a bit thin.

■ 4 July 1994 • Stanford, Palo Alto • 84,147 • Joël Quiniou (FRA)

▲ **BRAZIL (0) 1**
Bebeto 74
USA (0) 0

● BRAZIL *Taffarel, Jorginho, Leonardo, Mauro Silva, Aldair, Márcio Santos, Mazinho, Dunga (c), Bebeto, Romário, Zinho ['Cafú' (Marcos Evangelista) 68].*
USA *Meola (c), Clavijo, Caligiuri, Ramos [Wynalda HT], Lalas, Balboa, Dooley, Hugo Pérez [Wegerle 65], Sorber, Jones, Stewart.*
▼ SENT OFF: *Leonardo 44, Clavijo 87.*

Brazil dropped Raí, who'd had a poor season with Paris St Germain, settled for solidity in midfield, and needed it after Leonardo was sent off (and banned for the rest of the tournament) for fracturing Ramos' skull with his elbow. Balboa and Lalas again played well, and the US team had made its contribution to the finals, but Brazil's extra guile told in the end. Romário ran from deep and beat a man before slipping the ball wide to Bebeto, whose shot skidded under Lalas' tackle and just inside the far post. Clavijo, an American sent off on the 4th of July, was the oldest to be dismissed in a finals match: 37

years 162 days. Carlos Alberto Parreira and Milutinovic, already the only two coaches to take charge of three different countries in the finals, have both been appointed by a fourth in 1998.

REFEREES: MOST SENDINGS-OFF			
5	Joël Quiniou	FRA	1986–94
4	Jamal Al-Sharif	SYR	1986–94
3	Paul von Hertzka	HUN	1938
3	Arthur Ellis	ENG	1954
3	Jesús Díaz Palacio	COL	1986
3	Michel Vautrot	FRA	1990
3	Arturo Brizio Carter	MEX	1994

Von Hertzka and Ellis in a single match.

■ 5 July 1994 • Foxboro, Boston • 54,367 • Arturo Brizio Carter (MEX)

▲ **ITALY (0) (1) 2**
R. Baggio 88, pen 102
NIGERIA (1) (1) 1
Amunike 26

● ITALY *Marchegiani, Roberto Mussi, Benarrivo, Berti [D. Baggio HT], Costacurta, Maldini (c), Donadoni, Albertini, Signori [Gianfranco Zola 64], R. Baggio, Massaro.*
NIGERIA *Rufai (c), Eguavoen, Okechukwu, Nwanu, Emenalo, George, Oliseh, Okocha, Yekini, Amunike [Thompson Oliha 56], Amokachi [Adepoju 34].*
▼ SENT OFF: *Zola 76.*

Leonardo (16) is shown the red card for elbowing Ramos, which is one way of getting him away from an American lynching party. (l–r): Meola, Balboa, the bearded Lalas, and Stewart.

Again everything was stacked against the Italians. A corner bounced off Maldini's shins to set up Amunike's volley for the opening goal, Dino Baggio hit a post, and Zola was controversially sent off after being on the pitch only 12 minutes on his 28th birthday. There were only two minutes left when Mussi handed off a defender on the right, took a lucky rebound, and set up the finest moment in the competition.

Roberto Baggio was the current European Footballer of the Year and FIFA Player of the Year, yet here he'd been anonymous in two matches and taken off in the other. When Mussi rolled the ball across, it's hard to believe anyone else would have done anything but

hit it as hard as possible. Instead he aimed for the absolute bottom corner of the goal, between goalkeeper and defender. If he'd missed, they'd have said he didn't even have the bottle to go for his shot, leaving a big minus against his career. In all the pressure, Baggio backed his talent to the end, scored, and resuscitated his and Italy's World Cup. Courage and class, rewarded with a touch of good fortune: his penalty, for Eguavon's clumsy challenge on Benarrivo, went in off a post.

Nigeria were an enormous let-down. Stacked with class players, a goal down in extra-time, they kept five or six defenders back against ten men. Perhaps it's time for some more home help. None of the black African countries have employed an African coach in the finals, even though the likes of Charles Gyamfi and Fred Osam Duodu consistently won the African Nations Cup.

The bristling Stoitchkov, tournament joint top scorer, celebrates his goal against Mexico.

■ 5 July 1994 • Giants Stadium, New Jersey • 71,030 • Jamal Al-Sharif (SYR)

▲ **BULGARIA (1) (1) 1**
Stoitchkov 7
MEXICO (1) (1) 1
García Aspe pen 18,
Bulgaria 3-1 pens.

●

BULGARIA *Mikhailov (c), Kremenliev, Borimirov, Hubchev, Kiriakov, Letchkov, Yordanov, Balakov, Stoitchkov, Sirakov [Boncho Genchev 103], Kostadinov [Petar Mikhtarski 118].*
MEXICO *Campos, Rodríguez, Suárez, J. Ramírez, R. Ramírez, Bernal, García Aspe, Ambriz (c), L. García, Galindo, Alves Zague.*

▼ SENT OFF: *Kremenliev 50, L. García 58.*

□ PENALTY SHOOT-OUT: *García Aspe shot over, Balakov saved, Bernal saved, Genchev 0-1, Rodríguez saved, Borimirov 0-2, Suárez 1-2, Lechkov 1-3.*

By common consent, a match ruined by the referee. After Stoitchkov had sprinted on to Kostadinov's through-ball to thrash it over Campos, Al-Sharif awarded a penalty for a fifty-fifty tussle between Kremenliev and Alves Zague. As well as sending off two players for offences barely worthy of the name, he showed eight yellow cards in a match that was never rough. Bulgaria deserved to go through, if only because Kostadinov hit the post with a free-kick. In their last two finals tournaments, 1986 and now this, Mexico were eliminated on penalties.

1994

Quarter-finals

■ 9 July 1994 • Foxboro, Boston • 54,605 •
Sándor Puhl (HUN)

▲ **ITALY (1) 2**
D. Baggio 26, R. Baggio 88
SPAIN (0) 1
Caminero 59

● ITALY *Pagliuca, Tassotti, Benarrivo, D. Baggio, Costacurta,
Maldini (c), Donadoni, Albertini [Signori HT], Massaro, R.
Baggio, Antonio Conte [Berti 65].*
SPAIN *Zubizarreta (c), Ferrer, Sergi [Salinas 59], Alkorta,
Nadal, Abelardo, Caminero, Otero, Bakero [Hierro 64],
Goikoetxea, Luis Enrique.*

Italy's first goal was good (Dino Baggio scoring from
well outside the area) and Spain's was lucky
(Caminero's shot deflected over Pagliuca) – but it was
still another great Italian escape. Spain should have
had a penalty when Tassotti elbowed Luis Enrique in
the face, and Salinas prodded the ball against Pagliuca
when clean through. Italy immediately scored at the
other end, Signori accepting a clattering as the price
for lifting the ball beyond the last defender, Roberto
Baggio swerving past Zubizarreta to score from a
tight angle. Tassotti, not even booked for that elbow,
was banned for eight matches, long enough to end
his international career.

REFEREED MOST MATCHES

8	Joël Quiniou	FRA	1986–94
7	John Langenus	BEL	1930–38
7	Mervyn Griffiths	WAL	1950–58
7	Juan Gardeazábal	SPA	1958–66

■ 9 July 1994 • Cotton Bowl, Dallas • 63,998 •
Rodrigo Badilla (COS)

▲ **BRAZIL (0) 3**
Romário 52, Bebeto 62, Branco 81
HOLLAND (0) 2
Bergkamp 64, Winter 76

● BRAZIL *Taffarel, Jorginho, 'Branco' (Cláudio Vaz)
[Cafú 89], Mauro Silva, Aldair, Márcio Santos, Mazinho
[Raí 80], Dunga (c), Bebeto, Romário, Zinho.*
HOLLAND *De Goey, Winter, Valckx, Wouters, Rijkaard
[R. de Boer 64], Koeman (c), Jonk, Witschge, Overmars,
Bergkamp, van Vossen [Roy 53].*

How the Dutch must have wished for one or two
better players (the absent Gullit or the injured van
Basten) and a different referee. When Bebeto went
round de Goey for the second goal, Holland fully
expected a whistle as Romário strolled back from an
offside position directly in the goalkeeper's line of
vision. The two strikers had combined for the first
goal, Romário's half-volley meeting Bebeto's cross.

Against a defence that had conceded only one
goal in four matches, Holland did tremendously well
to get back on level terms. Bergkamp chested the
ball past a weak challenge before beating Taffarel,
who'd been off form for years and allowed Winter to
head in a corner from under his nose. But Brazil had
another shot in their locker, a low 25-yard free-kick
from Branco, the veteran replacing the suspended
Leonardo. The ball swerved between Raí and Valckx,
who both deliberately avoided it, and went in off the
bottom of the post.

Cruel for Holland, but not a patch on Bebeto's
goal celebration, the dreaded baby-cuddling which
later found its way into the English league. Bergkamp
had proved he could perform on the big stage, but the
once-mighty Koeman wasn't capped again.

1994

■ 10 July 1994 • Giants Stadium, New Jersey •
72,416 • José Torres Cadena (COL)

▲ **BULGARIA (0) 2**
Stoitchkov 75, Letchkov 78
GERMANY (0) 1
Matthäus pen 48

● BULGARIA *Mikhailov (c), Ivanov, Hubchev, Tsvetanov,
Kiriakov, Letchkov, Yankov, Sirakov, Balakov, Stoitchkov
[Yordanov 84], Kostadinov [Genchev 90].*
GERMANY *Illgner, Helmer, Matthäus (c), Kohler, Berthold,
Buchwald, Hässler [Brehme 83], Möller, Völler, Wagner
[Strunz 59], Klinsmann.*

In the end experience wasn't enough. Germany,
including nine players from the 1990 Final, had an
average of 57 previous caps each and took the lead when
Letchkov clearly fouled Klinsmann in the area (he
remonstrated but Klinsmann impatiently waved him
away). For the second successive quarter-final Matthäus
scored from the spot, and we waited for German
professionalism to do the rest.

But Stoitchkov equalized with a sweet free-kick
and Germany's slack marking let them in for the
winner. When Yankov crossed
from the right, only little Hässler
was left to challenge Letchkov as
his diving header scored the most
important goal in Bulgaria's
football history. For the second
time in the tournament, a player
(Matthäus) equalled the record of
21 appearances before being
stopped short. It was the end of
Völler's glittering international
career, sprinkled with successful
comebacks, in which he scored
47 goals.

■ 10 July 1994 • Stanford, Palo Alto • 81,715 •
Philip Don (ENG)

▲ **SWEDEN (0) (1) 2**
Brolin 79, K. Andersson 115
ROMANIA (0) (1) 2
Raducioiu 88, 101
Sweden 5-4 pens.

● SWEDEN *Ravelli, R. Nilsson (c), Ljung, Schwarz,
P. Andersson, Björklund [Kåmark 83], Brolin, Mild,
K. Andersson, Ingesson, Dahlin [Larsson 106].*
ROMANIA *Prunea, Petrescu, Prodan, Belodedici,
Lupescu, Popescu, Selymes, Munteanu [Pandaru 83],
Raducioiu, Hagi (c), Dumitrescu.*
▼ SENT OFF: *Schwarz 102.*
□ PENALTY SHOOT-OUT: *Mild shot over, Raducioiu 0-
1, K. Andersson 1-1, Hagi 1-2, Brolin 2-2, Lupescu 2-3,
Ingesson 3-3, Petrescu saved, R. Nilsson 4-3, Dumitrescu 4-
4. Sudden death: Larsson 5-4, Belodedici saved.*

*Brolin fires the ball over Prunea for the first goal of Sweden's
quarter-final against Romania.*

Once again Romania played their part in a memorable match, which neither side deserved to lose. Dahlin hit the post with a header in the third minute, Ingesson had a goal disallowed for pushing, and Sweden eventually went ahead with an imaginative free-kick. Schwarz ran over the ball, Mild pushed it around the wall, Brolin sprinted behind it to shoot into the roof of the net.

That seemed to be that, but a deflected free-kick found its way to Raducioiu, who celebrated his return from suspension by shooting high into the net. In extra-time he scored with a fierce low shot after a dreadful error by Patrik Andersson – but then it was Sweden's turn to score a late equalizer, Kennet Andersson towering over a hesitant Prunea to head in Roland Nilsson's long cross. Ravelli, wild-eyed and still elastic at 34, made two saves in the penalty shoot-out, but it was sad that the second was at the expense of Belodedici, one of the great defenders. Applause for

Sweden's resilience and skills, but Romania's absence would rob the tournament of flair and colour, and make things easier for the eventual winners.

Semi-finals

■ 13 July 1994 • Giants Stadium, New Jersey • 77,094 • Joël Quiniou (FRA)

▲ **ITALY (2) 2**
R. Baggio 20, 25
BULGARIA (1) 1
Stoitchkov pen 44

● ITALY *Pagliuca, Mussi, Benarrivo, Berti, Costacurta, Maldini (c), Donadoni, Albertini, D. Baggio [Conte 55], R. Baggio [Signori 70], Casiraghi.*
BULGARIA *Mikhailov (c), Kiriakov, Hubchev, Ivanov, Tsvetanov, Letchkov, Yankov, Sirakov, Balakov, Stoitchkov [Genchev 78], Kostadinov [Yordanov 71].*

No luck involved this time. Italy stayed strong throughout and Roberto Baggio scored two exceptional goals, the first a minor classic. Turning his marker in the process of collecting a throw-in on the left, he swerved to the right past another defender, the 'divine ponytail' flapping, before bending his shot around Ivanov and beyond the keeper. John Motson was lost for words and eloquent at the same time: 'Oh, look at that! Just look at that!' Five minutes later Albertini chipped a nicely weighted pass through the inside-right channel for Baggio to hook a low volley across the keeper.

[Top left] *Ravelli saves Belodedici's penalty to put Sweden in the semi-final for the first time since 1958.*

[Left] *Mikhailov and Ivanov of Bulgaria can't stop Italy's Roberto Baggio scoring his second goal in the semi-final.*

Against that sort of inspiration, Bulgaria could manage only a penalty for a foul on Sirakov by Costacurta, who was later booked for the second time, missing the Final just as he'd missed the European Cup Final in May. The much-maligned Sacchi had taken Italy almost all the way but now had to sweat on the fitness of Roberto Baggio, who pulled a hamstring in the second half.

■ 13 July 1994 • Rose Bowl, Pasadena • 84,569 • José Torres Cadena (COL)

▲ **BRAZIL (0) 1**
Romário 80
SWEDEN (0) 0

● BRAZIL *Taffarel, Jorginho, Branco, Mauro Silva, Aldair, Márcio Santos, Mazinho [Raí HT], Dunga (c), Bebeto, Romário, Zinho.*
SWEDEN *Ravelli, R. Nilsson, Ljung, Mild, P. Andersson, Björklund, Brolin, Thern (c), K. Andersson, Ingesson, Dahlin [Stefan Rehn 68].*
▼ SENT OFF: *Thern 63.*

If Romania had won that penalty shoot-out, Brazil would have had some serious counter-attacking threats to cope with – but Sweden didn't carry the same kind of threat, despite the talents of Brolin, Dahlin and Kennet Andersson. Tired and listless, they held out only because Zinho and Mazinho missed open goals and Ravelli had a good game. The goal, in the end, was very basic, little Romário getting between two defenders to head Jorginho's long cross just inside a post. Thern, Sweden's playmaker, was sent off for

a careless foul on Dunga. After seven matches (a record between any two countries), Sweden have yet to beat Brazil in the World Cup finals.

3rd-place Final

■ 16 July 1994 • Rose Bowl, Pasadena • 83,716 • Ali Mohammed Bujsaim (UAE)

▲ **SWEDEN (4) 4**
Brolin 8, Mild 30, Larsson 37, K. Andersson 39
BULGARIA (0) 0

● SWEDEN *Ravelli, R. Nilsson (c), Kåmark, Schwarz, P. Andersson, Björklund, Mild, Brolin, K. Andersson, Ingesson, Larsson [Anders Limpar 78].*
BULGARIA *Mikhailov (c) [Plamen Nikolov HT], Kiriakov, Hubchev, Ivanov [Kremenliev 41], Tsvetanov, Lechkov, Yankov, Sirakov [Yordanov HT], Balakov, Stoitchkov, Kostadinov.*

Romário gets between Patrik Andersson (3) and Roland Nilsson to head Brazil into the Final for the first time since 1970. Ljung, Björklund and Raí look on.

Jolly but strange, no reflection of what the teams had achieved so far. Ingesson, Sweden's midfield mule, went past Kiriakov, Mikhailov came out too far, and Brolin's downward header bounced in. Mild confidently pushed Brolin's quick free-kick past the advancing keeper. Larsson went round Mikhailov and waited for the covering defender to dive past before scoring. Finally Kennet Andersson got his last reward for a skilful and selfless tournament by heading into an empty net. Bulgaria, who spent the second half trying to set up Stoitchkov for the goal that would have made him outright leading scorer, suffered the biggest defeat in a World Cup 3rd-place Final, but everyone knew they were better than that.

The 'divine ponytail' looks mortal and God is a Brazilian again.

Final

■ 17 July 1994 • Rose Bowl, Pasadena • 94,194 • Sándor Puhl (HUN)

▲ **BRAZIL 0**
ITALY 0
Brazil 3-2 pens.

● BRAZIL *Taffarel, Jorginho [Cafú 21], Branco, Mazinho, Aldair, Márcio Santos, Mauro Silva, Dunga (c), Romário, Bebeto, Zinho ['Viola' (Paulo Sérgio Rosa) 105].*
ITALY *Pagliuca, Mussi [Apolloni 34], Benarrivo, Berti, Maldini, Baresi (c), Donadoni, Albertini, Massaro, R. Baggio, D. Baggio [Evani 94].*

□ PENALTY SHOOT-OUT: *Baresi shot over, Márcio Santos saved, Albertini 1-0, Romário 1-1, Evani 2-1, Branco 2-2, Massaro saved, Dunga 2-3, R. Baggio shot over.*

Yet again Sacchi had to send out a patched-up team, only more so. Costacurta was suspended, Roberto Baggio still feeling his injury, Mussi hurt early on. But at least, amazingly, Baresi was back. Not only had he missed every game since the first, he'd had a knee operation in between! Even McGrath couldn't match that.

Baresi played a monumental game, forcing Romário and Bebeto to forage further back. After Mussi's injury, Maldini simply switched back to the left, where he had an intriguing duel with the pacy Cafú. And the Italian midfield stuck to their task. But there was little happening up front, where Roberto Baggio was literally hamstrung. In a poor match, which the tournament didn't deserve, Brazil made the better chances and more of them. Mazinho should have scored when Pagliuca saved Branco's free-kick, Romário missed an open goal, and Pagliuca fumbled Mauro Silva's shot on to a post. When Italy had their one golden chance, it was too late in the day. A one-two with Massaro gave Roberto Baggio a clear shooting chance, but injury and weariness took their toll and Taffarel made an easy save. The match had been billed as a showdown between Baggio and Romário and they'd both missed in front of goal. But this was the first scoreless World Cup Final and both would have a second chance in the shoot-out.

If this was FIFA's idea of deciding the World Champions for the next four years, it was based on the slimmest evidence. About the width of a goalpost. While Italy's two injured heroes shot over the bar, Romário put his penalty in off an upright, a reminder of how close the two imposters of success and failure can be. Baggio's penalty against Nigeria had also gone in off a post, and Massaro had scored two goals in that year's European Cup Final. Italy had now lost a World Cup semi-final (1990) and Final on penalties. With a fraction more luck, they would have won the Cup twice in a row and five times in all. Instead their opponents became the first team to win it four times, and Italy took no comfort from the Brazilian captain's Italian surname.

Dunga, whose nickname means Dopey (of the Seven Dwarfs), lifted the trophy on the same ground where he'd played on the losing side in the Olympic Games final ten years earlier. Carlos Alberto Parreira, after taking two lesser countries to the finals, had won the big one with the big one, but with a team that wouldn't live in the memory.

LEADING GOALSCORERS 1994

6	Oleg Salenko	RUS	1 pen
6	Christo Stoitchkov	BUL	3 pen
5	Jürgen Klinsmann	GER	
5	Roberto Baggio	ITA	1 pen
5	Romário	BRZ	
5	Kennet Andersson	SWE	

The leading scorers in the last five tournaments have scored six goals.

Several dry spells had come to an end. Brazil, the only country to take part in every finals tournament, won the World Cup for the first time in 24 years; Bulgaria won a match; Bolivia scored a goal. But once again FIFA had sacrificed the tournament to the demands of television, forcing players to play in extreme heat and high humidity. The conditions made recovery all the harder (both semi-finals were won by the teams who had a day's extra rest) and wrecked the Final as a contest and spectacle. When Viola came on and caused havoc, people wondered where Carlos Alberto had been hiding him, but it was just a case of fresh legs. And what was the point of staging indoor matches at the height of summer?

Those who believed Mexico were happy to play the Irish in the midday heat of Orlando should have listened to their coach Miguel Mejía Barón. 'I would tell those gentlemen of FIFA to take their suits off and play football ... if FIFA were to think about the player, if it were to think more about football and less about business, there would be night games.' Footballers rarely show how much conditions take out of them (except perhaps poor Steve Staunton) so we can persuade ourselves they're not suffering all that much – but some lungs were burning out there. It was vivid, it was indelible, but it wasn't right.

Still, the world's great players keep rising above the machinations of their governing body (who, to be fair, helped by banning the tackle from behind and the pass back to the goalkeeper). There were sparkling goals, some fancy haircuts, and always someone in the news. Those with nothing to prove, except to sections of the press, proved it anyway: Hagi, Stoitchkov, Romário, Brolin, Dahlin, Bergkamp, Klinsmann. Defenders too: Babb, Belodedici, Maldini, Philippe Albert, the amazing McGrath, the bionic Baresi. France '98, swollen to 32 teams, has a hard act to follow.

Who's Dopey now? Dunga lifts the prize as the other dwarfs wait in line.

1998

Timetable

France 1998

Paris SF: Stade de France, Saint-Dénis. Paris PP: Parc des Princes.

GROUP A

BRAZIL (SEEDED), MOROCCO, NORWAY, SCOTLAND

Brazil v Scotland	Paris SF	10 June	5.30
Morocco v Norway	Montpellier	10 June	9.00
Norway v Scotland	Bordeaux	16 June	5.30
Brazil v Morocco	Nantes	16 June	9.00
Brazil v Norway	Marseille	23 June	9.00
Morocco v Scotland	St Étienne	23 June	9.00

GROUP B

ITALY (SEEDED), AUSTRIA, CAMEROON, CHILE

Chile v Italy	Bordeaux	11 June	5.30
Austria v Cameroon	Toulouse	11 June	9.00
Austria v Chile	St Étienne	17 June	5.30
Cameroon v Italy	Montpellier	17 June	9.00
Austria v Italy	Paris SF	23 June	4.00
Cameroon v Chile	Nantes	23 June	4.00

GROUP C

FRANCE (SEEDED), DENMARK, SAUDI ARABIA, SOUTH AFRICA

Denmark v Saudi Arabia	Lens	12 June	5.30
France v South Africa	Marseille	12 June	9.00
Denmark v South Africa	Toulouse	18 June	5.30
France v Saudi Arabia	Paris SF	18 June	9.00
Denmark v France	Lyon	24 June	4.00
Saudi Arabia v South Africa	Bordeaux	24 June	4.00

GROUP D

SPAIN (SEEDED), BULGARIA, NIGERIA, PARAGUAY

Bulgaria v Paraguay	Montpellier	12 June	2.30
Nigeria v Spain	Nantes	13 June	2.30
Bulgaria v Nigeria	Paris PP	19 June	5.30
Paraguay v Spain	St Étienne	19 June	9.00
Bulgaria v Spain	Lens	24 June	9.00
Nigeria v Paraguay	Toulouse	24 June	9.00

GROUP E

HOLLAND (SEEDED), BELGIUM, MEXICO, SOUTH KOREA

Mexico v South Korea	Lyon	13 June	5.30
Belgium v Holland	Paris SF	13 June	9.00
Belgium v Mexico	Bordeaux	20 June	5.30
Holland v South Korea	Marseille	20 June	9.00
Holland v Mexico	St Étienne	25 June	4.00
Belgium v South Korea	Paris PP	25 June	4.00

GROUP F

GERMANY (SEEDED), IRAN, USA, YUGOSLAVIA

Iran v Yugoslavia	St Étienne	14 June	5.30
Germany v USA	Paris PP	15 June	9.00
Germany v Yugoslavia	Lens	21 June	2.30
Iran v USA	Lyon	21 June	9.00
Germany v Iran	Montpellier	25 June	9.00
USA v Yugoslavia	Nantes	25 June	9.00

GROUP G

ROMANIA (SEEDED), COLOMBIA, ENGLAND, TUNISIA

England v Tunisia	Marseille	15 June	2.30
Colombia v Romania	Lyon	15 June	5.30
Colombia v Tunisia	Montpellier	22 June	5.30
England v Romania	Toulouse	22 June	9.00
Romania v Tunisia	Paris SF	26 June	9.00
Colombia v England	Lens	26 June	9.00

GROUP H

ARGENTINA (SEEDED), CROATIA, JAMAICA, JAPAN

Argentina v Japan	Toulouse	14 June	2.30
Croatia v Jamaica	Lens	14 June	9.00
Croatia v Japan	Nantes	20 June	2.30
Argentina v Jamaica	Paris PP	21 June	5.30
Argentina v Croatia	Bordeaux	26 June	4.00
Jamaica v Japan	Lyon	26 June	4.00

THE COMPLETE BOOK OF THE WORLD CUP

1998

2ND ROUND

GAME 2

| Winner Group B v Runner-up Group A | Marseille | 27 June | 4.30 |

GAME 1

| Winner Group A v Runner-up Group B | Paris PP | 27 June | 9.00 |

(Yes, Game 1 takes place after Game 2)

GAME 3

| Winner Group C v Runner-up Group D | Lens | 28 June | 4.30 |

GAME 4

| Winner Group D v Runner-up Group C | Paris SF | 28 June | 9.00 |

GAME 6

| Winner Group F v Runner-up Group E | Montpellier | 29 June | 4.30 |

GAME 5

| Winner Group E v Runner-up Group F | Toulouse | 29 June | 9.00 |

(Game 5 takes place after Game 6)

GAME 7

| Winner Group G v Runner-up Group H | Bordeaux | 30 June | 4.30 |

GAME 8

| Winner Group H v Runner-up Group G | Saint Étienne | 30 June | 9.00 |

QUARTER-FINALS

GAME B

| Winner Game 2 v Winner Game 3 | Paris SF | 3 July | 4.00 |

GAME A

| Winner Game 1 v Winner Game 4 | Nantes | 3 July | 9.00 |

(Game A takes place after Game B)

GAME C

| Winner Game 5 v Winner Game 8 | Marseille | 4 July | 4.00 |

GAME D

| Winner Game 6 v Winner Game 7 | Lyon | 4 July | 9.00 |

SEMI-FINALS

| Winner Game A v Winner Game C | Marseille | 7 July | 9.00 |
| Winner Game B v Winner Game D | Paris SF | 8 July | 9.00 |

3RD-PLACE FINAL

| Paris PP | 11 July | 9.00 |

FINAL

| Paris SF | 12 July | 9.00 |

ALL-TIME WORLD CUP XI

Very subjective, as these things always are, but one of the perks of editorship. Here goes. I've tried to keep to a loose 4-3-3 line-up, with a back four and a midfield tackler, rather than simply including as many skilful players as possible.

Sepp Maier	WG	1970–78
Victor Rodrigues Andrade	URU	1950–54
Nílton Santos	BRZ	1954–62
Johan Neeskens	HOL	1974–78
Obdulio Varela	URU	1950–54
Bobby Moore	ENG	1966–70
Garrincha	BRZ	1958–66
Diego Maradona	ARG	1982–94
Gerd Müller	WG	1970–74
Pelé	BRZ	1958–70
Mário Zagallo	BRZ	1958–62

Coach: Vittorio Pozzo (ITA).

TEN BEST MATCHES

Italy v Brazil	1982
Uruguay v Brazil	1950
Hungary v Uruguay	1954
West Germany v France	1982
West Germany v Hungary	1954
Northern Ireland v Spain	1982
Uruguay v Argentina	1930
England v Cameroon	1990
Romania v Sweden	1994
Brazil v Sweden	1950

# Bibliography

BOOKS

5000 Goles Blancos, historia del Real Madrid, La Gran
   Enciclopedia Vasca, Bilbao, 1969

Allaway, Roger, *The International Line-ups of the USA,*
   Soccer Book Publishing, Cleethorpes, 1995

Almanacco Illustrato del Calcio 1979 & 1991,
   Panini, Modena

Banks, Gordon, *Banks of England,* Arthur Barker Ltd,
   London, 1980

Bestard, Miguel Angel, *International Football in South
   America,* Soccer Book Publishing, Cleethorpes, 1992

Camkin, John, *World Cup 1958,* Rupert Hart-Davis Ltd,
   London, 1959

Cazal-Oreggia-Cazal, *L'Équipe de France de Football,*
   FFF, 1992

Clayton, David & Jan Buitenga, *The International Matches
   series, Czechoslovakia, East Germany, Holland,
   Romania, Turkey, USSR, Yugoslavia*

Cullen, Donal, *Ireland On The Ball 1926-93,* ELO
   Publicatons, Dublin, 1993

Das Bilderbuch von der Fussballweltmeisterschaft,
   Vienna, 1954

David, Lubomir, *Rocenka Futbal 1983–84,*
   Bratislava, 1984

Davies, Gareth & Ian Garland, *Who's Who of Welsh
   International Soccer Players,* Bridge Books,
   Wrexham, 1991

Ellis, Arthur, *Refereeing Round the World,* Hutchinson &
   Co., London, 1954

Escartin, Pedro, *Lo De Brasil Fue Asi,* 1950

Federação Portuguesa De Futbol Review 1972–73

FIFA News 1927–78

FIFA Official Reports, 1962–94

Finney, Tom, *Football Round the World,* Museum Press,
   London, 1953

Fraiponts, Norbert, *Onze Rode Duivels,* Helios NV,
   Antwerp, 1982

Franta, R., *Fussballweltmeisterschaft 1938,* Agon
   Sportverlag, Frankfurt, 1995

Gowarzewski, Andrzej, Encyklopedia Pilkarska: Copa
América, GIA, Katowice 1995

Gowarzewski, Andrzej, *Encyklopedia Pilkarska: Herosi
   Mundiali,* GIA, Katowice, 1993

Gregg, Harry, *Wild about Football,* Souvenir Press,
   London, 1961

Hammond, Mike (ed), *European Football Handbook
   94–95,* Sports Projects, Warley, 1994

Haynes, Johnny, *It's all in the Game,* Arthur Barker Ltd,
   London, 1962

Hilton, Tony & Barry Smith, *An Association with Soccer,*
   Sporting Press, Auckland, 1991

Hollander, Zander (ed), *The American Encyclopedia of
   Soccer,* Everest House, New York, 1980

Hoof, Van & Herrera Villareal, *Colombia: The National
   Teams,* 1991

Hurst, Geoff, *The World Game,* Stanley Paul,
   London, 1967

Jeffery, Gordon, *The Report from Chile,* Souvenir Press,
   London, 1962

Jennings, Pat, *Pat Jennings: an autobiography,*
   Willow Books, London, 1983

Kicker-Almanach 1992, Copress Verlag, Munich, 1991

Lamming, Doug, *A Scottish Internationalists' Who's Who,*
   Hutton Press, Beverley, 1987

Lee, Francis, *Soccer Round the World,* Arthur Barker Ltd,
   London, 1970

MacLeod, Ally, *The Ally MacLeod Story: an autobiography,*
   Stanley Paul, London, 1979

Mallam, Colin, *World Cup Argentina,* Collins,
   London, 1978

BIBLIOGRAPHY

Marquis, Max, *Anatomy of a Football Manager –
   Sir Alf Ramsey*, Arthur Barker Ltd, London, 1970

McIlroy, Jimmy, *Right inside Soccer*, Nicholas Kaye Ltd,
   London, 1960

McIlvanney, Hugh & Arthur Hopcraft (eds), *World Cup '70*,
   Eyre & Spottiswoode, London, 1970

McIlvanney, Hugh (ed), *World Cup '66*, Eyre &
   Spottiswoode, London, 1966

McParland, Peter, *Going for Goal*, Souvenir Press,
   London, 1960

Miller, David, *World Cup 1970*, William Heinemann,
   London, 1970

Miller, David, *World Cup: The Argentina Story*, Frederick
   Warne, London, 1978

Mundial 1930–1982, La Gazzetta dello Sport, Milan
   Official Report, 1934

Official Review (Brazil), 1950

Oreggia, Michel & J. M. Cazal, *Équipe Nationale d'Israël
   1948-89*, ASFS 1990

Ossola, Franco, *I Grandi del Torino*, MEB, Torino, 1975

Pele & Robert L. Fish, *My Life and the Beautiful Game*,
   New English Library, London, 1977

Powell, Jeff, *Bobby Moore*, Everest Books, London, 1976

Puskás, Ferenc, *Captain of Hungary*, Cassell & Co.,
   London, 1955

Ramsey, Alf, *Talking Football*, Stanley Paul, London, 1952

Raynor, George, *Football Ambassador at Large*, Soccer
   Book Club, Norwich, 1960

Soar, Phil & Richard Widdows, *Spain '82*, STW & Hamlyn,
   London, 1982

Soar, Phil, *World Cup 78*, Marshall Cavendish,
   London, 1978

Stiles, Nobby, *Soccer my Battlefield*, Stanley Paul,
   London, 1968

Taylor, Jack & David Jones, *Jack Taylor World Soccer
   referee*, Pelham Books, London, 1976

Tyler, Martin, *Boys of '66*, Hamlyn, London, 1981

Voetbaljaarboek 1991–92, KVBV, Belgium

Wright, Billy, *Captain of England*, Stanley Paul,
   London, 1950

NEWSPAPERS & MAGAZINES

Balón (Mexico)
El Mercurio (Santiago)
El Pais (Montevideo)
Football (France, June and July 1938)
Glasgow Evening News
Guerin Sportivo
IFFHS Fussballweltzeitschrift (1930 and 1934 finals)
Il Corriere della Sera (Milan)
L'Équipe Guide 84–85
La Nacion (Buenos Aires)
La Prensa (Buenos Aires)
La Prensa (Lima)
New York Times
Official World Cup Final Programme (1966)
Official World Cup Programme (1954)
Plaçar (80 Anos de Seleção Brasileira)
Soccer America
Soccer News (USA)
St Louis Post-Dispatch
Tempo (Yugoslavia)
The *Guardian*
World Soccer (various, 1982-94)

Acknowledgements

First and foremost, three World Cup specialists – Ron Templeton, Mervyn Baker and Alejandro Rodón – for throwing light on the most contentious areas. This is their book as much as mine, except of course for any errors, which are all my own work.

Others who helped separate fact from fiction include some of the leading statisticians and commentators in their fields: Colin Jose and Alex Shnerer in Hamilton, Ontario; Hector Luis Sicco in Montevideo; Carlos Yametti in Buenos Aires; Tito Ticerán Guerra in Lima; José Moretzsohn in Rio de Janeiro; Duilio Domingos Martino in São Paulo; Gilbert Rouselle in Ostend; the great Michel Oreggia in Nice; George Glass in Belfast, for generously allowing the use of his photographs from the 1954, 1958 and 1962 tournaments; Bryan Horsnell for supplying memorabilia, David Barber yet again, for throwing open the FA's increasingly extensive library; Brian Mellowship as always; Phil Cornwall; Keith and Lesley Millar; David 'Kaiser' Bayliffe; Harry Hatfield; Luigi Freddi; Arianne Fox Mortimer.

Anna Grapes, picture researcher at HarperCollins, and the editorial team of Mike Doggart, Tom Whiting, Nick Wells, Sonya Newland and Charlie Richards.

Last but not at all, David Godwin, for putting one and one together.

Picture Credits

ROMAN NUMERALS REFER TO COLOUR PLATE SECTION.

Allsport: Hulton Getty 20, Hulton Getty 53, Pressens Bild 114 (m), 277 (b), David Leah 288 (b), David Cannon 294, David Cannon 316 (b), Simon Bruty: 330 (t), Shaun Botterill 322, Shaun Botterill 336, Ben Radford 339, Hulton Getty II (bl), Steve Powell IX (b), XI (tr), Billy Stickland XII (r), David Cannon XIII (tr), XIII (tl), Simon Bruty XIV (l&br), David Cannon XV (br), Simon Bruty XV (t), Billy Stickland XV (bl). **Associated Press:** 111 (t), 193, 194, 210 (t), 232 (t), 254. **Beejay Soccer Enterprises:** 43, I (tr&b), II (t&br), III (tr), IV (l), V (tl). **Colorsport:** 8, 113 (t), Pica Pressfoto 114 (t), John Varley 162 (b), 188, John Varley 191, 192, 201, 202 (l), 207, Olympia 209, Olympia 210 (m), 218 (all), 223 (b), 229, 232 (b), 246, 253, 255, 257, 258 (t&m), 259, 272, 273, 276, 282 (l), 284 (b), 288 (t), 293, Gadoffre 306, 308, 309, 312 (all), 311 (b), 314 (2&5), Olympia 314 (4), 316 (t), 338, 342 (t), 343, 344, 346, III (tl), John Varley IV (r), John Varley V (b), VI (tl&bl), John Varley VII (br), IX (tl&tr), Olympia X (bl), XII (tl), XVI (tl). **Empics:** Neal Simpson XVI (b). **Hulton Getty:** 30, 42 (t), 54, 71, 78, 82, 89, 110 (l), 136, 150, 152 (t), 161 (b), 162 (t), 173, 179, 203 (t), 258 (b). **MSI:** 7, 9, 139, 144, 145, 180 (r), 220, 222, 223 (t), 260 (b), 282 (r), 304, 315, III (b), V (tr), VI (r), VII (l&tr), VIII (b), XI (bl), XIV (tr). **PA:** 156. **Popperfoto:** 12, 13, 14, 24, 25 (all), 26 (all), 27 (all), 28, 29, 35, 36, 38, 41 (all), 42 (b), 55, 59, 60, 61, 62 (all), 65, 76, 83, 85 (all), 87, 90 (all), 92, 93, 94, 97, 101, 102, 103, 106, 108, 110 (r), 111, 112 (b), 113 (b), 114 (b), 115, 120 (all), 123, 126, 128, 129, 130, 131, 132, 133, 134 (all), 137, 146, 149, 152 (b), 153, 154, 157, 158, 159, 160, 161 (t), 167, 171 (all), 176, 177, 180 (r), 181, 182, 183, 184, 185, 186, 198, 202, 206, 208, 210 (b), 214, 221, 231, 234, 241, 242, 260 (t), 275, 277 (t), 281, 283, 284 (t), 287, 311 (t), 313, 314 (1&3), 330 (b), 331, 341, 342 (b), I (tl), VIII (t), X (tl&r), XI (l&br), XIII (b), XVI (tr).